THE
CORNISH
FAMILY

THE
CORNISH
FAMILY

The Roots of Our Future

BERNARD DEACON

with Sharron Schwartz and David Holman

CORNWALL EDITIONS

FOWEY

DEDICATION

To all those nineteenth-century Bosankos, Crosses, Gribbles, Harrises, Horas,
Neals, Pascoes, Pearces, Penroses, Robbins and Rodds, without whom the author
of the bulk of this text would not be here

CORNWALL EDITIONS LIMITED

8 Langurtho Road

Fowey Cornwall

PL23 1EQ UK

Telephone: 01726 832483

Email: cornwalleditions@cornishinternet.com

www.cornwalleditions.co.uk

Publisher Ian Grant

This edition first published in the United Kingdom in 2004
by Cornwall Editions and is limited to 1,100 copies of which 1,000 are for sale

Number......... *631* ....

ISBN 1-904880-01-0

Typeset in New Caledonia 11/18PT

Designed and edited by Asterisk Design and Editorial Solutions, Cornwall
Art Director Roger Bristow
Editorial Director Yvonne McFarlane

Illustrations David Ashby
Maps Arka Graphics
Index Sue Lightfoot
Production Madeleine Day

Colour origination by Radstock Reproductions Ltd, Midsomer Norton, UK
Printed in China by WKT Co. Ltd

Papers used by Cornwall Editions are natural, recyclable products made from wood grown in sustainable forests;
the manufacturing processes conform to the environmental regulations of the country of origin

CONTENTS

SPECIAL ACKNOWLEDGEMENT
VI

FOREWORD
LADY MARY HOLBOROW
VII

INTRODUCTION
8

CHAPTER ONE
THE CHANGING FAMILY
18

CHAPTER TWO
BY TRE, POL AND PEN WILL YE KNOW MOST CORNISHMEN?
56

CHAPTER THREE
CORNISH FAMILIES ON THE MOVE
94

CHAPTER FOUR
TO GO OR TO STAY?
136

CHAPTER 5
'WHAT WE BELONG TO BE'
172

TIMELINE
202

FAMILY HISTORY RESEARCH IN CORNWALL
212

NOTES AND REFERENCES
232

LIST OF SUBSCRIBERS
244

INDEX AND ACKNOWLEDGEMENTS
249

Special acknowledgement

This was a truly collaborative venture. Some of those people who helped – wittingly and unwittingly – in the writing of it are acknowledged at the end of the book. But here I would like to take this opportunity to acknowledge the valuable work of my two colleagues, Sharron Schwartz and David Holman, whose input into the book was crucial. In doing so, I will also briefly tell how the book was written.

The Introduction and the first three chapters were written by me and I am ultimately responsible for any shortcomings they have. In the light of the surprising lack of interest shown by the academic world in Cornish by-names and surnames, Chapters Two and Three required a lot of new data extraction and analysis. In this, I was greatly aided by Sharron, who extracted some of the data that allowed me to re-capture the changing geography of the surnames discussed in Chapter Three. The book could also not have been completed without the cooperation of the Cornwall Family History Society and David Holman's help in accessing the Society's invaluable computerised databases of parish register and census data. These underpin the eighteenth- and nineteenth-century analyses in Chapters Two and Three.

While Sharron read a draft of the Introduction and Chapters One to Three and provided helpful suggestions for re-drafting, she was much more directly involved in the writing of Chapters Four and Five. In fact, she produced the first draft of Chapter Four and this chapter is about three quarters Sharron's work and one quarter mine. Chapter Five also directly incorporates some of Sharron's work, although there I was the author of the bulk of the text.

When working on a project, one positive experience is to have one's preconceptions shifted. During the writing of this book, Sharron succeeded in convincing me of the important role of transnationalism in the broader development of modern Cornwall, a role about which I had hitherto been rather more sceptical. More generally, writing the book has alerted me to the possibilities of name studies in uncovering aspects of the social history of Cornwall.

I hope that *The Cornish Family* will also convince the reader that there is a lot more to family history than family trees.

Bernard Deacon

FOREWORD

This is a fascinating book on a fascinating subject. It is not only an essential read for those who are Cornish, but also for everyone who either lives in Cornwall or who has an interest in the history of Cornwall, particularly the social history.

I am a great believer in the present and the future being shaped by the past – and this book tells us so much about the reasons why the Cornish are so passionate about their ancestry and their Cornish identity.

Cornwall itself is a very special place, loved by all those who live here, and the place of the family in the social structure over the centuries has helped to make it what it is.

In reading Dr Deacon's text, I learnt a great deal about Cornwall's social structure, the links between family and place, the difference the Cornish language made, and the strong links with so many countries through the migration of so many Cornish men and women in search of work in the nineteenth century.

This book gives us reasons why the Cornish family is unlike others, looks at the derivation of Cornish surnames, gives us reasons why the Cornish identity has stayed so strong through the ups and downs of population and economic prosperity and decline, and I am sure that all who read this will realise why the Cornish have such pride in their identity.

I am very proud to be the Lord-Lieutenant of Cornwall – a place which has such a strong community spirit and, even though the population has been swelled by a large number of newcomers, the Cornish people will never lose their strong sense of identity, and family ties, which is why Cornwall is such a unique place.

I commend *The Cornish Family* to you, the reader, and know that you will find it as interesting a book as I do.

Mary Holborow
Lord-Lieutenant of Cornwall
April 2004.

INTRODUCTION

O N MAY 15th, 1976, the Cornwall Family History Society held its inaugural meeting in Truro, having attracted around fifty founder members. From this modest beginning, the Society has grown to over 12,000 members and is now one of the leading family history societies in the British Isles.

It is not in any way difficult to suggest reasons for this phenomenal growth, given such an enduring interest in family roots in Cornwall and amongst the Cornish. First, there is the depth of attachment to the place. The genealogical tree provides incontrovertible evidence that the family is entrenched in Cornwall; its roots deep in the Cornish past validate and endorse contemporary feelings of pride in being Cornish, of being a member of what is sometimes referred to as an extended family with a unique and celebrated history.

Second, that extended family reaches well beyond the county borders. The mass migration of Cornish men and women and whole families overseas in the nineteenth and early twentieth centuries was central to Cornwall's modern history. One long-term impact of this emigration was to produce large numbers of people with Cornish roots in North America and Australasia, in particular, a potentially enormous symbolic family, all of whom might wish to discover their Cornish ancestors. And many thousands do. In the new environment of 'hyphenated' Americans or Australians, being Cornish-American or Cornish-Australian gives those people of Cornish descent a marker that commands respect.

Thirdly and more broadly, the family occupies a strategic position in more global, end-of-century social change. Some observers have argued that there is a 'transnational and global transition toward a wholly new kind of society, a society based on individualism, multiculturalism, consumerism, mass migration, and mass communications, which was everywhere displacing the older landmarks of family, occupation, religious belief and local and national identities'. Viewed this way, the family could be seen somehow threatened, or under attack. And certainly, for some, family values are co-opted into a litany of conservative nostalgia that yearns for a return to an older (and supposedly better) place, a world of stability and certainty rather than one of ceaseless change and uncertainty.

It would be foolish to deny that such longings for a past that is probably impossible to resurrect (and which is, in any case, to a degree fictitious) might lie behind some of the burgeoning interest in family history in some societies. But, while 'the family' in the abstract can stand in for a nostalgic past, real families are also very much part of a changing present. Furthermore, most of us are still brought up in families and continue to live within them, and they remain an inescapable part of modern society. Therefore, even if we wish to avoid families and want to reject the

OPPOSITE

Vine Cottage, Newlyn, the pretty thatched home of the Kitchen family at the beginning of the last century. The small boy was named 'Peter, called Edward.'

8

'Dear wife and children' - this extract from a letter by a Cornish émigré to his family at home speaks of the illness, hardship and homesickness suffered by many who migrated overseas in search of work.

A headstone in memory of Cornish-born Richard Rogers(1824-69), in Virginia City, Nevada. Many cemeteries in the western US are full of Cornish memorials.

reactionary use to which 'the family' is often put, we cannot ignore the family entirely. Moreover, the argument of this book is that the Cornish family is rescued from a fate of being purely a vehicle for nostalgia by two aspects of contemporary Cornwall.

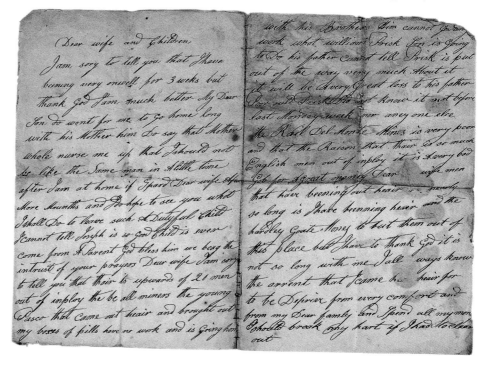

First, the 'transnational' aspect of the Cornish family, created by the great emigration of the past two centuries, crucially opens up our horizons, takes us beyond Cornwall and reminds us of the global reach and links of our lineage. It is a rare Cornish person who traces their family tree and fails to discover at least one example of overseas migration in the nineteenth century.

This extra-Cornish dimension of Cornishness, this Cornwall beyond Cornwall, both feeds on and informs another development, a feeling that Cornwall and the Cornish deserve more respect as a place and as a people. This is an identity that doesn't just look back to lost glories but also forward to possible opportunities. In any future project to re-build Cornwall, the strength of its cultural heritage and the depth of its sense of place will have to play a central role. Clearly, there are many shackles that still have to be cast aside and many old assumptions and myths that are long overdue for discarding if we seek to re-invigorate Cornish society. But in any such project, the Cornish family and Cornish family history will be called upon to play its part, not only to provide an inward contemplation of the foliage of the family tree but as an active instrument of cultural rejuvenation.

The aims of this book

While we might immodestly hope that this book is a small part of that rejuvenation, it is important to clarify at the start what it does *not* set out to do. This is not a 'how to do' guide to family history. David Holman, chairman of the Cornwall Family History Society, does supply plenty of pointers on how to go about this in the last section (pages 214-233). But equally, there are plenty of excellent such guides available and some references to these can be found in the bibliography there as well as useful internet links and information about relevant societies. Neither is it a comprehensive history of every family in Cornwall. That would be a mammoth task well beyond the capacity of any single volume, or even series of volumes. Again, many one-name studies have been published in recent decades, although of varying quality. The Cornish Studies Library at the Cornwall Centre in Redruth holds a very comprehensive selection of these. More surprisingly, perhaps, for a book entitled *The Cornish Family*, there is not much focus on genealogy. Such a book could be written, although it would be the devil's own job to make it interesting.

Instead of focusing on genealogy, this book provides the broader context of Cornish family history for the genealogist. In particular, we aim to open up an area hardly touched on so far in Cornwall - although there have been hints - and that is the historical geography and local history of Cornish surnames. Local historical study of names, their distribution and their origins, has made a lot of headway in Yorkshire, under the leadership of David Hey of the University of Sheffield. Cornwall, with its stock of distinct surnames, is a place that cries out for similar treatment. *The Cornish Family* is the first fruit of some research along these lines. It is the first, not the last, word on the Cornish family and its historical context. No doubt many of the conclusions reached in its pages can be and will be challenged. And that is all to the good. For the conclusions that we reach here are very much preliminary statements. Thus, the book aims to set a context for family historians. But we also contextualise the Cornish family, to say why it remains of such abiding interest and enduring significance and how it is tied up with larger issues of identity in Cornwall. In both these ways we trust the book will begin to inform a deeper understanding of how we might flesh out the bare branches of the family tree.

Chapter One begins by recounting something hitherto not attempted - a social history of the family in Cornwall, examining how far the Cornish family was unique and how far it has changed over time. The chapter commences with the verities of life, the vital events of births, marriages and deaths, and how these were experienced in the past. It then looks at other issues, such as kinship links and the quality of emotional life within the family in past times, before moving on to a look at the institution of the Cornish family. Here it is possible to identify what we call the 'Cornish customary family', which left its distinct legacy well

BELOW
Three generations of the Polkinghorne family at Carn Marth c.1909. David migrated to the US in 1895 to work as a miner. He returned with enough money to buy land and build a new house to replace this cob and stone cottage.

into the nineteenth century and combined with the effects of emigration to produce some familiar aspects of the late-nineteenth and early-twentieth-century Cornish family. Much of this is tentative and some of it speculative, as research has not been done in depth. However, perhaps these speculations just might encourage historians and sociologists to do more to probe the Cornish family and Cornish family life.

Chapter Two proceeds to a study of the stock of Cornish surnames and discusses their derivation. In this context, Cornish surnames means not just Cornish language

RIGHT

The Lanyon dynasty - artist Peter Lanyon and his five children (left to right: *Andrew, Peter, Matthew, Anna, Martin and Jo*) *perch on Lanyon Quoit. Photographed by his wife, Jane, in 1961.*

surnames, but also surnames traditionally common in Cornwall. There are four different types of surname; locational, those that come from a placename or from a broader description of a location; personal names, from first names; nicknames, and occupational names. It becomes clear what an important role the Cornish language has played in our surname history, for it is widely accepted that the Cornish language, both directly and indirectly, through Cornish placenames, has bequeathed us a unique stock of names. Moreover, Cornish language surnames are one of those aspects that make Cornwall more than a mere English county. Yet the precise role of the language in producing and structuring Cornwall's surname stock is less well-known. In researching this book, it still came as a something of a surprise to realise the extent of the influence of the Cornish language. Indeed, naming customs were a major component of cultural distinctions between Cornish- and English-speaking areas of Cornwall in the past. These included a late stabilisation of surnames (which in many cases did not become hereditary until after the 1540s and in some cases were not finally fixed until the seventeenth century in west Cornwall) and, secondly, an intimate link between surnames and placenames in Cornwall, echoing a wider connection between people and place.

Close study of early-sixteenth-century second names provides new evidence for the state of the Cornish language at that time and of the historical geography of Cornish-speaking communities. *The Cornish Family* reveals that evidence. But it is not just a question of examining sixteenth-century history and dissipating the mists of the past, fascinating though that is. For the shadow of the Cornish language extends well into the present and even helps to explain the modern distribution of non-Cornish language names, especially personal names, in ways we are only beginning to understand. Surnames are not static, however, because people do not stay forever in the same place. Just as people in the past changed the way they spelled their names, so they regularly changed the place where they lived. Chapter Three reminds us how Cornish families moved. They have, of course, not just moved location and the chapter begins by briefly noting some examples of upwardly mobile Cornish families in the past before concentrating on what is, in some ways, the core of the book - a discussion of what surname analysis reveals about the origins and geographical mobility of some selected ordinary Cornish families. This examination uncovers the expected predominance of short-distance moves. Prior to the nineteenth century, when they moved, people usually relocated no further than to the next parish or at most, six miles away and then, during the twentieth century, this was replaced by moves from villages and countryside to the towns, a process that surname distributions also illustrate. Yet families were not alike. Some family names ramified over the length and breadth of Cornwall, while others were less dispersed, remaining tightly tied to one district. And as we shall see, while the current distribution of some surnames still reflects their historic core, for other names, the twenty-first century distribution gives no clue to this at all. Studying the changing surname patterns over time also shows that longer distance moves occasionally transplanted families to distant towns or to new mining districts.

In the nineteenth century, such long-distance migration became more common and co-existed with the traditional pattern of shorter moves. The most dramatic movement was overseas to mining and farming frontiers on other continents - principally North America, Australia, Africa. Chapter Four summarises this process, examines some of the reasons for it and some of the consequences it has had for the distribution of Cornish names. Furthermore, unlike other accounts, it treats long-distance migration as a single process, combining a discussion of overseas moves with

BELOW

The hunt meets at Tehidy - a photograph from the family album of the Bassets, wealthy copper mine owners whose home this was until 1916.

moves to England and Wales. For, in the later nineteenth century, especially in the 1870s and 1880s, these two varieties came together, as families and individuals moved temporarily to mining and industrial regions in the north of England and South Wales, before eventually departing for overseas. Such long-distance migration was crucial in transforming the nature of Cornish identity, not just in the nineteenth century but, indirectly, in the late twentieth century as well.

ABOVE
Not all Cornishman
were miners and not all
migrated overseas. This
is John Henry Inch, a
butler, flanked by the
two footman at the
home of Mr Latilla in
Horsham where they
were all in service,
photographed c.1921.

The final chapter turns the spotlight on the Cornish identity and the place of family and family migration in it. Chapter Five aims to do something not attempted hitherto. It provides a narrative history of the Cornish identity and its roller-coaster ride over the centuries. It argues that identity is not, as we might imagine, a fixed, essential and unchanging aspect of our lives but, on the contrary, has been reproduced socially over time, constantly made and re-made by Cornish people reacting with and against their environment and in response to broader social change. From a linguistic identity, which in the sixteenth century was associated with unruliness and 'rebellion', the Cornish identity became a territorial one, by the early eighteenth century loyal and subdued. But overlying this, industrialisation and Methodism provided two triggers for a re-energised regional identity in the late eighteenth and early nineteenth centuries. This identity, resting on industrialisation, was undercut by economic crisis after the 1860s, but it was maintained partly through links with Cornish emigrant communities overseas which had remained synonymous with mining and industry into the early twentieth century. This was the first phase of Cornwall's 'transnational' identity, yet this phase evaporated after World War One and the Cornish identity in many ways contracted to resemble a 'county' identity by the mid-twentieth century, albeit a 'county' suffused with a rosy and romantic glow of mystery and superstition suitable for luring tourists. Only the Celtic Revivalists served to remind Cornish people that they were once something else. And the Cornish Revival remained on the fringes of Cornish life.

But then, in the 1970s, something new began to emerge. The influx of large numbers of newcomers stimulated many Cornish people to re-discover and re-assert their Cornishness. Some, too few, engaged in political activity, fighting the process of centralisation; some turned, as we have seen, to the solace of their family roots; others re-invented Cornish culture, discovering new musical and art forms that began to blend old and new in the process. To this ferment was added a parallel growth of Cornish consciousness in the Cornish communities overseas, by now re-named a 'diaspora'. Re-stating their Cornishness, a transnational Cornish identity was re-born. This provided wider horizons for Cornish families, compensating for the introspective, nostalgic parochialism and sense of loss that can bedevil Cornish

14

society. Cornish transnationalism, expressed in family links, thus has an important part to play in the on-going project to build a mature Cornish identity for the twenty-first century: outward-looking, but secure and confident about its past; assured of its uniqueness, but with a capacity for inclusiveness; an historical European region, but one with real global associations.

Before launching on the account of the Cornish family, we need to define its parameters. Families are part of a wider society and that society includes a certain number of people. It is from this stock that surnames have emerged; it is this stock that is replenished over the generations by families and everyday family life. But what are the parameters of the Cornish family? In other words we need to pose a simple question. What has been the size of the Cornish population in the past?

Changes in Cornwall's population

Numbers have fluctuated considerably over the past millennium. Remarkably, Richard Polwhele, one of the 'fathers of Cornish history' almost got it right in 1807. Like modern demographers, he saw a major turning point in the Black Death of the middle of the 1300s. At the time of Domesday Book in 1086, the population of Cornwall was not much more than 25,000 - little bigger than present-day Penzance or the St Austell district. This population was, furthermore, concentrated in the east. In the west, on the damp, unenclosed downlands stretching west of present-day Newquay, far from the castles of the Norman overlords, and especially north of the central spine of Cornwall, people were scattered thinly across the landscape.

However, numbers then rose steadily, indeed spectacularly, when compared with neighbouring southwest England. By the 1330s, the population was perhaps as high as 90,000 people, with the greatest growth seen in the west. It was in these centuries that the Cornish towns emerged. Some, like Bodmin (the only named borough in Domesday Book), Helston and Liskeard grew from villages to become small towns of maybe a thousand or more. Others, such as Truro, Lostwithiel and Camelford, were planted by landlords and their growth lovingly tended as potential income earners. But most Cornish people lived in the countryside, pushing their settlements well up into the hills. By 1327, a farm was recorded at Fernacre, 900 feet up in the lee of Rough Tor on Fowey Moor (Bodmin Moor). The limits of settlement had been reached.

By 1349, the consequences of inadvertently landing a cargo of plague-carrying black rats in a Dorset port were being fully felt across the British Isles. The Black Death, which had been cutting a scythe of disease and death throughout medieval Europe, had reached Cornwall. The immediate effect may have been mortality rates of up to a third. Moreover, once established, the plague became endemic, recurring with horrible regularity into the seventeenth century. This was one reason for the fall and then stagnation of population in western Europe through the second half of the 1300s and the 1400s. Somewhere between 1480 and 1510, numbers bottomed out.

In Cornwall, this may have been at around 45,000 persons, only a half of what it had been at its pre-plague peak. A population rise then set in, one that continued with only short-term interruptions through to the 1800s. There were around 69,000 people living in Cornwall in 1570. By 1660, this had grown to 108,000, exceeding the previous early fourteenth-century peak. Our estimate here is somewhat higher than previous ones. Population continued to rise in Cornwall at a time when growth slowed down in England. By 1750, there were 128,000 Cornish people, a growth that reflected the later eighteenth-century expansion of tin mining and a precociously early industrialisation based on the exploitation of copper ore reserves beginning in the 1730s. This increase, which had been concentrated almost entirely in the western (mining) Hundreds of Kerrier and Penwith, then became generalised after the 1750s as the population steadily grew in both farming and mining parishes. By 1841, 342,000 people were living in Cornwall.

At that point growth, in contrast to east of the Tamar, slowed down drastically. The reason is simple. People had begun to migrate in large numbers from the mid-1840s onwards, many overseas,. Natural growth, fuelled by exceptionally high

THE 1851 MOUSEHOLE CENSUS

A census has been taken annually in England and Wales every decade since 1801 - with the exception of 1941. Each census return includes the full name, age (or alleged age) and occupation of the household members as well as their birth place and relationship to one another plus the house number or name and the street name.

fertility amongst the mining population, just about kept pace with the outflow until the 1860s when the price of copper fell, precipitating mine closures and triggering the longer-term, gradual rundown of Cornish mining. Population peaked at somewhere around 375,000 in 1865 and then went into reverse, drifting down to around 315,000 by 1939. Despite a short-term surge in numbers during the Second World War, the Cornish population resumed its long-term decline in the 1950s. But then, confounding the planners, things changed radically in the following decade. At a time when the population growth of Britain had fallen to very low levels, numbers in Cornwall began to rise sharply, with growth rates close to those of the early nineteenth century. The 342,000 residents of 1961 had grown to 501,000 by 2001. Unlike earlier population rises, the late twentieth-century expansion, one that placed Cornwall near the top of the league table of population growth, was entirely fuelled by in-migration. Thousands of people, two-thirds of them from the southeast of England, moved west, some inspired by holiday experiences, some by romantic dreams of a life away from the 'rat race', others just to take up a job. For, contrary to popular myth, this movement was not restricted to people of retirement age. The average migrant of the 1970s and 1980s was likely to be of working age.

Cornwall after the 1960s became a society in flux, with thousands of people arriving and at the same time many, although not so many, were leaving. A large proportion of these were part of a long-established culture of out-migration amongst

BELOW
Archetypal Cornwall -
crab and lobster fisher-
man (and film-maker),
John Potter attends to
his boat on the slipway
at Priest's Cove, near
Cape Cornwall.

Cornish youngsters moving east in search of degrees and careers. They were joined by those who, quickly disillusioned by wet and windy winters, lack of urban infrastructure and low wages, fled back to the suburbs. Nevertheless, many hardier souls remained to stake a claim to be the 'new' Cornish.

While, economically, the excessive rate of in-migration exacerbated problems, culturally, it stimulated a re-appraisal and rejuvenation of Cornish identity as those already established looked to their roots for security and solace in the face of rapid and, apparently, uncontrollable change. Indeed, it is in large measure as a result of these population changes that so many Cornish people have returned to their family trees, for reassurance, consola-

tion and certainty in an increasingly uncertain and unstable world. Of course, both 'old' and 'new' Cornish were also affected, after the 1960s, by fundamental changes in the way we live. The family, as an institution, was changing fast, paradoxically just at the time that people began to look to the past and to their family roots. In fact, there may well be a connection between the two and it seems clear that the idea of family has become more important to us at the very time that the practice of family seems somehow less clear-cut and more brittle. In many ways, the concept of the 'traditional' family clearly appears to be splintering and fragmenting. But what exactly was this 'traditional' family? That is the subject of the first chapter.

THE CHANGING FAMILY

THE FAMILY IN CORNWALL may appear as a stable part of our history, but, while some aspects of family life remain the same, others change. Cornish men and women still marry and start a family, though not necessarily in that order. Babies are born, but virtually all now survive their first few years. Children leave home, but now for college rather than for work on a farm or an apprenticeship. Family life still contains both times of affection and times of argument. In this chapter, we discuss some of the ways in which family life has remained the same and some of the ways it has changed. We will also reflect on whether and how far Cornish families were different from families in other places. But first, what about those rites common to all societies and to all families: getting married, being born and dying? What was the experience of these in Cornwall before the nineteenth century and how different was this experience from other places?

Rites of passage: births, marriages and deaths

In former times, marriage was central to the formation of new families and the transmission of property from one generation to the next. Before the late nineteenth century, the vast majority of births occurred within marriage. Where birth control was not an option, the principal control on the numbers of births was the age of marriage. The Shakespearian notion of young marriages, even child marriages, is now known to be a myth. By the time the baptism and burial registers appear in the 1530s, the normal age of marriage for women was around twenty six years old, slightly older for men.[1] While those who married did so relatively late, many never married at all. It is estimated that before the late eighteenth century, up to a quarter of people remained single.[2]

In pre-industrial times, before the nineteenth century, people delayed marriage until they had amassed sufficient resources to rent or build a house, obtain some furniture and set up a new household. Sons and daughters of landowners, smallholders and craftsmen would expect to receive some at least of their parents' possessions. It may be no coincidence that the average age of marriage for such property-holding groups was near to thirty, just about the time when parents were reaching their sixties, the expectation of life for the average adult (ignoring for the moment the appalling toll of infant and child mortality). But children clearly did not always have to wait for their fathers and mothers to pass on. Redistribution of household goods, land and stock to the next generation often began when the parents were in their forties. Thus, Alexander Daniel, a minor landowner, settled property at Penzance on his

BELOW

The arms of the Rowe family. The lamb and flag was a symbol later popular with tin smelters.

BELOW

The arms of the Tredigue family with three Cornish choughs.

son, Richard, in the middle of the seventeenth century, only to find to his dismay that Richard later sold off this property. He wrote to his son in 1665:

'how false you have been in your performances … it doth grieve both your mother and myself … that you … should deal so unkindly and unnaturally with us.'[3]

Redistribution of assets from one generation to the next was not always so acrimonious. When John Clemens of St Buryan died in 1724, he left only token sums of a shilling to each of his three eldest sons, John, William and James, while leaving the rest of his estate to his youngest and unmarried son, Thomas.[4] But it is most likely that the three married sons had received previous legacies. As in this case, the normal practice was to leave equal amounts to each surviving child who was not the main beneficiary. Thus Elizabeth Hicks, a widow at Withiel in 1690, left her estate to her son, John Hicks, and £6 to each of her five daughters.[5]

For the poor, with little or nothing to pass on to the next generation, such arrangements were less important. If young men were more dependent on wages, then they could marry earlier as there was no advantage in waiting. Because of this, marriages were extremely sensitive to economic circumstances. Low wages could delay marriage. Conversely, opportunities to increase earnings made marriages more likely. This explains the early Cornish population growth from the 1660s to the 1750s. Expanding tin- and then copper-mining provided new opportunities for labourers and smallholders and encouraged earlier marriages. And, of course, earlier marriages meant that more children were born.

Weddings and courtship

But whether rich or poor, it seems that there was freedom, certainly by the sixteenth century, to choose one's marriage partner. Nevertheless, love was socially constrained. The heart could point in one direction, but the wealth and status of the intended might be unacceptable to other members of the family. This would usually be the parents, although Alexander Daniel's possible match in 1621 was scuppered by the fact that 'my sister would not endure to hear of it'.[6] If the young couple persisted in their choice, revenge could be exacted in wills. In 1707, Thomas Budge of Linkinhorne decided to leave some money to his married daughter, but gave it to two others who were to pay her, thus bypassing her husband, 'one John Smith, a tailor', who she had married 'contrary to my advice and direction, and considering with myself that if I should give her a legacy in money that her husband will soon spend it'.[7]

Arranged marriages, or certainly highly encouraged marriages, were more common among the well-to-do, seeking in-laws who might enhance the status or wealth of the family. For such groups, the practice of marriage 'portions' (dowries brought by the bride into the marriage contract) injected an unavoidable business element into proceedings. If portions were too low, negotiations could founder. Choice of

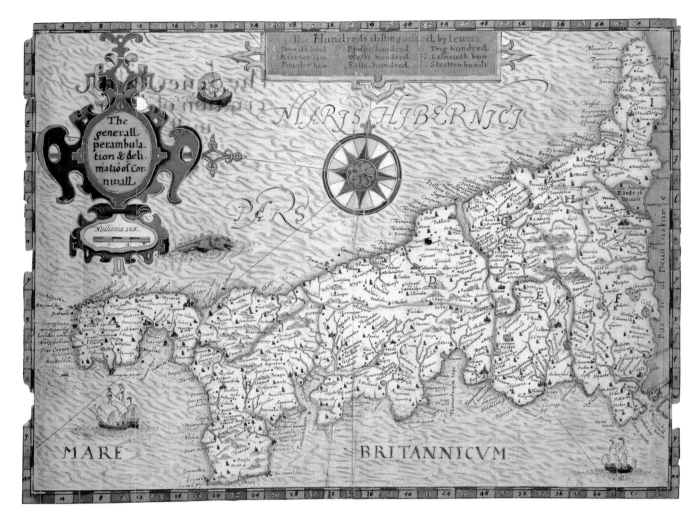

husband or wife was also constrained in a broader way. It remained normal practice to marry partners from the same social level well into the modern period. Thus, in Sennen in the 1850s, in forty-six per cent of marriages, the fathers of both bride and groom shared the same occupation.[8] This was particularly noticeable among fishermen, where 'marrying-out' seems to have become gradually rarer as the nineteenth century proceeded, incidentally producing high concentrations of surnames, as, for example, at Sennen Cove, where by 1881, over half the population shared the two surnames of George and Nicholas. A restricted choice of marriage partners, as people moved in networks bounded by occupation and class, led to the emergence of recognisable farming, legal and clerical dynasties, among others. In this manner, the Harveys of Hayle inter-married into the Wests and the Trevithicks to produce an early-nineteenth-century engineering dynasty.[9]

Weddings, usually in the bride's parish, peaked at certain points in the calendar. These could be January/February, before Lent and ploughing; April to June, when farm contracts ended, or October/November after the harvest was brought in.[10] In pastoral areas, the early summer peak was more likely; in arable areas, the early winter one. But in pre-industrial Cornwall, as elsewhere, the church service was less central to marriages. It has been estimated that by the 1750s, around half of weddings were sealed by a simple folk ceremony, something that state and church attempted to control by Hardwicke's Marriage Act of 1753. This made marriages in

ABOVE
John Norden visited Cornwall in the late sixteenth century and drew the first detailed map of the county and its settlements. His Generall Charte *or* Mappe of Cornwall *was presented to James I early in the seventeenth century.*

21

ABOVE

Portrait of Richard Glynn Vivian (1835-1910) by K. van Havermaet. Richard was the descendant of John Vivian who at the end of the 18th century moved from Truro to Swansea. There he established the copper smelting works that contributed to Swansea becoming the centre of the copper smelting industry.

the Anglican Church the only legal form and demanded that banns be read on the three preceding Sundays. In contrast, in popular culture it was the betrothal and the pledging to a partner that had been and was to remain for many years the more important aspect of the marriage process. Pledging a troth took place in an environment policed by community sanctions rather than the law. Those who flouted the rules of betrothal would suffer the consequences of being publicly 'outed' through *charivari* or 'rough music', and became the butt of community disapproval. Such disapproval was also extended to wife-beaters, cuckolded husbands and anyone who transgressed the unwritten moral codes of local communities.

Such community involvement in weddings and in married life more generally was frowned on by the Puritans of the seventeenth century and declined in vigour in some parts of England. But it remained strong in Cornwall, relatively unaffected by Puritanism, into the early nineteenth-century. Richard Polwhele (1760-1838), clergyman and Cornish historian, described Cornish weddings in 1806:

> After the wedding at midnight, all parties were armed ... with dram-glasses ... and proceeding to the chamber of the bride and bridegroom (who are at that time placed in bed and sitting up to receive their guests) drink off successively a dram, and dance around the room like bacchanals; then kneeling at the foot of the bed with their backs to the new-married couple, throw the bride's stocking behind them at a venture, assured that he who makes the best hit at the bridegroom or bride has the chance of being first married; then dance about the room again; and, bidding the happy couple goodnight, toss of another dram all round, to close the ceremony.[11]

According to George Henwood (died 1875), mine captain and journalist of the 1850s, drink had still been central to proceedings at Cornish miners' weddings in the 1810s and 1820s, when

> the wedding was then little better than a drunken spree for the bridegroom and his companions, continuing their orgies for three or four days ... After the ceremony (properly so termed), the wedding party repaired to the public house at the church-town in their best array, where a fiddler or two were

provided; eating, drinking, dancing and smoking being the order of the day as long as they could stand their effects.[12]

By the 1850s, Henwood claimed, such scenes of debauchery had been dissipated. Miners' wedding parties were more sober affairs – by mid-century sometimes involving a trip by train to the coast.

> From Redruth or Camborne they come by rail [to Penzance], as smart and hilarious as can be, with well-filled baskets of eatables and a fiddle or flute'. After walking to Marazion and visiting the pub, for 'we will not ... claim all as teetotallers', the wedding party would ramble around St Michael's Mount and eat their picnic. Returning by train, there would then be 'an hour or so at the "old people's", where a supper is usually provided, and the glass handed merrily round until 10 or 11 o'clock, at which period the young people repair to their new abode' and the wedding guests left, clutching their pieces of wedding cake.[13]

A customary attitude towards betrothals as being equally, if not more, important than the actual church ceremony, meant that communities also widely sanctioned pre-marital sex and the resultant conceptions. It has been estimated that in England, around fifteen per cent of brides were pregnant at the time of marriage in the 1680s, a proportion that rose to thirty five per cent by 1800. In Cornwall, this was even higher, reflecting a basic distinction between the west and north of the British Isles, where bridal pregnancy was common, and the south and east, where it was less so. In Camborne and Mawnan, before 1660, for example, bridal pregnancy rates could be as high as thirty to thirty-six per cent, double the English average. This practice continued well into the nineteenth century, prompting Henwood to comment as late as the 1850s that, 'the wedding-day was generally postponed as long as decency would permit; this was the rule not the exception, and was carried out with unblushing 'effrontery ... a shocking laxity ... still to be regretted'.[14]

ABOVE
The arms of the
Polwhele family.

It was the sterner moral teachings of nonconformist Victorian Cornwall that slowly changed the customs of the labouring classes. Pre-marital conceptions meant that, if for any reason the marriage was postponed or called off, illegitimate children were born. In the years before the Civil Wars of the 1640s, the Cornish illegitimacy rate was regularly one or two percentage points higher than south-west England, peaking just before the 1640s. However, during the eighteenth century, although bridal pregnancies remained common, the proportion of illegitimate births fell below that of England. A combination of economic circumstances and community disapproval meant the vast majority of promises resulted in actual marriages.

Moreover, illegitimacy carried a social stigma. The fate of illegitimate children, and even more so their mothers, remained grim. Under the terms of the Poor Law (which provided support for the poor from parish funds), women who were likely to give birth to an illegitimate child, who would then have a right to be supported out of the local rates, could be removed from a parish if they had no settlement rights there. Parish authorities could and did eject heavily pregnant women in a desperate bid to keep the rates down. That said, it is likely that the majority of single mothers were sheltered by their families, with grandparents or other kin giving a home to mother and child and sometimes, just child. Those single mothers who had no family or who had moved away from their kin were most vulnerable and exposed.

Births and baptisms

Once a couple married, children quickly arrived. Nonetheless, the universal pre-industrial practices of breast-feeding and late weaning (which seemed to occur at between a year and fifteen months), restricted pregnancies and produced a usual two-year gap between births, some-thing apparent in Cornish parish regis-ters.[15] This two-year gap – in addition to the relatively late age of marriage – meant that the average married woman might experience six or seven pregnancies.

ILLEGITIMATE BIRTHS

	Cornwall	England and Wales
1841	3.8%	7.0%
1851	5.5%	6.8%
1861	5.5%	6.3%
1871	6.6%	5.6%
1881	6.6%	4.9%
1891	5.7%	4.4%

Before the Reformation of the sixteenth century, children were baptised very quickly. When John Colshull was born at Tremadlart in the Hundred of West in 1416, a witness 'saw messengers sent to seek godfathers and godmothers, and immediately afterwards on the same day he was baptised' at Duloe church.[16] One reason for this hasty baptism was the medieval belief that unbaptised souls were consigned to limbo or, even worse, went straight to Hell if the child died. This was coupled with a high infant mortality that made the first few days of life very fragile ones. After the Reformation, the gap between birth and baptism gradually lengthened.

RIGHT

An examination form for Mary Eustis in Helston in 1779. Examinations established people's legal right to settlement (and therefore poor relief). But Mary's examination established the father as Richard Burgess of South Molton in faraway Devon. It is likely that the Helston authorities would have tried to pursue Richard Burgess for some maintenance costs.

Death and funerals

One in seven babies died in their first year in pre-industrial times; one in four did not live to see their fifth birthday. Death was a familiar, if unwelcome, guest. For adults, too, life could be ended with little warning, as plague or other endemic diseases, such as smallpox, typhus or dysentery periodically swept through communities. Hunger, even famine caused by harvest failure and food shortages, could still strike the British Isles into the sixteenth and seventeenth centuries, the last major famine in Britain outside Ireland being in Scotland in the 1690s. The local historian, Todd Gray, has claimed that 'the last period of severe food shortages in Cornwall' was a century ear-lier, in the 1590s, raising the possibility that famine may then have stalked the land.[17]

However, although there was a dearth of food in that decade, the burial registers indicate there were no widespread famine deaths. Mortality in a sample of six parish-es from east and west Cornwall in the years of poor harvests from 1594 to 1597 was no higher than usual. Only in St Erth in 1596 was there a hint of rather higher mortality. A bigger killer in the 1590s was plague, which appeared in 1591 in Redruth and neighbouring Illogan – where death rates were reputed to have been ten times the norm – as well as in mid- and east Cornwall at St Columb Minor, Morval and St Neot.[18] But even this epidemic was not universal. In fact, the last really major mortality crisis in Cornwall was just two years before the Prayer Book rising of 1549 and could have been an important factor in causing it. In September of 1547, forty-nine

people died in Camborne, compared with a normal monthly mortality of a mere one or two. Burial registers at St Columb Major in mid-Cornwall and Stoke Climsland in the east mirror this sharp peak in 1547/48, evidence of a virulent, pervasive outbreak of plague. But despite the disappearance of such spectacular visitations, the Grim Reaper continued steadily about his work. Even the gentry were not immune from sudden death at a young age, John Pendarves Basset dying of smallpox at Tehidy in 1739 aged only twenty five.[19] Death may, to some extent, have been a leveller, but it struck harder and earlier at the poor. In 1840, the Truro doctor Charles Barham produced some expectation-of-life statistics that proved the existence of shocking inequalities between the classes in the town. Professional people could expect to live to the age of forty, tradesmen some seven years less, while for labourers and artisans, expectation of life was just twenty eight.[20] While this dramatically shows that, in order to live longer, it helped to be better off, such statistics should be read with caution, since they relate to expectation of life at birth and do not allow for the huge waste of infant and child mortality. Taking the latter into consideration, such bald figures can be misleading. The reality, even for the poor, was that if people were lucky enough to survive childhood diseases and reach their late teens, then they might expect to live, on average, until their early sixties. Some, of course, lived a lot longer. Richard Polwhele reported a woman, Elizabeth Woolcock, aged 105, who 'on Sunday last … rode single to Bodmin church, a distance of three miles, and back again to dinner'.[21]

However, in the absence of high levels of literacy, ages could be subject to considerable guesswork at this time. Polwhele's account of Maurice Bingham, a

INFANT MORTALITY

In Victorian Britain, the levels of infant mortality (the number of deaths of children under a year old for every thousand live births), remained at a very high rate. This was due to a combination of poor sanitation, health care and housing plus poor diet and poor parenting skills and lack of knowledge. Despite a gradual fall in adult mortality from the 1860s onwards, the appalling toll of infants did not decrease the Edwardian period and the early twentieth century. In general, the Cornish rate was a little better than the average for England and Wales, being between 135 and 150 in the third quarter of the nineteenth century. Nonetheless, this picture masked variations within Cornwall; infant mortality in the mining and industrial districts being higher than the agricultural areas.

fisherman at St Just who died in 1780 aged one hundred and sixteen and, even more so, Christian Marchant who expired at Gwithian around 1676, 'one hundred and sixty-four years old, of good memory, and healthful at that age' (and, incidentally, the last reputed monoglot Cornish speaker) look a little bit more dubious.[22]

Childbirth carried the most risk for adult women and Cornish women in the late nineteenth century had a rate of death at childbirth that was almost fifty per cent higher than the English norm. This may have been partly due to the difficult economic conditions caused by depression in the mining industry. Deaths of adult men could be more unusual. William Trevarthen was buried at Camborne in August, 1705, 'being destroyed to a hurling with Redruth men at the high downs'.[23] Fatalities such as this gave the game of hurling across country between men of different parishes a bad name; as Daniel Defoe wrote in the early eighteenth century: 'a game fit only for barbarians'.[24]

Deaths showed a marked seasonality, peaking at the end of winter, just when food prices were usually at their highest and diet and weather at their worst. The constant presence of death, the high infant and child mortality, and the ever-present risk of a fatal illness striking out of the blue produced the Victorian obsession with death, funerals, mourning attire and florid memorials, an obsession that seems to have reached its height in the 1850s.[25] One can understand why. In 1851 for example, Nicholas Pedler, a chairmaker born in 1799, lived at Higher Market Street, Penryn, with his wife Elfrida, two sons and a daughter. Another three daughters lived away from home. In just under a decade between 1853 and 1862, the unfortunate Nicholas lost his wife, one son and three of his daughters to various illnesses.[26]

In the nineteenth century, funerals were common occurrences and, when the deceased was well known, very public events. According to George Henwood, the journalist and mine captain, in the mid nineteenth century people might travel as far as fourteen or fifteen miles to attend a burying. As an example, he recounted the funeral at Stithians of Nicholas Hill, a miner – or perhaps a mine captain – which, it was claimed, was attended by some three thousand people. The mourners formed a large procession of 'neatly, plainly clad persons of both sexes, the majority in respectable mourning, headed by the … Methodist minister, who gave out a hymn by verses, which was admirably sung by the choirs of the different chapels in the neighbourhood'. Following the minister and singers, numbered at over eighty, came the captains of Tresavean Mine and the relays of bearers needed to carry the body the three miles from his home to the church. Behind the widow came a 'long string of relatives' and then 'thousands of miners and rustics'. After the ceremony, the 'choirs repaired to the various public houses, and sing their songs over again'.[27] Other funerals, such as those of members of the Thomas family in Camborne, suppliers of Dolcoath's mine captains, attracted crowds. Clearly not every funeral was so well attended as this. In contrast, Robert Hichens of St Ives remembered a burial of 1736; 'in those days the family were always buried at night by torchlight and the body borne to the church not by hired bearers but by intimate friends of the deceased who after the funeral returned to the house where a cold collation was prepared'.[28]

It was death that broke up families and ended marriages before the early twentieth century. It has been estimated that half of children had lost one or both parents before they reached the age of marriage.[29] The implication of this is that many people, perhaps even a majority, never knew their grandparents. High death rates also meant high rates of widowhood. As many as one in five of the adult women in Lanner in 1851 were widows.[30] But, as half of the widowers and a somewhat lower proportion of the widows re-married within a year, there was also a large number of stepchildren as well as orphans.

Earlier deaths plus high child mortality kept family sizes down, even though many more children were being born than nowadays.

Family continuities

Sociologists once believed that, before industrialisation, families lived in households as an extended family with other kin including grandparents and even aunts, uncles, nephews and nieces – all under the same roof. This myth has long been exploded. Historians have replaced it with another: that the family in north-west Europe remained fundamentally unchanged over hundreds of years. This notion – that the nuclear family of parents and children sharing a household has been the usual form throughout recorded history – shades easily into the belief that such a family form is somehow the 'natural' way of organising domestic life, an unchanging and revered norm lying at the core of society. To an extent, this explains the panic that set in after the 1960s about the 'decline' of the family, as changing family structures were viewed as tantamount to changing society itself, a dissolution of natural ways of doing things.

But a longer perspective reveals that the way the family is organised has undergone continuous change. Continuities have always co-existed alongside change. Unusually, the early and mid twentieth century were periods of remarkable stability. The changes of recent decades perhaps herald a return to more normal fluctuating patterns. But what elements of family life have remained unchanged since earlier times?

The role of kinship

As well as extending the nuclear family way back into the mists of medieval times, historians now tend to downplay the role of kinship in England before the nineteenth century. It has been assumed that boundaries around the core family unit were drawn fairly tightly. Social historians note that there were few binding obligations to relatives beyond the immediate family and cultural historians observe that, before the nineteenth century, contemporaries rarely distinguished between first, second, third cousins etc. Similarly, all 'affinal' kin (those linked by marriages) were lumped together as 'in-laws', without the modern distinction between step-relations and in-laws.[31] Even so, wider kin could still provide a 'reserve account' which could be drawn upon when necessary.[32] We know as much from the example of the contents of a letter which Thomas St Aubyn of Clowance wrote in 1604 to John Trevelyan, interceding on behalf of his 'poor kinswoman', Tamsyn Pollard, concerning a disputed will. Tamsyn's mother was a sister of his cousin.[33]

But how far did Cornwall in the years before 1800 share the weak kinship network claimed for lowland England? Were there any hints of the wider kinship networks assumed to be more common in Celtic Britain? In his study of wealth and society in the early sixteenth century, Julian Cornwall suggested that in Cornwall the family was a 'larger, more cohesive unit than in the Saxon shires, keeping its property undivided'. In earlier times, he claims that Cornwall had been a place where 'partible inheritance (dividing land equally among all heirs) was practised', something that for him explained a greater fragmentation of landholding.[34] But, by the 1500s, it was the uniform practice to pass on land to the eldest son or other heir. Supporting this, there are no examples from Cornwall of the long name-chains of Celtic Wales, (such as Rhys ap Einion ap Tudur ap Griffith), striking evidence of the importance of genealogical memory in a society of partible inheritance. Granted, it is possible to find examples of bequests to wider kin in wills. Stephen Skues, a tinner of Redruth, left money to a nephew and niece as well as his own immediate family in 1752.[35] But the more usual pattern was, as in England, for only the immediate family to appear as the beneficiaries.

One place where kinship networks were supposedly strong was among the gentry. In his *Survey of Cornwall (1602)*, antiquarian Sir Richard Carew (1555-1620) observed that Cornwall's geography had made 'all Cornish gentlemen … cousins'; 'this angle, which so shutteth them in, hath wrought many interchangeable matches with each other's stock'.[36] Oiling this inter-marriage was a 'complex web of

OPPOSITE
The family of William Paddy Prophet and Kitty Whetter c.1867 before they emigrated to Canada. Back row, left to right: *their children, Sophia, Salmon, Sarah, Sylvanus, Susan and Silas.* Middle row: *William Paddy Prophet, his wife, Kitty, John Prophet, father of William, and Jennifred Paddy, his mother. Their son, Salathiel, is sits in front of William.* Front row: *Their grandson Samuel, Elizabeth Thomas, wife of Silas, holding their infant son. But they would not all have shared the same house.*

relationships' among sixteenth-century Cornish gentry, who were 'for ever in one another's houses, dining, playing at bowls or gambling into the night; travelling for business or pleasure in one another's company; quarrelling about land boundaries and inheritances, and marrying and arranging marriages among themselves'.[37] For example, William Carnsew, gentleman farmer of Bodilly in St Kew, recorded in his diary in the mid-1570s that he spent one night in ten sleeping over at the various houses of his fellow gentry.

In earlier times, a wider kin network was certainly centrally important for some Cornish gentry. Historian of medieval Cornwall, James Whetter, has unravelled the kin who were involved in the activities, legal and illegal, of prominent Cornish landlord, William Bodrugan, in the early 1400s.[38] But, by the 1800s, some voices at least were raised lamenting the decline of such kinship links. Polwhele reported in a letter written in 1822 that 'yesterday, in a conversation respecting "Cornish cousins" … we observed with regret, that the fellowship of affectionate kinsmen was now almost done away with'.[39] By the end of the eighteenth century, there was a notice-able increase in the proportion of children of the greater gentry marrying partners from outside Cornwall. In 1775-1825, forty five per cent found spouses in Cornwall, nine per cent in Devon and forty five per cent elsewhere in Britain. In the previous fifty years, as many as seventy three per cent had married into Cornish families. And yet, if we go further back to 1675-1725, we find that only forty per cent of greater gentry marriages were to Cornish partners, with thirty five per cent to partners in

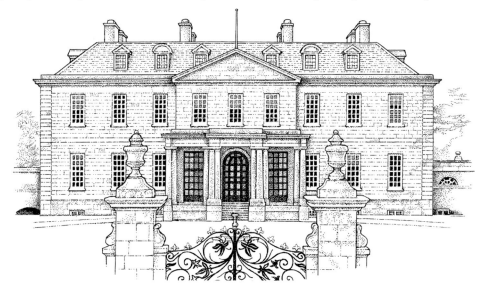

Devon. What seems to have happened at the end of the eighteenth century is that the horizons of the gentry widened but, in the 1600s, there had been considerable inter-marriage with Devon gentry, despite what might be implied by Carew's oft-quoted remark about Cornish cousins.

Family sentiments

While the evidence for extensive kin networks in the pre-industrial period remains ambiguous, relations within the family seemed to have mirrored those elsewhere. A

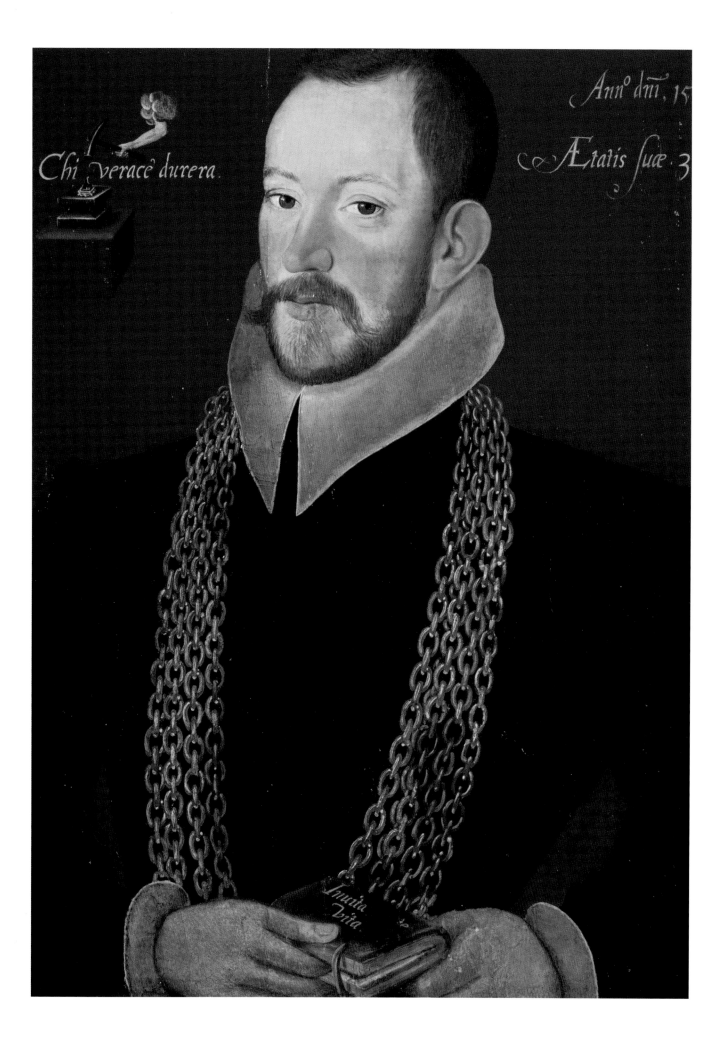

Chi verace durera.

Ann⁰ dñi. 15
Ætatis suæ 3

CHAPTER ONE

heated debate erupted among historians of the family at one point about whether relations between husbands and wives and parents and children in the sixteenth and seventeenth centuries were colder and more distant than later. High child mortality, child-rearing practices and the early age at which children left home were all seen as evidence for an emotionally starved environment. However, the majority view now is that there was considerable consistency into the nineteenth century. It is true that there was not much sign of affection for his wife or children in the diary of William Carnsew at St Kew in 1576/77.[40] But the workmanlike entries, which note his wife's comings and goings and little more, may just indicate that 'linguistic frugality' noted for more humble classes in later centuries.[41]

Historians have made a lot of the widespread practice of swaddling infants in tight cloth for the first few months of their lives. This, it is argued, prevented mother-child bonding in the crucial early months. Similarly, the practice of wet-nursing among the landed élites into the eighteenth century has been held to have had the same effect, establishing a remote relationship with children, one marked by domination rather than affection. But swaddling declined during the seventeenth century and, more broadly, the proposition that parent-child relations were distant and unaffectionate is now questioned. Indeed, it is not difficult to find examples of real affection. Thomas Gwyn of Falmouth remembered his late-seventeenth-century father with somewhat ambivalent affection; his merchant father 'tenderly loved me' but 'yet kept an exact government over me that I could not say whether I loved or feared him most'. But he grieved deeply over the deaths of his own children, expressing for example 'intense' grief in his journal in 1707 on the death from smallpox of his four year old daughter Jane. His daughters in their teens became his 'companions' and were taken with him on trips out of Cornwall.[42]

Affection between married couples

The frequency of second marriages could complicate relationships with parents. Alexander Daniel of Alverton at Penzance had several disagreements with his father over financial matters in the 1620s, arguments exacerbated, at least according to Alexander, by 'the maliciousness of my stepmother towards me'.[43] Yet even children who behaved badly towards their parents could be forgiven. The son of John Pearce, a St Ives merchant, stole his father's goods and had been 'undutiful'. Nevertheless, he was still made the executor of this father's will in 1656. 'I freely forgive him', wrote John in his will.[44] Perhaps neither domination nor affection were the most important principles underlying parent-child relationships in earlier centuries. Others have proposed that the more relevant motivation was reciprocity.[45]

Parents cared for their children and bestowed affection on them but expected children to be 'dutiful', to help add to the family income as soon as they were old enough (which could be very young in the households of the poor) and to care, in turn, for their parents if they reached old age. The failure of Henry Bodrugan to re-marry for eight years after the death in 1465 of his first wife, Joan Beaumont, who had borne him his first and only (and illegitimate) son is viewed by James Whetter as an 'indication, perhaps, of his attachment for her'.[46] Two hundred years later, Sidney Godolphin's wife, Margaret, died after childbirth in 1678, leaving a tender and pathetic letter for her husband.[47] Reportedly distraught at her death, Sidney

TRELOWARREN *c.* 1825

The duties of servants

The butler

To control the pantry, superintend the men in the servants' hall, report their conduct when necessary. The stable as well as the indoor servants are under his authority.

The housekeeper

All female servants are under her management. With the exception of the cook she may hire and dismiss them 'without applying to me' (i.e. Lady Vyvyan).

To regulate the expenditure in the house.

To receive and distribute articles of consumption.

To see that no 'improper' persons come into the house.

To keep the house in order (she had a carpenter under her orders for small jobs).

To mention all irregularities of conduct 'to myself or Mr Shaw'.

To superintend the dairy and poultry court.

No new linen to be purchased for the house without directions from myself, or some-one for me.

In the absence of the Ladies - to superintend the girls' school at Colenso and choose children when there are vacancies.

To attend to the poor and distribute small charities. Nothing to be given to vagrants.

To keep three accounts; housekeepers, dairy and poultry.

ABOVE

Arms of Trelowarren of Trelowarren. It was a common Cornish custom for landed families to name themselves after their estate.

never re-married, instead putting his energies into becoming Britain's first de-facto Prime Minister. Again, while Robert Hoblyn, a clergyman of St Columb, made little mention of his wife in the diary which he wrote in the 1690s,[48] Thomas Gwyn, from a Falmouth merchant family, wrote with feeling on the death of his wife in 1716; they had lived together with a great deal of hearty love and true faithfulness and with a growing affection all that time (they were married in 1687). She was not a woman of ostentation but a substantial good wife … a very tender good mother and very loving and helpful to me … great was our tenderness.[49]

No doubt, just as in present-day Cornwall, some couples got on amicably and affectionately, others got on less well, living together with more trouble and tempestuousness. Richard Grenville's marriage to Lady Mary Howard was a definite example of the latter. Grenville, soldier and later Cornish Royalist civil war leader, married Mary Howard in 1628, partly, it was alleged, to solve his financial problems as she was an heiress, bringing with her property of 4,000 acres and £1,000-a-year income. But Mary was strong willed and had already out-lived three previous husbands. The marriage was a stormy one. There was soon a law suit and a case to obtain a legal separation. During this, Mary claimed that Richard had confined her to a corner of the house, had broken down her door, given her a black eye and knocked her down. He had also ordered a servant to burn horse hair, wool, feathers, and the parings of horses' hooves and cause the resulting smoke to go into her chamber through a hole in the wall. Richard, in response, claimed she had taunted him for the meanness of his fortune and 'sung unseemly songs to his face'.[50] Mary eventually departed and was granted a separation in 1631, ending this short-lived and ill-fated partnership.

Care of the elderly

Those who survived into old age at a time when there were no pensions made up a group at serious risk of poverty and destitution. When ability to earn wages or otherwise make a living failed and independence was lost, the lot of the elderly poor before the twentieth century was not easy. Despite attempts by the authorities to force children to take responsibility for their aged parents, this was by no means guaranteed. Indeed, the wider community was more often after 1600 the provider of the basic means of existence for the elderly through the Poor Law and charity.[51] Moreover, when family members were involved directly, the burden was likely to fall upon younger children who often remained home to look after elderly parents or took a widowed parent into their own homes.

To avoid dependence on poor relief, complex arrangements were sometimes made with children for the care of their parents in return for handing over assets to the next generation. In 1682, William Truebody, a yeoman farmer at Tremar in St Cleer, settled all his land on his son, William, who was about to be married. In return, William agreed to pay his father '£4 per annum in quarterly installments … and finding meat and drink for him and Joan his wife, or in lieu thereof £10 at his (the father's) election'. His parents would 'enjoy the chamber over the shop parcel of the premises and use of the room or house called the Hall in common with William junior and wife and his heirs'. The younger William also had to cut and carry wood for his parents, on demand.[52] Twenty years earlier at St Teath, Giles Bawden retired and made similar arrangements with his son. In return for receiving all his property, apart from the clothes of the parents, goods to the value of £6 and six sheep, the son agreed to supply 'good and sufficient houseroom, meat, drink, lodging, fire, candlelight, washing and starching and £8 a year in quarterly installments' to be increased to £20 if the parents 'dislike or refuse to live with or be at the finding of' their son.[53]

Family and household size

It has become a truism that 'for as far back in time as records go, English families have taken the form that is familiar to us in the twentieth century', that is two generations of parents and children sharing a household.[54] Before the eighteenth century, it was rare for households to include other relatives. Only five to ten per cent did so and then it was usually aged parents, orphaned children and younger unmarried brothers and sisters. It was even rarer to find two married couples sharing the same house. Households had, on average, four and a half family members in late-medieval and early-modern times,[55] an average that has been raised to the status of an unalterable (and largely unquestioned) norm. Nonetheless, family size can and could vary widely over the family cycle. When two people before the late nineteenth century married and formed a household, children would soon follow and family size gradually rise from two to as many as seven or eight within ten to twelve years. But then, the practices of young people going into service and apprenticeship meant that they would start leaving home at a relatively young age. For a few years, those leaving would be balanced by those being born, though sooner or later, family size would fall again.

In the third decade of the marriage, the family would be back to four or five or fewer and this would also be when the chances of one or both parents dying would increase.

Service and apprenticeships

This cyclical pattern of rise and fall in family size was a generalised one, but among better-off households, numbers were also boosted by the presence of employees and servants. Living-in service had emerged by the 1500s as a regular part of the life course, a transitional period for many between the family home and setting up a new household. Apprenticeship was urban, service was rural; apprenticeship common among the artisan and craftsman classes, service among the labouring class, although before the nineteenth century, farmers and even some gentry sent their sons to live in other households for a period. Both farm service and apprenticeship served as a solution to the problem of controlling youth, and a way to socialise and educate young people.[56] They entered service – the terms of which were usually re-negotiated annually – sometimes as young as eight or nine years old, although more usually around thirteen. Living-in farm service, where the farmer provided a small wage,

ABOVE

Hester Polkinhorne (1863-1951), right, working as a domestic servant in Plymouth in the late 19th century. She set up a grocery business in Devonport before returning to retire in Cornwall

board and lodging, began to decline in the arable areas of south-east England in the late eighteenth century. But in Cornwall, as in other more pastoral regions, such farm service continued well into the late nineteenth century. As an example, William Thomas was born in 1841 at Trevescan in Sennen to a family headed by an agricultural labourer. By the age of ten, William was living at a neighbouring farm, that of Richard Trembath at Trevilly, along with two other farm servants. Unusually, he was still there ten years later, in 1861. Soon after this, however, he married and by 1871, was living back at Trevescan with his wife Mary and four children. He was still working on a farm (perhaps even the same one), but by this time, was selling his labour by the day or week and finding his own keep.

Unlike service, in apprenticeship, a child – usually a boy – would be bound to a master for a period of up to seven years. In most cases, the parents would pay for his apprenticeship and in return, the master would teach him the skills of his trade while exercising the powers of a parent. This occasionally involved meting out considerable punishment, as the recurring notices of runaway apprentices in early-nineteenth-century newspapers imply.

The household size of the labouring poor was reduced by such practices while those of farmers and craftsmen were raised, but it was the presence of servants which produced the largest households of all – among the landed gentry. At Tregullow, Scorrier, in 1861, William Williams and his wife and unmarried son and daughter shared their home with his married daughter, her husband and their daughter. These seven were waited on in turn by thirteen female servants and three male servants who lived in the servants' quarters. The women's roles ranged from tutor, housekeeper and cook through eight maids to nurse and washerwoman. These were all backed up by a butler, footman and valet. Gardeners also lived in the lodge and nearby cottages. Similarly, at Carclew House in 1891 Arthur Tremayne employed two footmen, a groom and a stableman, together with a housekeeper, lady's maid, still-room maid, scullery maid, kitchen maid, two laundry maids and three general housemaids.[57]

The changing family

These days, the larger proportion of people who survive to a greater age than formerly, the far lower infant mortality rate, smaller completed families, the one third of babies born outside marriage, the one third of marriages that end in divorce, would all suggest that the modern family has undergone considerable change. The apparent stability of the nuclear family should not be allowed to blind us to the changes that have occurred in family life since the medieval period. For example, as we have seen, it was extremely rare in early modern England for households to consist of more than one married couple. When a child married they left home to establish a new household. Yet, it has been claimed that in West Penwith in the 1500s and 1600s things may have been very different.

Cornish extended-family households

This startling conclusion was reached by David Cullum in a study of the economy and demography of West Penwith.[58] He argued that the *St Just Easter Book* entries of 1588-96 show that half of the households contained two or more married couples. In similar fashion, he argues that the taxation lists of the seventeenth century imply as many as ten persons per household, double the norm, in the parishes of St Just, Sancreed, Gulval and Paul. Based on this, Cullum concluded that 'large, joint or extended (households) commonly existed in the west Cornwall region' from the sixteenth to the early eighteenth century. To explain this, he points to the treeless, granite landscape with its lack of building materials, the scarce resources of fuel for

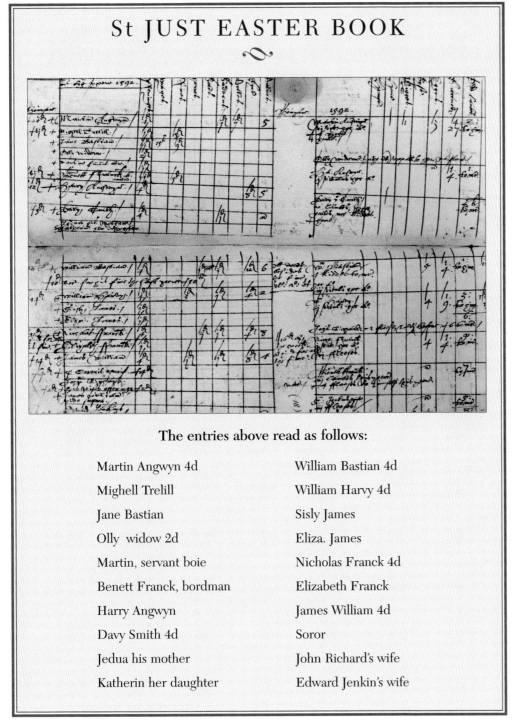

St JUST EASTER BOOK

The entries above read as follows:

Martin Angwyn 4d	William Bastian 4d
Mighell Trelill	William Harvy 4d
Jane Bastian	Sisly James
Olly widow 2d	Eliza. James
Martin, servant boie	Nicholas Franck 4d
Benett Franck, bordman	Elizabeth Franck
Harry Angwyn	James William 4d
Davy Smith 4d	Soror
Jedua his mother	John Richard's wife
Katherin her daughter	Edward Jenkin's wife

LEFT

An extract from the St Just Easter Book recording the Easter offerings paid by adult parishioners at Boiuyan (today, Bojewyan) near St Just in Penwith in 1592. Hard to decipher from the Elizabethan script, it is claimed that the record shows adults and children from different families sharing the same house. The 4d against a man's name shows that he was married and his wife living. A return of 2d that he or she was a widow or widower. Those names against which no sum of money is shown indicate a single man or woman.

cooking, economies of scale in childcare and the presence of tinning as well as agriculture. 'A large household engaged in both mining and farming could more finely tune its efforts to prevailing economic harmonies than could a smaller unit'.[59] For example, young men could work in tin streaming to gain a capital stake to buy or rent

land, with the older generation more involved in working the smallholding. But such extended two-couple households may not be quite as unusual as historians of the family claim. In the framework-knitting area of Leicestershire in the eighteenth century, there was a similar pattern of more complex households, with families huddling together for survival at particular times of stress in the family cycle.[60] Here it is suggested that the older generation took on domestic tasks and the younger laboured outside the home. What eighteenth-century Leicestershire and seventeenth-century West Penwith had in common is that they were both areas where industrial growth produced extra earning opportunities and relatively high levels of population growth. In such circumstances, the extended household might be seen as a transitional response to early industrialisation, a short-lived phase in the family cycle and one soon broken by the death of the older generation. What we cannot claim is that such extended families in West Penwith were somehow the survivors of an older medieval pattern. They were not the leftovers of an old society, but the harbingers of a new one.

Industrialisation and family change

By the middle of the eighteenth century, a recognisably new kind of family was emerging in Britain. Amongst the upper classes, a more domestic family is implied by family portraits of the later eighteenth century.[61] In the labouring classes, parallel changes were occurring, partly in response to profound economic change. West Penwith may have been in the vanguard, but a century later, other regions were experiencing the birth pains of industrialisation. Technological change created new jobs, many (though by no means all) outside the home, and also new earnings

opportunities for women and children. Meanwhile, a smaller proportion of families retained access to land. More became entirely dependent on markets for their food needs and on employers for the income to buy it. In the south and east of England, a decline in the institutions of farm service and apprenticeship accelerated.[62] All this shifted economic power towards the young. Peaks of earning ability for unskilled labourers came early, when they were at their fittest. As more people became dependent on labour power rather than property or land, constraints on early marriage now evaporated. As a result of this, the age of marriage fell sharply in the later eighteenth century. At the same time numbers not marrying were at a historic low. Disruption of the previous courtship-and-marriage pattern is indicated by the steady rise in the illegitimacy rate in England and Wales, which peaked at around seven per cent in the 1840s.

The Cornish 'customary' family

In this respect, Cornwall was different. By the 1840s, the illegitimacy rate in Cornwall was around four per cent, much lower than that in England. A remarkable turnaround had occurred in the two centuries since 1640 when Cornish illegitimacy rates were among the highest. This may be related to the cultural effects of Methodism which emphasised a domestic piety and domestic responsibilities (though it should be noted that it failed to dent the custom of pre-marital sex) or it

'THREE-LIFE' LEASES

By the eighteenth century, it had become common for tenants to rent property for the term of 'three lives'. On taking the lease, the tenant would name three people (they were often himself, his wife and his son but not always - if you were clever you might name someone in the royal family as their life expectancy was longer). When the three named persons were dead, the tenancy would end. Naming your immediate family was therefore a guarantee of security of tenure during your own and their lifetimes. On some leases, it was possible to replace a deceased life by another - at a charge - but this was up to the landlord. The majority of smallholdings and houses in the west of Cornwall were let out in this way in the early nineteenth century. However, many - if not most - farm leases, especially in the east, had become fixed-term. Three-life leases died out towards the end of the nineteenth century, partly because emigration made it increasingly difficult to monitor them.

may be due to greater economic security on the part of the Cornish labouring poor in the eighteenth and early nineteenth centuries. One element in the latter was the continuation in the eighteenth century, perhaps even expansion, of the practice of leasing out smallholdings on three-life leases to mining families.[63] This way, many mining families in west Cornwall retained access to a plot of land and their own food supply, thus reducing dependence on wages. Around 1840 as many as forty-seven per cent of households in St Agnes and over fifty per cent in Carnmenellis in Wendron leased smallholdings of an acre or more. Even in the more urban Redruth parish, twenty-six per cent of all households occupied such smallholdings.[64]

In the period from 1800 to 1840, access to smallholdings was supplemented by various other 'collateral aids', maintaining the independence of many families.[65] In West Penwith, these could include shares in fishing boats or the part ownership of a cow; more generally, the practice of granting potato allotments to labourers became common amongst farmers after 1800. In this transaction, no money changed hands. Farmers allowed labouring families to use a portion of their fields to grow potatoes, the size depending on the amount of household manure the family could supply. This way, the farmers' land was improved, the labouring family obtained a supply of food and everyone gained. Through such practices, Cornish families were sheltered from the worst effects of volatile and globalising markets for tin and copper and new households were perhaps less subject to unexpected disruption than elsewhere. The fact that illegitimate births were lower in the districts where 'collateral aids' were most extensive, in west Cornwall rather than in the east, must be significant.

While avoiding the worst disruptions of this period, in Cornwall, the 'customary' family also resisted wider changes that were transforming family life elsewhere. A central aspect of the 'traditional' family as it emerged in nineteenth-century England was the concept of the male-breadwinner wage.

The 'traditional' family – male breadwinners

This linked to emerging middle-class notions of what constituted an 'ideal' family – one in which gender roles were starkly differentiated, where the wife took all responsibility for domestic tasks and child care and did not earn money outside the home and where the husband worked away from the home and then returned to his domestic haven of peace away from the bitterly competitive world of work. Such an ideal depended on a male wage that was sufficient to maintain a family. It was an ideal that was rarely attained in working-class communities where most men's wages, until the 1870s at least, were just too low. But, by that decade, the emerging trade unions were beginning to demand a 'family wage', thus embedding ideas about the ideal family.

The concept of the breadwinner wage stabilised patriarchy in the nineteenth century, enhancing the financial power of men over their families.[66] It also reinforced the role of women in guaranteeing domestic conditions, and in so doing, it exposed even further the vulnerability of groups outside these family norms. The idea of the male breadwinner became most firmly ensconced in the towns and cities in Victorian England. which, by 1851, was mainly urban (Scotland even earlier). But Cornwall remained predominantly rural. Even by a generous definition of 'urban', seventy-eight per cent of miners still lived in rural parishes as late as 1851, and the largest Cornish towns of Penzance, Falmouth, Truro, Camborne and Redruth only contained between them thirteen per cent of the total population. In such towns, gender relations and family life, at least among the middle classes, may have begun to resemble that in the larger English population centres. But in the rural, industrial districts there was a strong element of continuity from the pre-industrial family.

Along with the Victorian ideal family had also come the double standard of morality. In the eighteenth century, what was expected of men and women within marriage seems to have diverged. This was given legal substance in the 1857 Divorce Act, under the terms of which men could sue for divorce on grounds of adultery alone, but women had to prove adultery plus some other reason. Little wonder that, in such a context, marital violence persisted, protected both by the dominance of patriarchy and the Victorian ideal of the private, domestic family, free from interference by outside agencies. Community sanctions against practices such as wife-beating gradually ebbed, condemned by the respectable. But legal sanctions were slow to take their place and as a result, marital violence may even have increased in the nineteenth century. We have little evidence from Cornwall about this aspect of family life. Occasional cases turned up in the local courts, such as John Sleeman of St Austell, bound over in 1852 for twelve months to keep the peace towards his wife.[67] Of course, violence was not always one way. In 1858, also at St Austell, Sarah Menear was committed for breach of the peace towards her husband, James. She had thrown a knife at him but in her defence, she claimed he 'used to get drunk and go to the wrestling'. The couple had separated since the assault and the case was dismissed.[68] In 1820, Sarah Polgrean was less lucky. She had poisoned her husband in order to re-marry and was charged with murder.[69]

In the early nineteenth century, there was considerable regional distinctiveness in family life and gender relations. In the Cornish mining districts, it is likely that women were less bound by patriarchal norms than elsewhere. The widespread employment of girls and young unmarried women as 'bal maidens' (surface workers at the mines) from the early eighteenth century onwards ensured women a taste of economic and social freedom and independence between childhood and marriage. This independence was symbolised through conspicuous spending on clothes and, it is suggested, by a lack of deference towards men.[70] Once married, women continued to participate in the smallholding economy, leading to a situation where 'boundaries between the world of work and the world of home were less rigidly drawn'.[71] It seems that, unlike the patriarchal hierarchy that was being embraced by many industrial artisans in other regions,[72] in early-nineteenth-century Cornwall the persistence of older, customary, 'traditions' established during the previous century, guaranteed some cooperation between the genders. It may be significant in this respect that by the 1850s, 'respectable' male writers such as George Henwood were beginning to criticise the independence of the bal maiden as producing poor domestic skills. Such criticisms heralded a growing condemnation of the Cornish customary family and can be viewed as an attempt to enhance the power of men within the family.

Growing kinship ties

If the Cornish family into the 1840s and 1850s was marked by greater cooperation between the genders and more muted patriarchy than was seen in urban, Victorian England, did it share the increase in kin ties associated with industrialisation? Anderson has found that kin support was important in mid-nineteenth-century Preston, where relatives helped family members to get jobs and housing and where kin often lived nearby in the packed working-class terraces of this expanding town.[73] Reay also discovered a similar pattern in rural Kent, which he describes as a 'kin-based environment'.[74] Kin may not have been living in the same house, but sixty per cent of the families in his parishes were related to others in the same parish. Similarly, Ruggles discovered that the proportion of extended families rose in Lancashire, a finding mirrored in other mid-nineteenth-century industrial communities.[75] By 1851, other relatives made up eight per cent of family members in England and Wales, compared with only five per cent (excluding servants) in the period from 1650-1749.[76]

The pattern of kinship, or neighbourly, networks helping people move to bigger places to find jobs is also found in Cornwall. For example, between 1868 and 1870,

Thomas French, a carpenter originally from Davidstow, moved with his family from Altarnun to Redruth, where he worked in 1871 as a labourer at the Redruth Brewery, living in nearby Pond Lane. This brewery was owned at the time by the Wickett family who came from Davidstow and had obviously brought with them several of the workforce from that parish. For whatever reason, however, we also know that industrial Redruth was not to the liking of Thomas and his family and, by 1881, they had moved back to Trewassa in Davidstow and to farm labouring.

But how important were kin ties more generally in nineteenth-century Cornwall? What should we make of the entry of Dolcoath mine captain, William Petherick, in his day book on 20 December, 1822: 'I have an opportunity of sending a letter to my newly married cousin at St Blazey Highway'?[77] Does this indicate an everyday awareness of wide kin connections in Cornwall? John Harris (1820-1884), the mining poet

of Camborne and brought up in a classic smallholding, 'customary' family environment, certainly peppered his autobiography with several references to aunts and uncles,[78] and it was an uncle who first employed him outside the family home, at the tender age of nine. Perhaps this growing nineteenth-century involvement in kinship networks actually helped pave the way for overseas migration, where kinship connections were to prove a valuable asset.

Economic crisis and changing family structure

Whatever the situation in 1851, by 1881, many Cornish families were experiencing serious strains. The crisis in mining from the 1860s had increased the proportion of households that contained extended families and decreased the proportion of nuclear families. In Tywardreath, for example, in 1851, seven per cent of families contained three generations; by 1881, this proportion had doubled to fourteen per cent. Calculations based on a sample of households reveal that in most west Cornish registration sub-districts in 1881, the proportions of all types of extended family households were a lot higher than the English norm of eighteen per cent (a figure also found in rural Kent). In contrast, in Cornwall a quarter of all families were extended in Redruth, Gwennap, St Buryan, Paul and Penzance (the highest at twenty seven per cent). Within nuclear families in west Cornwall, there was a lower proportion of households with children and a far higher proportion with just one parent and children. Over one in five of all households contained one parent with children

RIGHT

John Richards Branwell and his wife Elizabeth (née Tyack) in their garden home at Penlee House, Penzance in the late 19th century. The Branwells were a prosperous merchant family in the town. Maria Branwell married the Reverend Patrick Brontë and was the mother of writers Charlotte, Emily, Anne and Branwell.

in Redruth, St Austell, St Ives and Gwennap and almost one in five in Illogan and St Just in Penwith. This contrasted markedly with the fewer than one in ten average for England. The difference is explained by the absence of men, forced to leave home to seek work. As early as 1871, as many as thirty-five per cent of young married women in Redruth and twenty-six per cent in St Just were living apart from their husbands. Another effect of the economic problems of the later nineteenth century was the disruption of customary courtship practices. This was reflected by the fact that, while illegitimacy rates in England and Wales fell throughout the later nineteenth century, those in Cornwall began to increase in the 1840s, overtook the English rate by 1870 and peaked in the 1870s at a rate of about seven per cent, compared to an English average by then of just under five per cent.[79]

Such statistics hint at a very distinctive working-class family structure in later nineteenth century Cornwall. Relationships between husband and wife were more likely to be conducted over a distance, perhaps even over thousands of miles, grandchildren or grandparents more likely to be sharing the home and children more likely to be born out of wedlock. Did this affect the way husbands and wives, parents and children, children and grandparents, related to each other? Did it make people less willing to show affection or more willing? Did it lead to more emotional self-suffi-ciency? Did it lead to a greater reliance on kin? Some of these consequences might logically be forecast although conclusions await detailed research. But whatever that research proves, we can say that the traumatic social and demographic changes of the later nineteenth century fundamentally transformed Cornish families.

The compassionate family

In the late nineteenth century, signs began to appear in England of the gradual replacement of the 'traditional', patriarchal domestic family by a more compassion-ate, more egalitarian and relaxed family form. What allowed this to happen was a fundamental shift in family behaviour, producing what is known in academic circles as the 'nineteenth-century fer-tility transition'. Basically, the numbers of children being born began to fall and family size became smaller. This had a strong social dimension, with professional groups leading the way and labouring couples bringing up the rear. Thus, in the 1880s, the average number of children born to the fami-lies of doctors and clergymen was three. But the average for railway labourers was still 5.2. While in 1850, seven children born alive was a common thing, by 1900, five or six was beginning to be thought of as large.[80]

ABOVE
The Pender family at
Rosevean on Bryher in
the Scillies, c.1930.
Left to right,
William Ellis, Sarah
(1846-1944), Sarah jnr
(1871-1944) and James.

After the 1860s, smaller families were encouraged in turn by the growing avail-ability of consumer goods and rising standards of living. Given choices of expendi-ture and restrictions on child labour, parents, began to make that common, modern, 'life-style' choice between children or other consumption goods. In particular, it is suggested that middle-class families felt the social pressures to 'keep up with the Joneses' towards the end of the nineteenth century. This led to attempts to stop pro-ducing children in order to free resources for servant-keeping or to rent or buy a house in a better neighbourhood, or send at least the eldest son to a prestigious (and expensive) private school. With heroic ingenuity, given the absence of widely avail-able and effective barrier methods of contraception until after the First World War, the trend set by the urban middle classes gradually filtered through the rest of soci-ety. Simultaneously, it is claimed, 'progressive' child-rearing and more affectionate parent-child relationships began to emerge by the early 1900s.[81] This more compas-sionate family was the result of new views of children that had crystallised by the 1870s. Juvenile courts, ragged schools (bringing formal education to the very poor-est children in the cities), and restrictions on children's work had all resulted in changing attitudes to childhood. And this was followed later in the century by the emergence of that troubled category, 'adolescence'. The 'gentle, home-centred, working-class family of two or three children' that Paul Thompson claims to observe in Edwardian Britain was a product of these new ideas, as well as rising living standards.[82] Yet it should be noted that this picture does not go unchallenged, with other historians pointing to autobiographical evidence that suggest the happiest memories of childhood actually came from those who grew up in large families with few luxuries.[83] Gender differences continued. The more affectionate term, 'mum', is supposed to date from the 1880s,[84] indicating the central role of mother in this compassionate family. The working-class mum, it is claimed, was by the end of the nineteenth century and through the first half of the twentieth, deferential yet at the same time assertive.[85] With the apparent victory of the Victorian family ideal, women had accepted their withdrawal into domestic privacy. But, in return for this, they had demanded and obtained power within the home, in most industrial regions controlling the purse strings even if not directly filling the purse. It was mother who set codes of behaviour and often threatened and meted out corporal punishment on their errant offspring.

Cornwall and the 'compassionate' family

The domestic, yet assertive mum is a figure familiar to many Cornish working-class families of the twentieth century. However, it is likely that in Cornwall, with high numbers of men absent from the 1860s, mum had to be a great deal more assertive and less privately deferential than in many regions. The physical distance from men may well also have engendered an emotional distance, inhibiting the affection that Cornish men were able to bestow on their children from whom they were separated for considerable amounts of time. Of course, differences in emotional performance across the genders were hardly limited to early-twentieth-century Cornwall. And not all Cornish men found it difficult to express feelings. Alice Brannlund, born in Truro in 1902 and third child of a large family of ten, remembered her father who worked for the Truro Steam Laundry as 'always happy … He seldom got cross and never shouted or swore at us'.[86] And it wasn't just working-class men who were emotionally challenged. Indeed, perhaps this was even more of a problem for middle-class men, used to pursuing their careers while the children were left to the care of wives and servants. An example was the Reverend Sabine Baring-Gould (1834-1924), author of the hymn, *Onward Christian soldiers* and an early enthusiast of the Celtic Revival in Cornwall (though he was actually a Devonian). He was also the father of sixteen children. The story goes that Baring-Gould asked one small child at a party, "And whose little girl are you?" She burst into tears: "I'm yours, Daddy".[87]

Earlier, compassionate relationships were already in evidence in the Cornish customary family. At mid-century, for John Harris, 'children became my companions. They were never happier than when with me, nor I than when with them'.[88] His poem, written on the death of his young daughter, shows his deep emotional involvement with his children:

On the Death of My Daughter, Lucretia

(who died December 23rd, 1855, aged six years and five months)

And art thou gone so soon?
And is thy loving, gentle spirit fled?
Ah! is my fair, my passing beautiful,
My beloved Lucretia numbered with the dead?

I miss thee, daughter, now,
In the dear dells of earth we oft have trod;
And a strange longing fills my yearning soul
To sleep with thee, and be, like thee, with God!

I miss thee at thy books,
Lisping sweet Bible-accents in my ear,
Showing me pictures by the evening lamp,
Beautiful emblems thou didst love so dear.

I miss thee at thy prayers,
When the eve-star is looking through the sky,
And thy lone sister kneels in sorrow down,
To pray to her great Father up on high.

I miss thee by the brook,
Where we have wandered many a summer's day,
And thou were happy with thy loving sire,
More happy here than at thy simple play.

I miss thee mid the trees,
Where we have hasted in the twilight dim
To wake the echoes of the silent dell,
And mark the glow-worm 'neath the hawthorn's limb.

I miss thee on the Hill,
The dear old hill which we have climbed so oft;
And O, how very happy have we been
In the still bower of the old heathy croft!

I miss thee at day's close,
When from my labour I regain my cot,
And sit down sadly at the supper board,
Looking for thee, but, ah! I see thee not.

I miss thee every where,
In my small garden, watching the first flower,
By the clear fountain, – in thy Sunday class,
Running to meet me at the evening hour.

Farewell, my beautiful!
Thy sinless spirit is with Christ above;
Thou hast escaped the evils of the world:
We have a daughter in the meads of love.

When I and little Jane
Walk hand in hand along the old hill's way,
Shall we not feel thy cherub-presence near,
Singing our sad psalms in the twilight grey?

Companion of the bard,
Mid rocks and trees, and hedges ivy-crossed!
At morn and eve in Nature's presence-cell
We oft have entered with our musings lost.

How thou didst love the flowers,
The darling daisy and the buds of Spring,
The brooks and birds, the hush of solitude,
The moon and stars, like some diviner thing!

Ah! thou wert like a rose,
Dropped by an angel on earth's feverish clime,
To bloom full lovely, till December winds
Blasted thy beauty in its morning's prime.

Hush, murmuring spirit, hush!
It is the Lord, He only, who hath given:
And He hath taken – Thus I kiss His rod!
– The gem, which fell from paradise, to heaven.

Harris's idyllic family life, though perhaps exceptional, reflected his close relations
with his mother – 'the gentlest mother the world ever saw' – and grandmother – 'the
dearest, kindest grandmother in all the world'. Relations with his father were, however, more distant. In contrast to his mother, he makes little mention of his father's
death and comments that his father 'expressed himself in few words'.[89] A contemporary, John James, who spent much of his working life overseas and separated from
his family, included many references to his wife and children in his journal, written
between the 1850s and 1870s. They were clearly central in his thoughts.[90]

Other evidence may suggest that Cornish working-class communities were more affectionate, certainly more tolerant, towards children than the patriarchal, reserved, distant, middle-class English norm. The writer W.H.Hudson (1841-1922) concluded after his visit to Cornwall in the early years of the twentieth century that 'one of the most pleasing traits of the Cornish people ... is their love for little children ... The rudest men exhibit a strange tenderness towards their little ones; and not only of their own, since they regard all children with a kind of paternal feeling'. Hudson thought that west Cornwall was, 'compared with other parts of England ... a children's paradise' for the corollary of a love for children was a lenient toleration of them. 'A common complaint made by English residents is that the children are not

Richard Davey, the centre of controversy over the Davey legacy (see next page), *pictured here with his cousins.*
Back row, from left: *Amy Rooke, an American cousin, Florrie Rooke,the husband of the American cousin, and Violet Rooke. Mary Rooke is seated in front beside Richard Davey.*

taught to know their place – that they do just what they like'. 'The children', according to a schoolmaster, 'are masters of the situation in these parts: the way they lorded it over their parents had amazed him when he first came from a Midland district to live among them'.[91] The survival of the more egalitarian, domestic, Cornish cottage relations of the eighteenth century long into the nineteenth century and the migrations and domestic upheavals of the end of the nineteenth century may have combined to produce this situation, where authoritarian and patriarchal relations, both of men over women and parents over children, were relatively restrained in early twentieth century Cornwall.

Cornish middle class families – legacies and inheritances

More organised families can also be identified. Charles Trevail, born of a farming family at Luxulyan in 1854, experienced a typical, late-nineteenth-century, middle-class family upbringing within a 'traditional' family. His 'father and mother were thrifty, careful and worked hard, and brought their children to work'.[92] In such families, the ownership of property and its transmission from one generation to the next remained an important, all-consuming topic of conversation, speculation and planning.

Cornwall's own version of Charles Dickens's interminable law suit of Jarndyce and Jarndyce in *Bleak House* came to public attention in 1914.[93] In 1872, Captain John Davey of Busveal Farm in Gwennap, mine agent at various mines, died, leaving his estate to his son, also called John and also a mine captain, at Wheal Buller. The story is that John junior persuaded his father to alter the will in his favour. John senior regretted this and on his deathbed, asked another mine captain relative, Paul Toy, to go to Redruth to change it. This was prevented by the younger John who,

RIGHT

John Davey, whose son triggered a twenty-one-year court case. Davey was captain at several Gwennap mines. He died in 1872. This photograph speaks volumes for the solid self-confidence and independence of the 19th-century Cornish mine captain.

with the aid of a four-barrelled revolver, stopped him leaving the house until his father was conveniently dead. Inheritance safely secured, the surviving John travelled to Australia on a trip for his health in 1881-82, but died on the way home, reputedly after hearing he had been jilted and having thrown his ring into the Red

Sea. John left his estate, valued at £60,000 plus at his death, to the unborn eldest son of his nephew, Richard Davey, who, in the meantime, was to receive £200 a year until his son was born. However, although Richard married, he remained childless. John Davey's six sisters commenced a court case to overturn the will and this dragged on in the Chancery court for twenty one years before it was decided that the accumulated interest on the capital, by then £30,000, should be distributed to the growing families of the six sisters. In 1914, Richard Davey's death renewed the whole question and the courts were again asked to determine the validity of the will. It was eventually judged to be valid, and the property went to form the Davey charity. The descendants of the six sisters were left to rue their losses. According to the newspaper, 'the whole matter is viewed with the deepest interest locally'[94] and the perceived injustice of the outcome became an enduring fixation for the families robbed, as they saw it, of their rightful heritage.

For middle-class Cornish families like this, such events took on major, indeed, traumatic, importance. Furthermore, the role of legacies and inheritances possibly became even more important, given the long-term stagnation of the Cornish economy in the early twentieth century. This may have induced an inward-looking defensiveness and a suspicion of outsiders beyond the family. Amongst such families the values of hard work and obedience remained strong.

The modern family

In both middle- and working-class families, there was a reaction in the 1950s against the residual authoritarian streak of the 'traditional' family, an environment that some argued had merely succeeded in producing an authoritarian personality, repressed and anxious, easy fodder for the first fascist or populist demagogue who might come along. Those seeking less rigid styles of parenting were encouraged by Dr Benjamin Spock's 1946 publication, *Common Sense Book of Baby and Child Care*. This emphasised reacting to children in a relaxed and instinctive way in place of discipline and habit training and the book was eventually to outsell the *Holy Bible*.[95] Anecdotally, it would seem that trends in Cornwall were similar. But comparative research on child rearing has not been undertaken in Cornwall and is a task that cries out for the attention of oral historians.

The small-scale research actually done on family life in modern Cornwall suggests that 'complex households', with two families or three generations sharing the same house, were still somewhat over-represented in Cornwall in the 1970s. The most recent studies also find some slight evidence for more frequent kin assistance among Cornish families than incomers and closer kin relationships with a 'further hint that the intensity of relationships is especially high in west Cornwall'. However, it is also true that 'traditional' gender expectations existed both among Cornish and non-Cornish families in Cornwall.[96] More indulgent parenting paved the way for yet more change after the 1960s. The emphasis came to favour relaxed discipline along with

RIGHT

Mrs John Batten and son, painted in 1830 by Mousehole artist, Richard Thomas Pentreath. Her husband was Mayor of Penzance several times during the 1830s and 1840s and was the principal shareholder in the town's first bank, Batten, Carne & Carne.

warmer and more companionable family relationships. For some, this smacked of over-indulgence, with the golden age of the nuclear family in the 1950s giving way to the chaotic, de-moralised 1960s. But such fears – lack of discipline, juvenile delinquency, quality of parenting, broken homes, the 'emancipation' of women – had all been raised before, at the height of the Victorian family ideal.[97] What was really new were changing attitudes to marriage and a soaring divorce rate after the 1960s. Family structures are, as a result, again less predictable and more fluid, with stepfamilies, the new extended family, making up a growing proportion of households.

Images of the family

But the modern family is a family in change rather than in a state of complete collapse. The continuing popularity of marriage as an institution and the role of cohabitation as pre-, rather than non-marital behaviour, suggests a considerable degree of continuity with earlier times.

We have seen in this chapter how families in Cornwall have been influenced by wider changes and how attitudes within the family reflect this. But, in addition, we have also discovered that there were significant differences. Cornwall's early industrialisation produced earlier extended families, at least in the far west. The society produced by rural industrialisation in the eighteenth century appeared to produce something we have called here the 'Cornish customary family'. Then, just as Cornwall began to be more influenced by the Victorian 'traditional' family ideal, economic depression combined with a culture of migration to disrupt both 'customary' and 'traditional' families in Cornwall. As a result, patriarchy never really unquestioningly embedded itself in the late-nineteenth-century Cornish family and women continued to play a more strategic role in family decision-making, not just managing the domestic budget.

Nonetheless, married women had to exercise more autonomy in the absence of their menfolk. Those who received regular remittances from abroad may even have been empowered, freed from child-rearing and able to spend the family income as they wished. Their husbands, too, had considerable freedom, ultimately controlling the flow of income back to Cornwall. In this respect, married Cornish women had less opportunity than elsewhere to negotiate how much of the earnings passed into the family purse. In such a context, kin support may have been more prominent. Furthermore, the nineteenth-century 'absent father' may have had more profound effects on the emotional repertoire of twentieth-century Cornish men and on the intimate details of family life.

And, crucially, the Cornish family retains one difference: it is seen by the Cornish themselves to be different. Some people in modern Cornwall still argue that kin is more important and that family members have a stronger sense of obligation towards each other. Family anecdotes are introduced into conversations in order to reinforce a sense of family solidarity and to emphasise difference from those who are unable to place themselves on this map of family connections and belonging.[98] A sense of family difference is claimed, although the evidence for this is patchier than the claims warrant. What empirical work has been done does, interestingly, show that young people today are more likely to be involved in family enterprises and that the proportion of extended households in Cornwall is still somewhat higher than the norm.[99] (However, this could be the result of the high price of housing and low local wages rather than choice, just as economic necessity underpinned the extended households of sixteenth-century Penwith.)

This perceived centrality of the family in modern Cornwall has many historical echoes. We have already met Richard Carew's characterisation of the Cornish gentry as 'cousins'. After the 1580s and into the seventeenth century, Cornish lesser gentry families seem to have had a greater predilection for raising funeral monuments that memorialised their family lines.[100] In 1836, Hugh Tremenheere, himself born and brought up outside Cornwall, was surprised when, on joining the Western Circuit as a judge, he was reminded by William Arundell Harris that 'we were Cornish cousins' and promptly introduced to others as of 'good Cornish stock'.[101] Lineage was clearly important in nineteenth-century Cornwall. And not just for the gentry. The mining population was also claimed to have a 'certain pride of ancestry, a boast of descent , and a veneration for heirlooms'.[102] On the other hand, John Harris wrote in the 1880s that: 'I have tried, but cannot trace back our ancestry any further (than to his

THE CHANGING FAMILY

These photographs of three generations of the Deacon family display changing attitudes to marriage over the course of the twentieth century. *Left*, the marriage (somewhere around 1913 to 1915) of farm labourer Lewis Deacon to Beatrice Dymond at Coads Green. The importance of the day is implied by the symbols of the wedding, which took place at the local Methodist chapel, the couple being staunch Methodists. *Centre*, Bill Deacon and Gertrude Cross, photographed in a Launceston studio just before their marriage in 1945. The War had not yet ended and both are dressed in their military uniforms, Bill having just returned from Germany. *Right*, the wedding ceremony at Camborne Registry Office in 1994 of Bernard Deacon and Penny Davies. Their daughter, Merryn, was with them on the day.

grandparents), and know not whether my grandfather was a Saxon or a Celt'. [103] An interest in genealogy had flourished in the eighteenth century. And the space given by C.S.Gilbert in his *Historical Survey of Cornwall*, published in 1817, to heraldry and pedigrees is a reminder of the growing nineteenth-century passion to identify one's historical kin. As a result, licences to display coats-of-arms rose six-fold from 1830 to 1868.[104] In Cornwall as well as in nineteenth-century England, this was evidence of a wider talismanic role for the family in general and the values invested in it by the Victorians. But even this had its distinct Cornish twist. When a family tree of the Carnes of St Columb was drawn up in 1882, care was taken to extend the line back to 'Clemens ap Blodri, king of Cornwall'.[105] This may well have been 'wild nonsense',[106] but interest in family roots in Cornwall always carried with it the possibility of transporting Cornish people back to golden ages of independence, or at the least, perhaps, to dreams of them. Finally, one indisputable fact that made and makes some Cornish families distinctive resides in the very names they bear. Cornwall has generated a unique stock of surnames originating only in Cornwall and nowhere else in Europe. This, in turn, led to the well-known and regularly cited couplet:

> By Ros-, Car-, Lan-, Tre-, Pol-, Pen-
>
> Ye may know most Cornish men.

But how precisely did this distinct stock of surnames emerge – and when? The next chapter explores this aspect of the Cornish family in more detail.

CHAPTER TWO

BY TRE, POL AND PEN WILL WE KNOW MOST CORNISH MEN?

W HAT'S IN A NAME? It would appear an awful lot to those thousands of family historians poring over the parish registers, puzzling out seventeenth-century handwriting, or ruining their eyesight on the micro-film reader. Our surnames guide us through the historical traces, tell us who we are and where we have come from. They are the taken for granted core of our being. It is our surname that links us to our parents, our parents' parents and to that line of ancestors that recedes ever more dimly into the past. Our surnames also unite us to other lines, providing the links in a chain of connections backwards and outwards. Our names therefore define who we are in the present, who we were in the past and the imagined community to which we now belong and once belonged.

This chapter will look at how Cornish surnames arose. After setting the adoption of hereditary surnames in context it looks at examples of Cornish surnames of the nineteenth century, divided into four different categories. The distribution of surnames in the past will then be used to shed light on some puzzles of Cornish surname history. Moving on to the historical distribution of the different types of surnames, it becomes obvious that the former presence of the Cornish language cast a long shadow over the history of naming in Cornwall. The second part of this chapter uses the distribution of sixteenth-century surnames in the Cornish language to reveal the historical geography of that language. Finally, after reviewing which first names have been popular in both earlier and more recent periods, the chapter ends by briefly noting the continuing changes in the stock of our Cornish surnames.

From by-names to surnames

Names are the very essence of who we are. But this wasn't always the case. Hereditary surnames, passed on from one generation to the next, were unknown in Cornwall before the Norman Conquest of 1066. It was the Norman ruling class who brought the fashion of hereditary surnames with them. Names such as de Dunstanville, Pomeroy and Boteraux were introduced into Cornwall in the eleventh century, referring originally to places in Normandy but retained by their bearers until the line ran out, which it often did, for example the Boteraux, who gave us the place name Boscastle, died out in 1461.[1] The practice of the Norman barons gradually percolated through the rest of society, but only slowly. It has been claimed that in the thirteenth and fourteenth centuries 'there was little or no prestige attaching to the

RIGHT

Part of an early-16th-century stained glass window at St Neot church donated by Nicholas Borlase, a small landowner. This window is devoted to St Leonard. Before the Reformation, landowning families paid for the glazing of windows as a display of devotion and as a public monument to their family.

possession of a hereditary surname. A surname was not a status symbol'.[2] Although the process is still somewhat unclear, surnames arose after people adopted, or were ascribed, second names. This arose when the various Johns or Richards needed to be distinguished from each other. By-names must have therefore grown in use, such as John of Redruth or John, the son of James, or John of the bald head. Moreover, the presence of aliases in the records alerts us to the fact that individuals might carry a number of such by-names and not just one, use depending on context. The process by which such by-names, relating to an individual, solidified into a surname, passed on within a family, was gradual and hesitant. And it owed as much to the ascription of names by state or church for tax-exacting or rent-collecting purposes as it did to the desire to unite the members of a family through a common surname.[3]

Use of second names began in the south of France among the elite and then spread north.[4] For a shorter or longer transitional phase, second names were in use but changed from one generation to the next, before becoming fixed surnames. This process occurred in western Europe over a very long period from the eleventh to the eighteenth centuries (and still not everywhere – in Iceland names are not inherited

BELOW

The Ancient Parishes
of Cornwall
Cornwall's ecclesiastical
parishes before the
Victorians began adding
new ones in the 1840s.

Key to The Ancient Parishes of Cornwall map

St Levan **1**

Sennen **2**

St Buryan **3**

St Just in Penwith **4**

Paul **5**

Sancreed **6**

Madron **7**

Morvah **8**

Gulval **9**

Zennor **10**

St Michael's Mount **11**

Ludgvan **12**

Towednack **13**

Lelant **14**

St Ives **15**

Perranuthnoe **16**

St Hilary **17**

St Erth **18**

Phillack **19**

Breage **20**

Germoe **21**

Crowan **22**

Gwinear **23**

Gwithian **24**

Sithney **25**

Camborne **26**

Mullion **27**

Gunwalloe **28**

Cury **29**

Mawgan in Meneage **30**

Wendron **31**

Helston **32**

Illogan **33**

Landewednack **34**

Grade **35**

Ruan Minor **36**

Ruan Major **37**

St Keverne **38**

St Martin in Meneage **39**

Manaccan **40**

St Anthony in Meneage **41**

Constantine **42**

Mabe **43**

Stithians **44**

Gwennap **45**

Redruth **46**

St Agnes **47**

Mawnan **48**

Budock **49**

St Gluvias **50**

Perranarworthal **51**

Kea **52**

Kenwyn **53**

Perranzabuloe **54**

Falmouth **55**

Mylor **56**

Feock **57**

Truro, St Mary's **58**

St Clement **59**

St Allen **60**

Newlyn East **61**

Cubert **62**

Crantock **63**

St Columb Minor **64**

St Anthony in Roseland **65**

St Just in Roseland **66**

Gerrans **67**

Philleigh **68**

St Michael Penkivel **69**

Merther **70**

St Erme **71**

Veryan **72**

Ruan Lanihorne **73**

Lamorran **74**

Cornelly **75**

Cuby **76**

Probus **77**

Ladock **78**

St Enoder **79**

Colan **80**

Mawgan in Pydar **81**

St Eval **82**

St Merryn **83**

St Michael Caerhays **84**

St Ewe **85**

Creed **86**

St Stephen in Brannel **87**

St Dennis **88**

St Columb Major **89**

St Ervan **90**

Little Petherick **91**

Padstow **92**

Gorran **93**

Mevagissey **94**

St Mewan **95**

St Austell **96**

Roche **97**

Withiel **98**

St Wenn **99**

St Issey **100**

St Breock **101**

St Minver **102**

St Blazey **103**

Luxulyan **104**

Lanivet **105**

Bodmin **106**

Egloshayle **107**

St Kew **108**

Endellion **109**

Tywardreath **110**

Lanlivery **111**

Lostwithiel **112**

Lanhydrock **113**

Helland **114**

St Mabyn **115**

St Tudy **116**

Michaelstow **117**

St Teath **118**

Lanteglos by Camelford **119**

Tintagel **120**

Trevalga **121**

Forrabury **122**

Fowey **123**

St Sampson, Golant **124**

St Winnow **125**

Cardinham **126**

Blisland **127**

Temple **128**

St Breward **129**

Advent **130**

Minster **131**

Lanteglos by Fowey **132**

St Veep **133**

Boconno **134**

Braddock **135**

Warleggan **136**

Davidstow **137**

Lesnewth **138**

St Julio **139**

Lansallos **140**

Pelynt **141**

Lanreath **142**

St Pinnock **143**

St Neot **144**

Altarnun **145**

St Clether **146**

Treneglos **147**

Warbstow **148**

Otterham **149**

St Gennys **150**

Talland **151**

Duloe **152**

St Keyne **153**

Liskeard **154**

St Cleer **155**

Laneast **156**

Tresmere **157**

Tremaine **158**

Jacobstow **159**

Poundstock **160**

St Martin by Looe **161**

Morval **162**

Menheniot **163**

St Ive **164**

Linkinhorne **165**

North Hill **166**

Lewannick **167**

Trewen **168**

Egloskerry **169**

North Petherwin **170**

Week St Mary **171**

Marhamchurch **172**

Stratton **173**

Poughill **174**

Kilkhampton **175**

Morwenstow **176**

St Germans **177**

Quethiock **178**

South Hill **179**

South Petherwin **180**

Launceston, St Mary Magdalene **181**

St Thomas by Launceston **182**

St Stephen by Launceston **183**

Sheviock **184**

St Erney **185**

Landrake **186**

Pillaton **187**

St Mellion **188**

Callington **189**

Stoke Climsland **190**

Lezant **191**

Lawhitton **192**

Werrington **193**

Boyton **194**

North Tamerton **195**

Whitstone **196**

Bridgerule West **197**

Launcells **198**

Rame **199**

Maker **200**

St John **201**

Antony **202**

St Stephens by Saltash **203**

Saltash **204**

Botus Fleming **205**

Landulph **206**

St Dominick **207**

Calstock **208**

RIGHT

The Cornish Hundreds
*Cornwall was divided
into nine Hundreds by
the medieval period.
Originally it is likely to
have been six.*

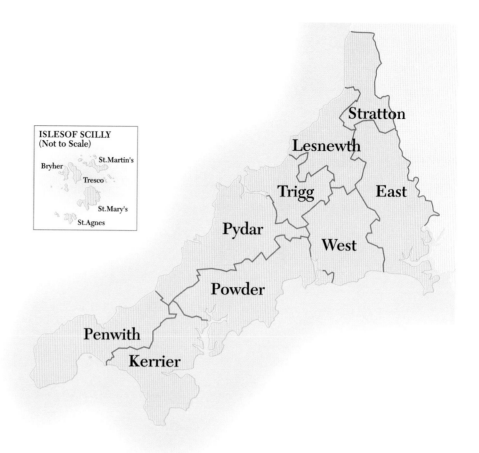

in the same way as elsewhere). Broadly speaking, people in the south and east of the British Isles were quicker to adopt hereditary surnames, before the mid-fourteenth century in the case of most people in Oxfordshire, Norfolk and Suffolk for example.[5] In the north, hereditary surnames came later. In Lancashire and Yorkshire, a considerable minority remained without inherited surnames into the Tudor period and the early 1500s. Things do not seem to have been so tardy in Devon, where hereditary surnames are claimed to have been the norm for the majority of the population by the 1350s and been almost universal by 1400.[6] The evolution of hereditary family names in Devon also clearly illustrates the effect of status. Inherited surnames first appeared before 1200 among the landholding families and by 1250 'most landed families of any consequence in Devon already possessed hereditary surnames'. Unfree tenants (those tied to their landlords and manors by bonds of serfdom) lagged behind by about another generation.[7] As is often the case, things were not quite the same in Cornwall, as we shall discover in the course of this chapter.

Surname types

We can divide surnames into four main types based on their meanings: locational, personal, nicknames and occupational. Locational names are those derived either from a distinct place or from a description of the landscape where the individual lived, for example Wood or Heath. In nineteenth century Cornwall three common locational names were Bowden or Bawden, Bray and Lobb. There are seventeen places, at least, called Bowden in Devon, although we are told that there was some confusion between the place name Bowden (which meant either a hill shaped like a bow, or the top of a hill) and the Norman first name Baldwin, with the two names perhaps falling together in the sixteenth to eighteenth centuries.[8] This example should alert us to the difficulties of ascribing surnames to watertight compartments, as alternative possible meanings co-exist for many modern surnames. Bray was another fairly widespread locational name in nineteenth-century Cornwall. This was

SOME CORNISH PLACE-NAME ELEMENTS AND THEIR MEANINGS

awel – breeze	marghas – market
bal – mine work	nans – valley
bod/bos - dwelling	nowyth – new
kelli – grove	onnen – ash tree
ker – a round	pen – end
du – black	pons – bridge
faw – beech trees	rid - ford
fenten – spring	ruth - red
goon – downland	sans – holy
gwern – alder trees	sowson – Englishman
gwyns – wind	tal – brow
heligen – willow tree	toll – hole
hendre – old farm	ughel – high
lowarth – garden	vean - small
lowen – happy	wheal - mine working

also a placename in Devon, but one with a possible Celtic root *bre*, meaning hill.[9] There were also two places called Bray in east Cornwall, at Altarnun and Morval and a Bray Hill at St Minver, as well as the more well-known Carn Breas at Illogan and St Just-in-Penwith. Third, we have Lobb, a Domesday manor in Devon. However, Lobb could also derive from a middle English word for spider,[10] so again this apparent locational name could in some instances be an example of a nickname. Less ambiguous are Cornish-language locational names, such as the modern Treloar, based on the placename of Treloar in Wendron, and written in the early sixteenth century as Trelowarth, a spelling that makes the meaning clear – farmstead of the garden.[11] Placenames could become surnames either when a person left the place, thus distinguishing Mary of Treloar from Mary from somewhere else. Or they could be adopted when the person lived at the place with that name, *i.e.* Mary living at Treloar. As we shall see, the vast majority of Cornish-language locational names seem to be examples of the latter. It is logical that surnames derived from small places – hamlets and farms – were related to actual residence at that spot whereas surnames

Headstone of M. Brown of Botusfleming, who died in the early months of 1735 (the 1734/35 of the old Julian calendar changed in 1752). But what did skull and cross bones mean?

RIGHT

In an early-20th-century photograph, Breton and Cornish fisher boys sit together in Newlyn harbour. The surname of the local lad second from the right was Harvey, a name derived from Breton and still well known in the town.

that came from larger villages, towns, parishes or even counties were assumed on settling in a new spot. Such names as Gwennap, Maddern (originally Madron), Gluyas (Guvias), Hartland (from the parish just across the border in Devon) or Kent and Devonshire are examples of this type.

Relatively common examples in nineteenth-century Cornwall of topographical names, those taken from a landscape feature, were Hill, someone who lived by or on a hill, Holman, a person living in a hollow, or Hall, an individual who lived at or near to a hall or large house. On the other hand, the name Hall could have been given to someone who worked at a hall or manor house and in this instance be an occupational name.[12] Similarly, does Warren indicate someone who lived near to a game park, or who was actually employed in one, warren in its original Norman French being applied to any game, not just rabbits? To confuse things further there is also a Norman placename La Varenne, which could have given rise to this surname![13] In names from the Cornish language it is difficult, if not impossible, to distinguish between locational names that come from places and those from topographical features. Candidates such as Kelly and Kellow, from *kelli* or *kelliow*, the Cornish for grove or small wood and its plural, also crop up as the names of actual places.

The second form of surnames emerged from given names, as in John, son of Edward. Sometimes these were Middle English names, such as Piers, a form of Peter, giving rise to Pearce.[14] Sometimes they were Norman in origin, as was Rowe, a short form of either Rowland or Rollo, the Norman versions of English Rolf or Ralph.[15] Another common surname from a personal name is Harvey, this time from the Breton name Haerviu.[16] A given name popular in Cornwall was Pascoe, itself

derived from Pask, the Cornish form of Easter and also a name held by a pope and saint in the ninth century.[17] Sometimes, given names could spawn large numbers of variants. Jenkin, for example, was a diminutive, a minor version, of John, literally John's kin.[18] John could also give rise to Jane, via Jan, a name not confined to girls until the 1600s and probably later in Cornwall.[19] Sometimes -en was added to the end of a name, as in Batten, a popular form of Bate, which was itself the shortened Bartholomew. The given name Richard, gaining great popularity through its association with the English royal family, had a short vernacular form amongst ordinary people – Hich – the result of the English struggling with the French sound 'r' in Richard. This in its turn led to Hitchen or Hichen, which then produced Hitchens/Hichens, the final 's' here standing in for 'son'. Meanwhile, there were Hicks and Richards, not to mention Rickard, to add to the complexity. Given names such as William, Robert, Stephen and Henry or Harry became increasingly popular in the late medieval

and Tudor times in the 1400s and 1500s, this popularity presumably reflecting their connotations with royalty.

Surnames could also emerge out of more fleeting and ephemeral descriptive names or nicknames. Nicknames were in wide use in medieval and early modern Cornwall as elsewhere, and sometimes the nickname given to an individual would stick and become the hereditary surname. But Cornwall lacks the very expressive range of nicknames of the north of England. The most widely held nickname-derived surnames in the nineteenth century were the comparatively restrained Brown, White and Rundle, the latter purportedly being a variant of round.[20] Another equally widely distributed nickname was Cock, from the bird. This was apparently, 'applied to a young lad who strutted proudly like a cock (and) soon became a generic term for a youth'. It could also have applied to an early riser, a natural leader or a 'lusty and aggressive' individual.[21] The dialect term 'cock', applied to a young man, can still be found in west Cornwall. This also gave rise to surnames such as Willcock or Hancock, in these cases being added to Will or Hann, the latter a short form of Johan, or perhaps a vernacular form of the name Randolph.[22]

The Cornish language could also add its quota of nicknames, the most common one often being cited as Moyle, given the original meaning of bald man.[23] However, this is unlikely to be a Cornish word, partly because it is not attested in the Cornish texts and partly because the Welsh word *moel*, of which it is supposed to be the

ABOVE

Part of a manuscript on the state of the Cornish language, compiled in the early 1680s by William Scawen, Cornish patriot and gentleman of St Germans.

BELOW
Detail of a page from
the Fowey parish regis-
ters showing marriage
entries from 1638-40.
It looks as if some of
the entries for 1639
are missing.

equivalent, should actually have given rise to a Cornish word *mool*, not *moyle*.[24] This conclusion is strongly supported by the historical distribution of the name. Although now found predominantly west of Truro, in the early sixteenth century the name was confined to mid Cornwall, with most occurrences being found within an area bound by St Austell in the south, Newlyn East in the west and St Kew in the north. An early example of the name – John Moyle – occurs in 1350 in connection with the Padstow area,[25] implying that the origin of the name may lie in that area and that it might have arrived from Wales.

Nicknames could also include descriptive names such as King, Pope, Bishop or Knight. However, these names do not necessarily imply the bearer is descended from a distant king, pope, bishop or even knight, either legitimately or illegitimately. It is more likely that the name was given as a nickname to someone who had the characteristics of such exalted people and, for some reason, it stuck. Clearly here there is some overlap with our final class of surnames, those derived from occupations. The most common such name in nineteenth-century Cornwall, though not nearly as common as in England, was the ubiquitous Smith. Other relatively common surnames were Tucker and Taylor. To the modern observer, less obvious occupational surnames are Chapman, originally meaning a merchant or trader – the chap part being related to the word 'cheap' – and, more surprisingly, Parsons, meaning not an actual priest but either a servant of a parish priest or a servant at a parsonage.[26]

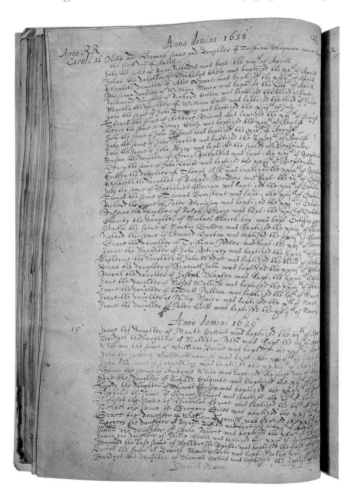

The distribution of surnames

Surname studies before the 1970s were dominated by those who pursued the origin and development of the name, its etymology. Such writers, led by Percy Reaney, a prominent writer on the origin of surnames, produced both the classification used above and a number of widely consulted dictionaries of surnames. However, such an approach, resting primarily on the study of language, had its drawbacks. Reaney himself pointed out how the spelling of modern surnames only stabilised relatively recently – in the 1700s and 1800s. Therefore, drawing links between the modern form of a surname and a name of the fourteenth century, when many were becoming inherited, is not an easy task. In the 1970s, another approach gained ground, led by a group centred on the Department of English Local History at Leicester University. There, Richard McKinley produced a series of volumes on the surnames

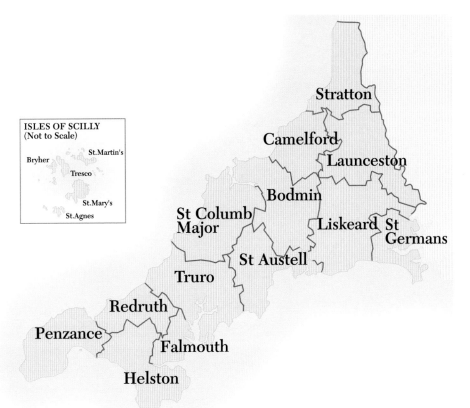

ISLES OF SCILLY
(Not to Scale)

St.Martin's
Bryher
Tresco

St.Mary's
St.Agnes

Stratton

Camelford
Launceston

Bodmin

St Columb
Major

Liskeard St
Germans

St Austell

Truro

Redruth

Penzance

Falmouth

Helston

LEFT
The Cornish
Registration Districts
In 1834, Poor Law
Unions were set up to
administer the New
Poor Law and its associ-
ated workhouses. These
districts after 1837
became the basis for the
civil registration of
births, marriages
and deaths.

of various English counties, concentrating on the period before the sixteenth century and focusing on the origin, development and ramification of surnames. Studying how surnames spread and how they were distributed introduced a more dynamic element into the equation. It revealed that locational surnames were most common in the early period of surname formation. But, as surnames spread to the poorer sections of society, patronymics (naming after the father's first name) and nicknames became more likely. It was this work that established the geographical pattern underlying the timing of inherited surnames, the thirteenth and fourteenth centuries in the south of England, later in the north.

More recently, the genealogist and surname specialist, George Redmonds, has suggested that the Leicester School approach needs supplementing by closer genealogical work.[27] He claims that the fluidity of spellings and the presence of aliases was more common to a much later date than is often assumed. This means that if we are to seek the origin and development of names, more attention has to be given to family genealogies and the sixteenth century and after. Such criticism echoes the work of the local historian, David Hey. He has shown how the historical study of surname distribution, tracing the occurrence of surnames back over the centuries, can reveal the geographical origins of family names.[28] Using Yorkshire as the basis of his case studies, Hey has shown that not just locational names are traceable back to single places. Nicknames and occupational names also have a geography and examination of that geography can uncover a district or even a specific point of origin.

Some Cornish surname puzzles

Adopting David Hey's approach helps us shed light on some puzzles of Cornish surname history and at the same time raises questions about commonly held assumptions about surnames in Cornwall. For example, the name Jago is usually viewed as
a Cornish language version of James, cognate with the Welsh form *Iago*.[29]
Furthermore, it seems similar to the many Cornish surnames that end in -o or -ow,
such as Clemo, Sandow, Bennetto, Perrow or Varcoe. Yet the distribution of the

THE SIXTEENTH-CENTURY SUBSIDIES

The subsidies were a form of Tudor taxation. In 1523, the subsidy raised finances
for the government by a tax of 4d in the £
on wages, those earning less than £1 a year
being exempt; 4d in the £ on goods valued
between £1 and £2; 6d in the £ on goods
from £2 to £20 and 12d in the £ on goods
over £20 and on income from land over £1
a year. The significance of this rather progressive tax is that it resulted in taxation
returns that contain lists of the names of
the actual individual taxpayers, the first
listing since the taxation of 1327 (which
was restricted to a much wealthier group).
Two of the 'most substantial, discrete and
honest inhabitants' of each parish were
appointed to assess the wealth of the
inhabitants and two more acted as local
collectors.

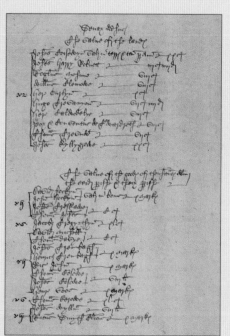

A detail from the subsidy list of 1530.

name Jago in the 1520s is curious for a Cornish-language name. For the rest of the
names listed above were all heavily concentrated in mid and west Cornwall with no
examples east of St Dennis. In stark contrast, nine of the fourteen Jagos in the 1520s
were living to the east of Hensbarrow Downs, in parishes such as Jacobstow,
St Gennys, St Thomas by Launceston, St Mellion and Liskeard. And, again
most unlike the other Cornish language names, there were no examples west of
Gwennap. It is possible that someone named Jago had moved from west Cornwall in
the fourteenth century when surnames were stabilising in the east and produced
a number of widely scattered family branches. But that scattering hints at multiple
origins. And, if Cornish, why was this name relatively unpopular in the west by
the sixteenth century? In the absence of early examples of the name its origins

remain a mystery.

Crago looks like a similar name. But it isn't. In the 1520s, there were three Cragos listed in the subsidy rolls. Two – Richard Cragowe and William Cragowe – lived at Lanreath and nearby Boconnoc in the Hundred of West. The other, Thomas Cregow, was found at Gerrans. The western Cregos almost certainly took their name from the placename Cregoe in Ruanlanihorne, or perhaps Creggo in Mylor.[30] An earlier example, Thomas Cregow, lived in the 1480s at St Columb, and this may have been a separate derivation from a lost *crego* placename in Creed.[31] This implies that the eastern Cragowes were migrants or the descendants of earlier migrants from mid Cornwall, or perhaps point to yet another lost placename somewhere further east.

Some names that look at first glance to be from the English language are sometimes in Cornwall claimed to derive from the Cornish language instead. One example is Blight or Bligh, in English the nickname for a cheerful person, but in contrast in Cornish that of a wolf-like individual, from the Middle Cornish *blyth*.[32] That the two surnames were indeed interchangeable is shown by Richard Blygh in the Lezant subsidy list who also appears as Richard Blyght in the 1520s muster roll (the list of people who could be called upon to defend their communities).[33] Apart from a lonely Bligh in Bodmin, the name was heavily concentrated in the early sixteenth century in the far east, along the Tamar, with around two-thirds of all Blighs/Blights living in just five parishes – South Petherwin, Lezant, Stokeclimsland, South Hill and Calstock. This strongly suggests two things. First, it hints that the origin of the family name in the medieval period was somewhere on the western bank of the Tamar. Second, as this area, between the Lynher and Tamar rivers, is one of the two parts of Cornwall where the Cornish language was already supplanted by English before 1100,[34] its origin is extremely unlikely to have been the Cornish word *blyth*.

Moon is another nickname (in English from monk) that is claimed to have a parallel and separate Cornish derivation – from *mon*, the Cornish for thin or slender. Unlike Bligh/Blight, Moons (usually spelt Mone) in the 1520s were dispersed across the east Cornish countryside around the edges of Bodmin Moor, from Landulph, St Stephens and St Germans in the south east, through St Neot and Braddock in the south west, St Breward, Michaelstow and St Juliot in the north west and St Stephens and Egloskerry in the north east near Launceston. This distribution could indeed indicate that the surname arose simultaneously in a number of locations, exactly what one would expect with a nickname. But again, this geography also means that, if from the Cornish language, the name must have taken on a hereditary form at an early stage, in the thirteenth or fourteenth centuries.

The absence of Moons from mid and west Cornwall is paralleled by a third surname claimed to be from a Cornish language nickname – Keast. This has been linked to *kest*, Cornish for paunch, with the suggestion the nickname was applied to a fat man.[35] But unlike Moon, the distribution of Keasts in the 1520s was more localised. Putting aside a single Keste in St Mewan, Kestes or Kests were found on the south

ABOVE
The tombstone of
Agnes, wife of
John Gard, who died
aged 76 at Forrabury.
Gard, also spelt
Guard is an
occupational name
from the Old
French for guard
or watchman.

eastern edge of Bodmin Moor, in a string of parishes from Lewannick and South Petherwin in the north, through Linkinhorne, St Cleer and St Ive to St Germans in the south. This suggests an origin somewhere to the east of Bodmin Moor, again an unlikely scenario for a surname from the Cornish language. Unless it had been adopted very early.

Other surnames are more puzzling. For example, nothing in the 1520s seems to resemble the surname Ough. But did Ough develop as a local spelling variant for Howe? By the mid seventeenth century when the name does appear it is found in south east Cornwall, at St Cleer, St Ive, Antony and St Germans, in precisely the area that Howes were concentrated in the previous century. There is clearly no link with another surname with no suggested etymology – Uglow. This originated in Stratton, where Christina and John Uglowe bore the name in 1543.[36]

Soady is another east Cornish name, the origins of which are shrouded in uncertainty. In the early 16th century, three Sawdys are listed – Walter Sawdy at St Cleer, John Sawdy at South Petherwin and William Sawdy at St Germans. By 1641, two spelling variants had emerged – Sawdy and Sowdy.[37] They shared a similar distribution, one by this time more akin to the modern pattern of Soadys, centred on the south coast around Looe. (More than half the Soadys in the current telephone book still live in Looe and surrounding parishes.) But what does the surname mean? One possibility is that it was a variant of the name Sowden, also found in south east Cornwall in the 1520s. This is supposed to be a nickname from the word sultan, applied to someone 'who behaved in an outlandish and autocratic manner, or for someone who had played the part of a sultan in a pageant'.[38]

Another intriguing name found overwhelmingly in Cornwall is Kneebone. In 1881 fifty-four per cent of all Kneebones in Britain were living in Cornwall and another fifteen per cent in Devon. But in that year, another one in three of the Kneebones who lived outside Cornwall (and Devon) had actually been born in Cornwall.[39] If we look this one up in the surname dictionaries, we are offered two possibilities. The first is the English nickname for someone with knobbly knees; the second sees it as a locational name, placing its origin in the place called Carnebone (recorded in 1298 as Carnebwen) in Wendron in west Cornwall.[40] However, the distribution of the name in the early sixteenth century hardly bears out this link to Carnebone as there were no Kneebones living anywhere near the place. John Kneebone could be found at Tregony and a couple of Kneebones at Padstow and St Merryn. But the main concentration was in the east, again to the north and east of Bodmin Moor. There were four Kneebones living at Linkinhorne and North Hill and others at St Neot, Altarnun and Advent. The concentration around Bodmin Moor may be the result of a prolific and proliferating branch of early migrants or it may infer a different origin for the name and one we should seek amongst the moors and valleys of east Cornwall rather than the uplands of the west.

Finally, one of the most puzzling names is also one of the commonest surnames in Cornwall – Hocking or Hockin/Hocken. If we search for the meaning of this name in a surname dictionary, we are likely to be disappointed. The *Oxford Names Companion* makes no mention of it and neither does Reaney's classic *Dictionary of British Surnames*. The -kin is clearly a diminutive, with an extra -g being sometimes added by the seventeenth century. But a diminutive of what? One possibility is Hodge, a pet form of Roger; another is Hick, a pet form of Richard. Yet another is Hawke, which gave rise to the very similar name of Hawkin.[41]

RIGHT

Distribution of Hockyns and Hawkyns in the early 16th century
It seems likely that these common surnames originated in a number of different locations in Cornwall.

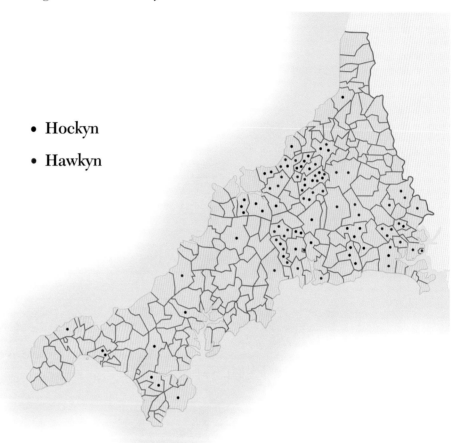

- Hockyn
- Hawkyn

Both Hockyn and Hawkyn were well established by the early sixteenth century, there being three main concentrations of Hawkyns. The first was to the south west of Camelford, the second to the east of St Austell, centred on Luxulyan, and the third to the south east of Bodmin Moor. Hockyns were also found in the first two of these districts, interspersed with the Hawkyns. In addition, in Liskeard and to the south west of that town running towards Duloe, there was a concentration of Hockyns with no Hawkyns. And a few Hockyns could also be found in some parishes in the west. Such a distribution doesn't preclude the possibility that Hawkyn and Hockyn had the same origin, both concentrated in east Cornwall, even though it is likely that these surnames emerged in a number of different locations.

The distribution of surname types

The geographical distribution of single surnames clearly tells us a lot about their history and we will return to this in the next chapter. But the distribution of surnames more broadly also sheds light on how far Cornwall differed from other places in Britain. In some of the earliest work on the distribution of surnames in the late nineteenth century, which was based on the entries in trades directories, listing inhabitants county by county, it was found that the number of locational names based on placenames were higher in Cornwall (and in Devon) than in most other places. At least forty per cent of the farmers in Cornwall and Devon bore placenames as their surnames.[42] For Cornwall, this continued a long tradition of by-names and surnames based on placenames.

MOST POPULAR MALE FIRST NAMES IN THE 1520s

Penwith Hundred	Trigg Hundred	Stratton Hundred
1. John	1. John	1. John
2. Richard	2. Thomas	2. William
3. William	3. William	3. Thomas
4. Thomas	4. Richard	4. Richard
5. Henry	5. Robert	5. Nicholas
6. James	6. Henry	6. Robert
7. Robert	7. Nicholas	7. Roger
8. Nicholas	8. Stephen	8. Walter
9. Ralph	9. Peter	9. Henry
10. Stephen	10. Walter	10. Simon

The first listing of the inhabitants (or at least some of them) that we have, is the 1327 lay subsidy roll, a list of taxpayers. Oliver Padel, former Institute of Cornish Studies Placenames Research Fellow and author of the major work on Cornish placenames, found that forty-seven per cent of Cornish bynames in 1327 were locational, relating to known and unknown placenames. This was a higher proportion than has been found in eastern England and nearer the levels of Lancashire. Within Cornwall in 1327 the proportions of placename by-names ranged from sixty one per cent in Kerrier Hundred down to just thirty-one per cent in Trigg and thirty-eight per cent in East. Proportions in the other Hundreds clustered between forty four and fifty-four per cent.[43] Some areas in Devon also had high proportions of locational by-names in the tax list of 1332, notably Hartland at sixty-one per cent and Black Torrington at fifty-seven per cent.

These Hundreds, just over the border in north west Devon, were the districts with the most dispersed settlement. High rates of locational names are associated with just such areas, where farms and houses are scattered across the landscape rather then being concentrated in villages. Proportions of such names were much lower in the east and south of Devon, which brought the overall proportion of locational names in Devon down to thirty-four per cent, well below that of Cornwall.[44]

The far lower proportion of locational names in the small towns of fourteenth century Cornwall is taken to mean that people at this time were still naming themselves from the place they lived at rather than being named after the place they had come

RIGHT

**Subsidy lists of the
1520s and 1540s**
*This map excludes
locational names and
provides a snapshot of
the distribution
of bynames and
surnames in the
Cornish language in
the early 16th century.*

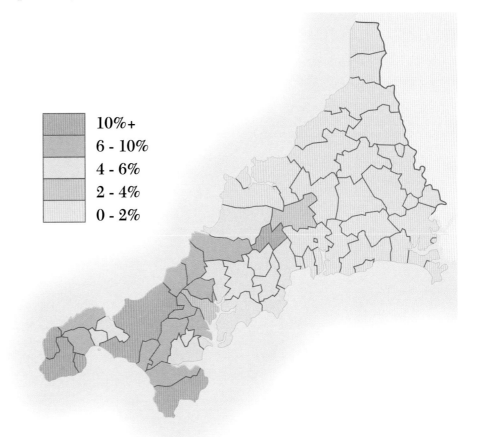

10%+
6 - 10%
4 - 6%
2 - 4%
0 - 2%

from. Oliver Padel notes that this appears to have been a distinctive Cornish naming practice, continuing well into later centuries. It is not difficult to find examples. At some time in the middle ages, the Taillefers, a family of Norman French origin, adopted the name Borlase, after their farm in St Columb Major.[45] As late as 1585, the Thomas family, who had taken a tenancy at Carnsew in Mabe, began to call themselves Thomas alias Carnsew. By 1641, they had moved to neighbouring Budock, but by this time were known simply as Carnsew, taking their placename with them.[46] The connection between family name and placename was a strong one in Cornwall, so strong that the Trelawneys in east Cornwall, with an origin in Altarnun parish, deliberately bought the manor of Trelawne at Pelynt in the sixteenth century, presumably attracted by the similarity of the placename to their family name. Though in Cornwall surnames could still be discarded in favour of the name of a new home in the sixteenth century and even later, families like the Thomases/Carnsews, were also by this time taking the placename with them when moving. Another interesting example of this was a family living at Trewartha in St Agnes in the early sixteenth century. Their family name was taken from the place, with the addition of the Cornish *an* (the) to become Andrewartha (the higher farm). At some point in the 1500s, they moved west to Gwithian. But there they named or re-named their new farm Upton

Farm, a direct translation of Trewartha. For some reason, perhaps for reasons of status, they preferred the English word to the Cornish name for the place, keeping the latter as their family name.[47]

In the Arundell estate papers of the fourteenth to sixteenth centuries, locational by-names remained the most important type, amounting to forty-six per cent of all the different names found, a proportion that suggests little change over 200 years. However, the continuing link between place and family in late medieval and Tudor Cornwall was accompanied by an important change. From the 1400s onwards there was a growing use of personal names as second names and the consequent multiplication of names derived from a rather limited stock of first names. Although such personal names were fewer in number than locational names a much larger proportion of individuals bore them as more people began to answer to by-names and surnames such as Stephens, Williams, Harris, Hicks or similar.

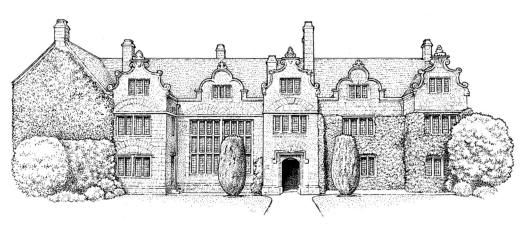

LEFT
Trerice, home of the Arundells, a cadet line of the Arundells of Lanherne, who could trace their ancestry back to the marriage of Ralph Arundell to a Trerice heiress in the 14th century. Unlike the senior Arundells, this family embraced the new Protestant religion in the 16th century and duly prospered.

This can be illustrated by looking at the distribution of surnames in the nineteenth century. By 1861 as many as two-thirds of the one hundred most common surnames in Cornwall were personal names. Only twelve per cent were locational names while fourteen per cent were from nicknames and seven per cent occupational in origin. This naming pattern was not, however, evenly distributed across Cornwall. As many as thirty-two per cent of the most common names were locational names in Stratton Registration District whereas in most registration districts (RDs), they made up between sixteen per cent and twenty-three per cent of the most common one hundred surnames. The lowest proportion was thirteen per cent at St Germans. Descriptive and nickname surnames were most common in St Austell RD and uncommon in the west, in Redruth and Helston. Occupational surnames were also least common in the west where they were less than half as frequent as in Launceston or St Germans RDs in the east.

Meanwhile, the proportion of personal names was lowest in Stratton, at just thirty-six per cent, and highest in west Cornwall. In all RDs west of St Columb more than fifty-five per cent of the most common surnames derived from personal names. In north and east Cornwall this proportion was less than fifty per cent. This uneven pattern is clear when we map the three most common surnames of the nineteenth century, Williams, Thomas and Richards. Combining these, the map below indicates that they were increasingly likely to be found as we move westwards. The geography of surnames in the nineteenth century therefore betrays a clear east-west difference.

RIGHT

The three most
common Cornish
surnames in 1861
Note how the
proportion steadily rises
as we move to the west,
reflecting the popularity
of these names in the
Cornish-speaking areas
in the later 16th century
when surnames were
being stablised.

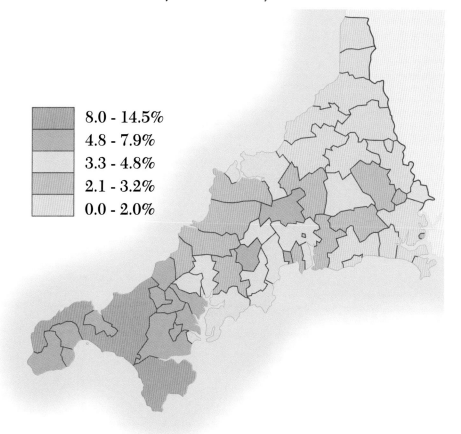

8.0 - 14.5%
4.8 - 7.9%
3.3 - 4.8%
2.1 - 3.2%
0.0 - 2.0%

What we are seeing here are the historical traces of the Cornish language, the influence of which affected the distribution of Cornish surnames, and not just the expected Cornish language surnames, right into the modern period.

Cornish surnames and the Cornish language

Before the eleventh century, Cornish was spoken across all of the territory save two districts, one between the Rivers Tamar and Lynher in south-east Cornwall and the other north of the River Ottery in north Cornwall. But even as the population continued to speak this Celtic language, they had begun to come under the influence of English, the language of their more powerful, organised and aggressive neighbours. An early example of this was felt in the names they gave themselves. Just as parents in contemporary Cornwall might consider the rich and famous, sports stars or over-hyped media creations when choosing a name for their new baby, the Cornish started in the later tenth century to adopt the more prestigious names of their overlords. Such motives were strengthened by a somewhat more prosaic and understandable factor, the greater rights the English kings of Wessex granted their English subjects in contrast to their 'west Welsh' or British subjects. Changing one's name was a simple and relatively painless way of changing one's ethnicity – at least on paper – and easing discrimination. As a result, the prevalence of English names amongst the sub-tenants at the time of Domesday in 1086 should not be taken to mean that all these landlords were English or even English-speaking. Instead, Cornish people, perhaps especially the landowning group, were giving themselves English names and abandoning their Cornish ones.[48]

One document survives which records some British first names used by the Cornish people before the eleventh century, a list of manumissions (freeing of slaves) written into a gospel book of St Petrock's monastery at Padstow or Bodmin from the 950s into the 1000s.[49] This contains both Celtic and English names, the former including names such as Costentin, also the name both of the saint who gave his name to Constantine and of an earlier Cornish king, and Cantgueithen – or 'hundred trees' in English. The other main source for early Cornish names is Cornish place-names. Places beginning with *Tre-* were very often named after someone, perhaps the person who founded them, at some point between the sixth and tenth centuries. Thus, for example, the place Tremail in Davidstow gives us the name Mel while Tresillian near Truro, spelt Tresulyan in 1325, provides the name Sulyan. *Lan-* (holy site) names may also contain a personal name, this time that of a saint; for example Lamorran on the Roseland contains the name Moren.[50]

By the time of the taxpayers' list of 1327 all these distinctive names had long ceased to be used. But so had most of the English names that pepper the Cornish entries in the Domesday Book, swept aside in the rush to adopt the names of a new ruling class, the Normans, during the twelfth and thirteenth centuries. By the fifteenth century, Norman first names, along with Biblical ones, were the most frequent. Only one Celtic name survived as a by-name into the fourteenth – that of Luke Modres, the Cornish form of Modred, a character in the Arthurian legends.[51] Two hundred years later, even this name had disappeared. Yet Arthur, re-popularised by the medieval romances, was by this time used as surname, most obviously in Pydar Hundred in parishes between Newlyn East and Padstow and most evocatively in one example, John Arthur, living at Tintagel in 1543.

We have already seen how Cornish families were keen to adopt their place of residence as their surname and how families were still changing their second name to that of their new home as late as the end of the sixteenth century, two centuries after surnames had stabilised further east. This transitional pattern of relatively unstable by-names, not yet inherited, is found in mid and west Cornwall to a late date and resembles Welsh naming customs rather than the system in southern England. Together with this fluidity, Oliver Padel has drawn attention to the presence of two-part surnames in mid and west Cornwall in the fifteenth and early sixteenth century.[52] These were normally formed from Christian names. Thus Henry John Jack was recorded living in Redruth in 1524. The probability is that this was Henry son of John, grandson of Jack. His son, in turn, may then have been named Henry John or

ABOVE

The headstone of John Williams of Launcells, who died in 1849. In the early 19th century, it is estimated that only around one in ten families could afford headstones like this. But the details of Susan, who died in 1881, suggest this was a later headstone, perhaps replacing an earlier one.

a variant thereof. Actually, in Redruth in 1545 there was a John Harry Jenky(n), who was perhaps Henry John Jack's son, the change of Henry to the more colloquial Harry and Jack to Jenkyn (both pet forms of John or Jan) being quite plausible at a time when names were not fixed. Other examples of this process appear in the Arundell papers. In Gorran Churchtown in 1451-64 William Toma Davy held a tenancy. In 1499 the tenancy was held by John Will, in all probability William Toma Davy's son.[53] A similar fluidity is suggested by the entries for Thomas John, holding a tenancy at Treloy in St Columb Minor in 1480 and that of John Treloy, the entry in 1499, possibly the son of Thomas John who adopted (or was given) the placename as his by-name, or even the same person.[54] This suggests that aliases were common, perhaps more common than family historians, wedded to the fixity of surnames, would like to think. For example, Richard Trebervet, living at Trebarveth in Stithians in 1480 is called Richard Jacktom, a disguised two part surname, in 1499.[55]

Two-part names, the final part of which could sometimes be a placename, as for John Thomas Trethall at Crowan in 1543, are not found in the five eastern Hundreds. Oliver Padel makes the intriguing proposal that this naming custom was thus 'distinctive of areas where the Cornish language was still spoken'.[56] It would appear that in the English-speaking areas of Cornwall by the early sixteenth century surnames had long been hereditary, possibly as early as the fourteenth in a similar fashion to Devon. But in the Cornish-speaking districts hybrid naming customs remained. Before the fifteenth century some families adopted hereditary surnames along the same lines as in England, this being most likely among the landowning groups and most clearly seen for locational surnames. Thus William Lannergh at Lamarth in Mawgan in Meneage in 1499 was the son of Ralph Lannergh; at Clies, also in Mawgan, Ralph Clies in 1499 was the son of Henry Clies recorded in 1480.[57]

But these families still lived at the place from which they were named. It is not impossible that had they moved, they would have changed their surname. Better evidence of hereditary surnames is provided by those individuals of different generations who either held a locational name and did not live at the place named or had another type of surname. One such example could be Richard Skeberyowe, who had a garden at Strete Newham in Truro in 1480. In 1499, this plot of land was rented by John Skeberiow, presumably son of Richard.[58] Other surnames had become hereditary even in the west. At Stithians, Martin Enys was one of the heirs of Ralph Enys in the late fifteenth century, while Thomas Briand (derived from the Norman or Breton name, Brian), held the corn mill at Lower Woodley at Lanivet in 1499 and his father, Reginald Briant, had held it in the 1450s.[59] Although some families had therefore adopted inherited surnames in the Cornish-speaking areas, and perhaps as early as the fourteenth century, this practice co-existed with a more fluid and unpredictable pattern of changing by-names, two-part surnames and aliases. This marked a distinct cultural zone, where naming customs differed from English-speaking regions to the east and where the English pattern of hereditary surnames in the sixteenth century jostled with the Welsh pattern of fluid by-names and patronymics. There was also no doubt a status dimension to this, with the richer families quicker

to adopt hereditary surnames than poorer tenant farmers. The continuing irregularity of by-names and use of aliases may explain why, in many west Cornish parishes, it seems so difficult to trace individuals from the subsidy rolls of the 1520s just a couple of decades further to those of the 1540s.

Family names and the geography of Cornish

This cultural difference in naming customs raises the exciting possibility that we can use the presence of both two-part surnames and the distribution of actual names in the Cornish language to map the extent of Cornish-speaking communities in the early sixteenth century, something no-one has hitherto attempted to do. This was a crucial period in the history of the Cornish language, just as it was moving into a period of territorial and social decline during the sixteenth century. The Protestant Reformation and the growing use of the English *Holy Bible* and *English Prayer Book* were either the causes of or the final seal of the ultimate destruction of this language community. It appears from other evidence that, after a contraction in the two hundred years following the Norman Conquest, a period which saw the spread of the English language in east Cornwall, the linguistic border was stabilised from about 1350 until the sixteenth century. But where was this border precisely? Here the evidence of surnames allow us both to assess and to qualify the conclusions drawn from placename evidence that place the language divide somewhere between the Camel and Fowey estuaries in mid-Cornwall.[60] In many ways, given the lack of widespread contemporary comments on the state of spoken Cornish, early-sixteenth-century surnames may be the most direct guide to the presence of the Cornish language. This is because, as many surnames were still not fixed, they 'meant what they said'.[61] Use of a Cornish version of an English name should be evidence that Cornish was understood and used in that parish.

We begin by mapping those parishes where, in the subsidies of the 1520s and 40s, there was evidence of two part-personal surnames, i.e. with both parts from first names rather than placenames. The map opposite shows that it does indeed correspond to the notion of some sort of linguistic boundary in mid Cornwall, with no examples being found outside the four Hundreds of Penwith, Kerrier, Pydar and Powder. It is here that we should therefore expect to find distinctive Cornish non-locational names. For surnames based on Cornish placenames could occur anywhere, as most places in east as well as west Cornwall were named in the Cornish language. Although old Celtic first names had gone long before the period when surnames were formed in Cornwall, there were several examples in the early sixteenth century of distinctively 'Celtic' names. Uryn or Urin was one, found in eight parishes, all west of Budock, save one – Richard Uryn – listed in the tinners' muster roll of 1522 at St Columb Major.[62] That this was an old Cornish name is suggested by the placename Treurin (Urin's farmstead), which became the modern surname, Truran. But the name Urin in the 1520s is unlikely to have been in use as a by-name continuously from the ninth century.

It is more likely that it was re-introduced during the 'second Armorican return', the migration of large numbers of Bretons to Cornwall during the fifteenth century. This 'second return' was principally of craftsmen, labourers and servants, low-status 'economic migrants' in search of better wages in a relatively prosperous Cornwall. In contrast, the 'first Armorican return' of the eleventh century had been of high-status Breton landowners who had thrown in their lot with William the Conqueror. They were more likely to have come from eastern than western Brittany, districts which may already have been French-speaking. These fifteenth-century Bretons,

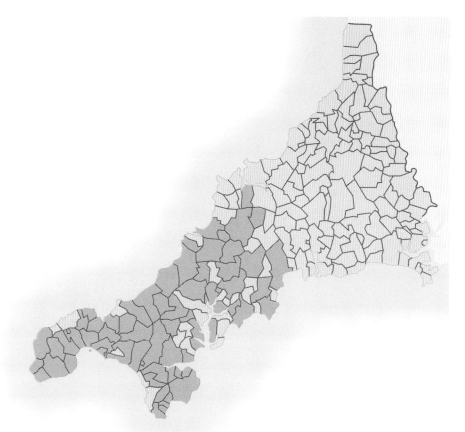

LEFT
**Parishes with two-part
personal surnames**
*The map gives an
overview of the Cornish
parishes where two-part
bynames appeared
in the 16th-century
subsidy lists. These are
predominantly in the
west of the county.*

speaking a language still close enough to Cornish to be mutually intelligible, both bolstered the Cornish language in the years before the Reformation, and gave us several new surnames. Urin was one; Tangye was another, found in the 1520s in just two parishes in west Cornwall, Breage and Cury. But by far the most popular one, present in 35 parishes in the early sixteenth century, was Udy. The surname Udy, however, spread from Marazion and St Ives eastwards, implying it also found popularity in some English-speaking parishes as it was being used as far east as Lanivet, Fowey, Cardinham, Helland, St Pinnock, Saltash, Otterham, Jacobstow and Stratton. It is possible Cornish was still understood in the first two of these in the 1520s, but it is stretching credibility too far to imagine many Cornish-speakers in the others.

The indigenous Cornish method of expressing that a person was of the family of X was to add the ending –ow to a first name. Morton Nance pointed out that old British names were also found ending in -oe or -ou, names such as Uthnoe (as in Perranuthnoe), Cathno or Iudicou.[63] However, there may be no link between this and later naming customs as the ending -ow is also one Cornish way of making a plural word, as in *cader* (chair) and *caderiow* (chairs). Is it a coincidence therefore that this ending is used where the English added -s to first names to denote son of? Perhaps the Cornish form was a conscious copy of the English.

Whatever the exact reason, we get Cornish surnames such as Clemo (of Clement), Kitto (Christopher), Sandow (Alexander) or Benetto (Bennett). In the sixteenth century among the most common names like this were Hegow/Higow, from

Penzance borough diver,
Omar Pascoe, front
right. Omar was
retained to repair the
harbour and sea walls.
His helmet and diving
suit are now on display
in the town's Penlee
House Museum.

Hick, short for Richard, and Perrow (from Peter). While a few examples of Higow turned up as far east as St Endellion and Lanivet, most Higows and all Perrows were confined to Cornwall west of Truro. By 1641 Higgow or Hegaw was confined to a much smaller area, including Breage and Germoe, Constantine and St Keverne, with Richard Higgoe in solitary splendour way to the east at St Blazey. By the nineteenth century this formerly common surname seems to have been lost, perhaps translated into the English Hicks or converging with the name Hugo. Another surviving name of this type is Daddow, the origin of which is unclear (perhaps from David?) but which was found in the early sixteenth century in mid-Cornwall at St Austell, Roche, Probus and St Stephen in Brannel. Nowadays there are no longer Daddows in mid-Cornwall, virtually all of those in the phone book being located further west, in the Camborne-Redruth district. Another sixteenth century surname of this type was Dogow and this has not survived although there was still one person – Richard Dogoe – at Withiel with this name in 1641. While we cannot be certain about the origin of this name, it is at least interesting that there had been an older Celtic name – Docco or Doghow – a saint who gave his name to Lanhoghou or Lanow, an alternative name for St Kew churchtown.[64]

Sometimes the ending -ow became an -a. Thus, Hegow is found spelt as Hicca in the far west in the 1520s. Eva, Sara and Rodda are other examples like this, although the origins are less clear in these cases. Sara might be from the female name. On the other hand, there was a Breton with the first name Yvo living at St Ives in 1524 and Richard, Earl of Cornwall's brother, was called Yvo in the 1230s.[65] Meanwhile, Rodda could be the Cornish version of the English surname Rodd, itself given a topographical derivation as a name for someone who lived in a woodland clearing.[66]

When adopted into the Cornish language, English loan words often took on a extra -a,[67] an example being *cota* – coat. This also seems to have happened with personal names, two common examples in the early sixteenth century being Jacka and Tomma. While Jacka survived into the modern period as a hereditary surname, most common in the Redruth area, with most families of that name being south and west of the town, Tomma did not survive, despite being as common as Jacka in the 1520s. Tomma does not appear in the Cornwall Protestation Returns of 1641, by that time no doubt falling in with the very common surnames Thomas or Toms.

But the most commonplace name with an ending in -ow or -a was the name Pascoe, also used as a first name and derived from the word *Pask* or Easter. This was found in as many as fifty-seven parishes in the early sixteenth century subsidy lists and muster rolls. Some of these were to the east of Bodmin, for example at Lanteglos by Fowey, Saltash, Davidstow and Morwenstow and one or two of these may have been a locational name from a place called Paschoe in Colebrooke in Devon.[68] But ninety-two per cent of all those listed with the Pascoe surname lived in the four western Hundreds. This name was clearly a popular one in Cornish speaking communities.

Is it too fanciful to view this as evidence for their commitment to the Easter rites associated with Christ's crucifixon and resurrection and the associated local customs? The popularity of Pascoe might indicate that such rituals were clung on to with particular devotion in Cornish speaking Cornwall, something that may in turn explain the high level of support in these communities for the Prayer Book Rising of 1549.

LEFT
The distribution of
Pascoes in the early
16th century
Most Pascoes at this
time lived in the four
westernmost Hundreds,
though a few were
located east of Bodmin.

This is probably the place where we should re-emphasise something pointed out by Henry Jenner a century ago and Robert Morton Nance half a century ago.[69] Names such as Pascoe, Jago, Benneto or Jose, usually spelt Joce in the 1520s and widely found in Cornwall, including many places in east Cornwall, are not evidence of Spanish influence. Jose is in fact another example of a borrowing of a Breton name, this time Iodoc. Iodoc was a Breton prince whose brother was Iudicael, which name gave rise to the surname Jekyll.[70] All these names were attested well before the Spanish Armada of 1588 or the burning of Paul by the Spanish in 1595, events which in nineteenth century popular memory were associated with the introduction of Spanish blood. Indeed, Clemou is found as early as the fourteenth century.[71] The stubborn persistence of this popular myth of Spanish origins seems to be the result of a combination of a search for romantic origins – usually overseas – and an ignorance of the Cornish language. But isn't the Cornish language itself sufficiently distinctive and romantic to meet this need without resorting to the Spanish myth?

The Cornish language also gave rise to distinctive nicknames and other descriptive names. Often, these were found with the Cornish definite article *an* or *en* (the) attached. Thus Gilbert Engwyn of Sancreed in 1524 was a bearer of the name that became Angwin, literally 'the white', like the English White meaning a blonde or fair haired person. There was also Enhere, the later Annear, for a tall person, Cornish *here* meaning long. Anhell, as in John Anhell of St Gluvias in 1543, may mean Brown, although it could be the Cornish equivalent of the name Hall. Other such examples in the early sixteenth century include Reynold Enowre at Perranuthnoe (Gold), Matilda Endeves (tongue or perhaps sheep) at Truro and Udy Anglasse (Green) at Penzance, the last a Breton immigrant. There are several examples of this

THE PROTESTATION RETURNS

In 1641, tensions were rising as parliament brought the Earl of Strafford to trial against the wishes of Charles I. The House of Commons drew up a 'protestation' to declare their loyalty to the King and the reformed Church of England but also their opposition to 'popish innovations'. This was a device to smoke out closet Catholics and a sign of paranoia about Catholicism as well as a means of opposing what were seen as conspiracies to persuade Charles I to use the army to overawe Parliament. After the MPs had signed the Protestation they passed a bill obliging all subjects of the King to sign it as well; any refusing to sign were to be ejected from all church and state offices.

Early in 1642 the Protestation was sent to local sheriffs. All male parishioners over 18 signed. In Cornwall the lists of only four parishes are missing, while in St Mabyn and St Tudy the women signed as well. Just 48 'recusants' or Catholics are explicitly named – half of these in Pydar Hundred.

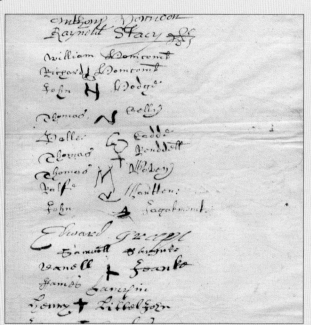

Detail from the 1641 Protestation Return for Callington.

type of name, but none had more than a handful of bearers and only a few of this type have survived. Two of the three Angwins in the sixteenth century were found in West Penwith, still home to almost half the Angwins in the modern phone book. Annears were living in the early sixteenth century mainly in the three parishes of Probus, Gwennap and Mylor and their main location in the early twenty-first century still appears to be centred on Truro-Probus. Finally, the modern distribution of Angell, with the majority in Kerrier between Redruth and Coverack, might indicate that this is the same name as Anhell, whose three bearers lived at St Gluvias, Helston and Breage in the early 1500s. The attrition rate of other descriptive names has been high. Epscob, the Cornish for Bishop, was found at Crowan, Mana (Monk) at St Columb Major and Menyghy (Monkhouse) at Grade and Wendron. There was a John Tegawe (Toy) at Gulval, a John Cotha (Older) at Gorran and Scovarns (Ear) at

Ludgvan and Crantock. All of these nicknames have been lost, swept away in the transition to English and the fashion for using personal names as by-names and sur-names in the later sixteenth century. There are hints of others. Morton Nance cites Cogden (worthless man) as the nickname of a James Symons at Breage and suggests that the John Ergudyn who was named as an actor in the Camborne feast play Bewnans Meriasek, was named after the Cornish words for snowlock.[72]

Yet some did survive. The names Teake (pretty or handsome) and Tallack (large-browed) were found more widely in the early sixteenth century and perhaps because of this managed to hold on into the period of inherited surnames. Marrack (Knight), a name clustered east and west of Carnmenellis in Kerrier in the 1520s, was also handed on as a hereditary surname into the seventeenth century. Perhaps more sur-prisingly, as there appears to be only one bearer of the name in 1524, so was the splendid name Baragwaneth. This family originated in Zennor, perhaps with Richard Baragwaneth. Its meaning is literally wheat bread and it is more likely to be a nick-name than an occupational name for a baker, perhaps given to someone who pre-ferred wheaten to the more usual breads of the time which were baked with barley or oats.[73] Later, the name was given to a hospital at Soweto in South Africa, regular-ly in the news during the struggle against apartheid in the 1980s and no doubt equal-ly regularly assumed by news-consumers outside Cornwall to be an African name. Meanwhile, the surname Legassick, sometimes held to be a nickname for 'big-eyed',[74] is probably not. The name does not appear in the sixteenth century lists and in the seventeenth century is only noted as Legossack in relation to St Issey parish. This indicates that it's more likely to have come from the placename Legossick in that parish, the meaning of which comes from *logaz* (mice) rather than *lagaz* (eye).[75]

An interesting nickname of the sixteenth century is that of Sais, or Says. This means English and could have been applied to an English speaking person or some-one who put on English airs. It occurred twice as frequently as the most common of the other Cornish nicknames, with thirty-three people so named in the 1520s and 1540s lists. It is unlikely to have been given to anyone in areas which were not Cornish-speaking and its distribution clearly reflects this. The most easterly example was William Sais at St Dennis. For some reason the name was rarely adopted as a surname. In the 1640s there were only three people listed in the Protestation Returns with this name – John Sise at Truro, Thomas Size at St Ives and Beatrix Sise at Egloshayle. The surname Size does not appear in the 2001 phone book.

Another Cornish nickname is a little more perplexing. The modern name Curnow is usually taken to be the Cornish for Cornwall. In the early sixteenth century this name was spelt variously but the first four letters were invariably Corn-. It was also found widely from Camborne in the west, St Keverne and Mawgan in Meneage in the south, through Probus and Bodmin to Duloe and North Tamerton in the far east, a rather curious distribution for a Cornish-language name. And why should someone

- **Sais/Says**
- Anhere
- **Tallack**

be named Cornwall while still living in Cornwall? It may have been given to a Cornish-speaking person from another part of Cornwall but in this case why was it found in English speaking parishes? Were these migrants from the west who had already acquired their surname, perhaps early examples of step migrants? Morton Nance tentatively offers another explanation. Perhaps the origin was not Cornwall at all, but the plural of *corn*, meaning either corners, trumpets or horns. Even so we are still left with the puzzle of two bearers of this name so far east. Or perhaps names like John Cornawe of Duloe and Richard Cornowe of Mawgan in Meneage just look the same but hide different roots.

The most frequent Cornish nickname, with sixty-one bearers across fifty-five separate parishes in the early 1500s was Vean (also spelt Vyghan, Vyan and Vian). The word *vean* in Cornish means little or small but when applied as a by-name presumably meant 'younger' or 'junior'. By the 1660s this name was restricted to just four parishes; St Mewan and Gorran in mid-Cornwall and Talland/Morval in south east Cornwall.[76] This limited later hereditary usage of Vean as a surname demonstrates that those with this name in the early sixteenth century for the most part bore it as a temporary by-name. At that time it was distributed widely across mid and west Cornwall, again indicating that the Cornish language was actively used in those parts of Cornwall. However, in addition, people called Vyan lived in a string of parishes along the south east coast of Cornwall, from Lanteglos by Fowey through to St Germans and Quethiock, with a single Vyan at Landulph on the banks of the Tamar.

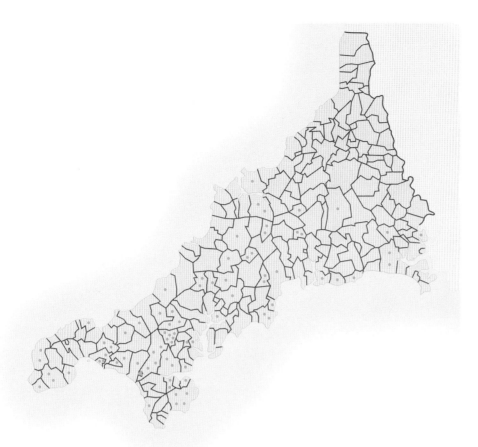

LEFT
The distribution of
Veans in the early 16th
century
By the second half
of the century the
name Vean (also spelt
Vyghan Vyan or Vian),
meaning 'little' or 'small'
in Cornish, was
restricted to mid- and
south-east Cornwall

There are two possible explanations for the presence of the name in this English speaking part of Cornwall. First, it may have been adopted in the fourteenth century when hereditary surnames began to be used and when the Cornish language may still have been in use here. Alternatively, those Vyans living there in the early 1500s may have been migrants from the west, people engaged in coastwise trade from Cornish speaking districts. The persistence of the surname in the coastal parishes of Talland and Morval into the seventeenth century suggests that the surname was either already inherited in the sixteenth century or became so as some at least of the lifetime migrants stayed on.

If Vean gives us a snapshot of Cornish-speaking Cornwall, occupational second names, at a time when they could mean 'what they said' rather than refer to the calling of an ancestor, tell us even more about the geography of the Cornish language. The most common Cornish language occupational name by far was Angove, found in 34 separate parishes in the early 1500s. At the same time the English equivalent Smith occurred in roughly similar numbers and in forty parishes. Mapping the distribution of these two names therefore provides a possible map of the two languages. It is immediately apparent from the map above that the Cornish name is found only west of a line of mid-Cornish parishes from Crantock in the north through Colan and St Dennis in the centre to Creed and Gorran in the south. On the other hand the name Smith appears in various parishes in the 'Cornish' areas. It is noticeably commoner in the small towns – Penryn, Helston and St Ives – despite these places being

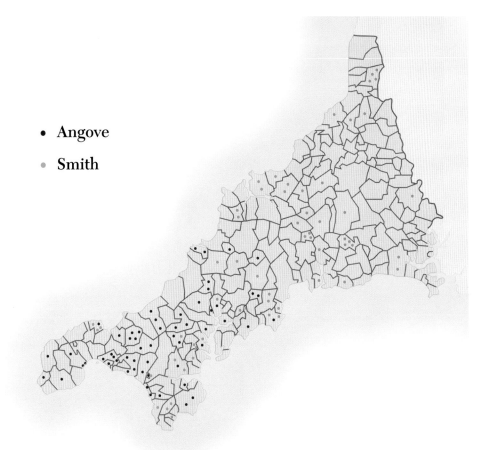

- Angove
- Smith

ABOVE
The tombstone of mine
captain Edward Angove
of Gwinnear. He died in
1810 at the venerable
age of 72.

home to many people with Cornish language names at this time. This is taken, along with the appearance of the English occupational names of Carter, Saddler, Skinner and Tanner in urban places in the fifteenth century, as evidence that towns in mid and west Cornwall were 'more English speaking than the surrounding countryside'.[77] But, another explanation could be that the subsidy assessors in the towns were more influenced by the English language and translated some Cornish Angoves to Smiths when making their lists. This may also be the explanation for the pockets of neighbouring parishes in otherwise Cornish speaking rural Kerrier where Smith seems to have been used in preference to Angove. It is very likely that, given the status difference between the two languages, Cornish names would get translated into English rather than the other way around. Of course, a second reason for the presence of Smiths in west Cornwall may be migration from eastern, English-speaking districts of people who already had the inherited family name of Smith. Longer-distance migrants would also be more likely to have homed in on the towns rather than the countryside.

A number of Cornish language occupational names are found in the early-sixteenth-century subsidies and these reinforce the picture provided by Angove, matching its geographical distribution. The most common occupational name was Trehar (cutter, tailor), which appeared in parishes from St Just in Penwith to Bodmin. There is also a hint among the Trehars of the way Cornish could be converted to English names at the whim of the scribes. In Ruan Major a John Treher was listed in 1543. Nineteen years earlier, in 1524, there were no Trehars but there was a John Taillor. Was this the same John but given the English version of his name in the earlier listing? A hundred years later Trehars had virtually disappeared. In 1641 there was just a Hannibal Treer at Philleigh and a Thomas Trear in nearby Probus. At St Issey John and William Trayer might seem to offer further examples. However, the name Trayer could have had a separate origin, as in 1525 there was a John Treyer in St Issey and other people called Treyre in St Eval and in Bodmin. The modern telephone book still includes one entry for Traher, and there are several for Trahair. Morton Nance felt that Trahair was a variant of Trehar but its modern distribution implies an origin in west Penwith rather than in mid Cornwall where the seventeenth century Trehars tended to be found. If Trahair is a variant of this name,

- Treher
- Melender
- Gweader

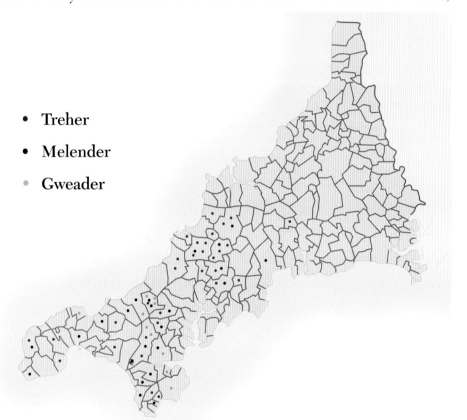

Some Cornish language occupational names in the 1520s and 1540s
Trehar, also spelt Trehair or Treher, means 'tailor' or 'cutter'; Melender was a miller while Gweader was the Cornish name for a weaver.

the stress on the name has also shifted over time – from the first to the second syllable. Many of the other relatively common sixteenth century occupational names have disappeared entirely. Melender was one, applied to a miller. This is not listed in the 1641 Returns. Neither is Trockyer, Cornish for fuller and found in several parishes west of Gwennap in the 1520s, nor Gweader, the Cornish for weaver, also found in Redruth, Illogan and Wendron, St Ives and parishes on the Lizard peninsula. The name Tyer or Tyar, meaning roofer (perhaps thatcher) was still found in St Erth in 1641 and may have assimilated itself to the similar sounding English name Dyer, but one originally referring to a completely different occupation. Rather surprisingly, Tyack, the Cornish version of farmer, which has survived into modern times, was only the name of one individual in 1524, John Tyak of Wendron. By 1641 this name could be found at Germoe, Lelant and Ludgvan in the west, Gorran in mid-Cornwall and Forrabury in the north. At first glance it is even more surprising that there appears to be no Cornish language occupational names relating to the mining industry. However, this may not be so surprising as it seems. Sometimes in other places leading occupations were avoided as second names, presumably because they would not have served to identify different people. (This was the case in medieval Kings Lynn in Norfolk where there few names relating to the dominant cloth trade.[78]) At the same time neither Kigoer (Butcher) nor Mablean (Clerk) became inherited surnames although, like Tyak, each was the name of one person in the sixteenth century subsidy lists.

A somewhat more common name that looks like another occupational by-name was Meneger, found in west Cornwall at Kenwyn, Constantine, Helston, Breage and Lelant. This was still found as a surname in Breage parish in 1641 but has not survived into the twenty-first century. Its meaning is obscure but it may relate to the Cornish word *meneges*, meaning to mention or relate something. Rather than a straightforward occupational name could this be a nickname applied to a story teller or perhaps someone who played a role in the miracle plays? Other similar by-names in the early sixteenth century were Pebar or Pybar (Piper) and Taborer (Drummer). These, too, did not manage to survive the cultural changes of the mid and late sixteenth century when miracle plays fell into disuse, ridiculed by cosmopolitan gentry like Richard Carew of Antony, author of the *Survey of Cornwall*, and undermined by religious reforms which put the emphasis on private bible-reading rather than public biblical play-acting.

Before that happened, however, the evidence of Cornish surnames in the fifteenth and early sixteenth centuries informs us that the language was still widely spoken in the majority of Pydar and Powder Hundreds in mid Cornwall. This undermines the arguments of those who seem, on the basis of scanty data, determined to compress the Cornish language as far west as they can at this point.[79] There was, in the generation just before the Reformation, a fairly clear linguistic boundary running north to south to the east of St Columb, Roche and St Austell. This is perhaps slightly further to the west than some have concluded based on placename evidence; in particular it does not include the district just south of the Camel estuary. There is also some indication that the Cornish language was made more use of in by-names west of Truro, although this may be an impression created by a rather more fluid second name situation in the two western Hundreds. In contrast, Pydar and Powder could have been more influenced by the English liking for inherited surnames, had more of these than further west and in consequence fewer Cornish language names. Nonetheless, as population began to rise after the late fifteenth century there was a growing need for by-names and nicknames in order to distinguish between people and this need had been met in mid and west Cornwall partly through the medium of the Cornish language.

Unfortunately, much of this rich cultural heritage was then lost in the second half of the sixteenth century when, badly shaken by the social changes accompanying the Reformation, consigned to a low status and deserted by the gentry, Cornish was no longer the language of choice when considering by-names, just at the point these were stabilising into inherited surnames. This can be illustrated by looking at the 1569 muster roll. Cornish occupational names and nicknames were still present but much reduced from the 1520s.[80]

Interestingly, their geography was very similar to that of the early decades of the century, implying there was no sudden east-west shift in the sixteenth century of what had been a relatively stable linguistic boundary (a little like the division between Breton and Gallo, a dialect of French, in Brittany). It is more likely there was a gradual dilution or thinning out of the Cornish language in mid Cornwall as use became increasingly restricted to certain social contexts and particular groups.

As a result of this history Cornish surnames are complex and hybrid. On the one hand they show long-standing influence in the east from English patterns. On the other they include names from a Celtic language, with surnames reminiscent of neighbouring Brittany surviving into the modern period. In addition there are also a large number of families bearing simple patronymics like Williams, Richards, Thomas, Hicks, a pattern similar to that in Wales where late surname formation on the English pattern has given rise to an even larger proportion of people called Williams, Evans, Davies and the like.

That said, it should be remembered that the largest class of Cornish surnames in the Cornish language were and are

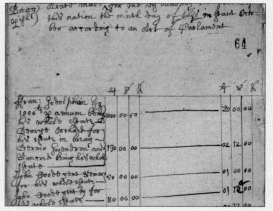
not nicknames, occupational or personal names at all but locational names, those taken from Cornish placenames. As such placenames are dominant across most of Cornwall save the far east and north and as such locational names seem to have been as popular in east as in west Cornwall in the fourteenth century we might expect that the distribution of surnames made up from Cornish placename elements would have been relatively evenly spread across Cornwall in the early sixteenth century. But we would be wrong. A map of the proportion of Cornish language locational names in the subsidy lists shows a strikingly close correlation with the Cornish language areas. East of Pydar and Powder such names were never more than seven to

eight per cent of all those listed. West of the Camel and the parishes of Lanivet, Lanlivery and St Blazey the proportion was uniformly over fifteen per cent. This is striking evidence both of that long-standing linguistic frontier and of differing naming customs in English and Cornish speaking Cornwall. In the former the period of surname formation in the fourteenth century had introduced many non-locational names. In the latter placenames retained their attraction much later, even being adopted afresh as new by-names and surnames well into the sixteenth century. Nevertheless, there was one area where the percentage of locational names was high but that of other Cornish language names low and that was immediately west of Padstow and Wadebridge. What this implies is that this district had, in the early sixteenth century, only recently experienced language change, perhaps the first indications of the more profound and widespread linguistic change that was to follow in the course of the next century.

The Cornish language did not just leave its traces in those obvious surnames, whether locational or other types, derived from that language. As we gave seen, those parishes which in the nineteenth century had the highest numbers of the three most common Cornish surnames – Williams, Richards and Thomas – were predominantly found in the west. This is precisely because it was in the Cornish-speaking areas that surnames were stabilised latest, and by that time the commonest way of forming a surname was to take a first name from the rather limited stock available, although there was much ingenuity in using pet forms and diminutives such as Hicks, Rickard, Hitchens and similar. The implication is plain. If your family name is Williams, Richards or Thomas, then the likelihood that your ancestors were Cornish-speaking is as high as, if not higher, than if you have a Cornish locational name of the Tre, Pol and Pen variety.

The use of first names

Across western Europe from the twelfth century onwards the stock of male names began to shrink. Furthermore there was a marked concentration on just a handful of first names.[81] In England old English names went out of use, discarded in favour of trendier Norman ones like Robert or William or a new fashion for Biblical names such as John and James. In the 1100s thirty-eight per cent of recorded male Christian names in England were accounted for by the five names Henry, John, Richard, Robert and William. By the 1300s these same five names were carried by sixty-four per cent, or almost two thirds, of those men whose names were recorded.[82] Things were no different in Cornwall. The four most common male names in the 1520s were held by almost two thirds of all men in the west and as many as three quarters in east Cornwall. In Cornwall both west and east John was by far the most common first name at this time. Around a third of all men in west Cornwall were called John and that proportion rose in east Cornwall. It was as high as forty-four per cent in Stratton Hundred. William and Thomas each tended to account for just over another ten per cent everywhere, but Richard was somewhat more popular in west than in east Cornwall. Nicholas, Robert and Henry were the next most common names, though lagging well behind the other four.

The arrival of new names

Although completely new surnames became rarer after the sixteenth century there was, nonetheless, continuing change as nicknames became inherited surnames and aliases continued in use. In addition, spelling variants of the same name settled down into apparently separate names. So, Stephens/Stevens and Hitchens/Hichens are obvious examples of this process in Cornwall. But new names could also appear through the migration of families into Cornwall.

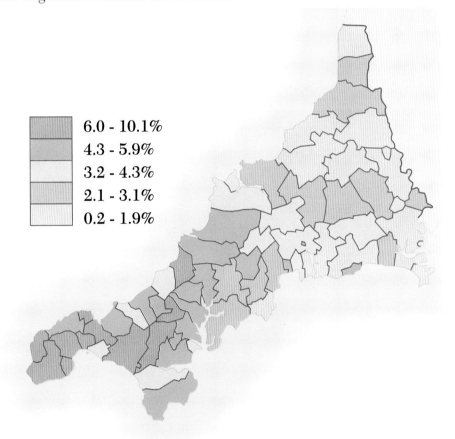

6.0 - 10.1%
4.3 - 5.9%
3.2 - 4.3%
2.1 - 3.1%
0.2 - 1.9%

LEFT
Tre, Pol, Pen
names in 1861
This map again shows
an increase from east to
west, a result of the
greater popularity of
such locational names in
mid and west Cornwall
in the 16th century.

One fascinating name is Ugalde, a family name currently found in the Liskeard/Menheniot area. This name does not appear in the seventeenth century lists, while a check in the surname dictionaries suggests it might be a Basque name for someone who lived near water.[83] Were the first Ugaldes Basque immigrants to Cornwall? Vandersluys is a name still extant in the Redruth area. The first mention of this surname, a Dutch topographical name for someone living by a lock or a locational name after a town in Zeeland, first appears in Cornwall in Lostwithiel in 1783. The name Rouffignac in west Cornwall also speaks of older trading links. This was first found in 1795 in the Paul area of Penwith, the name coming originally from the Dordogne region of France and presumably brought to Cornwall by late-eighteenth-century traders. Another surname with French origins which is not to be found in

RIGHT

Dolly Pentreath of Paul (1685-177), reputedly the last speaker of Cornish (though this is inaccurate). Painted in the style of Nicholas Condy, it hints at the later romaticisation of fishing communities. The surname Pentreath was found in a relatively wide area of west Penwith in the 16th century, as far east as Breage and north as St Ives. By 1641, it was concentrated on Paul parish.

seventeenth-century Cornwall is Blanchard. This nickname (from *blanc* – white), although now found only in north Cornwall, may possibly be related to an episode in the late 1750s when many French settlers were deported from Nova Scotia, some stopping at Falmouth/Penryn on their way back to France.

Other Cornish names are evidence of more recent twentieth century migrations. Kaczmarek is a Polish name either occupational in its roots – for innkeeper – or a place in the Kujawy district of Poland.[84] Polish surnames are mainly found in the Camborne-Redruth district and are the result of Polish miners being employed in the remaining tin mines at the end of Second World War. Italian names such as Nuciforo can be explained in the same way. Meanwhile the large influx of English surnames since the 1960s has added greatly to the stock of Cornish names. Some of these may become established in the same way as Ugalde, Kaczmarek and Nuciforo and, in due course of time, could even come to be seen as 'Cornish' names as well.

Conclusion

This chapter has uncovered the crucial role Cornwall's Celtic language has played in the production of its surname stock, both in the obviously 'Cornish' locational names and the less obviously 'Cornish' English personal names of modern Cornwall. We have seen how a study of Cornish language surnames in the early sixteenth century, many now long gone, can both remind us of the richness of our heritage and also help to explain the names we bear in the twenty-first century. In addition it sheds valuable new light on the state of Cornish in the crucial period of the early sixteenth century.

Moreover, the final section alerts us to the fact that surnames in Cornwall, as elsewhere, are subject to constant change. New surnames are introduced as new families arrive, to add their own quota to that diverse place we call Cornwall. Surnames can therefore tell us about change and movement as well as tradition and stability. It is to this more dynamic aspect of surnames that the next chapter turns.

CHAPTER THREE
CORNISH FAMILIES ON THE MOVE

WE SAW IN CHAPTER TWO how Cornish by-names became surnames at some time before 1400 in English-speaking east Cornwall, but that a hybrid pattern with more fluid second names continued in the Cornish-speaking west well into the late 1500s. There, some family names made the transition from by-names to hereditary surnames before 1500 but others had to await the 1600s before becoming finally stabilised. There was a long period of transition when different names and aliases could be used. John Chynoweth, in his book *Tudor Cornwall*, gives a good example of this. John Richard, who lived at Bosavarne in St Just in Penwith in the 1520s to 1540s was called John Richard, John Bosavarne and John Richard Bosavarne. His son, who only appears once in the historical record, was called Thomas Bosavarne. But John's grandson was still known as both Martin Thomas and Martin Bosavarne in the early seventeenth century.[1] The moral of this is that family historians must not assume that those people who bore their names in the 1500s are necessarily their relatives. The instability of names, plus the tendency to change the surname to fit a new location means that, before the Protestation Return of 1641 at the earliest, we cannot be at all sure about this.

Early ramification of names

However, after the sixteenth century, some family names ramified, multiplying outwards from their early origins to become spread over the length and breadth of Cornwall and, for some in the nineteenth century, over several continents. Yet surnames could also remain tightly restricted to small districts within Cornwall. Both the spread of names and their continuing concentration in certain areas reflect patterns of movement. The predominant short-distance moves of the centuries before the twentieth confined names to certain districts, while occasional longer-distance moves leap-frogged names into new areas, far from their origin.

This chapter looks at some examples of surname ramification and non-ramification amongst Cornish families, mainly using the lists of names that were compiled for purposes of central government in the 1520s and 1641, together with the distribution of marriages from the 1720s to 1750s, the 1861 Census and the modern telephone directory. (As this latter source is becoming increasingly unrepresentative with the growing use of mobile phones and ex-directory entries, the 2001 telephone directory was used in preference to more recent editions.) But geographical movement is only one way families could move. They also moved

RIGHT

Tucking a School of Pilchards 1897, *by Percy Robert Craft (1856-1935). The artist used local Newlyn fishermen as models for this study of emptying a seine net. The back of the canvas is inscribed with some of their names: Thomas Tregurtha Bone, James Johnson, William Maddern, William Glasson and Andrew Harvey. The fisherman second from right whose hands are on the boat's edge is called Kitchen and the family lived at Vine Cottage (see page 9).*

ABOVE

The arms of the
Rashleigh family.

ABOVE

The arms of the
Robartes, Earl of
Radnor, acquired in the
later 17th century.

socially, up and down the scale of wealth and status. Therefore, we begin by recounting a few examples of socially mobile families in past centuries before focusing on the more commonplace ramification of a selection of Cornish surnames since the sixteenth century.

Social mobility

The sixteenth century saw the rise of the gentry. In the 1500s, population growth encouraged trade and in so doing, provided opportunities for profits for those entrepreneurial families well-placed to pursue them. One such family was the Rashleighs, who originally came from Devon, but settled in Fowey around 1540. Profits from trading ventures and expeditions against the Spanish meant that John Rashleigh, who died in 1578, was well placed when the government began to sell off property taken from the monasteries in the 1530s. John bought Bodmin Priory in 1567 and the Menabilly estate in 1573. His son, also John (1554-1624) built on this by developing interests in the Newfoundland cod fishery and marrying into the Bonythons of Carclew, an established gentry family. He was knighted, represented Fowey in Parliament in 1589 and 1598, was Sheriff of Cornwall in 1608 and a Justice of the Peace from that year. In 1600, he also commenced the building of a mansion at Menabilly, to where the family moved from Fowey, sealing its transition from merchant to gentry status.[2]

Another family that bought property out of the profits of trade were the Robertses of Truro. This was perhaps the most dramatic sixteenth- and seventeenth-century example of social mobility. Richard Roberts was a Truro bailiff who traded in wood and furze. This seemingly inauspicious base allowed him to pass on £5,000 (equal to at least £500,000 now) to his son John, on his death in 1593. John managed to transform this already considerable estate into a spectacular £300,000 by the time of his death in 1615. The family had, within two generations, effectively become the equivalent of modern multi-millionaires. John achieved this by lending money to tin producers on the security of the tin produced. It was his son Richard (?-1634) who then transformed financial riches into social standing. He had married into a gentry family, the Henders of Boscastle, in 1598, became Sheriff of Cornwall in 1614 and bought a knighthood for £12,000 in 1616. At around this time, Richard also changed the spelling and pronunciation of the family name, from the prosaic and undistinguished personal name, Roberts, to the more pretentious Robartes, with its hint of Norman-French connections.

With a suitable surname, the sky was the limit. In 1621, Richard became a baronet and in 1625 a baron, after handing over another £10,000 to a cash-hungry government. In 1620, he bought the former monastic estate of Lanhydrock and in 1630 began building one of Cornwall's premier great houses there. His son John (1606-1684), married into the influential Warwick family and was MP in the Short Parliament which only met for a few months in 1640. Unusually for the Cornish gentry, though not unusually for a Puritan family like the Robartes, he fought on the side of Parliament in the wars of the 1640s. But John Robartes was able to swim with the tide and, increasingly disillusioned with the English Republic, survived to take on a role in the Restoration government of Charles II in 1660.[3]

ABOVE

Lanhydrock House,
originally built around
a courtyard. The fourth,
east wing was pulled
down in the 1780s to
give it its present shape.
In 1881, a disastrous
fire destroyed all but
the north wing, on the
right in this drawing,
but the rest of
the house was
soon rebuilt.

Of course, just like those warnings to twenty-first-century investors in shares – that prices may fall as well as rise – dabbling in mining was not guaranteed to bring riches. Sometimes it brought no end of problems. For example, Piers Edgecombe (1536-1607) of Cotehele lost £4,000 in mining ventures in the 1560s and left debts for his heirs to sort out.[4] Thomas Kestell of Egloshayle (died 1626) reputedly managed, through gambling and extravagance, to reduce an estate worth £1,000 a year in rent to a tenth of its former value, and the gentry Enys family of Mylor were forced to sell most of their land to pay off debts in the early seventeenth century.[5] The Enyses were saved by a younger son, Samuel, who made considerable money as a merchant in Spain and was able to re-build their estate.

This family in the eighteenth century also made a lot of money, estimated at £20,000 (around £2 million in modern terms) out of mining, and the great rise of copper mining in that century restored the fortunes and added to the vaults of other older landed families, the most obvious being the Bassets of Tehidy.[6] Whereas such families would make fortunes to some extent from the pure luck of possessing the mining rights in new copper districts, others hauled themselves up the slippery ladder through their own efforts. And spectacularly so.

The rise of the mining gentry

William Lemon (1696-1760) was born in Breage of an ordinary mining family and spent his early years learning the tricks of mining in that district. When still a young man, he was involved in the discovery of Wheal Fortune, near Marazion, a tin mine that lived up to its name by providing a fortune for William.[7] With this money he was able to move into other profitable ventures such as Angarrack tin smelting house near Hayle.[8] Moving to Truro, William Lemon became a leading citizen of that town and, outliving his son, passed on his growing wealth to his grandson, also named William (1748-1825), who was educated at Oxford and then undertook the European Grand Tour.[9] It was during the lifetime of this William that the family completed its meteoric rise from miners to landed gentry in just three generations. William junior was involved in setting up the first Cornish banks in 1771, and in 1774 became a baronet. In the same year, in a landmark election that marked political recognition

RIGHT

Almshouses in Truro in the late 19th century. The memorial is to Henry Williams, a local draper and charity benefactor unrelated to the mining gentry family of the same name.

of Cornwall's mining interests, he became a County MP, a position retained until his death. He also made the physical move from Truro to the mansion at Carclew, from where his son Charles (1784-1868) retained a key role as one of Cornwall's leading political figures. Charles was incidentally the ninth child of twelve, but became the heir as six of his older siblings were girls, one of the boys died in infancy and the eldest brother, William (born 1774) shot himself in his London lodgings in 1799 after a spell in the Coldstream Guards.[10]

The Lemons' rise was followed in the early nineteenth century by the two families who became the richest in later nineteenth century Cornwall – the Williamses and Bolithos. The Williams family were tinners in Stithians in the 1600s. Moving to Gwennap, at the centre of the expanding copper industry, John Williams (*c.*1684-1761) became manager of Poldice Mine and was heavily involved in the building of the Great County Adit, miles of tunnels that drained the mines of the central mining district. By 1800, the Williams family 'controlled or managed over a quarter of the copper mines in Cornwall'.[11] John Williams' grandson, another John (1753-1841) moved into other fields, establishing in 1822 the partnership that later became Williams, Foster and Company, investing in copper smelting in Swansea and opening places of business in London, Liverpool, Manchester and Birmingham. By 1840 the company's capital was £400,000 and John Michael Williams (1813-1880) left a massive £1.6 million in his will, being described as 'probably the most wealthy man in Cornwall'.[12] It was John Michael who made the symbolic leap into the landed class in 1853, purchasing Caerhays from the old gentry family of the Trevanions, fallen on hard times. This has been the main family home to this day,

while the family has diversified from mining and smelting into nurseries and horticulture. Meanwhile, further west, the Bolithos rose on the strength of their tin-smelting and merchanting interests.

Before 1740, the family had been tanners and merchants in Penryn, but moved west to Madron. By 1805, Thomas Bolitho (1765-1858) had joined in a tin-smelting partnership at Chyandour and the family's trading company was also involved in shipowning, lime pits, dealing in hemp, cordage and tallow and exporting pilchards.[13] But their most astute move by far was to enter banking, in 1807 setting up the Mounts Bay Commercial Bank and becoming partners in the East Cornwall Bank, based at Liskeard. From this base in both halves of Cornwall they bought shares in various tin mines. Thomas Simon Bolitho (1808-1887), Thomas's son, bought Trengwainton House in 1866 and had become a magistrate by the 1870s. His son in turn, Thomas Robins Bolitho (1840-1925) received the Harrow and Oxford education by this time deemed essential for membership of the upper classes. By 1885, the family had become wealthy enough to be given the title of the 'merchant princes' of Cornwall.[14]

But, again, families could fall as well as rise. In 1828, for example, Thomas Daniell, one of the Truro merchant dynasty which ended up owning the country house at Trelissick, found himself in financial difficulties just two years after serving as County Sheriff. He was forced to flee to Boulogne in order to avoid bankruptcy

ABOVE

Caerhays Castle was a romantic project begun by the Trevanions in 1810. Unfortunately, it bankrupted them and was bought, half-finished, by the Williamses who completed the construction work.

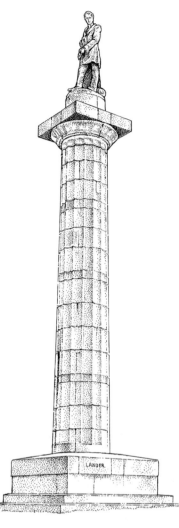

ABOVE

The Lander Monument,
1890, Lemon Street,
Truro. Richard Lander
(1804 - 34), born in the
city, discovered the
source of the River
Niger.

proceedings.[15] Nevertheless, mining underpinned social mobility well into the nineteenth century. As an example, William Teague (1821-1886) was a working miner in Tincroft in the 1840s. He had been born in Ludgvan, the son of a mining captain who later died on a voyage to America. William had become a mine captain by 1850 and was managing St Day United in 1852. After this, he took a controlling interest in Tincroft mine and became its manager just as the mine began to reap large dividends from the transition from copper to tin reserves as it went deeper. Coupling control of Tincroft with that of neighbouring Carn Brea mine, William Teague was reputed to have made up to £30,000 a year (the equivalent of almost £3 million nowadays) in the halcyon years of the 1850s and 1860s. With the proceeds of this, he bought estates at Camelford and Wadebridge, the manor of Crackington at St Gennys and Treliske estate near Truro, where he built a mansion on the site of the present-day hospital.[16] Though Teague lost considerable money in mining ventures in the more difficult years after the early 1870s, diversification into banking and tin smelting made him secure. This man, who had begun his working life as a miner, ended it living in a country house, having entertained the Duke of Cornwall there in 1880. Politically, he was approached to become Conservative candidate for West Cornwall, but wisely declined. And in religious terms, he gave up his early Primitive Methodist allegiance in favour of becoming a staunch member of the Church of England. The Primitives, particularly associated with a working-class membership, were hardly appropriate for such gentry aspirations.

Mining families

Other Cornish families could, in the nineteenth century, experience similar mobility, courtesy of mining. Charles Thomas (1794-1868), a working miner at Dolcoath, like William Teague became a mine captain and manager and founded a dynasty of Dolcoath captains and managers.[17] The Thomas family were also prominent Methodists, regularly appearing in the pulpit as lay preachers. This religious role complemented and extended their secular role as captains of men. Such families made up the new Cornish middle class, confident self-made men who exercised their position of social leadership in the occasionally turbulent towns of west Cornwall and buttressed this through a dominant position in both chapel and mine.

Sometimes, later in the century, social mobility could interact with geographical mobility in striking ways. Perhaps the last of the old-style mining adventurers was Francis Oats (died 1918) of St Just in Penwith. Oats had left Botallack Mine, where he was a captain, for the goldfields of Kimberley in South Africa in 1876. There, he built up a diamond mining company, eventually taken over by De Beers. But Oats was rewarded by a place on the De Beers board and a considerable income. In the 1880s, he returned to St Just, became a major shareholder in Levant Mine and in Wheal Basset in Illogan and built himself a mansion in a splendid location at Cape Cornwall. Oats was able to fund a series of ventures, all of which ultimately failed, in the Cornish mining and explosives industries, his energy being sustained by the retention of a base in South Africa, to and from which he commuted regularly.[18] Here was a striking example of the 'new Cornwall' overseas being used for a time at the end of the nineteenth century to bankroll the 'old Cornwall' of home.

The industrial middle class

Some Cornish families made their money out of non-mining activities, even though these were often indirectly stimulated by Cornwall's mining economy. John Harvey (1730-1803) for example, a blacksmith at Carnhell Green to the west of Camborne, moved his forge to Hayle in 1779 and established Hayle Foundry. This was later to grow into the largest engineering company west of Bristol, enjoying its heyday in the early nineteenth century when John's son, Henry Harvey (1775-1850) built up the business. Another, later, family engineering concern was that of the Holmans at Camborne. William Holman was the son of a farm servant of the Basset family at Tehidy. He became a mine smith and began to build boilers at Pool. It was his son, Nicholas (born 1777), who started a works to produce the boilers for Richard Trevithick's high-pressure steam engine. And his grandson, John (1819-1890), set up the business at Camborne in 1839 which was to survive the decline of Cornish

ABOVE

Harvey's Foundry, Hayle, showing the (expensively miscast) 144-inch cylinder made there in 1843 for a Cruquis pumping engine destined for Holland.

101

mining and eventually employ as many as 3,000 workers at its height in 1962 before being 'downsized' by a succession of up-country owners after the 1970s, finally closing in 2003. Meanwhile, a branch of the family had moved to St Just in Penwith in the 1830s, starting a foundry there and later a dry dock at Penzance.[19]

Not all socially mobile families made money from making things. Others were able to prosper by selling things. In 1854, two brothers, Samuel and Thomas Trounson, sons of a Cury farmer on the Lizard, moved to Redruth and took over a grocer's shop in the middle of Fore Street just up the road from the Clock Tower. This shop, rebuilt in 1869 and extended in 1901, flourished and became the major grocery store in the Camborne-Redruth area. The money gained from this enabled the family to open shops and a bakery in Helston and a corn store in Truro. The Trounsons were also devout attenders at the Methodist Free Church and closely involved with the construction of the new Fore Street United Methodist chapel, later known as Flowerpot Chapel, in 1863. They also helped to set up the Coffee Tavern in Alma Place, Redruth, as a temperance tavern. The Trounsons became one of the leading middle class families of the early twentieth century town, before selling their business in 1940 to Peak Frean, the biscuit company.[20]

While the families discussed here moved a considerable distance socially, other families also experienced both good and bad times, although their ups would not be as lucrative or as memorable as these were. Though not moving so far socially, most families also moved geographically and it is to this movement, as revealed in the changing distribution of surnames, that we can now turn.

Surname ramification

Historians of surnames have studied the ramification, or spread, of surnames as well as their meaning, in order to shed light on the origin of family names. Some Cornish surnames have ramified widely since the sixteenth century, yet others remain surprisingly concentrated on a relatively limited area. Sometimes their present-day distribution hints at their origin, but in other cases, current homes do not provide a good guide to the previous locations of families.

Locational names that are derived from placenames ought to be traceable back to an actual place or places. Tresidder is a surname now more likely to be found in the Camborne-Redruth district, this district accounting for more than half of the Tresidders in the 2001 phone book. But in 1524, Michael Treseder was the only person of this name in the subsidy lists. Michael lived in Constantine, probably at a place called Treseder. In 1641, there were three men called Treseder still living in Constantine, while one had drifted south to St Keverne. The early-eighteenth-century pattern suggests the name had still not moved far beyond Constantine, Wendron and Helston. But, by 1861, the centre of gravity of the Tresidders had definitely shifted north-westwards to Wendron, possibly drawn by mining opportunities in that parish. The rural depopulation that set in after the 1860s pushed the

Tresidders further north again, to the towns of Camborne and Redruth. Thus, despite some ramification the name Tresidder and its variants is still mainly confined to Kerrier District, although north of its origin among the fields of Constantine.

Greenaway or Greenway is an English name, originally for someone who lived by a grassy path.[21] In Cornwall, no Greenaways were found in the early sixteenth century. But in 1641, there were eight listed, seven of them living in the far north east, centred on Kilkhampton, with one adventurous soul at Truro. The name, which seems to have arrived in Cornwall during the sixteenth century, then moved gradually westwards. It was still confined mainly to east Cornwall in 1861, but then spread into the west by 2001. Greenaway/Greenway is also one of the few names that showed a growth in numbers from 1861 to 2001, perhaps indicative of more recent movement into Cornwall of Greenaways. The name has no obvious geographical focus and is one of the less concentrated surnames of Cornwall.

Another English language locational name, and one that had ramified in Cornwall before the nineteenth century, was Yelland, formerly spelt Yolland or Yeoland. There are several places in Devon named Yelland and the name Yeo is common in Devon and Somerset, meaning someone who lived near a stream.[22] There is also a placename, Yelland, in Cornwall, at Linkinhorne. But it might not have given rise to the Cornish Yellands. Admittedly, in the early sixteenth century the only Yelland is found living just ten miles from Linkinhorne, close to the Tamar at Pillaton. But by 1641, there was also a small group at St Stephen in Brannel. It was this latter branch of the family that then increased rapidly in numbers. In 1861 more than one in three Yellands in Cornwall were living in St Stephen. Over the twentieth century, the surname has drifted away from St Stephen towards the urban centres of Newquay and St Austell.

Locational names with two or three origins

Unlike Yelland, most Cornish locational names have more than one possible point of origin. An example is Skewes (also spelt Skewis and Skuse). The placename comes from the Cornish word *scawen*, or elder tree, and means place of the elder tree.[23] There are three possible candidates for the origin of this surname, at St Wenn, Cury and Crowan. The current distribution of the name, centred on Camborne and Illogan, might suggest that it originated in one or both of the western parishes. Its early distribution bears this out. In 1545, there was a John Thomas Skuys at Crowan and in 1524, a Thomas Skewis at Cury. Other Skewes were living in west Cornwall, though there were also strays at St Blazey and Launceston. But it was the western Skewes who ramified, the name being most common in 1861 in Gwennap and Kea, as well as Cury. This indicates two branches of the family, one originating in Cury and ramifying on the Lizard and the other with its point of origin in Crowan. The Lizard branch gave rise to a coastwise migration of Skewes eastwards, as in 1641 there were Skewes living on the Roseland and at Gorran. Again, like many Cornish

THE MOST NUMEROUS SURNAMES

The most numerous surname in each Registration District in 1861

Bodmin
1. William
2. Rowe
3. Thomas
4. Hicks
5. Stephens
6. Harris
7. Bray
8. Lobb
9. Chapman
10. Bate

Camelford
1. Brown
2. Hawken
3. Bray
4. Stephens
5. Hoskin
6. Parsons
7. Rowe
8. Prout
9. Baker
10. Davey

Falmouth
1. Thomas
2. Williams
3. Martin
4. Richards
5. Pascoe
6. Rowe
7. Roberts
8. Dunstan
9. Stephens
10. Rogers

Helston
1. Williams
2. Richards
3. Thomas
4. Pascoe
5. James
6. Johns
7. Moyle
8. Roberts
9. Pearce
10. Treloar

Launceston
1 Parsons
2. Martin
3. Harris
4. Rowe
5. Jasper
6. Dawe
7. Sleep
8. Stephen
9. Symons
10. Gregory

Liskeard
1 Stephens
2. Williams
3. Harris
4. Symons
5. Rowe
6. Pearce
7. Hicks
8. Richards
9. Hooper
10. Roberts

Penzance
1. Williams
2. Thomas
3. Richards
4. Rowe
5. James
6. Harvey
7. Eddy
8. Hosking
9. Stevens
10. Roberts

Redruth.
1 Williams
2. Thomas
3. Richards
4. Harris
5. Martin
6. Michell
7. Rowe
8. Rogers
9. Hocking
10. Pascoe

St Austell
1. Williams
2. Thomas
3. Truscott
4. Richards
5. Stephens
6. Rowe
7. Pearce
8. Hancock
9. Rundle
10. Hooper

St Columb
1. Williams
2. Stephens
3. Trebilcock
4. Chapman
5. Hicks
6. Brewer
7. Rowe
8. Osborne
9. Hawken
10. Roberts

St Germans
1. Williams
2. Rowe
3. Harris
4. Bennett
5. Stephens
6. Rickard
7. Pearce
8. Smith
9. Snell
10. Hosking

Stratton
1. Heard
2. Bray
3. Harris
4. Baker
5. Brown
6. Cornish
7. Jewell
8. Gilbert
9. Sandercock
10. Stacey

Truro
1. Williams
2. Harris
3. Mitchell
4. Roberts
5. Richards
6. Thomas
7. Stephens
8. Pascoe
9. Martin
10. James

Cornwall total
1. Williams
2. Thomas
3. Richards
4. Rowe
5. Harris
6. Pearce
7. Roberts
8. James
9. Martin
10. Stephens

families the Skewes moved towards the industrial district of Camborne after the 1860s. And overseas. There were eighteen Skewes households in the United States in 1880, and these names or families were dispersed across eleven separate states.

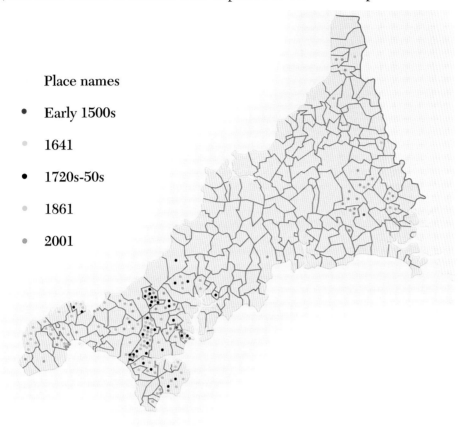

Place names

● Early 1500s

◦ 1641

● 1720s-50s

◦ 1861

◦ 2001

LEFT
Bolitho, an example of
a ramifying name.

According to Symons' nineteenth-century *Gazetteer*, there are two places in Cornwall called Bolitho, meaning *bod* or *bos* (home) plus a lost personal name, at Crowan and Menheniot. It appears that both these gave rise to the surname Bolitho. In 1544/45 Geoffrey Bolythow was living at Crowan and, at the other end of Cornwall, in Menheniot there was a John Bolloytho. In between a John Bolythow was also found at Penryn. Both eastern and western branches ramified, although that in the west at a quicker rate. Although the best known Bolithos of the nineteenth century were the banking family living around Penzance, the surname was most likely to be found further east, in Wendron parish, next door to Crowan, as it had been in 1641. By 2001 the family name was less concentrated, but the two branches can still be traced, as there are very few Bolithos in mid-Cornwall, while a significant scattering of Bolithos still live in Liskeard and to the east of the town.

Another name that looks to have ramified from two distinct origins is Chegwidden (white house). For, at first glance, the spelling variants Chegwidden/Chegwin and Chirgwin/Chergwin would seem to be connected. But they are not. A place called Chygwyne in Constantine had given rise to most Chigwyns and a Chegwidden by 1641. But, in St Levan Richard and William Chywargwyn, also spelt Chergwyn, were listed in 1524 and 1545. Chirgwines, all spelt this way, had spread by 1641 to other parishes in West Penwith, to Penzance, Towednack and Sancreed. And it is in Sancreed that we find the place Chirgwidden. Early spellings of this place confirm that it has a slightly different meaning from the Constantine Chygwyne, with three elements, *chy*, *gour* and *gwyn*, meaning house of the white man, or house of someone called Gourgwyn.[24] Originally then, Chirgwin and Chygwyn were two different surnames arising in two different places. It would not be surprising, however, if the two names had a tendency to fall together, although in 1861 it is noticeable that Chirgwins were still, with the exception of one in St Cleer, limited to West Penwith, Even in 2001, there was one Chirgwin family left in West Penwith and no Chegwiddens, and Chirgwin remains the usual spelling in the Redruth district, suggesting an eastwards drift of the Penwith Chirgwins.

Roseveare is a topographical name meaning 'great or large moor or down'. As such it could be applied to many parts of medieval Cornwall, with its large tracts of

RICK RESCORLA

Rick Rescorla was born in Hayle on May 27, 1939 and went to the United States to enlist in the Army in 1963. A brave and celebrated Vietnam veteran, he became a US citizen in 1967. As Vice-President of Security at Morgan Stanley Dean Witter, his office was on the 44th floor of the south tower of New York's World Trade Center.

On September 11, 2001 at 08:46 local time, a highjacked American Airlines plane was deliberately crashed into the North Tower and minutes later, a second passenger jet crashed into the adjacent South Tower. Rick Rescorla personally led the evacuation of the 2,700-person workforce, singing Cornish songs in an effort to keep spirits up. All but six of them survived. Rescorla was one of the lost six.

unenclosed downland. But, in fact, the surname Roseveare has a very distinct origin, one still suggested by its present distribution, although the name has ramified over a wide area of Cornwall. In 1522, John Rosvear, a tinner, lived at St Austell, while six miles or so up the road at Lanivet, there were two more John Rosevears, father and son. It is likely that all these were related and also possible that everyone with the name Roseveare could, if possible, trace their family trees back to these three. At every snapshot listing up to 1861, Rosevears were more likely to be found in the St Austell/Luxulyan/Lanivet district than anywhere else. By that time the main offshoots were a group of Roseveares in south east Cornwall, centred on St Germans, Quethiock and St Martin by Looe with another group in Padstow and St Merryn. However, the core stayed in St Austell, and this remains the most likely place in Cornwall to encounter Roseveares.

Roscorla is another surname which has its origins in one of two places called Rescorla, found in St Austell or in nearby St Ewe parish. This either meant the enclosure by the ford or the enclosure by the moor.[25] Looking at the modern map the former looks more likely for the St Ewe Rescorla while the latter seems the best bet for the St Austell version, perched on the hillside next to Kerrow Moor on the edge of the clay tips. Whatever the derivation, one or both of these places gave rise to the family name. In 1385, a Ralph and Henry Roscorlan were recorded living at the Rescorla in St Ewe.[26] And in 1525 there was a John Roscorla in St Austell. The St Austell Roscorlas had multiplied by 1641 and a branch appeared at St Columb Major. By 1861, the family was no longer found in St Austell, but were mainly just to the east from St Blazey through Lostwithiel to Bodmin, while some still stuck around St Columb and a branch had appeared far to the west at St Erth. However, although

LEFT

John Mudge and his wife, Marion (née Branwell), daughter of John Richards Branwell of Penzance. John Mudge worked for the Indian Civil Service.

the name never ramified to the same extent as Roseveare, present-day Roscorlas can still be found in St Austell, one of the original parishes of origin, and in west Cornwall, where family members had moved at some point, although the date is uncertain, in the eighteenth century.

Locational names with multiple origins

Chynoweth means new house in Cornish, a name applied to at least seven places from St Austell in the east to Madron in the west. The seven Chynowiths of the 1520s and 1540s, though not exactly matching the seven placenames, were equally spread out, from Luxulyan in the east to Madron in the west, suggesting multiple points of origin for the family name. In the fluid by-name/surname context of west Cornwall, several of these appear not to have ramified and, by 1641 Chinoweths were concentrated on just two districts, Cubert in Pydar and Mawgan in Meneage in Kerrier, with a single John Chinowith at St Anthony in Roseland, possibly a relation to the Meneage Chinoweths. The distribution in 1861 suggests that it was the Cubert and Roseland branches that had ramified over the previous two centuries. For, by the nineteenth century, Chynoweths were more likely to be encountered in a band of parishes from St Agnes through Kea to the Roseland. Other Chenoweths in St Blazey, Liskeard and Calstock may indicate the eastern movement of miners towards new mining districts in the second quarter of the nineteenth century. The surname is still most likely to be found in the western part of Powder and Pydar Hundreds, neatly reflecting the family history.

In the case of other locational names, it is sometimes more difficult to pin down the point of origin of the family name. Take Trevena as an example. This placename, possibly originally Trewarvena (farm on the hill) crops up far and wide across Cornwall from Tintagel and St Neot in the east to Breage in the west. But, while

there was a John Trefuna at Breage in 1524, it is unlikely he passed on this name. By the 1740s, Trevenas were heavily concentrated in the area of Stithians, Gwennap, Perranarworthal, St Gluvias and Budock in Kerrier. This might suggest that the origin was somewhere in this district. And yet, according to Symons' *Gazetteer*, there is no place with the name Trevena in this area. However, an Oliver Trewennow was living at Perranarworthal in 1524 and this Oliver could have spawned the later Trevenas in this area. By 1861, members of the family were represented in mid-Cornwall and this, together with the older heartland from Falmouth through to Camborne, remains its stronghold.

Tregonning is a name that more clearly has multiple roots. The placename, originally Tregonan (Conan's farm), appeared early as a surname in several parishes, for example in 1336 in Newlyn East,[27] most of these being close to the places of the same name. By 1641, the name had ramified in two distinct districts, presumably reflecting two distinctly separate geographical origins. These were Luxulyan/Lanlivery in mid Cornwall and the Constantine/Gwennap district in the west. By the early eighteenth century, Tregonnings, now with the -ing spelling, had made inroads further west, at Breage, Sithney, Crowan and St Erth, although only detailed genealogical research could tell us whether this marked a third point of origin, based on the Tregonning placename at Breage, or if it was westwards migrants from eastern Kerrier. By the nineteenth century, both main centres of the family name had continued to ramify, although it remained concentrated in Gwennap, where there were twenty-four households headed by a Tregonning in 1861. The expansion of mining had kept the Tregonnings here in the eighteenth and nineteenth centuries. Its demise has, conversely, meant that Tregonnings are now less concentrated, forsaking Gwennap for nearby more urban Redruth, while St Austell remains a centre of the name. It is likely that the majority of the eighteen Tregonning family heads living in the US in 1880, half in California and Nevada, hailed from the Gwennap branch.

Other families have, like the Tregonnings, ramified, but are dispersed more extensively within Cornwall. For example, there are several places called Tremain (farm of a stone). More people seem to have called themselves Tremain in earlier centuries, with one of the earliest examples being a de Tremaen at St Martin at Meneage in 1262-66. Others were found at St Columb in the 1350s and St Ewe in 1376.[28] In the first of these parishes there was a place called Tremain, while the St Ewe family may have taken its name from the Tremain in Ruanlanihorne, about seven miles to the west. Rather strangely, however, very few of the sixteenth-century Tremains seem to have ramified. The exceptions were the Tremains of St Martin, who, moving north across the Helford, were flourishing by 1641, and those of St Ewe, where the name had also begun to multiply by the seventeenth century. Constantine remained the parish with the most Tremains in 1861, although by this time, the name had spread over all of mid-Cornwall and as far north in the county as St Teath. Tremaines/Tremaynes are now, in the early twenty-first century, distributed widely across Cornwall in a very dispersed pattern, the older focus on Constantine having evaporated.

- Early 1500s
- 1641
- 1720s-50s
- 1861
- 2001

RIGHT

Dingle, a name that
has spread steadily
from its south-east
Cornish origin.

Some English ramifying names

Some English-language surnames also display this greater level of dissemination. The first is Dingle, purportedly a topographical name for someone living in a wooded dell or hollow.[29] Dingle was already well established as a surname, then spelt Doyngell, in south-east Cornwall in the early sixteenth century, with one or two strays north of Bodmin Moor. In the seventeenth century, south-east Cornwall continued to be home to the majority of Dingles, but branches had moved westwards and appeared in coastal places like Lanteglos by Fowey and, in particular, Gorran, and as far west as St Just in Roseland. This again implies the existence of a vigorous coast-wise movement of shipping and people in the sixteenth and seventeenth centuries. In the eighteenth and nineteenth centuries, the westwards move continued apace, with Dingles by 1861 appearing as far west as Breage, although the place with the largest number – eighteen households – remained in the far east, at Stoke Climsland, bordering on the Tamar. The surname Dingle persists as one of the less concentrated in Cornwall, by 2001 being found in many parishes in east and mid Cornwall, although still not so common in the west.

Langdon, an English locational name meaning long hill, and a common placename in Devon, is also a placename in at least three Cornish parishes, at Boyton, Jacobstow and St Neot. The early-sixteenth-century distribution of the surname in Cornwall strongly suggests that it was taken from the placenames at Jacobstow and St Neot, all Langdons being found within ten miles of these two parishes and six of the eight Langdons living either in them or their neighbours. By 1641, the name had ramified quite widely, but with a patchy distribution, with groups of Langdons being found at Liskeard and Jacobstow in the east; Withiel, St Columb Major and the Roseland in mid Cornwall; and St Agnes in the west.

The eighteenth-century pattern mirrored this distribution, with the addition of a new branch near to Camelford. By 1861, the Camelford branch had become one of the most numerous, along with distinct concentrations at Launceston; just south of Truro; and at St Agnes-Redruth. The number of Langdons fell away in the twentieth century, although the name remains well dispersed but with a definite tendency to be found in urban rather than rural Cornwall. Another surname that has spread far afield across Cornwall is Henwood. There is one place in Cornwall called Henwood – in Linkinhorne, and the name has been claimed to be English, meaning, not surprisingly, hen's wood.[30] In 1327, this was spelt Hennawode and in 1544, we find, sure

LEFT

Mr Tippett of Kelynack, photographed in the mid-1860s, riding a velocipede which he built himself. He was the first man in the area to make bicycles.

enough, a John Hennawood living in Linkinhorne, presumably at the place so named on the eastern slopes of Bodmin Moor. The name would appear to have already spread but only sparsely, with others living at Egloshayle and Helland, at Braddock and at St Germans. Only the surname of Robert Hennawood at St Germans was spelt the same way as John's, the other three being versions of Henwood. The seventeenth- and eighteenth-century distribution reflects that of the sixteenth century, with Henwoods spread in an arc between St Germans, through Menheniot, St Neot, Cardinham to Helland. One more branch had appeared in St Ewe and Gorran by

1641 and another by the 1730s in the centre of Pydar Hundred, at St Columb Minor, Newlyn East and St Enoder. This last area was still one of the favourite locations of the Henwoods in 1861, along with the area to the south east of Bodmin Moor that may have been their origin and St Blazey and Tywardreath, a mining district that had grown rapidly in population in the interim period and, presumably, attracted some Henwoods. Henwoods are still widely distributed, although in 2001, there were concentrations with this name in Newquay and in Looe.

RIGHT

Trevorrow, one of Cornwall's most concentrated surnames.

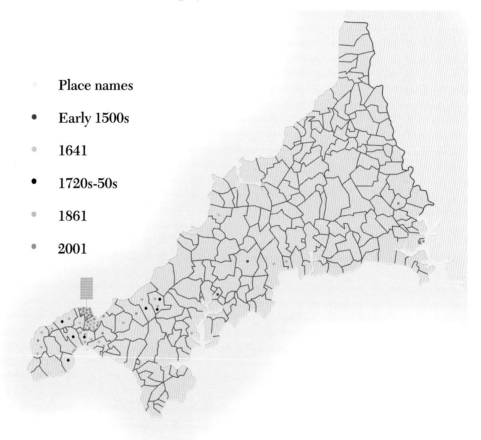

- ○ Place names
- ● Early 1500s
- ○ 1641
- ● 1720s-50s
- ○ 1861
- ○ 2001

Nucleated surnames

In contrast to this fluctuating and broad ramification, some locational names have remained much more concentrated, though not necessarily around their points of origin. Perhaps the most striking example of this is the surname Trevorrow, a surname we shall meet again in Chapter Four. This remains one of the most concentrated Cornish surnames, around two thirds of the Trevorrows in the 2001 telephone book living around St Ives Bay.

This reflects a pattern already established by 1861, when a similar proportion of Trevorrows were found in just one parish – St Ives. Having set themselves up in this fishing port by the early nineteenth century, the Trevorrows seem to be a prime example of the lack of migration, both in and out, that came to characterise such communities in the nineteenth century.[31] However, in earlier times the concentration on St Ives was less marked. The eighteenth-century marriage registers are not such a comprehensive source as they tell us about just one age group. Nevertheless, they suggest that at that time only around half of the Trevorrows recorded were in Lelant, and none in St Ives. Earlier sources are even more intriguing. In 1641, there were just two Trevorrows, Martin at Towednack, next to St Ives, and Michael, way to the east at Mawgan in Pydar. Earlier, in 1543, there were no Trevorrows listed at all. But there were two Trevorvows, a name that should have changed to Trevorrow. Yet these two, both named Richard, were living not in west Cornwall, but at Merther and St Stephen in Brannel in Powder Hundred. Does this imply that the Trevorrows originated in Powder, or do we have two separate points of origin, or two different names? To confuse matters further, the one example of the placename Trevorrow appears at Ludgvan, conveniently close to Towednack but a long way from the sixteenth-century Trevorvows. Again, only close family history research could, and perhaps already has, solved this puzzle.

Treloar is a name that was once almost as concentrated as Trevorrow. But the origin of this is clearer, being Treloar in Wendron parish. This was originally Trelowarth (garden farm) and the surname was spelt this way in the sixteenth century. By 1641 the -th had been lost, but all the listed Trelowers or Treloars were still living in Wendron. Spellings such as Trelooer and Treluar in the eighteenth century show that the pronunciation was still more like Trelower. Twenty of the twenty-eight brides with this surname were found in Wendron, Helston and Sithney, within five miles of the origin of the name. These three parishes accounted for just over a third of all Treloars in 1861, while the largest number still lived in Wendron.

It was the rural depopulation that set in after the 1860s that destroyed this long-established pattern. Nowadays, there is only one family listed in the telephone book living in Wendron, but the numbers in Camborne, Helston, Falmouth, Truro and even Penzance speak volumes about the process of townward movement over the course of the twentieth century. Moreover, the name Treloar, though no longer concentrated in Wendron, is still virtually confined to the Penwith and Kerrier Districts, a distribution that reflects the short-distance moves from the birthplace of the name in Wendron.

Locational names that migrate

Some names move over time in unpredictable ways. Trebilcock is one. The placename Trebilcock is found in Roche parish and we might assume this to be the origin of the surname. And we do find an Odo Trebylcock living there in 1525. But the name seems to have already ramified by this time, with other Trebilcocks in nearby St Stephen in Brannel, St Mewan and St Columb Minor, one further west at Perranzabuloe and two as far west as Stithians. But this early ramification then disappears. Only the St Columb Minor branch had multiplied by 1641, when Trebilcocks were found just there and in Cubert, three miles away. By the early eighteenth century, numbers of the family had increased, with two main foci outside

ABOVE

Polperro, 1904, a young woman stands at 'the Peak' knitting as she watches out to sea.
In the 1851 census, 28 women and girls from the town were listed as contract workers, hand-knitting Cornish guernseys or 'knit-frocks'.

St Columb Minor/Colan being St Issey to the east and Gwennap/Kenwyn to the west, perhaps attracted by the booming copper mines of this district. In 1861, St Columb Minor and Major vied with Gwennap as the main centre of the name, although by this time it was found in parishes from Gwinear to St Breock along the north coast, with strays further afield. Its current distribution is more diffuse, although a clutch of Trebilcocks around Newquay and a distribution mainly in mid-Cornwall still reflects the historical pattern.

Polglase was a relatively common name in the early sixteenth century, reflecting the fact that there are at least twelve places of this name (meaning green or blue pool) across Cornwall. However, most of the early Polglases clearly did not pass on this name to their offspring. Only one of the early families of this name success-fully ramified and that was at Breage/St Hilary. By 1861, Breage had five times as many Polglase households as any other parish in Cornwall and the name was restricted to this area, with some at Paul, the Camborne-Redruth district, at Falmouth and at St Cleer, where a branch appeared to have established itself by the early eighteenth century. The twentieth century saw the dispersal of the Polglase concentration at Breage and, although some Polglases still live in that district, more are now found in the towns of Penzance and Camborne.

This twentieth-century shift to the towns was also a marked feature of the history of the Penrose family. Like Polglase, this name (meaning end of the moor) is a common placename and there are multiple possible places of origin for the surname. In the fourteenth century, Penroses were recorded in Bodmin and possibly Sennen,[32]

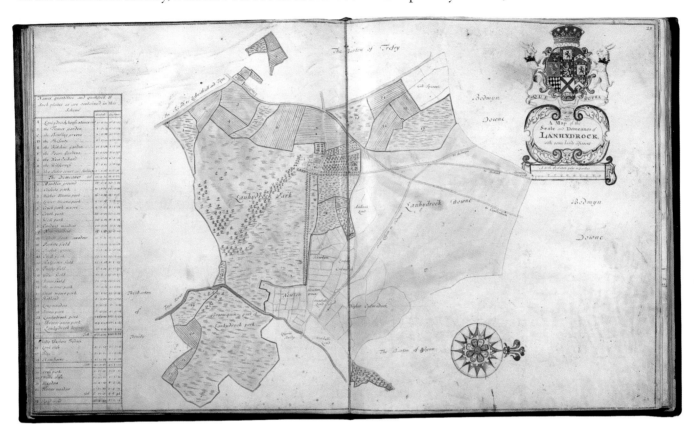

while in the 1450s and 1460s, there were Penroses in Powder Hundred and at Phillack in the west. However, none of these seem to have given rise to hereditary surnames. Penrose has always been somewhat less concentrated than some other locational names. By 1641, there were Penroses in the Cubert area of Powder, to the south and east of Truro, in St Keverne and neighbouring parishes and in Breage and Germoe with some solitary Penroses in other parishes. The name was by this time a west Cornish one, and did not appear east of Probus or Newlyn East. The vast majority of Penroses of the early eighteenth century were still in the west, with clusters at St Just in Penwith and Redruth, perhaps indicating early mining-related migration. By 1861, the industrial Penroses, at St Just and Redruth, were the most numerous, although there were by this time considerable numbers in Truro, Kenwyn and Perranzabuloe. Over the twentieth century, the Truro-based Penroses have prospered, with this area now accounting for almost a quarter of the Penroses in the telephone book. Meanwhile, the Penroses in West Penwith have declined markedly, suggesting that many of the thirty-three Penrose households to be found in the US in 1880 were from that mining district.

ABOVE
Predannick on the Lizard, from the Lanhydrock Atlas, *a late-17th-century survey of the Robartes lands scattered through Cornwall, all 40,000 acres of them.*

Non-ramifying locational names

While many locational family names in Cornwall have ramified in numbers, whether remaining concentrated in one area or moving more widely across Cornwall, there are several that have hardly increased at all.

In the 2001, telephone book there were only two Penglazes –and of them were in the Redruth district. This surname at first looks like a bit of a mystery as there were no Penglases in the sixteenth-century subsidy lists or the 1641 Protestation Lists. Light is shed on this when we realize that the Cornish elements *pen* and *pol* have, over time, been interchangeable. And thus the placenames that we know as Penglaze were originally, as at Lansallos, Poleglaze,[33] which explains the absence of

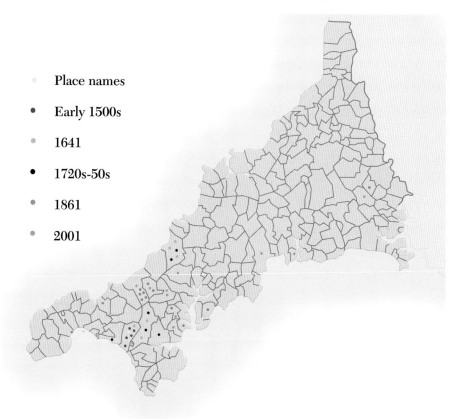

Place names

Early 1500s

1641

1720s-50s

1861

2001

early Penglases. The surname underwent the same shift as the placename and is actually a variant of Polglase. Although Penglases were recorded in St Hilary and St Ives in the early eighteenth century, the name failed to multiply in great numbers, in 1861 only being found in Camborne-Redruth, around Penzance, in Helston and also at St Blazey.

Another *pen* name, Penpraze (end of the meadow) is more unique. There are two examples of the placename, in Illogan and Sithney, and it is likely the Sithney placename gave rise to the surname, with five Penpras men being recorded there in the early sixteenth century. By 1641, the family had ramified into neighbouring Helston and Wendron, and a branch had gone further north, to Perranzabuloe. But numbers never really took off. In the early eighteenth century, the name was still restricted to these two areas. By 1861, after a century of population growth, there were a few more Penprazes, and by this time the surname had clearly moved to the Illogan and Redruth district, where we find over half the Penpraze households. Since then the name has become somewhat more dispersed, although most Penprazes are still found west of Truro.

Roskruge and Trethowan are also surnames with single points of origin, but names that never became very numerous. Roskruge (barrow moor) is found at St Anthony in Meneage, where three Roskrukes in the early sixteenth century show the early spelling. The name was still confined largely to this parish in 1641, with three of the four Roskruges living there and one across the parish boundary in St Keverne. By the eighteenth century, there had been some ramification as family members were drawn northwards towards the early industrial district of Redruth and the growing port of Falmouth. But in 1861, more than half the thirteen Roskruge households in Cornwall were still on the Lizard peninsula, with others not that far away in Helston and Falmouth. However, the Meneage Roskruges now seem to have disappeared from the phone book, with three of the four Roskruge subscribers living in the Camborne-Redruth district.

Trethowans also have a single point of origin in Constantine, home of many Cornish location names, where Nicholas Trethewyne was found in 1543. Trethowans were slightly more adventurous than the Roskruges and by the eighteenth century they even turned up in the far north of Cornwall, at Otterham in Lesnewth. But none of the wanderers gave rise to large numbers and in 1861 a third of Trethowans were still living in Constantine, with a scattering found in parishes within ten miles distance. More Trethowans than Roskruges live in early twenty-first-century Cornwall. but the distribution of Trethowans in 2001 was not that different from the pattern of the name in 1861, although Constantine, while still the parish with most Trethowans, now accounts for less than a quarter of the name group.

Penhallurick is a splendid surname, and a placename (meaning of the end of the marsh or moor of Urick or Lurick). Thomas Penhalurek was named after the place in Stithians in 1524 and in 1543, he was joined by his brother or son, Richard Penhaluryk. Another Penhalurek, John, lived in Helston, implying that he had moved there or that the name may already have been hereditary. It was certainly so by 1641, by which time it had ramified strongly, with eighteen men called Penhallurick or variants, and one Penelerick, hinting at the later spelling variant of Penlerick. Two-thirds of these were still living in Stithians, Wendron and Helston. But a Pennalericke at St Agnes, another at Philleigh, across the Fal, and one at Mevagissey are evidence of longer distance moves. However, in the early eighteenth century, the name was only found in Wendron and in 1861, there were only twenty households of this name, still spelt seven different ways. The distribution had not changed much in two hundred years, however, with Gwennap and Wendron being

ABOVE
The arms of the
Tregenna family.

ABOVE
The arms of Treffry. The
surname was taken
from the place in
Lanhydrock, from
which the family moved
to Place near Fowey.

the main centres of Penhalluricks. Over the next century and a half, the surname contracted further, with most of the ten Penhalluricks and Penlericks in the telephone book being found in the towns of Truro, Falmouth, Helston and St Austell.

Penwarden is a place in South Hill parish near Callington and there are a number of families with this name in modern Cornwall strung out, apparently randomly, across mid and east Cornwall. But the name does not seem to have originated in South Hill. In fact, there were no Penwardens in the sixteenth-century subsidy lists. But there were Penwarnes. The placenames Penwarne and Penwarden have a shared derivation; both were originally Penwarn, meaning the end of the alder trees.[34] However, none of the places called Penwarne easily explain the three Penwarens of the 1540s as these were all found in north Cornwall, at Advent, St Gennys and Poundstock. Nonetheless, at some point between the 1540s and 1641, Penwarens became known as Penwardens and, although some families named Penwarne were still found in 1641, it was the name Penwarden that grew in numbers. In 1641 there was quite a concentration of Penwardens in two parishes – Poundstock and Camelford, with one or two elsewhere.

By the eighteenth century, the Camelford Penwardens had disappeared and the name was spread rather more extensively over east Cornwall. But, like Penhallurick, the number of Penwardens seems to have declined, there only being eleven households in 1861, and more than half of these were in the two towns of Liskeard and Launceston, forsaking their previous northern rural home around Poundstock. Tremeer is another name with multiple possible points of origin and again one where none of those bearing the surname or by-name in the sixteenth appear to have lived at actual places called Tremeer (big farm).

It may be significant that the five places with this name are all in east Cornwall, where Cornish died out in the medieval period and where locational names, as we saw in Chapter Two, were not so common in later centuries. For some reason, the placename was not adopted as a hereditary surname in early times, apart from the Tremeer in St Tudy. This may have been the home of a de Tremur of St Kew in 1328 [35]. By the sixteenth century, there were two Tremures in St Teath and another in Egloshayle. But oddly, given the eastern placenames, there was a Richard Tremer at St Buryan in 1524 and a Roger Tremere at Breage in 1543. John Tremeur, a cottager, at Carbis Bay in Lelant in 1499, is also testimony to the presence of the name far to the west at an early date,[36] suggesting, perhaps, a lost placename. But neither eastern nor western Tremeers reproduced themselves in great numbers after the seventeenth century. In 1641, there is evidence of some ramification in the west and pockets of Tremers in east Cornwall, notably at St Mellion and Lanivet. But by 1861, there were only three Tremeer households - in Newlyn East, St Ive and St Juliot. The western Tremeers had died out entirely. There were actually more Tremeer households (four) in the United States in 1880 (all in the north-eastern industrial belt). Yet nowadays, the handful of Tremeers in the telephone book are, puzzlingly, all found in West Penwith, The unpredictable leaps of this name back and forth from east to west to east and back again requires a lot more detailed genealogical research to unravel.

Less confusing are two names with similar geographies. Trewavas is a placename that means farm of the winter-dwelling and is found in Wendron and Breage. Both these places had given second names to people in the sixteenth century and others named Trewhafos, the contemporary spelling, lived in between at Sithney. By 1641 the family had moved west, to St Buryan, where they were still found in the eighteenth century. But little ramification took place and in 1861, there were only six Trewavas families, five of whom by then lived in Paul parish, where it had become a well-known Mousehole name. In 2001, however, there was just one Trewavas, who was living at Falmouth.

ABOVE

A plaque commemorating the first Cornish VC, Joseph Trewavas, at his home in Mousehole.

Tremethick (doctor's farm) can also be pinned down to Madron parish, to a farm halfway between Penzance and Newbridge (where today there is a crossroads of that name). However, there was no person with this name in the sixteenth-century lists. But by 1641, Tremethicks had made an appearance in nearby Gulval and Paul. In the eighteenth century, the distribution remained centred on Madron and Paul. But again, the name did not ramify far. Only seven households were headed by a Tremethick in 1861 and six of these were in Paul, only a mile or two to the south of the origin of the name. (The other was equally near – at Penzance.) By 2001, the three Tremethicks in the phone book had finally broken from the family's very limited geographical circuit, living at Falmouth to the east and St Just in Penwith a short way to the west.

Parish names

Madron parish, as well as being the origin of the Tremethicks, is one of those Cornish parishes that give rise to a surname, which in most cases became Maddern over the years. The name was relatively late to appear. There were no Madrons in the sixteenth century, but by 1641, the surname was well established and exactly where we would expect, in Sancreed and St Just in Penwith, places just to the west of Madron, the name presumably being given in the first instance to someone who had come from that parish. By the eighteenth century, Madderns had drifted back into Madron itself, no doubt pulled by the growth of Penzance, though the name was found right across West Penwith and, by this time, had percolated up into the copper-mining parishes of Gwennap and Camborne. By 1861, the surname was growing in numbers in a healthy fashion, but remained very concentrated. Twenty-three Madderns (a third of the total) lived at Paul, another fourteen in Madron itself and eight at St Just. The earlier migrants to Gwennap and Camborne had either returned to West

Penwith or their lines had died out, as there was only one Maddern east of St Erth, a solitary family at Luxulyan. Even now, Maddern remains essentially a West Penwith name, being found in particular in Penzance, although the name is also encountered in a number of parishes as far east as St Austell.

Another parish name is Gluyas, from St Gluvias. Again, no-one was found with this name in the early sixteenth century. But by 1641, there were four Gluviases in St Gluvias and Penryn and another two in Wendron. Although the name never grew to the same extent as Maddern, it remained equally concentrated, this time on Wendron, where over a third of people called Gluyas were to be found in 1861. Most of the others were in neighbouring parishes, with one in Truro and a couple at Liskeard and St Cleer, no doubt drawn there by the opening of the Caradon or Menheniot mines in the 1830s. Gluyas remains a name mostly found in the north of Kerrier District.

Mobile locational names

Sometimes the listings on their own are insufficient to explain the geography of a sur-name. Take the rather obscure placename, Lethlean in Phillack. The four Lethleans of the early sixteenth century might be an indication that this was adopted early as a hereditary name, as they were found well away from Phillack; in Constantine, Mawnan, Budock and Penryn. This geographical focus was maintained in 1641, although by now the name was also known in Redruth and across the Fal at St Just in Roseland; in the process the spelling (and pronunciation) had changed to Lelean or Lalean. Unfortunately, the eighteenth-century marriage registers reveal no Leleans. But something dramatic happened as, by 1861, only one Lelean family is left in the west, at Falmouth and the other eight were all living at Mevagissey. The name never ramified greatly and by 2001, the Mevagissey Leleans had gone again, to leave just one at St Mawes, not that far from the sixteenth-century Lethleans, and another at Camborne, but now with the original spelling of Lethlean restored.

Truran is a rather more common name with a clear point of origin but one that, like Lelean, underwent a startling change of location between 1641 and 1861. The placename Trewern is found in Madron parish, just to the north-east of Newbridge and near to the parish boundary with Sancreed. An earlier version of this name was Treuryn (or Urin's farm) and we find a Thomas Treowran in Sancreed in 1524, spelt Treyowren in the 1522 muster roll. By 1641. the name was being spelt Trevren or Treuren and, in most cases, Trewren. Two-thirds of Trewrens were found in West Penwith, most in Sancreed, although others with this name had moved east – to Breage, Penryn and Philleigh in the Roseland. These latter had clearly begun to branch out by the early eighteenth century, when Trewrens and Trurans were found in a number of parishes between Helston and Falmouth in the south and St Agnes in the north, as well as to the west at Sancreed. And then a strange thing happened. In 1861 there was just one Truran left in West Penwith – at Madron. Most were by now found in a belt of parishes further east, from St Agnes through Kea and Kenwyn to Penryn on the west side of the Fal and Gerrans on the east. But what had happened to the western Trurans? The answer is that they had changed the spelling of their name. For there were several Trewerns or Trewarns living in Paul, Madron, St Buryan, St Levan and St Ives. As there was no-one with this name in 1641, it appears that at some time in the two centuries between 1641 and 1861, the western Trewrens began to spell their name to match the placename, while the eastern Trewrens preferred Truran. This should warn family historians to be alert to spelling changes and spelling variants into relatively modern periods.

Our final locational name is Glasson. This does not originate from an actual place-name, but is a topographical name. The placename expert, Oliver Padel, points how *glasen*, which he interprets as 'greensward' or 'verdure', has a Breton equivalent *glazenn*.[37] Glizzon was also a dialect term for turf or a green place known in the nineteenth century. The Glasons that were found at Crowan, Paul and Helston in the early sixteenth century were therefore presumably so called from their living near to such a green place. The centre of gravity of the name was still Crowan and Camborne in 1641, although the Glassons at Penzance and Sancreed might have traced their origin back to another root. In the eighteenth century, Glassons were still mainly restricted to Penwith Hundred, but by 1861, they had ramified quite extensively, being found up to Crantock and Newlyn East in Pydar Hundred and in the Truro district, with odd strays further east. The parish with the largest number of Glassons had become Redruth, although there were another two concentrations of the name, at St Ives, Lelant and St Erth and in the Paul-Penzance districts. In this instance, there was less change in the twentieth century, and Glassons are still most likely to be found in Paul, Camborne and Redruth with the bulk of them in the west of Cornwall.

Cornish nicknames

We might have expected the Cornish word *glas* (blue-green) to have given rise to a nickname Anglase, like the English Green. However, this did not happen. One possible Cornish-language nickname that has survived as a surname (and most of those nicknames present as by-names in the sixteenth century did not) is Ennor, which Robert Morton Nance glosses as *en owre*, or gold, describing a man with golden hair.[38] There was a Reynold Enowr at Perranuthnoe in 1524. But Reynold does not seem to have passed his name on, for by 1641, the three Ennors or Enners

ABOVE

From a family of Luxulyan yeoman farmers, Sylvanus Trevail became one of Cornwall's most active late-19th-century architects. He designed hotels, schools and villas, and was elected Truro's mayor in 1894.

- Early 1500s

- 1641

- 1720s-50s

- 1861

- 2001

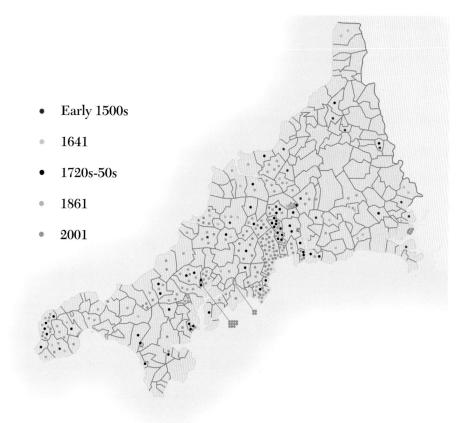

listed were found at Budock, St Agnes and further east, at Menheniot. One problem with early forms of this name is that they were quite close to Annear (originally Anhere) and may have been confused with that name. Whatever the precise genealogy, it was the St Agnes Ennor family that ramified and, by the early eighteenth century, all Ennor brides were living at St Agnes or Perranzabuloe. St Agnes remained home to about a third of Ennors into the 1860s, by which time another third were found in east Cornwall, in the mining parishes of St Cleer, Calstock and Linkinhorne. These may have been the descendants of the Robert Ennor who lived at Menheniot in 1641. Or, more likely, they were migrants from St Agnes, lured by opportunities in the mid-nineteenth century eastern copper mines. The half a dozen Ennors who were in the 2001 telephone book give no hint of the earlier link to St Agnes, being strung out across Cornwall from Lelant in the west to Liskeard in the east.

Although Ennor is a nickname that did not ramify greatly, Grose is another name that most certainly did. Morton Nance suggested that Grose might originate in the Cornish language *an grows* (the cross) and be a locational rather than descriptive surname.[39] This hypothesis might get some tentative support from the Pascoe Engrous who lived at Mullion in 1524 and 1543, as Angrouse appears in that parish as a placename. John Richard Engrose of St Columb Major in 1524 and Remfry Engros in the same parish in 1543 may also indicate a Cornish language derivation. However, in St Columb Major, we also find a Roger Grose.

The name Grose appeared in the historical record at an early stage. Roger Le Gros was a tenant, for example at Trenance, Newlyn East in 1249 and at Cragantallan, St Columb Minor in 1256.[40] But Grose was a name not confined to Cornwall. It was also found widely in Devon in 1332.[41] This all suggests that Grose could have two separate origins – Angrows in Cornish and Grose, as an English nickname for a big man ('the word did not develop the sense "excessively fat" until the sixteenth century'[42]).

The evidence of the distribution of the name Grose in the early sixteenth century strongly indicates that the origin of the name was English in the vast majority of cases. Eleven of the fourteen examples of the name turn up in English-speaking parishes. The multiple origins of this nickname resulted in a number of dispersed nuclei of the name by 1641; in Liskeard and parishes to the east of that town; in Luxulyan and Bodmin in mid Cornwall; around St Columb and finally, a small concentration in West Penwith. The name had ramified most strongly in the Luxulyan district by the eighteenth century, although by then Groses appear in the mining parishes of St Just in Penwith, Redruth and Kenwyn as well as in the towns of Falmouth and Truro. Remaining quite dispersed, Groses were most likely to be met in 1861 in mid Cornwall – particularly Gorran and St Austell, Luxulyan and Roche. From there they had struck out northwards into the parishes near the Camel estuary. A second centre had emerged in St Just in Penwith, while a third focus was the triangle bounded by Redruth, Truro and Penryn. Meanwhile, the numbers of Groses in east Cornwall had declined significantly. Grose is still a name centred on mid Cornwall, in St Austell and St Stephen in Brannel and neighbouring parishes, although Truro is home to a second concentration of the name. Contrasting with its early distribution, which was focused strongly on east Cornwall, there are now very few Groses east of Fowey and Bodmin, apart from a cluster at Saltash.

Pentecost is an interesting nickname, as the distribution of this name in the early sixteenth century bears relatively little connection to that of 1641. The name is a west Cornish one, but derived from an English word for Whitsun, and possibly applied to someone born at that time of the year.[43] The four examples in the early 1500s were at Helston, Gwennap, Constantine and St Just in Roseland. The two people in the latter places may have given rise to one of the two areas of Pentecosts in 1641, in the eastern part of the Lizard and the Roseland.

But the other area of Pentecosts was further west, at Penzance, St Ives and St Hilary. By the nineteenth century, the name was most common in St Keverne and in a band of parishes from Truro to St Ewe, just north of the Roseland. In addition there was a third area of Pentecosts between Breage and Camborne further west. Since 1861, unusually, this name became more rather than less concentrated, over a half of the twenty-two Pentecosts in the 2001 telephone book being in Falmouth and

Harry of Mullion

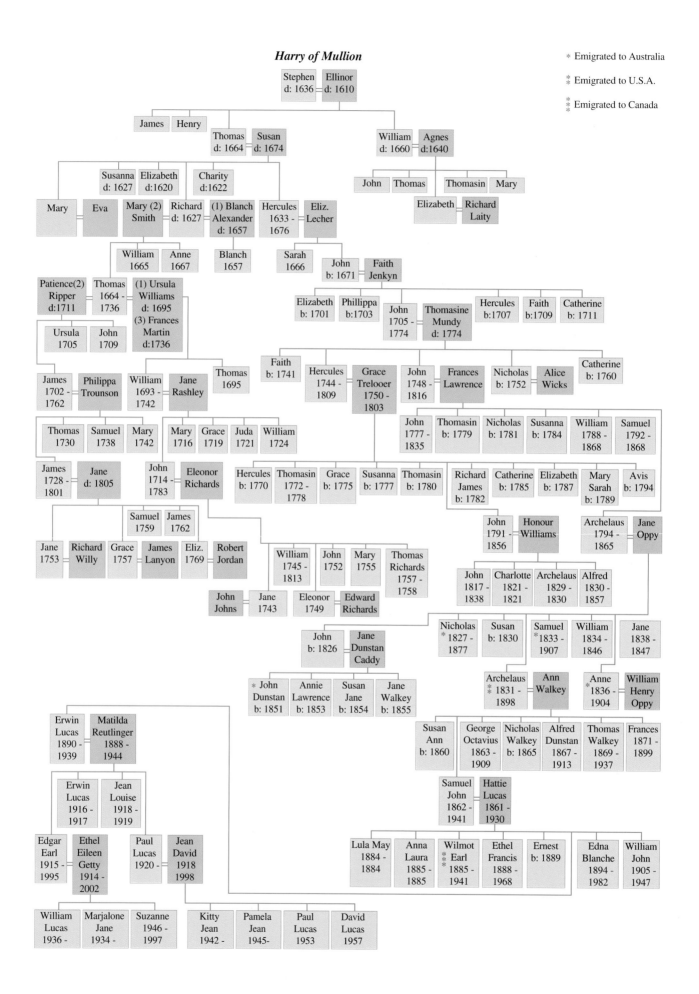

Legend:
* Emigrated to Australia
** Emigrated to U.S.A.
*** Emigrated to Canada

Stephen d: 1636 — Ellinor d: 1610

James | Henry

Thomas d: 1664 — Susan d: 1674

William d: 1660 — Agnes d:1640

Susanna d: 1627 | Elizabeth d:1620 | Charity d:1622

John | Thomas | Thomasin | Mary

Elizabeth — Richard Laity

Mary | Eva | Mary (2) Smith | Richard d: 1627 | (1) Blanch Alexander d: 1657 | Hercules 1633 - 1676 | Eliz. Lecher

William 1665 | Anne 1667 | Blanch 1657

Sarah 1666

John b: 1671 — Faith Jenkyn

Patience(2) Ripper d:1711 | Thomas 1664 - 1736 | (1) Ursula Williams d: 1695 (3) Frances Martin d:1736

Elizabeth b: 1701 | Phillippa b:1703 | John 1705 - 1774 — Thomasine Mundy d: 1774 | Hercules b:1707 | Faith b:1709 | Catherine b:1711

Ursula 1705 | John 1709

James 1702 - 1762 | Philippa Trounson | William 1693 - 1742 — Jane Rashley | Thomas 1695

Faith b: 1741 | Hercules 1744 - 1809 | Grace Trelooer 1750 - 1803 | John 1748 - 1816 | Frances Lawrence | Nicholas b: 1752 | Alice Wicks | Catherine b: 1760

Thomas 1730 | Samuel 1738 | Mary 1742 | Mary 1716 | Grace 1719 | Juda 1721 | William 1724

John 1777 - 1835 | Thomasin b: 1779 | Nicholas b: 1781 | Susanna b: 1784 | William 1788 - 1868 | Samuel 1792 - 1868

James 1728 - 1801 | Jane d: 1805 | John 1714 - 1783 — Eleonor Richards | Hercules b: 1770 | Thomasin 1772 - 1778 | Grace b: 1775 | Susanna b: 1777 | Thomasin b: 1780 | Richard James b: 1782 | Catherine b: 1785 | Elizabeth b: 1787 | Mary Sarah b: 1789 | Avis b: 1794

Samuel 1759 | James 1762

John 1791 - 1856 — Honour Williams | Archelaus 1794 - 1865 — Jane Oppy

Jane 1753 | Richard Willy | Grace 1757 | James Lanyon | Eliz. 1769 | Robert Jordan | William 1745 - 1813 | John 1752 | Mary 1755 | Thomas Richards 1757 - 1758

John 1817 - 1838 | Charlotte 1821 - 1821 | Archelaus 1829 - 1830 | Alfred 1830 - 1857

John Johns | Jane 1743 | Eleonor 1749 | Edward Richards

Nicholas * 1827 - 1877 | Susan b: 1830 | Samuel * 1833 - 1907 | William 1834 - 1846 | Jane 1838 - 1847

John b: 1826 — Jane Dunstan Caddy

Archelaus * 1831 - 1898 — Ann Walkey | Anne * 1836 - 1904 — William Henry Oppy

* John Dunstan b: 1851 | Annie Lawrence b: 1853 | Susan Jane b: 1854 | Jane Walkey b: 1855

Susan Ann b: 1860 | George Octavius 1863 - 1909 | Nicholas Walkey b: 1865 | Alfred Dunstan 1867 - 1913 | Thomas Walkey 1869 - 1937 | Frances 1871 - 1899

Erwin Lucas 1890 - 1939 — Matilda Reutlinger 1888 - 1944

Samuel John 1862 - 1941 — Hattie Lucas 1861 - 1930

Erwin Lucas 1916 - 1917 | Jean Louise 1918 - 1919

Lula May 1884 - 1884 | Anna Laura 1885 - 1885 | Wilmot *** Earl *** 1885 - 1941 | Ethel Francis 1888 - 1968 | Ernest b: 1889 | Edna Blanche 1894 - 1982 | William John 1905 - 1947

Edgar Earl 1915 - 1995 | Ethel Eileen Getty 1914 - 2002 | Paul Lucas 1920 - | Jean David 1918 1998

William Lucas 1936 - | Marjalone Jane 1934 - | Suzanne 1946 - 1997 | Kitty Jean 1942 - | Pamela Jean 1945 - | Paul Lucas 1953 | David Lucas 1957

Penryn, with another cluster at Truro. Like other old-established Cornish names, the change in the twentieth century was from a rural to an urban location.

Personal names

The least likely sort of surname that we would expect to have a single point of origin would be personal names. As we saw in Chapter Two, these arose later than locational names but the number of people with personal second names became very numerous over the sixteenth century. This was because, as such names came from first names, they were adopted simultaneously by many people in different places. Yet, as we shall see, even personal names have their own geography.

Take the name Harry, for example. William Harry, now living in Nevada, has traced his ancestors in Cornwall back to the parish of Gunwalloe on the Lizard. In doing this he has found a John Harry and a Margaret Harry, wife of Enty, living at Winnianton, the medieval manor that included Gunwalloe, as early as 1440.[44] The John Harry who lived at Nampean in Gunwalloe, paying rent on half an acre of land in 1480 and 1499, is also evidence of fifteenth-century Harrys in this parish.[45] However, it would be unwise to assume that the fifteenth-century Harrys are actually linked to a twenty-first century Harry living in the United States. This must remain conjectural for one very good reason. By-names like Harry had often, in the late fifteenth century in west Cornwall, not yet stabilised as permanent surnames passed on from father to children.

As Harry, or Henry, was a common first name, it was not surprising that in the fifteenth and sixteenth centuries it became a common second name. As a result, unlike the locational names we have discussed, there were scores of Harrys in the 1520s, and they could be found anywhere in Cornwall. But, also unlike most locational names, the number of Harrys decreased from the 1520s to 1641, despite the fact that the latter listing contains around three times as many names in total as the former.

HARRYS 1520 - 2001

	1520s/40s	1641	1720-59	1861	2001
Penwith	18 (11%)	56 (31%)	59 (64%)	63 (58%)	29 (54%)
Kerrier	32 (19%)	55 (30%)	18 (20%)	12 (11%)	11 (20%)
Pydar	24 (14%)	6 (3%)	0	5 (5%)	1 (2%)
Powder	37 (22%)	12 (7%)	3 (3%)	14 (13%)	5 (9%)
Trigg/Lesnewth/Stratton					
	35 (20%)	23 (12%)	9 (9%)	6 (6%)	1 (2%)
West/East	25 (14%)	30 (17%)	4 (4%)	7 (7%)	7 (13%)
Total	171	18	292	108	54

And this contraction has continued, with fewer Harrys in the 1861 census and even fewer in the 2001 telephone book. Indeed, the number of Harrys to be found in it is only a third of those in the sixteenth-century subsidies.

What has gone on here? The answer is that a lot of those men called Harry in the 1520s and 1540s did not pass their second name on to their children. A close look at the geography of their name in the table on page 125 shows that that the reduction was most pronounced in Pydar and Powder Hundreds in mid-Cornwall. Some of these, in the shifting naming customs of Cornish-speaking Cornwall, no doubt ended up with other names. But the majority probably made the shift from Harry to the much more common Harris, the numbers of which increased rapidly between the 1520s and 1641. It was only in Penwith and Kerrier Hundreds that people clung on to Harry, rather than Harris, a feature no doubt in some way linked to the later survival of the Cornish language in

ABOVE AND RIGHT

Winnianton Farm at Gunwalloe (above) *and* (right), *Winnianton Manor, the new home in Reno, Nevada, of William Lucas Harry, descendent of the Harrys of Mullion.*

those Hundreds. In 1641, while there were scattered Harrys in mid and east Cornwall, the distribution of the name is closely correlated with the surviving Cornish-speaking areas. By the eighteenth century, the zone of the Harry name had contracted even further, into West Penwith, a pattern that was reproduced in 1861, when the heartland of the name was in St Ives, Penzance/Paul and Redruth. Interestingly, the current geography of this surname has not changed greatly since 1861. From this we can see that the big change in the pattern occurred between the sixteenth century and the eighteenth, as the former even distribution gave way to one concentrated on Penwith.

Another personal name displaying an even sharper contraction was the more 'Celtic' name Udy. This was scattered throughout Cornwall in the sixteenth century and found in both Cornish- and English- speaking areas. By 1641, two centres of the reduced numbers of Udys had emerged, one in the west in Penwith and the other in mid Cornwall on a north-south line from St Issey and St Minver through St Wenn and Luxulyan to Tywardreath. However, by 1861 and perhaps as early as the 1750s, the Udys had disappeared from Penwith, where they may have changed the name to Eddy. By that date the name was focused almost entirely on the same mid-Cornwall area as in 1861. This area still accounts for the majority of the diminished numbers called Udy. A second personal name given Celtic origins is Pethick, supposedly from

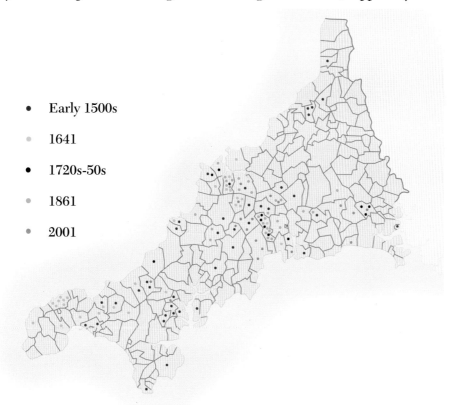

- Early 1500s
- 1641
- 1720s-50s
- 1861
- 2001

the given name Petroc or Pedrek, a shortened version of Peter.[46] The origin of the name can be pinned down in a way impossible for Harry or Udy. In the early sixteenth century, most Pethicks, or Pedicks, were found in north Cornwall, with a particular focus on Trevalga, to the east of Tintagel. This district remained a centre of Pethicks through to the eighteenth century, as did an area around Whitstone and Week St Mary further north, near the reaches of the upper Tamar. From these two bases, the name spread southwards to Camelford and Launceston and north towards Stratton in a classic ramifying pattern, although before the twentieth century, it was restricted entirely to east Cornwall.

Kitto is one of those names that look – like Clemo, Sandow or Perrow, to be a Cornish personal name – in this case from Kit, a short form of Christopher. And this is what Robert Morton Nance assumed.[47] However, like Jago, the early distribution of the name raises some questions about its derivation. For, in the sixteenth century, Kittos were entirely absent from Cornish-speaking Cornwall, a strange pattern for a supposedly Cornish patronymic. Instead, it was widely dispersed over east Cornwall, suggesting multiple origins in those parts. But, by 1641 a group of Kittos had appeared at Breage, well to the west. These must either have been a branch that migrated from the east or a separate line that had arisen between the 1520s and 1641. Whatever their ancestry, the Breage Kittos began to multiply enthusiastically and, by 1861, this parish was by far the major centre of the surname, with twenty-three Kitto households. Furthermore, Kittos had spread north-eastwards through the mining parishes of west Cornwall as far as Perranzabuloe. The name is now widely diffused across Cornwall, but this distribution hides the multiple points of origin in the east and a single, perhaps later and separate, point of origin in the west.

Bennetto is another name with a distinct geographical origin, although again the modern distribution of the surname gives absolutely no clue to this, as the name has moved well away from its original home. In the sixteenth century, it was restricted to West Penwith and was clearly a Cornish-language version of Bennetts. The distribution of the surname in 1641 was very similar, confined to just three parishes in the far west – St Just, St Buryan and Paul and with a solitary Stephen Bennetto in St Enoder (incidentally a parish with several men called Bennett). This Stephen's offspring may have produced the Bennettos of 1861 who were living in mid-Cornwall at St Dennis, St Blazey, Tywardreath and Probus. But strangely, by 1861 there were no Bennettos at all left in Penwith. What happened to the Penwith Bennettos? There seem too many in 1641 for the name just to have died out and, given the growth of tin mining in the west of Penwith at this time, it seems unlikely that all upped sticks and moved to mid-Cornwall. The mystery of the western Bennettos can only be solved by serious

ABOVE
Dr J.G. Moyle at
Tresco in 1880. Also an
accomplished artist, he
practised as a GP in
the Scilly Isles from
1849 - 90. He died
in 1893.

family history detective work. And that requires a close attention to the cognate names of Bennett and Bennetts as changes in spelling between 1631 and 1861 may well be at work here.

Unlike Bennetto, another Cornish name, Opie, ramified greatly in numbers between the sixteenth and nineteenth centuries. The name derives from a medieval

given name Oppy, itself possibly a form of Osborn or Osbert.[48] In the early sixteenth century, it was found in various places between Redruth in the west and Bodmin in the east. Several of these gave rise to fixed hereditary surnames, and the Opies in the west began to branch out beyond Redruth. By the eighteenth century, the name could be met anywhere from Breage and Gunwalloe to Altarnun in the east, but its main core was Redruth and Stithians. This remained the case in 1861. The vast majority of nineteenth-century Opies lived in the district between and including

ABOVE
A Fowler steam traction engine at work at a Mabe granite quarry, c. June 1885.

129

Camborne-Redruth in the north and Helston and Penryn in the south, a third of all Opies being resident in Stithians and Wendron. There was a secondary, much smaller, concentration around St Blazey, although some of these could have been migrants from the west. By 2001, the name had become, if anything, even more

ABOVE

Busveal Wesleyan
School Tea Treat, 1914.
Taken at Gwennap Pit,
this photograph shows
virtually all one family
– the children and
grandchildren of
Joseph and Martha
Harvey (née Inch).

concentrated. The eastern nucleus of Opies had gone, leaving the name heavily concentrated on Camborne, Illogan, Redruth and Gwennap, with some of this name in the nearby towns of Truro, Falmouth and Helston. So, although ramifying in a numerical sense, Opie has remained since the eighteenth century a geographically concentrated name.

Other personal names display a pattern more akin to locational names. One is Sandercock. This is a diminutive form of Alexander, Sander, with the ending -cock. While appearing in Werrington, then part of Devon, in 1462-70,[49] the name was rare in early-sixteenth-century Cornwall, being restricted to five occurrences, four in the far north of Cornwall and close to Devon. From this base, however, the name has spread to the west in classic fashion. By 1641, Sandercock branches had appeared in south-east Cornwall near to Looe and in mid Cornwall at Ladock as well as just to the west of its original north Cornwall setting. The name remained predominantly a north Cornish one into the nineteenth century, being most common in the coastal parishes between Tintagel and Stratton, and to the west of Launceston. Sandercocks were by this time found in many other places in east Cornwall, though there were few examples of the name west of St Austell. In modern Cornwall, Sandercocks have penetrated as far west as Camborne, continuing the process of ramification already begun in the 1500s, although the name remains most common in its

- Early 1500s

- 1641

- 1720s-50s

- 1861

- 2001

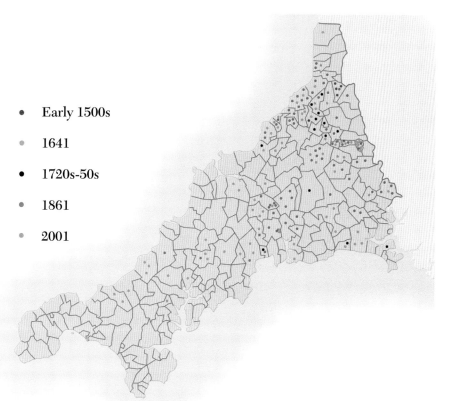

LEFT
Sandercock, an example
of a classic ramifying
surname, from its first
appearance in north-
east cornwall.

longer-established areas of north Cornwall. In Chapter Four, we follow the progress
of the name Sandercock name overseas.

Our final personal name is Varcoe or Vercoe. The name may come from Mark,
the mutation of m- to v- being a common one in the Cornish language, and mean
Mark's son. Its early distribution suggests this is a possibility as Varcoes were found
in the early sixteenth century in St Ewe and St Dennis. From these original points,
the name ramified predictably, gradually ranging outwards but retaining a core in the
St Dennis and St Stephen in Brannel district. Even now, Varcoe/Vercoe is a name
associated with mid-Cornwall, being most common in the St Austell district and relatively rare west of St Enoder and Newquay and east of Wadebridge, Bodmin and
Fowey. As such, it is an excellent example of the short-distance movements that have
characterised migration patterns in Cornwall since the sixteenth century.

Occupational names

The last category of names to discuss are those that stem from occupational descrip-
tions. These are least common in Cornwall. Some, like Hellyar or Hellyer, a
stoneworker, never really ramified although it was quite common in the sixteenth
century, particularly around the lower reaches of the Fowey River. It was still found
there, as well as at other places in south-east Cornwall and on the Roseland in 1641,
but never consolidated itself in those districts as a surname. Instead, what expansion
there was occurred in the Padstow, St Merryn and St Eval area on the north coast,
home to most Hellyars in 1861. There is a faint echo of this in the 2001 telephone

book, but now the distribution of Hellyars has changed again, the name being thinned out widely in both east and west Cornwall.

Gard or Guard, the occupational name for a watchman, is another surname where the current distribution is not a good guide to its history. Now strewn across Cornwall, this name has a distinct origin in the far north in Morwenstow and Launcells. However, by 1641 the name had made its appearance at a number of other widely separated places such as Constantine, Grampound, Boconnoc, South Petherwin and Forrabury and Minster. It would seem unlikely that all these would have been branches of the original family or families in the far north so it is likely the surname had been adopted in the interim period at some places in the west. However, none of these resulted in any great ramification, apart from some at Forrabury and Minster. Instead, Gards/Guards could be found by 1861 living in the west of Penwith, the far east and points in between.

Higman is an occupational name, a version of Hickman, meaning Richard's man or servant. In Cornwall, there was just one person with this name in 1525, William Hygman of Tywardreath. It is possible, though of course not proven, that all the Cornish Higmans can trace their ancestry back to this William, the distribution since 1525 being perfectly compatible with this. However, in the Protestation List of 1641, there is no Higman listed, so perhaps the line died out and was re-introduced from up-country at a later date. But if it was, the eighteenth-century distribution suggests they had settled in mid-Cornwall around St Austell or Roche, and/or in the far south-east. By 1861, almost a half of Higmans were living in St Austell and Roche, with another secondary cluster in the east, between Liskeard and Calstock. Since then, some Higmans have moved to the west but the name is still relatively uncommon west of St Austell and Newquay or in north Cornwall.

The surname etymologist, P.H.Reaney, tells us that Berryman, the final name reviewed here, is derived from someone who was a servant at a manor house.[50]

However, in Cornwall another derivation is possible; someone from St Buryan. The early-sixteenth-century distribution of the name would seem to point to the former rather than the latter explanation, as Berrymans were found at Redruth, Breage, Sithney and Tregony, none of these particularly close to St Buryan. Nonetheless, the 1641 data then confuses things by pointing more to the St Buryan explanation. For,

in 1641, all the Berrymans were living in West Penwith, at Madron, Paul, St Ives and Zennor, exactly within the area we might expect St Buryan men to move. Perhaps the name arose as a locational name referring to Buryan in the later sixteenth century, as seems to have happened with Maddern and Gluyas. By the early eighteenth century, the name had spread eastwards, as far as St Austell in one case. In 1861, either migration to the mining parishes of the central mining district or the multiplication of earlier migrants had resulted in a concentration of Berrymans at Crowan and Camborne, while the name was found in mid-Cornwall at St Austell and Newlyn East and in the east at Calstock, Linkinhorne and Altarnun, possibly linked to migrants following the mining industry. Nevertheless, the core zone for the surname

ABOVE
Newlyn fish-sellers c.1880. Note the brow-band which they used to support the fish cowls they carried on their heads.

133

UNSTABLE NAMES

Proportion of names traced

	1520s to 1540s	1520s/40s to 1641
Penwith	29%	39%
Kerrier	42%	34%
Powder	53%	26%
Pydar	46%	38%
Lesnewth	70%	50%
West	67%	35%

The low proportion of names that can be traced from the 1520s listings to those of the 1540s in Penwith shows the instability of second names at this time. More generally, there seems to be a correlation between the Cornish-speaking areas and second name loss in this period. Yet, over a century from the 1520s/40s to 1641, most Hundreds shown have a similar rate of loss. With the exception of Lesnewth, two-thirds or more of the second names that were present in the 16th century did not appear in the 1641 listings.

remained West Penwith, and almost half of all Berrymans were living there. The name is still a common one in west Cornish towns.

Conclusion

This extended journey through the highways and byways of Cornish surname history has taught us a number of things. First, the examples of upward (and for that matter downward) social mobility in Cornwall before the last century were inextricably entwined with mining. It was the presence of mining that gave Cornish society a volatility, that lent an air of unpredictability to the economy, that enhanced the run-of-the-mill ups and downs of family fortunes.

Second, and in contrast, the role of mining seems less crucial for understanding geographical patterns of surname shift. We have come across few examples of large-scale movement of family names from east to west Cornwall, as might have been expected with the growth of tin and copper mining in the centuries between the sixteenth and nineteenth. Look carefully though, and it is possible to discern a movement within west Cornwall, from agricultural to mining parishes, as in the cases of the Tresidders and the Penroses, while surnames which were already well ensconced in mining districts, such as Opie, flourished.

But, and this is the third lesson, the absence of dramatic long-distance movement to Cornwall's mining districts combined with the general process of a series of short-distance moves mean that a lot of surnames, though ramifying through the centuries, retained a distinct geography. Names such as Penhallurick, Maddern and Higman are still more common in some parts of Cornwall than others. This continuing concentration of surnames, though as in the case of Truran or Glasson or Bennetto, sometimes the exact location of the surname core has moved a considerable distance, exists alongside names that have ramified widely, such as Bolitho, Greenaway or Sandercock. More clearly, the fourth lesson of these geographies is that in the twentieth century many well-rooted Cornish names

migrated from rural Cornwall to its towns, a process reflecting a broader rural-urban migration, although Cornwall experienced this rather later than did places in industrial England.

Fifth and finally, underlying the details of moves within Cornwall we again found the presence of the Cornish language. By focusing on surnames still with us, as we have done in this chapter, we run the risk of playing down the fluidity of surname formation in sixteenth and seventeenth century Cornwall. But the example of the changing geography of the surname Harry, along with the discussion in Chapter Two, should again serve to remind us that the Cornish language has not just given us a stock of distinct surnames

but, less obviously, has also helped to structure, in ways that are still to a large extent unknown, the changing distribution of surnames within Cornwall.

However, the short-distance moves within Cornwall that lie behind the stories presented in this chapter have always co-existed with longer-distance moves. Indeed, the exodus of Cornish men and women in the nineteenth century to places in the New World has tended to focus attention on that drama to the detriment of the more mundane (and older) moves discussed here. Hopefully this chapter has done something to redress the balance and reinstate the importance of the Cornish context of Cornish family history. Nonetheless, that family history would be very incomplete if we stopped there. As we have already noted at several points in this chapter, in the nineteenth century moves within Cornwall accompanied moves out of Cornwall. It is to these longer-distance moves, both to the rest of the British Isles and overseas, that we turn in the next chapter.

ABOVE
Penzance Rifle
Volunteers. Back row,
left to right:
Goddard; Tancock;
Paul; W. Caldwell;
Jenkins; Stewart.
Front row, left to right:
W. Motten;
Col. Caldwell; Warren;
(name not known);
and Sergeant-Major
Sainsbury.

CHAPTER FOUR
TO GO OR TO STAY?

IN THE PREVIOUS CHAPTER we saw that some families in Cornwall stayed in the same parish over several generations. The persistence of localized surnames is evidence for the presence for such core families. Thus, in 1664, the only Tregembo who is listed is a George Tregimba, paying tax on two hearths in his home at Breage. In 2001, of the seven Tregembos subscribing to British Telecom's telephone service almost 350 years later, there was still one who could be found living in Breage. However, we have also seen that families regularly moved short distances, even in the seventeenth century and earlier, so it is not surprising that in 2001 one Tregembo could still be found on the borders of Breage parish – at Porthleven, while in the other direction another lived at Goldsithney, only a couple of miles away. This short-distance, 'circular' migration was commonplace before the twentieth century. But after 1700, it was joined by a growing number of instances when people moved much longer distances, both within Cornwall and, increasingly, further afield. Thus, by 1881, Tregembos could be found living not just in the rest of the British Isles (there were three in Lancashire and four in Ayrshire) but several from Breage and Sithney had established themselves at Ishpeming, Michigan.

In this chapter we move from a focus on the movement of families and the ramification of their surnames within Cornwall to the longer-distance moves for which the Cornish became famous. We first review the evidence for early long-distance moves, which is actually quite sparse, before noting how longer journeys began to become more frequent in the 1700s. This provided the foundation for the long-distance migration which took place in the nineteenth century, including the movement of many thousands of Cornish people overseas. However, almost as many people also moved long distances within the United Kingdom and, after recounting the reasons for the Cornish 'Great Migration', we add the picture of movement within these islands. Finally, the chapter concludes by examining the role that the nineteenth-century migration came to play in the Cornish identity, both by maintaining older forms of Cornishness and in helping to create new ones.

Early long-distance moves

Long-distance moves, although not unknown, were very much the exception in medieval Cornwall. A study of migration to London from 1147 to 1350 based on the presence of locational names revealed that, while migrants could be found from 'every part of England', there were none at all from Cornwall.[1] From the late 1200s, Cornish gentry may have been willing to make the eight-day trek necessary to attend meetings of the new-fangled Parliament at Westminster,[2] but very few Cornish men (or women) would have considered moving to London permanently. In a similar

OPPOSITE

Cornish migrants aboard the Union Castle liner RMS Walmer Castle en route from Southampton to Cape Town in South Africa, c.1915.

fashion, few people came to Cornwall. In 1327, only twenty six of the 5,769 taxpayers in Cornwall (a mere 0.5 per cent) bore names of clearly extra-Cornish origin. Several of these were from places just across the Tamar in Devon; the rest included two from Bristol, two from Canterbury (possibly from the same family) and one from London. At the same time, thirteen people had surnames that suggested Welsh origins, four were Breton and another five were called Seys – or 'Englishman'.[3] Taken together, this may be evidence that migration from Wales was almost as common at this time as migration from England east of Devon. In any case, whether Welsh or English, long-distance migrants in early-fourteenth-century Cornwall were relatively uncommon.[4] This continued to be the case through the following three centuries, with the significant exception of Breton movement to Cornwall in the fifteenth century. In a list of forty-three apprentices in Exeter from 1413 onwards, only six were from Cornwall, four of these from Bodmin, Liskeard, Tregony and South Petherwin. In Bristol in 1542-65, while there were twenty seven apprentices from Devon, there were only nine from Cornwall, and in Southampton even at a later period (from 1609-1740), four came from Devon while none at all hailed from Cornwall.

Changing patterns

This picture of limited long-distance movement began to change perceptibly in the 1700s. Earlier, long distance moves were most common among the landed classes and examples of these continued. Thus, the Reverend John Baron, eldest son of William Baron of Tregeare in Egloskerry, moved to Patishall, Northamptonshire, where he bought estates in 1730 at the age of forty nine, having left Tregeare to be inherited by his younger brother, Digory.[6] Such gentlemanly migration was joined in the eighteenth century by long-distance moves made by merchants and entrepreneurs. William Chappell, born in 1739, left Dobwalls and moved across the Tamar to Plymouth, taking a position with a merchant broker selling iron and hemp sacking in the inns around Plymouth Dock. By 1793, he had prospered sufficiently to be in a position to open the Plymouth Dock Bank.[7] Abram Cogar, born in 1772 in St Ives, moved to London some time before 1805. A boot and shoemaker, he gradually improved his position, moving his family from Petticoat Lane in the East End to Newgate Street in the City. By 1851, his son, William Abram Cogar, was described in the Census as a shoe agent who employed one servant.[8] In addition, growing trade during the eighteenth and early nineteenth centuries meant increasing contacts with strangers at home. For example, in around 1834, Mary Behenna from Lelant met a travelling salesman from Bristol, Samuel Brodribb. The twenty-six-year old Mary married her suitor in Bristol in 1835 and in 1838 their son, John Henry, was born there, later to become much better known as the celebrated actor, Henry Irving.[9]

By now, Cornish people were not only increasingly likely to move to Bristol, but were also leaving their home county in ever larger numbers for destinations far overseas, at first, principally in the Americas. Throughout the nineteenth century, many thousands of Cornish people took the decision to uproot themselves in order to seek a new life in the New World, far from the fields and cottages that generations of their predecessors had come to know intimately over the centuries. What caused this amazing outpouring of Cornish people to the four corners of the globe?

Reasons for migration

Until recently, historians of migration tended to focus on the study of individuals, but this ignores the importance of intermediate groups – village clans, households, and, most importantly, the family, since a significant proportion of migrations involve families or parts of families rather than individuals. Once settled in a new community, adjustment to life in a strange environment was often undertaken as part of a family rather than as an isolated individual. This seems a remarkable oversight on behalf of migration scholars since it has long been acknowledged that the family was not only the basic social unit, but that historically it has been 'the fundamental unit of economic organization'.[10]

Traditionally, a family's survival depended on its ability to maximise income and to minimise risk. As families learned to survive in difficult circumstances, or in order to improve their circumstances, they adopted particular mobility strategies.[11] They might decide to move as a family or perhaps send one or more of the family members away to work so that they could send money home. In the sixteenth and seventeenth centuries, we now know that some people would travel considerable distances in order to find employment and in more recent centuries, this long-distance movement multiplied and often took place across international borders.

Once settled in their new locations, families, extended kin groups and communities were held together by social or personal networks or 'migration chains', which bound migrants and non-migrants together. These migration chains provided channels of information and social and financial assistance that shaped further decisions – for example, whether or not to stay put, or return home, or move again. The decision to move did not occur in a vacuum. When a mining family in Perranporth, or farm labourers in St Pinnock, or the fisher folk from Polperro sat down to decide whether to go, they were influenced by all sorts of factors: international flows of

D.M Packet Lady Mary Pelham. 1818.

capital investment, the presence of a migration 'trade,' the development of labour recruitment programmes and, crucially, the state of transport and communications. Migration was easier if the labour market for a specific occupation was a global one and the decision to leave would be based on responses to broad economic, political and socio-cultural factors that elicited changing responses at different times from families across Cornwall. Cornish migration flows were therefore fluid and hetero-geneous, with movement from various parts of Cornwall occurring at different times, for different reasons and to a variety of destinations outside the county.

Eighteenth-century moves

As a peninsula situated at the heart of the Atlantic world, Cornwall has always had strong maritime links and a 'culture of mobility'. Trade undoubtedly stimulated many migration flows to the Americas. Well before the 'Great Migration' of the nine-teenth century, the Cornish could be found residing as settlers, agriculturists and merchants in the eastern seaboard colonies of North America and as seasonal residents in the fishing ports along the coasts of Newfoundland and the United States – for example, Falmouth, was founded in 1660 on Cape Cod as a shipbuild-ing and whaling harbour. In the sixteenth and seventeenth centuries, the Cornish

H. M. Packet _ Walsingham _ John Bulloch _ Commander 1823

were well represented among the settlers of the Virginia Company that gave its name to the state, and among those of the Plymouth Company in New England. Cornish surnames such as Bolitho, Cock, Harris, Penrice, Treherne and Trevethan appear among residents of the lower James River in Virginia, while in Maine and New Hampshire names common in East Cornwall were conspicuous, including Bonython, Edgcombe, Freethy, Herle, Jope and Treworgy.[13]

The demise of the Cromwellian regime in 1660 prompted dissenters who disliked High Church tendencies in the Church of England to migrate to North America. Quakers now settled in Pennsylvania and the Delaware River area and among the early Quaker families from Cornwall were the Billings, Rawles, Growdens and Foxes, who mainly came from the northern and eastern regions of the county. Migration chains became established between Cornwall and Pennsylvania, promoting emigration throughout the seventeenth and eighteenth centuries to such an extent that historian A.L. Rowse was prompted to speculate that this seriously depleted Quaker numbers in Cornwall.[14]

Some Cornishmen attained high-level governmental positions overseas, for example in Jamaica, which has many prominent Cornish connections including a county

Both studies of these Falmouth packets were painted by the Maltese artist, Nicholas S. Cammillieri, who was noted for the accuracy of his ship portraits.

141

of Cornwall with a town named Falmouth. This is the capital of the parish of Trelawney, and named in honour of Sir William Trelawny, the Cornish governor of Jamaica from 1767. Cornishmen and women worked on the sugar plantations of the Caribbean as indentured servants before black slaves were brought into the islands in large numbers. Often governmental positions arose because Cornishmen held prominent positions in the Royal and merchant navies, which had become vitally important as Britain became a great colonial power, its strength underpinned by naval prowess. Falmouth was one of Britain's premier naval ports and home to the Packet Service which, with its extensive transatlantic links, had been set up in 1688 to deliver the Post Office's overseas mail service. Naval men, such as Edward Pellew (1757-1833), who became Viscount Exmouth, and from Tregothnan, Admiral Edward Boscawen (1711-61), later Lord Falmouth [15] – in whose honour a place in New Hampshire was named – were responsible for the recruitment of hundreds of Cornishmen. Charles Penrose of the Royal Navy became Commodore of Gibraltar and Samuel Wallis of Lanteglos by Fowey discovered Easter Island and Tahiti in 1767.[16] Many Cornish began their careers with Captain James Cook. Midshipman James Trevenen of Camborne sailed with Cook in 1776 on his last voyage in HMS *Resolution*, while more famous still was William Bligh of St Tudy (1754-1817), who sailed with Cook on this final voyage and went on to captain the armed transport ship, the *Bounty* in 1787, gaining an unaccountably bad press in the

BELOW
Cornish wrestlers
William Chapman (left)
and Francis St Clair
Gregory photographed
before a bout in the
1950s at which the
purse was £25.

process.[17] Bligh later became the Governor of New South Wales and was succeeded by another Cornishman, Philip Gidley King of Launceston. King led expeditions to colonise Norfolk Island and Van Dieman's Land (later called Tasmania) for use as penal colonies. King's influence on the island is evident in the naming of Launceston in Cornwallshire and its River Tamar.[18] Yet it was not only the great and the good who left their mark and Cornish convicts also contributed to long-distance movement as they were sent to the penal colonies of Australia. One example was James Ruse of Lawhitton, described as a husbandman, or farmer, who was transported for burglary, but who served his sentence and became the 'father of Australian agriculture'. Another was Mary Bryant of Fowey. Known as 'the girl from Botany Bay', this poor woman was transported for highway robbery.[19]

By the late eighteenth century, too, Cornish miners were making long-distance moves: a group had been sent out to the Lake Superior area in the early 1770s to inspect copper deposits discovered by a British-backed expedition to the Ontonagon River in 1766.[20] More important still was the successful erection and operation of a Newcomen steam engine at the copper mines of New Jersey in 1753. This was the feat of engineer Josiah Hornblower of Penryn (1729-1809) who pioneered the revolution in mining engineering in North America by constructing the first steam engine at John Schuyler's copper mine in Belleville.

The extraordinary 'culture of mobility' which saw the worldwide movement of Cornish merchants and traders, plantation owners, naval officers, merchant seamen, colonial government officers, convicts, fishermen, and miners, undoubtedly underpinned and facilitated Cornwall's 'Great Migration' that began after 1815 and which was to give the Cornish their reputation as a migrating people.

Cornwall's 'Great Migration'

Between 1815 and the end of the First World War, an estimated sixty million people participated in a pan-European exodus. Great Britain lost eleven million people, more than any European country, primarily to destinations in the Americas and Australasia. Although migration was nothing new, having been an important component of European history for centuries, movement of people on this scale was remarkable. Some regions witnessed acute out-migration over a sustained period, others experienced large-scale exodus for only a relatively short time, while there were areas where little or no out-migration took place at all.[21]

Cornwall has been described as an emigration region comparable with any in Europe.[22] Between 1861 and 1891, Cornish men and women were three times as likely to emigrate than were people in England and Wales. Gross emigration amounted to about 20 per cent of the male Cornish born population every decade

*BELOW
Cornish wrestling
was exported to North
America, Australasia
and South Africa by
Cornish migrants.
This poster dates
from 1909 and
features William's
Chapman's elder
brother, Sydney,
fighting Tim
Harrington in a bout
at Calumet, Michigan.*

from 1861-1900 and about ten per cent of the female. Apart from the Irish and Scots Highlanders, both Cornish men and women were the most likely to leave British shores.[23] In addition, almost as many people migrated to England and Wales as overseas in this period.

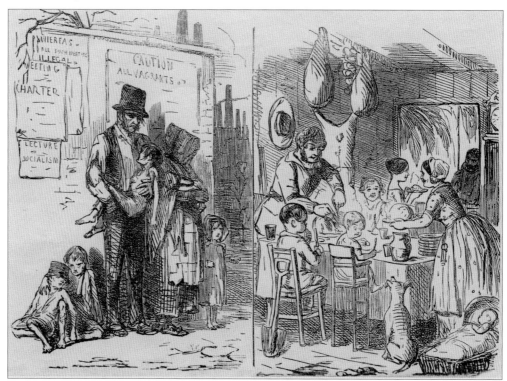

RIGHT

Before and After Emigration – *an early 19th-century cartoon caricaturing the expectations of emigration. The gloomy scene on the left depicts a ragged family huddled together in an English industrial town. On the right, the scene is one of plenty as a well-dressed immigrant farming family settle down to dinner. The shovel symbolises the rewards that accrue to those prepared to emigrate and work hard.*

By 1861, over 28,000 Cornish men and 33,000 women (around seventeen per cent of all Cornish-born people), were to be found living in England and Wales. About a third of these had gone to Devon, and many of those in turn had made only relatively short moves across the Tamar, especially to Plymouth. This kind of movement was not so very different from the constant short-distance 'churning' that had always taken place in Cornwall as families regularly adjusted their rent costs in response to changes in family circumstances. But two-thirds of Cornish migrants in the early nineteenth century had gone a lot further. The largest number – almost 8,900 men and 9,800 women – had moved to London. Five counties – Glamorgan, Surrey, Kent, Hampshire and Lancashire – accounted for the majority of the remainder. Early maritime links forged with the coal mining and copper smelting region of south Wales had resulted in conspicuous Cornish communities in the Welsh ports of Swansea, Cardiff and Newport. For example, in Cardiff in 1851 could be found, among others, Hodges from Lostwithiel, Redruth and Padstow; Jameses from Scilly, Ludgvan, Penzance, Madron and Launcells; Oateses from Penzance, Sancreed and Morvah; Treseders from Mylor, Gluvias, Redruth and Gwennap; Trounsons from Cury, Helston and St Ives and Truscotts from Phillack, Crowan, Phillack and St Stephen.[24] These people were part of the first wave of the 'Great Migration'.

With a population never exceeding 400,000 in the nineteenth century, Cornwall lost somewhere between a quarter and half a million people during the duration of the 'Great Migration' (roughly, the 1820s and 1920s). Today there are possibly in excess of six million people of Cornish descent worldwide. Yet, the decision to start life again in a new country was not an easy one to make and the dangers of a lengthy sea voyage were not to be taken lightly.

LEFT
St Blazey-born former domestic servant, Nell Bunney (1908-1995), left, *outside her Hayes tearoom in Middlesex, c. 1936. In 1949, Nell migrated to Australia where she opened a new tearoom, returning to Cornwall in the early 1970s. She is an unusual example of an unmarried, extremely mobile female Cornish migrant.*

Early agricultural movement

The first stirrings of mass overseas migration began in agricultural areas, particularly in the north and east of Cornwall. There had always been some people who were looking for a means of escape; from their families, the law, bad harvests and unemployment, but why did many more people than ever before migrate in the early nineteenth century? One thing that was new was the rate of growth of population, but this would not have mattered if the number of jobs had kept pace with population growth. In Cornwall, as well as in parts of rural England, a combination of elements produced a situation that made more and more families in rural parishes after 1815 consider seeking work overseas. Wages paid to farm labourers were scandalously low in the early 1800s and were in many cases supplemented out of the poor rates levied on all property owners in each parish. These rates, which had been introduced in the sixteenth century to provide a bare subsistence for the poor and managed at the level of the parish, had, by the late eighteenth century in some areas become a means to supplement low wages. This situation benefited farmers, whose wage costs were subsidised by the general ratepayers, farmers or not. Rising unemployment and poor harvests aggravated the situation. Even the relatively high price of grain guaranteed by the Corn Laws (passed in 1815 and intended to produce high prices for wheat which, indirectly, allowed landlords to maintain their rent income) did not much help farmers more reliant on other crops or on pastoral farming. Small farmers eking out a living on land with poor soil fared little better than their labourers, while plummeting wool prices decimated the domestic textile trade which had once thrived in parts of east Cornwall. Landlords sought to amalgamate smaller holdings to create larger farms with higher rental values, and began to evict their small tenant farmers who now, already burdened by taxes, rates and tithes (taxes for the upkeep of the Church) found increased rents were the final straw.

Social unrest

In 1822, a County Meeting (of ratepayers) at Bodmin called for the reduction of taxes, which in turn would enable tithes and rents to be reduced, the abolition of sinecure offices (those jobs which involved little work and which were obtained through influence or bribery) and protection for agriculture against foreign competition. Protection of landed interests had been the idea behind the Corn Laws, which taxed cheap grain imports, but these had now come under attack because of their effect on the living standards of the poor and because of a growing belief in the efficacy of free trade. A succession of Tory governments in the 1820s backed the large landowners, confronting the anger of the discontented and dispossessed labourers with a series of repressive measures which, in turn, produced growing support for constitutional reform. In 1830, the High Sheriff refused to convene another Meeting, fearing radical elements would whip up public discontent; in St Neot tithe troubles nearly resulted in rioting. Ernest Augustus, third earl of Mount Edgecumbe, the Deputy Lieutenant of Cornwall, writing to the Home Office in December, 1830, obviously expected trouble as he wrote:

> Around Callington and Launceston there have been meetings of labourers in bodies for the purpose of demanding an increase in wages, I fear that in many parts of that district great discontent exists, and it can be wondered at for in some parishes the wages are shamefully low. The most disagreeable circumstance is farmers instigating the people to riot to obtain lower rents or tithes.[25]

If we could ask Cornish emigrants of the 1820s and 1830s why they took the major decision to leave, many would probably have placed their dislike of rent-racking landlords and the Established Church, with its right to impose tithes, at the top of the list. A flavour of the discontent can be gleaned from a letter dated 1834. In it, Wendron native, John Gluyas, then a resident in South Wales but planning to migrate to the United States, grumbled to his brother:

> In this countrey [sic] ... if there is a bit of land or anything of note to be sold there is a plenty of Lawyers and Parsons and other lazy fellows who have money brought to them from the labouring class in Thousands so that a labouring person have no honest chance in anyway to do good for him self and family, but be a slave and rear his children in the same way.[26]

Other migrants might have cited the desire to escape under-employment, low wages, poor farmland and a fickle climate. Yet in the past, for example in the late 1500s, when people had been threatened by unemployment and starvation, they had not emigrated in such huge numbers. There was now a new factor stimulating movement in the early nineteenth century: the growth of British colonies seeking to strengthen their economic bases and needing an influx of immigrants to achieve this. News from earlier migrants in overseas colonies meant that something was known about what was involved in going to live abroad, which may have been seen by many as a welcome alternative to a miserable life at home, a belief captured by the satirical cartoonists of the day where emigrants are portrayed as living a life of plenty. An important new factor was the existence of regular shipping lines, at least across the Atlantic, and the slowly improving state of roads that facilitated access to ports. Yet, even given these improvements, we should not assume that it was easy to migrate or without risk. Would you survive the journey and find new friends to replace those left behind? Would it be possible to obtain work or a new home? Would you like the place you had chosen to settle in?

The desire for self-improvement and the 'rage for emigration'

We should not assume that all those who were migrating were down-and-outs for whom life in Cornwall had little to offer. On the contrary, the movement of people from agricultural backgrounds in the 1830s included a significant number of independent farmers who were challenging the *status quo*, men such as Peter Davey of St Neot who migrated to Coburg, Ontario, in 1830 to be master of his own 200-acre farm, purchased for £275:

> I shall have no rent to pay, no poor rates, no tithes, no Church rates, no land
> tax and only about 5 shillings a year to Government, I may fairly hope to do
> well…I would not return to England if I could have the land of the estate I
> rented in St Neot given to me.[27]

Families such as the Daveys could leave Cornwall because they had the financial means; they could raise enough capital to fund the Atlantic passage and onward journey in North America and still have enough money to purchase land and then survive until the first crops were harvested and sold. But they were also able to obtain good-quality information about when to migrate, where to settle and how much money they would need, so that the risk involved in migration for them and people like them was minimised.

Much of this information was contained in letters sent home to family and friends. William Peters, who had settled in Hope Township, Ontario, on a farm of two hundred acres, wrote to his brother in St Germans in 1831 about the opportunities to live 'a more homely and domesticated life (and) raise by industry the necessaries of life without the control of others'. Crucially, at this point, he urged his brother not to delay coming to Canada:

You can now bring a capital that I hope would procure you here a comfortable settlement, but if you put it off perhaps another year (it) may make considerable difference…as land here is on the advance in price.[28]

Davey's letter had been published – presumably as a piece of propaganda – by the radical *West Briton* newspaper which favoured migration, unlike the conservative *Royal Cornwall Gazette* that at first viewed migration with disquiet as something tending to create disaffection with conditions at home. Davey wrote that if Mallett and Keast, people known to him in St Neot, could get to Canada, their families would cease to be a trouble to them.[29] A common facet of these early migration networks was that they resulted in the movement of whole families, parts of families and their labourers, from one area in Cornwall to the same place overseas over the course of several years: the adjustment to life overseas was easier if made in groups.

The migration of discontented agricultural workers and those who serviced the farming districts prompted the *West Briton* to report in May, 1832, that there was a wholly unprecedented 'rage for emigration' in the north of the county; 'in different parishes from two hundred to three hundred persons each have either departed or are preparing to leave for Canada or the United States'.[30] This movement was facilitated by shipping agents who were quick off the mark in advertising passages to Quebec that sailed from Padstow, Fowey and Malpas, heralding the beginnings of an emigration trade.

RAILWAY FARE PAID TO LONDON.

T. L. RICHARDS is authorised by Messrs. Donald Currie and Co. to take passengers for their line of Mail Steamers to the Cape, Natal, and intermediate ports. Persons engaging their passage with the above will be allowed 3rd class fare from any Railway Station in Cornwall to London or Dartmouth. Apply to

T. L. RICHARDS,
Emigration Agent and Mineral Specimen Dealer,
Lanner Moor, Gwennap.

ABOVE

Train companies in league with shipping lines offered reduced travel rates to tempt customers in the late 19th century.

Religious reasons for emigration

Another factor prompting people to migrate from Cornwall was religion. North America was seen as something of a bulwark of civil and religious liberty. Lay preacher William Peters told his brother that he was employed each Sunday in 'labouring to spread the Saviour's name abroad', and informed him that a large chapel was about to be built in Hope Township not far from his residence 'which will make the neighbourhood very desirable for settlers'.[31] Such information was crucial as it lessened the psychological cost of migration; chapels often provided the basic needs of a community and migrants felt that they were travelling from the known to the known. Thomas Rundell of St Eval recorded in his diary that his arrival at Platteville, Wisconsin happily coincided with the departure of the congregation from a service at the Primitive Methodist Chapel on Second Street: 'Met with Stephen and Eliza (Carhart) here and went home with them. Glad we met with relatives and friends in a foreign land'.[32] The 'Little Cornwall' of Coburg became the heartland in Canada of the Bible Christians, a Methodist denomination that had prospered in north Devon and the neighbouring parts of rural northern and eastern Cornwall. By 1850, Coburg boasted a brotherhood of over one thousand souls and by 1854, had set up its own Conference – the annual formal meeting of itinerant Methodist preachers.[33]

Methodism, with its cherished belief in self-help and improvement, obviously provided a strong socio-cultural reason for early migration. Paul Robins and his family sailed from Padstow aboard the *Voluna* to Quebec in October, 1846, with forty other passengers. Of the twenty-three adult migrants, twelve were members of the Bible Christian Society drawn from Kilkhampton, Luxulyan, Padstow, St Neot and St Austell.[34] Many like Brother Hooper and his wife, who were mentioned in Robins' diary in 1846, used Canada as a gateway to the United States. A flood of emigrants from north Cornwall settled in the rich agricultural land of south eastern Wisconsin during the 1840s, founding a string of Bible Christian chapels.

That a migration stream to Canada was already well established by 1846 is evident in Paul Robins' diary: from this we learn that Brother Hambly, who had settled with his family in Canada from England and Wales some years before, was returning after visiting family and friends in Cornwall. He wrote further of one Betsy Powell and her son, Thomas, who were migrating to join two family members who had already settled in Canada and about two St Austell women, one named Husband and the other Whitehair, who were emigrating to get married.[35] Such details clearly show the fact that social networks linked communities in Canada to those in Cornwall, and that overseas settlements were being initiated and sustained by the strong ties forged by Methodism.

In 1841, the small north coast port of Padstow had witnessed the third highest number of emigrants to Canada after Liverpool and London, showing that there was indeed a mass movement of people from Cornwall.[36] But quantitative surveys suggest that agricultural migration to North America was taking place from other parts of Cornwall; farm workers accounted for almost half the migrants to the United States from the Redruth Registration District before 1840.[37]

The emergence of 'Cousin Jack': early mining migration

But, by the end of the 1830s, emigration was not just confined to farmers and farm labourers. Cornish miners had been used to migrating long distances for at least a hundred years. In 1841 the Government conducted an emigration census and in Cornwall it is noticeable that the bulk of Cornish emigrants were from either industrial Camborne-Redruth or from the agricultural Lizard. Similarly, applicants for free passage to South Australia in the late 1830s were more likely to come either from the agricultural district of east Cornwall between Launceston and Callington or from the mining parishes of Illogan, Redruth, Gwennap, St Agnes and Perranzabuloe.[38] By the early 1800s, Cornwall had become the acknowledged centre of mining and engineering excellence in Britain, while copper mining was entering its golden era. Yet Cornish miners were still prepared to migrate.

Several things help to explain this apparent paradox. Life for miners was often difficult as they worked in an industry subject to fluctuations of mineral prices that caused periodic unemployment and hardship. By the 1820s, the practice of living on smallholdings in rural-industrial parishes was threatened by rising population. This put pressure on finite resources of land and coincided with diminishing access to common lands. Pressures on common grazing and other rights lessened the opportunities of supplementing wages. As the population grew, families began to live in rows and terraces, some of which had no gardens for growing potatoes, the main staple.[39]

Cornish miners, who may have had some reasons for migration in common with agriculturists, were different in a particularly crucial way: they possessed skills that were highly tradable and in short supply in an industry that was undergoing global expansion. Furthermore, Cornish 'science' was believed to be the panacea for foreign mining ventures, Richard Trevithick (1771-1833) leading the way in 1818 with the successful installation of several high-pressure Cornish steam engines and boilers pumped out the flooded silver mines of Cerro de Pasco in Peru before 1820.[40] Over one third of the directors of the British-capitalised mining enterprises in Latin America which were set up during the Stock Market boom of 1824-5 had some connection with Cornwall. These included the Williamses of Scorrier, the Foxes of Falmouth and John Taylor of the United and Consolidated Mines in Gwennap, who began the trend of recruiting labour in Cornwall that resulted in the practical domination of the global mining industry by 'Cousin Jacks' for almost a century.[41]

In the 1820s Cornish miners from increasingly crowded mining parishes in what had become known as the central mining district (Camborne-Redruth and Gwennap) were enticed to migrate by the initially high annual wages offered to contract labourers by overseas mining companies. Also attractive was the system of 'home pay,' remitted in regular quarterly disbursements direct to a Cornish bank, offering the miner's family back home in Cornwall the prospect of long-term financial stability. As contracts ran for a fixed period, anywhere from three to five years, most miners hoped to return with savings sufficient to purchase a house and even some land. In addition, they expected to obtain better skills and to rise far higher up the mining hierarchy than was possible in Cornwall.[42]

Just as farmers relied on up-to-date and accurate information about migration, so did miners. In practice there was little choice in destination; miners simply went to the areas where the overseas companies had an interest, either in Latin America, or later, when they could join family and friends, in the mines of Wisconsin and Illinois. For example, the diary of William Merrett of Gwennap,

ABOVE

Richard Trevithick's statue in Camborne was unveiled in 1933 by William Booth Powell, then aged 93. Born in 1840, he was at school with Trevithick's grandsons and himself became a distinguished engineer.

who was recruited under a five-year contract in 1830 by the Williams family, wealthy copper magnates from Scorrier, reveals the benefits of company recruitment. Merrett's clothing was bought for him, and his journey from Redruth to Falmouth, an overnight stay there and the cost of his passage to Rio de Janeiro were all borne by the Imperial Brazilian Mining Company, which also arranged a passport, subsequent transportation from Rio to the Gongo Soco Mine and lodging at a pre-agreed rental. The company would gradually redeem the cost of his migration from his wages which were set at £102 per year.[43]

Unlike most early Cornish migrant farmers who had to bear the entire cost of emigration, Merrett risked virtually nothing. Even the psychological cost of migration was lessened as men were often recruited in groups. This eased the pain of parting from their families and provided friendship and solidarity that helped them collectively to address the problems arising from their being immigrant labour in unfamiliar surroundings. Merrett travelled with several other

Gwennap miners and on his arrival at the Gongo Soco Mines was delighted to see many of his fellow countrymen:

> Rode about twelve miles, and got to the village of Gongeo Socoa (sic). We were met by scores of Englishmen. We were received gladly. Soon after I dismounted the horse, several other men came forth and shook hands with me. Among them was John Lean, of Gwennap....[44]

Competition for contracts of this type was so great that when 12 miners were wanted for the National Brazilian Mining Company in 1829, two hundred and fifty men besieged their agent's Falmouth office.[45] Often mining migration patterns were extremely localised, linking specific parishes or even single villages in Cornwall with particular overseas communities. This implies the presence of family and community ties, the 'Cousin Jack' network, an informal system of recommendation for jobs by men who were related or knew each other in the local mines.[46]

Families on the move

It was not long before overseas mining companies permitted miners' wives and children to join them or migrate with them, their passage money redeemed from future wages. The arrival of families added stability to mining communities; women in particular were vital in ensuring the continuance of Cornish cultural life by creating the familiar in foreign surroundings, an added incentive for prospective migrants. This was an expedient move by the companies as it ensured that the next generation of Cornish miners could be raised *in situ*. The first 'Little Cornwalls' grew up at Morro Velho, Brazil and Real del Monte, Mexico, in the 1820s and 1830s. By the 1850s, about one hundred miners and their families resided at Morro Velho, which could

ABOVE

A headstone in the Pantéon de los Inglés at Real del Monte, Mexico. Although they have clearly become Hispanicized, some families there have Cornish ancestry and are the descendants of miners who first came to the area in 1824.

CHAPTER
FOUR

boast a church, a resident clergyman to perform the rites of life and a Protestant cemetery, three Sunday Schools and an amateur brass band. Many core families were related by marriage, creating a thriving and close-knit community that organised an annual miners' festival with Cornish wrestling matches and Sunday School anniversary, complete with parade and tea treat.[47]

Analysts of Cornish mining migration have traditionally interpreted such movement as a male-dominated affair; men migrated and their women waited behind. The decision to migrate was one of the most important, difficult and painful decisions a family could ever make. But the decision was not likely to have been taken lightly or to have been made exclusively by the male head of the house, as is evident from the correspondence of Alfred Jenkin who engaged William May to go to Cuba as a wheelwright in 1837. May's wife, not previously consulted, resolutely opposed his migration and the couple went to see Jenkin to beg he be freed from his contract, which was agreed.[48] This hints at the fact that migration decisions involving the whole family were not unusual; the migration of a son or husband overseas was sanctioned only after much consideration in order to maintain the integrity of the family as an economic unit, a practice that had a clear historical precedent.

On the surface, the early flows of Cornish migrants appeared quite different:

BELOW

A remittance cheque sent from Chile to Mrs. Esther A. Martin of Connor Downs near Hayle in 1879, by one of her sons. Many Cornish families became dependent on a breadwinner resident overseas and by 1900, as much as one eighth of the Cornish population was living on remittances from South Africa alone.

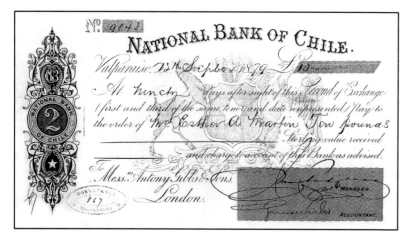

the less pronounced migration flow of miners to mining camps in the Americas was primarily of short duration, undertaken by male bread-winners who sent money (known as remittances) home to their families in mining communities in the west of Cornwall. Conversely, the mass movement of farmworkers was predominantly from the north and east of Cornwall and was characterised by families who intended to settle permanently in North America. But both flows were the result of rational decisions taken to better their lot by people who had the necessary capital or tradable skills to go: these were not mass groups of poor or unskilled people driven out by crisis.

Free and assisted passages

Poor, aged or unskilled workers, whose migration could not be sponsored by a family member, landlord or employer, would have found it difficult to migrate before the late 1830s. Historically, European governments believed that labour was a national resource and had discouraged emigration, arguing that the loss of labour would result in a decline of national wealth. But this attitude changed as population rose steadily. In 1826, a British government select committee on migration concluded, in line with Malthusian theory which stated that population growth was unsustainable and would produce lower living standards, that migration offered a solution to rising numbers.[49] The only way remote colonies in the southern hemisphere could attract settlers was to fund government-assisted passage schemes which eventually came into effect in the mid-1830s. This coincided with a tightening of government policy towards the poor, epitomised in the 1834 Poor Law Amendment Act which enabled parish vestries to send their long-term paupers

overseas. In such cases, funding for those travelling overseas was raised by parish ratepayers who in the long term would benefit as the collective costs of paying for the poor fell.

Mary Rapson, a pauper of Southill, wanted to join her son in Canada in 1837: '…My dear son as (sic) tried the farmers for them to help me to come to you. But it is all in vain. They cannot do now as they have done before in sending people to America…'[50] Farmers had previously sponsored people to migrate, but this had ceased because of the official system of migration introduced with the New Poor

ABOVE
Cornish miners at Wallaroo Mines in South Australia in the late 19th century. Here, it was said, they remained 'more Cornish than Cornwall'.

Law. Not all parishes operated the scheme and many poor migrants had little say in where they migrated; they simply went where their local vestry arranged for them to go. Some used an element of coercion, as an entry in the Gwennap vestry book for 1836 indicates: 'The Overseers are desired to inquire whether any of the young women who occasionally infest the workhouse will volunteer to go to Australia.' But a far tougher approach was adopted in 1840:

> That the list of paupers sent from the Union House be received and the re-
> commendation of sending the parties named therein to Australia be adopt-
> ed and that the overseers take such steps as are necessary for carrying out
> the same immediately.[51]

Such dispassionate treatment of the poor took place against the harsh socio-economic backdrop of the time. The 'Hungry Forties' witnessed the potato blight of 1846–48 that boosted migration. Although not of the same magnitude as Ireland's, the blight hit Cornwall's western mining districts hard, reliant as they were on potatoes not only as a main part of their diet, but also as a cash crop with which to help pay the rent. The political instability caused by revolutions in Europe drove the market price of copper ore down with adverse economic repurcussions at home. This in turn resulted in widespread unemployment as some Cornish mines were forced to close. Farmers were hurt economically in turn, for the miners had been the main consumers of their grain crops and now farmers began to abandon their small-holdings, unable to afford the rent.

Assisted migration and bounty schemes to the British colonies[52] offered a survival strategy for struggling Cornish families as the costs, both monetary and psychological, were deemed to be low. In such cases, the passage was either free or paid by the government, whether local or national, and as migrants often sailed in groups, friendships were made on the voyage and maintained at the destination. Pat Lay, historian of Cornish migration to New South Wales, has found that across that state, the Cornish settled in clusters. Indeed, many of the passengers aboard the *Florentina* who settled in the Bathurst area in 1838 knew each other in Cornwall, among them the Smiths, Nicholses and Rogers – all from the Lizard Peninsula.[53]

In the 1830s and 40s, government migration agents such as Isaac Latimer of Truro drummed up support throughout Cornwall for free and assisted migration to the colonies including South Australia, Van Diemen's Land, New South Wales and New Zealand. His posters, public meetings and favourable newspaper reports in the *West Briton* were a feature of the period.[54] Young married people without children were initially preferred and a variety of occupations were required at various times and places, but as Pat Lay has uncovered, many applicants lied about their occupation or age to obtain a passage.[55] An example of this occurred in 1872, when James and Mary Jane Bolitho of Wendron obtained an assisted passage aboard *The Ocean Mail* to New Zealand by stating that James, actually a miner, was an agricultural labourer.[56] Indeed, many miners had already used this ruse to leave Cornwall after the first mineral discoveries had been made in the southern hemisphere.[57]

EMIGRATION TO SOUTH AUSTRALIA

Her Majesty's Colonization Commissioners having determined to dispatch in the course of a few weeks a large number of Emigrants, all eligible persons may obtain, by making an IMMEDIATE application, a

FREE PASSAGE!

The classes of persons now in requisition are **Agricultural Laborers, SHEPHERDS, CARPENTERS, BLACKSMITHS** AND **STONE MASONS** And all Persons connected with Building. Application to be made to **Mr. I. LATIMER, Rosewin-row, TRURO.**

R. HEARD, PRINTER AND BOOKBINDER, BOSCAWEN-STREET, TRURO.

ABOVE

Latimer was one of a number of emigration agents that encouraged people throughout Cornwall to consider migration to the British colonies that were keen to attract young, able-bodied labour.

However, in spite of such schemes, not all people in apparently similar circumstances made use of them, underlining the fact that the reasons behind deciding whether to go or stay were different for every family. John Boaden, a farmer's son from Meneage on the Lizard Peninsula, witnessed the migration of his sweetheart, Eleanor Jane Orchard and her family, also farmers, for Australia in 1848. As both families were working the land, why did John himself, or the entire Boaden family, not also migrate? The Orchards were smallholders whose landlord could decide to rack up the rent in order to obtain their eviction so he could amalgamate their land: their farm was only a sideline, the head of the house being a tradesman who was more likely to obtain work in Australia than farmers, according to relations already settled there. What is more, one member of the Orchard family had been a sailor so was less averse to migration; another was consumptive and it was hoped that the Australian climate would improve his health. The Boadens were substantial farmers whose land provided a reasonable income. But the loss of a son would have meant the family would have had to hire a labourer, thus putting an extra burden on the farm's financial resources. Unless conditions worsened, his family was well advised to stay put, and although upwards of fifty people left Meneage around this time, there was never any suggestion of John Boaden joining them.[58]

Although the Cornish economy was relatively buoyant in the 1850s, by the middle of the decade, emigration figures rose. Prospects overseas, including the Victoria gold rush in Australia and rumours of riches in California, triggered a mad scramble for the emigrant ships in 1855, a pattern experienced right across Cornwall. A culture of migration was by now well and truly established. Local Cornish communities had become finely tuned to every tremor in world mineral markets, every rumour of gold

found in remote scrubland thousands of miles away. News of opportunities on the mining frontiers spread rapidly and people responded in their thousands.

We should not overestimate the numbers of Cornish people who were officially assisted migrants at this time. Cornwall sent 4,775 government migrants just to the colony of South Australia in 1846-50, about a quarter of the total of 17,750 for the United Kingdom.[59] The migration scholar, Dudley Baines, concludes that overall, assisted migration probably only accounted for around ten per cent of European migration, but that about a quarter of migrants were assisted by family, friends, landlords or former employers who sent them their fare.[60]

Presumably, the same is true of Cornish migration. John Scoble, formerly of St Cleer, paid £80 to finance the migration to South Australia of his sister-in-law, Mary Belman, and her two children, five-year-old William and an infant. Scoble was also paying for the passage of Mary's parents, a fine example of an extended family migration network.[61] Another method of financial assistance at this time was the pioneering, collective, community-financed emigration scheme formed in Breage in 1850. The capital was subscribed by local families to send a group of men to the rapidly expanding gold diggings in California in the hope that their families and the wider community would benefit through remittances.[62]

ABOVE

Born in Camborne a miner's son, Dr William Thomas Angove (1854-1912) emigrated to Australia in 1886 and went on to found the Angove winemaking dynasty. He is photographed here driving his 1904 six-horse-power Humberette at Tea Tree Gully in the Adelaide Hills.

Later nineteenth-century migration

Patterns began to change in the later 1860s when periodic slumps in Cornish mining caused migration to became more of a strategy of survival than one of advancement, particularly among mining families. By the last quarter of the nine-

teenth century there was a definite shift away from migration by agricultural families, as the pressure on availability of farms in Cornwall eased. Assisted migration had largely ceased by the mid 1860s and by the 1880s Canada, which had once attracted so many farming families, was struggling to entice settlers. Instead, we see the rise of lone male commuter-type migrants, so-called 'birds of passage', who made use of existing Cornish migration networks and an international reputation for excellence underpinned by the Cousin Jack network. Cornishmen headed many overseas mines and nearby settlements always seemed to contain a contingent of Cornish immigrants who welcomed new arrivals.[63] These individual migrants were now more inclined to make repeated sojourns overseas, not necessarily to the same settlement or even to the same country, maintaining their families at home through the system of remittances. This 'commuter' migration was the result of first the

ABOVE

Wilfred Bray (1883-1925), left, *with his brothers-in-law,* Thomas (centre) *and Bill Harvey, employees of the Calumet and Hecla Mining Company, Michigan, photographed c. 1905. Wilfred was a mine carpenter, the others were stonemasons. All three came from Carn Marth in Gwennap.*

decline, and then the dramatic failure of Cornish mineral production. Copper crashed in 1866, partly as a consequence of the failure of financial giants, Overend and Gurney. There followed a squeeze on tin mining in the following decades resulting from cheap alluvial production in South East Asia. Population declined rapidly in many Cornish areas, especially rural-industrial parishes such as Towednack, Crowan, Breage and Menheniot, all of which saw spectacular population falls of a third or more in a mere decade during the 1870s and 1880s. This caused alarm as the majority of migrants were the very 'bone and sinew of the county'[64]: young, skilled and resourceful. However, mass movement at this time was only made possible because of a number of different factors operating at home and overseas.

Although the industrial base in Cornwall was declining, metalliferous mining expanded rapidly worldwide after 1850, particularly in the United States and southern Africa. The copper mines of Michigan were booming, the Mother Lode in California and the Comstock Lode of neighbouring Nevada were being exploited and throughout the Rocky Mountains mining camps such as Butte and Central City mushroomed. In South Africa, copper was discovered in Namaqualand in the 1850s, diamonds were being mined in Kimberley by the 1870s and gold was found in the Transvaal in the 1880s. The rush to Africa was on and by the mid-1890s, 'Joburg', with its Cornish-run businesses and shops, was a word on everyone's lips. There, miners' wages before the Boer War of 1899-1902 were thirty to forty pounds a month at a time when wages in Cornwall could be as low as just two to three pounds. The rapid growth of overseas mining towns provided new migration opportunities for tradesmen and merchants. Stonemasons from Constantine migrated, returned and re-migrated to the United States in search of better pay and conditions; slate workers found employment in Cornish-owned quarries in Pennsylvania; while in the twentieth century many Cornishmen were happy to join the Michigan factory production lines of the Ford Motor Company for five dollars a day.[65]

The migration industry

As if in response to the quickening movement, migration had evolved into an organised industry, making it both cheaper and easier to migrate. In most Cornish towns and even some villages, agents were on hand to book a ticket direct to communities overseas; Lanner had at least three in the 1870s and 1880s and these provided up-to-date information for prospective migrants.[66] As steam-powered ocean liners superseded sail, the focus of travel now shifted from Padstow and Falmouth to larger ports beyond Cornwall such as Southampton and Liverpool and this aided rather than hindered migration. Ocean liners were cheaper, faster and safer than sail: the decision to migrate now became less daunting.

ABOVE

Gwennap emigrant, Joseph Winn, captain of the Sunday Lake iron mine, photographed here in his Sunday best suit at Ironwood, Michigan, where he was to settle permanently.

Moreover, the construction in 1859 of the Tamar Bridge at Saltash on the Cornwall-Devon border helped to make it easier, cheaper and speedier to get to English ports, as railway companies in league with the shipping lines offered reduced rail tariffs to customers. Railway stations in Cornwall were thronged in the 1890s with groups of departing migrants on their way to South Africa via Southampton aboard exotically named ships: *Spartan, Trojan, Tartar, Moor,* owned by the Union Castle shipping line.

The opening of railways overseas also made it easier to reach the mineral fields; the Union-Pacific Railroad in the United States facilitated journeys to western America that had previously entailed lengthy voyages by sea via Panama, or perilous overland journeys. Cornish-run hotels, whose employees met and took care of newly arrived migrants at ports and railway stations, prospered in England and abroad. The best known of these was the *Cornish Arms Hotel* in New York, a kind of Cornish 'gateway to America' set up by Sid Blake of St Austell in the early twentieth

ABOVE

Joseph and Emily Kemp's headstone, Park City, Utah. It carries masonic insignia – many Cornish were freemasons or members of friendly societies, another form of social networking.

RIGHT

A postcard to Mrs Hingston of Carn Marth from Cornish miner and migrant Joe Odgers. He was en route to South Africa aboard the Castle Line's steamer, Carisbrook Castle *seen here sailing off Madeira. The card probably dates from the late 1890s.*

century.[67] In addition, many Cornish became members of the increasingly popular masonic and friendly societies which thrived in the late nineteenth century, both in Cornwall and overseas. Close-knit Cornish Lodges provided mutual support networks that by the twentieth century spanned the globe and eased new arrivals into local job markets. Masonic and friendly societies with their expressed aims of social philanthropy and welfare served Cornish immigrants well as they provided solidarity, job opportunities and a degree of financial security for the families of those who were members. Indeed, it was Cornishman Charles A. S. Vivian who was the founder of the Order of Elks.[68]

The 'haves' and the 'have-nots'

Migrants left Cornwall secure in the knowledge that they could rely on a trustworthy and efficient banking and postal system enabling them to transfer money orders to their families in Cornwall. Left to head large families alone, those women who received regular remittance cheques had never had it so good, while others who did not receive such money had probably never been so miserable. Late-nineteenth-century migration patterns could thus have led to a widening gender gulf as the experience of Cornish men and women diverged, with families being literally separated by thousands of intervening miles.

Remittances could also divide communities: there were families of 'haves' and 'have-nots'. Some women with husbands abroad, and there were many examples in mining communities, openly flaunted their newfound wealth, prompting more migration as others sought to 'keep up with the Joneses'. Cornish high streets cashed in handsomely as businesses flourished in towns such as Redruth, where in 1896 the sum of 1,500 pounds (the equivalent in today's currency of almost 200,000 pounds) was received each week from remittances sent home from the Rand alone and a building boom occurred in the 1880s. By 1900, the equivalent

of nearly twelve per cent of Cornwall's population was maintained at a basic standard of comfort by remittances from South Africa.[69]

Migration networks

Across Europe in general, anywhere from a quarter to a third of migrants eventually returned home and the same was true of Cornwall. Return migrants brought back with them new ideas, politics, fashions – and information about migration. Certain families and communities contained a vast store of informal knowledge about migration networks, people who could help in receiving communities, job opportunities, wage rates, the price of accommodation and commodities and were thus tempted to go, ignoring the fact that many migrants before them had paid a terrible price through death, injury, ill health and disease. Historian A.L. Rowse wrote of the links that bound the mining villages near St Austell to the urban centres of South Africa, noting the regular comings and goings of people, the receipt of letters, postcards and books, the remittances sent home to wives and the exchange of newspapers and journals – 'people knew what was going on in South Africa rather better than what was happening "up the country" '.[70]

By the early 1900s, there had emerged what have been termed 'Cornish transnational communities', linking families and places across many thousands of miles. Those who had settled overseas remained interested and closely connected with the

ABOVE

Native and Cornish miners in South Africa, late 19th century. Before the Boer War (1899-1902), over 25 per cent of the white labour force in the Transvaal was Cornish.

159

RIGHT

The Man in the Panama
Hat, *a portrait of Herbert
Thomas, the legendary
newspaper editor, painted
by Leonard J. Fuller in
1949. Thomas was
Editor of* The Cornishman
*for fifty years. The main
Cornish newspapers were
in favour of emigration.*

affairs of their home communities. Migration was more likely to occur among families in communities of the type described by Rowse as they had previous migration experience. Indeed, dense migration networks radiated from Cornwall and along these people, goods, ideas and capital flowed, so that life for migrants and non-migrants alike had a transnational aspect. So familiar were families in some Cornish settlements with the mining camps and towns of the United States and South Africa that those countries were looked upon almost as the parish next door, even by those who had never set foot in them.

The end of the Great Migration

The period up to the end of World War One was the great era of the Cornish overseas. Almost a half of all the migrants to South Australia before the 1870s were Cornish and the Yorke Peninsula became known as Australia's 'Little Cornwall'.[71] By 1896 over sixty per cent of the six thousand residents of Grass Valley,

California, were Cornish, and before the Boer War one in every four white miners on the Transvaal had arrived from Cornwall.[72] This was the time when Johannesburg had a 'Cousin Jack's Corner' and a raft of Cornish societies and associations sprang up worldwide. Cornish journalist, W. Herbert Thomas, captured the spirit of the time when he wrote:

> Join hands, ye Cornish lads, across the main!
> Let Asia clasp Columbia's outstretch'd hand!
> Come forth, Australia! Swell the glad refrain!
> And touch the fringe of Afric's golden strand!
> Swift o'er the boundless ocean rings the call!
> The mystic girdle round the world is cast!
> Shout now with thund'rous voices 'One and All'!
> All hail! Old Cornwall, may thy glory last![73]

But it was not to last. Migration flows dropped rapidly during World War One and the economically depressed years afterwards when migration chains were severely disrupted, many Cornish families repatriated and their men were killed in action. These networks were not easily repaired, especially since overseas British-financed mining companies were not as numerous as once they had been. Cornish mine captains were fewer as a result and men native to overseas metalliferous mining fields were increasingly recruited. Crucially, Cornish 'science' was seen to be outdated, its miners and engineers in their technical dotage, added to which the skilled labour pool in Cornwall had shrunk so drastically that by the 1940s, miners from Poland and Italy had to be brought in to work local mines.

Going 'up-country'

However, emigrating overseas was not the only option for Cornish families in the nineteenth century. More than forty per cent of net out-migration was to England and Wales. It was perhaps less heroic, and has been certainly less visible in the historical literature, but is nonetheless an extremely significant part of the history of Cornish families. In some decades, such as the crisis-ridden 1870s, migrants to England and Wales outnumbered overseas emigrants. People sought out a more cost-effective option at times when it was a struggle to scrape together the resources needed for migration from a Cornish economy seemingly staggering from one disaster to another.

In the late 1860s and throughout the 1870s, large numbers of Cornish men and women travelled to the industrial heartlands of northern England and Wales. The process was not exactly new although the destinations were. Miners, their skills in demand in metal mines in England and Wales as well as overseas, had made such long-distance moves at an early date. In the 1740s, Cornish immigrants were reported to be in Derbyshire, introducing the natives to the mysteries of ore buddling.

Cornish investors were also instrumental in ensuring Cornish captains and miners worked their capital in the lead mines of central and north Wales in the later eighteenth century.[74] In the mid-nineteenth century, Cornish tin and copper miners began to move away in large numbers to work the coal mines in Wales and the north of England. The most visible of these were recruited to break strikes, as in 1844 when a number of miners from Cornwall, most of whom absconded when they became aware of the true conditions, were brought in during a strike at Radcliffe, Northumberland.[75] Again, in 1865, coal owners near Newcastle turned to Cornish miners to break a strike. Soon after this episode, which cannot have made Cornish miners at all popular with the local community and must have had a knock-on effect on their assimilation, large-scale movement of miners to collieries became more widespread. By the early 1870s, the flow of Cornish mining families to northern England and Wales was in full flood.

The cotton districts of Lancashire proved a popular magnet for many. Here there was the advantage of paid work for wives and daughters as well as husbands and sons. Burnley, with a buoyant demand for female labour in its booming weaving factories, coupled with local coal mining, attracted many. In 1871, its cotton factories were said to be enticing young girls away from the Camborne-Redruth district, while in 1873, Burnley, along with Cumberland and America, was stated to be the destination for a continuing exodus from St Just in Penwith.[76] As in the case of movement overseas, much of this migration was very directed, with clear 'chains' linking parishes at home in Cornwall to places in Lancashire. For example, Spotland in Rochdale exerted a particular pull on migrants from Redruth. In this part of Rochdale in 1881 there were as many as seven 25 year-olds who had been born in Redruth. William Dawe was a cotton weaver, married to a local woman from Bacup. Annie Earnshaw had gained her local surname from her cotton weaver husband. Annie had not moved directly but came via another town in Lancashire. Francis Eddy was living with his mother and the rest of the family plus another boarder from Redruth and worked as a varnisher. William Faull, who also lived with mother and family, was a foreman miller at an iron works. George Hicks had married a woman from Norfolk and was a cotton mule spinner. John Jenkin, another spinner, had married into a Lancashire family and had arrived as early as 1867 as a child of twelve, presumably with his parents. Finally, Frances Robins was a domestic servant to a cotton waste dealer.[77] Links via relations and friends had spread knowledge of the opportunities available in Rochdale back to Redruth and eased the transition for later arrivals. No doubt a host of similar discrete migration streams wait to be discovered.

The stream of migrant workers from Redruth to Rochdale appeared to have been pulled mainly by the opportunities of the cotton industry. Further north, the attraction was mining. In Northumberland and County Durham, metal miners made the shift to coal, recognising that as numbers of metal miners in the UK began to shrink from the 1860s the demand for coal miners was rising at a healthy rate. In Cumbria, however, the geographical move might not have entailed a great change in occupational practices. Here the iron mines drew in many Cornish miners. Indeed,

these were numerous enough in Millom and Moor Row to field their own cricket team in 1881.[78] But perhaps the most spectacular example was at Roose, a village in Furness built specifically to house iron miners in 1873. Here, sixty-nine per cent of the workforce in 1881 had been born in Cornwall. The historian of Roose, Bryn Trescatheric, writes that 'the fact that so many Cornish people came to Roose within a short space of time meant that they could transfer their community values and traditions to the new environment and thus create a "Cornish village in Furness"[79]. While they were more likely to have been born in the Central Mining District than elsewhere, Roose pulled its migrants from widely dispersed districts of Cornwall. From the records we know, for example, that Richard Allen, aged thirty eight, who was originally born in St Mewan near St Austell, had a Gwennap-born wife and five children, which suggests that he had probably moved from depressed Gwennap in the mid-1870s. A few houses down the row could be found twenty-nine-year old John Bant and his twenty-four-year-old wife, Elizabeth, both of whom had been born at Breage. The birthplace of their eldest son, James, implies that they came via Durham in 1879. In between, Thomas and Mary Hicks, aged thirty two and thirty

The London Cornish Association annual picnic, held in August, 1927 at Caerhays Castle. The LCA celebrated its first centenary in 1998.

five, hailed from St Just in Penwith and seem to have arrived in Roose via Westmorland (1875) and Northumberland (1880). On the other side of the street, John and Rebecca May, thirty seven and thirty nine respectively, had both been born in Liskeard and lived among the Menheniot lead mines before making the journey to Roose sometime between 1872 and 1877. Meanwhile, the slightly older John and Tamsin Bowden, aged forty six and forty four, had moved to Durham between 1872 and 1876 from Perranzabuloe and then again to Roose in the later 1870s.[80]

Stepping stones to the wider world

For many of the migrants to the industrial regions of England and south Wales, such moves were but the first step of a longer journey. Twenty-nine-year-old Andrew Thomas from St Just moved first to Cumberland in 1870, but then, presumably having raised sufficient cash for the trip, travelled on to Colorado to join the gold rush there in 1879. Samuel Hoar, born in 1858 at Jollys Bottom in Kenwyn began to work in the mines in 1867. Six years later, aged fifteen, he left home for south Wales, but quickly moved on to Halifax in Yorkshire, working as a railway navvy. By 1877, still under twenty, Samuel was in Dalton-in-Furness, shaft-sinking. In 1878, he left his young wife and two children to emigrate to Colorado and Nevada in the search for gold and silver. After some hard years, he was eventually able to save enough dollars to send for his family who joined him at Butte, Montana in 1882.[81]

Miners weren't the only ones who left Cornwall, moving first to England and then on to the United States or other places overseas. Having overcome the medieval distaste for London, several thousands of Cornish men and even more Cornish women – about four women for every three men – were heading for the 'Great Wen' and its suburbs by the middle of the nineteenth century. An early example was Michael Baragwaneth, who moved to London in the 1830s from Ludgvan. His move, echoing that of the famous Chartist William Lovett from Newlyn to London a few years previously, no doubt influenced the later move of his relation William Baragwaneth, born in Towednack in 1820. William married a local girl in 1844 in Hertfordshire and plied his trade as a blacksmith in the Bushey and Watford areas for several years. Then in 1850, he and his family left for America. Surviving a horrific wreck off Newfoundland, when they lost all their possessions, the family eventually settled in Chicago where William became a boiler manufacturer, eventually being elected onto the city council and becoming a respectable local citizen before his death in 1888.[82]

Of course, the tendency to concentrate on migrants' success stories should not blind us to the fact that, for many, the experience of long-distance migration must have been anything but a happy one. Movement over the Devon border, to Plymouth, a major destination for Cornish migrants, seems to have been the option for the very poor and the dispossessed, those without the family networks or material resources necessary to make the trip up-country or overseas. The anonymous author of *A Cornish Waif's Story* was brought up in Redruth in the 1890s by her grandparents. At five years old, she was re-united with her mother in Plymouth, but promptly farmed out to an organ grinder and his wife. The child was left by her mother in a large tenement room:

> … a dirty, evil-smelling apartment. Tired and bewildered as I was, I noticed a large cage in one corner of the room in which white rats disported themselves. One was treading at a wheel. The opposite corner contained a rickety-looking bed. The third corner of the room contained a dirty gas-stove, on the top of which a frying pan was standing from which came a savoury smell of something cooking. Later I learned that only one cooking smell ever pervaded that room – fried bacon scraps and cheese. The fourth corner contained a heap of dirty rags, old jackets etc. Very soon I discovered this was to be my sleeping quarters.[83]

Distinctive 'migration streams'

It is possible now for scholars to identify at least three distinct 'streams' of long-distance Cornish migrants to England and Wales, complementing the movement overseas.[84] The first was to south Wales and the north of England, often acting as a halfway stage in an onward process of emigration. This 'industrial' stream accompanied a smaller 'maritime' stream along the Channel coast to Hampshire, Sussex and Kent. It is likely this was related to Royal Navy connections and involved single men rather than family groups. For many years the coastal communities of Cornwall had supplied sailors for the Royal Navy and this tradition meant that many men were found in ship and shore facilities in places like Devonport and Portsmouth. In addition, links between Cornish ports and similar places along the Channel coast had facilitated a long-standing coastwise trade that engendered moves from Cornish maritime communities to coastal counties from Devon to Kent.

The 'service' stream

The third stream was the most heterogenous of the three types, including those forced to eke out a living in the slums of Plymouth along with those who became prominent professionals in the towns of middle England. The outcome of this stream was not Cousin Jack down a hole in the ground, but more often than not Cousin Jenny in the scullery or behind the shop counter. Shopworkers, casual labourers and professionals alike were drawn to the big cities, overwhelmingly London, but also Bristol. Such migrants were more dispersed than the industrial migrants, probably less likely to have moved in family groups and more likely to be women. For example, we know that one Mary Crease originally from Bude, was working as a cook at a boarding school in 1881 in Hendon, Middlesex. At around the same time, Helen Jewell from Sennen, who had exchanged the cliffs of Land's End for the terraced streets of Hackney, was servant to an elderly clerk and his wife. And Ellen Tresidder, a dressmaker born in Falmouth, was one of a large number of drapers' assistants working in an establishment in London's St Marylebone.[85] Migrants, whether to London or Michigan, took their surnames with them. Such movement has therefore resulted in the presence of recognisably Cornish names across the UK and much further afield.

Cornish names on the danger list

As a result of the Cornish emigration, names derived from the Cornish language as well as those common in Cornwall but not of Celtic derivation, are found across the world today. There are often many more bearers of a particular name overseas than in Cornwall, including surnames that are now either extinct or on the verge of extinction in Cornwall itself. Often these names survive overseas in clusters, revealing patterns of family and community settlement. Ustick, a surname applied to someone from St Just and once peculiar to the Penwith area of Cornwall, has vanished from the Cornish telephone directory, but lives on in North America: there are five entries in the Canadian white pages – one in British Columbia and four in Ontario – while in the United States there are seventy, with the highest concentration being twenty four – in California.

> ## CORNISH NAMES ON THE DANGER LIST
>
>
>
> The attrition of Cornish names in Cornwall since the sixteenth century continues apace. Just looking at Tre, Pol and Pen names, the following have four or fewer entries in the 2004-5 telephone book for the county:
>
> Pendarves, Penglase, Polgrean, Tredrea, Treen, Tregenna, Tregurtha, Tregust, Trehane, Trelawny, Tresadern, Trescowthick, Trevivian, Trewellard, Trezona

Tregeagle does not appear in the most recent telephone directory for Cornwall or that of the rest of the British Isles, but survives in the White Pages of the United States in two states only: California, with three entries and Utah with eighteen. It has fared rather better in Australia; there are fifty entries across the country, with the highest concentration being twenty two in South Australia, while seventeen are listed in New South Wales and a further nine in Victoria. It seems likely that some of the South Australian Tregeagles could be descendants of John and Ann Tregeagle of Tregony, who migrated there on the *Java* in 1839.[86]

Baragwanath is scarce indeed in Cornwall having just five entries in the telephone directory in three different spellings (Baracwanath, Baragwanath and Baragwnath, the last of which could be a typographical error), and a smattering of entries across England, including major cities such as London, Bristol, Liverpool and Manchester, with more being resident in Plymouth than anywhere else. But overseas, the name survives more strongly: twenty nine in Victoria and South Australia and twelve in New Zealand, with one quarter of the name bearers residing in Auckland. There are a further two in Ontario, Canada and sixteen listed across the United States, with the largest concentration in Michigan, some possibly the descendants of three brothers, Edward, George and John Perkin Baragwanath, miners from St Ives who arrived in the Keweenaw in the early nineteenth century.[87] A further two appear in Chile and fourteen are listed in South Africa, where the surname has been immortalised with the naming of the country's largest hospital serving the black population in Johannesburg in memory of Cornishman, John Albert Baragwanath, whose farm once occupied the site.[88]

Other surnames are clearly on the danger list in Cornwall itself. The England cricketer, Marcus Trescothick, for example, bears a name that appears just five times in the current telephone directory. In 1901, there were forty four Penhallows residing in the London and Oxford areas, none Cornish-born; the name appears just once in the recent telephone directory for Cornwall – in Flushing, just across the Fal from the location of the four Penhallows of 1641, at Philleigh, Ruanlanihorne, St Clement and St Just-in-Roseland. Other Cornish names that are endangered survive more strongly elsewhere. The residential telephone directories for South Australia and Victoria reveal thirty five Chynoweths while in Cornwall there are now twenty four Chenoweths and Chynoweths, Menadues number eighty in both states, as opposed to Cornwall's six entries, and the 154 Nankivells far outnumber Cornwall's fifteen.

BELOW
Pritchard Street in Johannesburg in the late 19th century. Both Heath's Hotel and the Chudleigh Brothers store were run by Cornish people.

Names as indicators of occupation

Family names can reveal where in Cornwall people are likely to have migrated from, or even what their occupations might have been. Sandercock has just two entries in the white pages of South Africa (in Johannesburg) and one for New Zealand. Yet, it has 168 entries in those of Australia, by far the majority in South Australia and New South Wales. Sandercock also has a further sixty eight entries in the United States residential telephone directory (amazingly, this is the same number as appear in the directory for Cornwall). These are spread across eighteen states, though over a third of them are clustered in Pennsylvania. Moreover, in Canada the number is 119, predominantly in Ontario (forty one), while the states of Alberta (twenty five), Saskatchewan (twenty one), British Columbia (sixteen) and Manitoba (thirteen) also account for significant numbers.

Sandercock is a name that becomes more prevalent the further east one travels in Cornwall, a fact which is borne out by the 1861 Census which reveals thirty four name bearers in the Camelford Registration District, sixty in that of Bodmin, seventy one in Stratton and eighty eight in Launceston. The distribution of Sandercocks in overseas states is probably not accidental. The north-eastern region of Cornwall was noted for its agricultural movement and the states in which Sandercocks are clustered overseas are also predominantly agricultural. Caleb and George Sandercock, who migrated to Pennsylvania in the mid-nineteenth century, came from St Teath and Jacobstow respectively, both agricultural parishes.[89] We can therefore conclude with a degree of certainty that the majority of Sandercocks overseas had ancestors who came from the north and east of Cornwall and were probably connected to the farming industry.

A significant percentage of the Trevorrows included in the recent United States White Pages reside in Michigan. Of the Trevorrows that entered the United States during the 'Great Migration' sixty four per cent headed for Michigan, beginning in the mid-1860s. Of those who emigrated, there with a known parish of departure, over ninety per cent were from St Ives, where the name still proliferates today. These were men such as Thomas Stevens Trevorrow, a miner born in 1879 who migrated in 1907 on the *Ivernia*.[90] His decision to migrate to Michigan was not accidental: a staggering eighty-eight per cent of Trevorrows from St Ives who migrated to that state were miners. Indeed, social networks linking many St Ives families with the mining towns of the Upper Peninsula of Michigan once existed. The only other state to attract significant numbers of Trevorrows was New Jersey, which also had a strong mining industry.

Again it seems fair to deduce three separate facts from this data: that the descendants of most American Trevorrows came from St Ives; that they were mainly miners and they were more likely to settle in Michigan than anywhere else.

HECLA DRIVE

Mis-spelt Cornish names

The examples just noted are of names with spellings that have remained relatively unchanged, but other surnames have been hybridized during the process of migration and/or altered beyond recognition, often through repeated mispronunciation.

LEFT
Cornish miners at the
Tamarack Mine,
Calumet, Michigan
c.1922. Wilfred
Harvey of St Day is in
the front row, fourth
from the left. This
Gwennap family had a
long association with
the Upper Peninsula
and today Wilfred's
descendents live in
Flint, Michigan.

English and Americans alike shift accents forward to the first syllable, thus Chenóweth becomes Chénoweth; this name has suffered further by becoming Chenworth or Chinworth, thus losing its meaning completely. Trenérry has become Trénerry, the name of a prominent female American ice skater in the 1980s. Trebílcock has mutated from Trébilcock to Trébilco, which could reasonably be assumed to be Italian! Uren, a name initially imported from Brittany and derived from the Breton personal name Urien, has been metamorphosed so as not to rhyme with urine, most famously by the well-known Oregon political leader, William S. U'Ren.[91] In Latin America, patronymic names such as Martin and Phillips have become Martín and Felipes, while Hispanic-sounding names such as Pascoe and Jose have become Pasco and José respectively, the latter surname most famously connected with Lanner-born migrant, Richard Jose, who became a famous American singer and was publicised in the western United States as Juan Ricardo José, the more to appeal to the resident Hispanic population.[92]

Yet mispronunciation is just one problem that has contributed to the hybridization of Cornish names; misspelling has also taken its toll and was doubtless quite common as people in destination countries were unfamiliar with 'foreign' names spoken in strange accents by people who were unable to read or write. When the *Marquis of Anglesea* entered the Argentine port of Buenos Aires in 1825 with some forty five passengers from Falmouth, the immigration clerk recording their details Hispanicised some of the surnames but completely corrupted others. Isaac Kellow

RIGHT

*Chits on the board at
South Crofty on the last
day of the mine. Among
the Cornish names there is
also evidence of some
English ones and a
few Europeans as well,
evidence of mining
immigration to Cornwall
(although most people
associate Cornwall
with the out-migration
of miners).*

became Isaac Kelor and Grovesnor Bunster became Grovesnor Brumer. One might be forgiven for believing both names to be German.[93] United States immigration officers at Ellis Island in the later nineteenth century also made mistakes when recording surnames which can make it extremely difficult for their descendants trying to make the vital link back through census and parochial records to Cornwall. For example, some descendants of a Cornish family that had migrated to the United States were trying to trace their ancestors whom they definitely knew to be from the Penzance area. They were looking for the name Ockon, which does not exist in Cornwall. The original name of this family had been Hockin, but had probably been corrupted beyond recognition through the innocent action of an immigration officer hearing the name spoken in a broad Cornish accent when the family first arrived in America.[94]

Conclusion

We have seen in this chapter how the Cornish have a long history of migration. In the early nineteenth century Cornwall's role as a world-renowned centre of metal mining meant that its miners were in demand as labour for mining districts in the New World. This helped to produce a culture of migration, one strongly embedded by the 1830s, when distress in agricultural areas led to emigration of farmers and agricultural labourers. This society, prone to migration, was ripe for the mass migration that set in during the 1840s when social changes in the mining districts combined with information from early pioneers who had already gone to propel families overseas. Recurrent crises in the mining industry from the later 1860s guaranteed that the steady flow of emigrants did not abate. On the contrary, migration out of Cornwall peaked in the 1870s, a decade of serious economic problems and one when many Cornish families were forced to leave for destinations in England and Wales as well as overseas.

The remarkable movement of people from Cornwall during the 'Great Migration' has resulted in possibly six million people of Cornish descent worldwide. Not all are aware that they have Cornish roots as their ancestors were recorded as English or British in official documentation, but the extraordinary resurgence in awareness of Cornish cultural identity in recent years has helped to make the Cornish ethnically visible in many countries across the globe. Increasing numbers of people are being made aware of roots and are keen to manifest and celebrate a Cornish cultural identity. But this has not always been the case. From a zenith in the early twentieth

century when there were numerous Cornish societies around the world, when Detroit and Johannesburg had informal 'Cousin Jack' meeting places and towns such as Moonta, South Australia and Grass Valley in California were invariably described as 'Cornish,' a nadir was reached in the post World War Two period. Many Cornish societies and organisations were disbanded, Cornish cultural traits diminished and in some cases disappeared, and the links that bound families in Cornwall with those overseas were weakened or broken.

How do we explain the rise, decline, and rise again of Cornish transnationalism, the feeling of belonging to a worldwide Cornish community spanning many borders? And how do we place this in the wider story of Cornish pride in identity and homeland? The final chapter of this book tackles these issues.

ABOVE
An 1897 view of Moonta Mines, in what was known as the Copper Triangle of 'Australia's little Cornwall', which included the townships of Kadina and Wallaroo.

CHAPTER FIVE
'WHAT WE BELONG TO BE'

THE SEARCH FOR ROOTS is deeply entwined with the quest for identity. We need to answer those questions of who we are, where we come from, how we fit into this world. As we have seen, our name links us to the past and helps us understand the story of who we are. In this sense the vast outpouring of family and one-name studies that have weighed down the library shelves since the 1970s are testimony to a renewed search for identity. And that weight of texts suggests, moreover, that this search has become more energetic, more frenetic, over the past generation. Why this should be the case is one of the issues this final chapter will probe. In doing this we will try to pin down what we mean by identity and examine the changing nature of Cornish identity and the place of the family within contemporary Cornish identity.

Attachment to place and to people varies, both between individuals, and even on the part of the same individual in different contexts. For example, many Cornish people are proudly Cornish when cheering on the Cornish rugby team or a Cornish entrant in a competition on television. But the same person might also feel proudly English when supporting a 'world' cup-winning England rugby union team. Or, inflamed by the myths of the popular and 'regional' press, they might prefer to label themselves 'British' when bemoaning the alleged attempts of 'Johnny Foreigner' across the Channel to undermine the pound sterling, imperial measures, 'our' unwritten constitution or other revered flotsam and jetsam of heritage.

Families, identities and Cornwall

Clearly, identities are, to some extent, personal, variable and difficult to understand if you don't share them. But they're also extremely powerful, particularly the Cornish identity, which exerts its pull over even the most self-professedly rational people. And others. Even hard-nosed social scientists can assert that 'residents of (Cornwall) fall into an extended kinship group that encompasses a Celto-Cornish essence of belonging'.[1] Although, as we have seen, the actual empirical evidence is slight – more because the research has yet to be done than the findings contradict it – it continues to be assumed that there must be something special about being Cornish.

To a large extent, such assertions about the Cornish family reflect similar assertions about Cornwall more generally. If Cornwall is a 'land apart' – different, special, unique – then the Cornish family, along with Cornish rugby, Cornish Methodism, Cornish humour, must also be 'different', 'special' and 'unique'. A moment's reflection might lead us to conclude that, in the cold light of day, this doesn't necessarily

BELOW
Fisherman Edward
Couch with his niece,
Bessie Phillips in St Ives
in the late 1890s.

follow. Nevertheless, the connection is both expected and regularly made. Such a link appears to follow naturally from the equally strong notion that the family is the building block of societies. We hear that families can be 'dysfunctional', but such a description suggests that, most of the time, families are, in contrast, functional. But functioning to what end? To keep society ticking over, to reproduce (relatively) civilised modes of behaviour, to instil moral values generally considered proper and 'normal' and, in the Cornish context, to reproduce Cornish society.

If families reproduce society in this way, they can also reflect and describe that society. Family life in Cornwall can evoke a wider social life. In the 1970s, Mary Lakeman recalled her Mevagissey childhood at the time of the First World War. The houses in the thickly packed streets of her fishing village 'emitted a stream of human beings, old, middle aged and young, all stamped with a family likeness, variations on a Cornish theme.' But these families were also part of a close-knit community where everybody knew everybody else's business, a 'classless society where ties of blood, of interdependence, of shared fear of death and joy-in-life were as strong as any human connections could ever be'.[2] In this fishing village environment, by the last century the preferred location for the most distilled sense of Cornishness, family and community melted indistinguishably into one another. The close families and equally close communities of the past acted as a foil for the very different society of the 1970s, which appeared less friendly, less open, less of a 'community'. Describing the Cornish family of early-twentieth-century coastal villages in this way, however, can exacerbate a sense of loss, a feeling that in some way the Cornish family has been diminished in the decades since.

Much is obviously being taken for granted in discussions of both family and identity in Cornwall. Yet, as this book has tried to show, family life has been as much about change as stability. Households now contain far fewer and less varied kinds of people. Families were and are continually being broken up and re-formed, whether through death, divorce or departures. Families have moved with bewildering frequency from place to place, sometimes in the past couple of centuries over many hundreds or even thousands of miles. Historians have shown that only a minority of 'core families' have stayed put, although that minority tended to provide more than their fair share of parish officers and what we now like to call 'opinion-formers'.[3] Yet the majority of people who did not stay in one place all their lives also lived within families and, even if they had wanted to, found it difficult to escape their influence.

Disentangling myth and reality when discussing family or identity is a well-nigh impossible task, but, in order to delve a little deeper into the 'Cornish identity' and the way families might relate to it, we must go beyond the superficial myths of families and family life or of Cornwall and Cornish life.

Defining 'identity'

Identity has two aspects. First, it involves understanding our own individuality – what it is that makes us different from other people – and this can apply both to an individual or a group. Secondly, and in contradictory fashion, we need to look at what makes us the same as others, part of a group with a shared identity. The implication of these two sides of the same coin is that, in the making of group identity, boundaries are drawn around groups and the behaviours, customs, attributes that are assigned to that group. Thus, since the early nineteenth century, there has been an ongoing search to define what makes the Cornish 'different'. More relevant here, the family, being such an integral part of society, is inevitably displayed as a part of this 'difference'.

Having defined Cornish as different (and the more regularly this is asserted the more that difference seems natural and above argument), the second element is to attribute particular symbols or behaviours to that group. Cornish people eat pasties, speak with a certain accent or go down holes in the ground. Or, according to some writers at the beginning of the nineteenth century, they were unimaginative, uncreative, prosaic, candid, pliant, 'delighted to serve you when pleased', (which was convenient news for the then infant tourist industry) or 'subject to petulant and stubborn fits, will brood in sullen resentment for days'.[4] Or the Cornish family is particularly close-knit, with a strong sense of kinship.

It is difficult to discriminate between stereotype and truth here. Indeed, some stereotypes, for example, that of the Celt as being poetic and emotional, irrational and argumentative, in contrast to the stolid, rational and somewhat boring English person, can be repeated so often that people begin to believe in them innately. Otherwise sane observers are liable to lose their critical faculties entirely and fall into such simple labelling. The historian A.L.Rowse could claim that 'anyone with discernment' had to admit 'the dualism of English and Celtic characteristics' – 'the extremism, the vivacity and temperament of the one, the reliability, the dogged qualities, the imagination, the sense of moderation of the other'.[5] Perhaps the order of 'English and Celtic' and the characteristics listed afterwards is a clue that Rowse was making one of his little in-jokes here, but no doubt his readers would not have needed too much help in jumping to the expected conclusion. It is best to try to avoid such romantic assertions (since, after all, there are many books where this can be read *ad nauseam*) and instead to review some ways in which the Cornish family has been characterised as different, discriminating between those attributes which appear to have a basis in the historical record and those that, while no less powerful, are more clearly symbolic attributes of difference. From this it is possible to assess the history of the Cornish identity, weaving the Cornish family into this at the appropriate points. For there have been many stories of Cornwall but no convincing account of the changing Cornish identity.[6]

The Cornish family as icon of identity

As we have already seen in earlier chapters, there are several ways in which the Cornish family appeared to be 'different' at various points in the past. Claims for an intense kin network have been put forward for certain times, for example among the gentry in the sixteenth and seventeenth centuries. It is also likely that the growth of kinship connections more generally amongst population of industrialising Britain provided a springboard for Cornish emigration in the nineteenth century, oiling those transnational links between Cornish families and communities. It is also possible that aid between family members is more common within modern Cornish families than within other families, although now it is more likely to be amongst immediate family members than a wider network of relatives as was the case in the past.

The Cornish 'customary family' of the eighteenth and early nineteenth centuries was a distinct kind of family organisation. In its early phase in West Penwith and possibly associated with larger households, such a family involved a relatively low division of household roles between men and women, a high degree of occupational diversity as income was won from a variety of different sources, close links (again) with nearby kin, and strategic decision-making on a family as opposed to an individual basis. In the later nineteenth century, the 'dispersed Cornish family', sundered by migration, was also a distinct phase, with husbands and wives often living separate existences, with a clear division of labour according to gender, greater likelihood of grandparents sharing the family home but with autonomy for women in decision-making and in the spending of family income. Both Cornish 'customary' and 'dispersed' families combined to limit the full expression of the ideal Victorian 'traditional' family in Cornwall, dampening the effects of patriarchy and male dominance and producing somewhat more equal, although, of course, hardly egalitarian, relations between men and women within the family.

Some Cornish families, were clearly 'different' in earlier centuries in that they they spoke Cornish and not English. The linguistic history of Cornwall provides Cornish families with a distinct stock of surnames that are peculiar to it, marking off some families as 'Cornish' in ways unavailable to others. The popularity of place-names as surnames, the way some families were still adopting places as their surnames as late as the sixteenth and seventeenth centuries, and the particularly high level of such names in Cornish-speaking mid and west Cornwall, all point to an especially close link between family and place in Cornwall. Some families are tied intimately to the landscape via their names in a unique sense, perhaps indicating wider connections in Cornwall between people and place. But we must be on our guard against the facile assumption that those families that bear Cornish placenames as their surnames are somehow 'more' Cornish than the rest, Quite the contrary. As the Cornish Revivalist Robert Morton Nance pointed out:

> 'Some of those who bear Saxon names may indeed be now more Celtic than those who carry a fine old Cornish Tre- name, for it must be allowed that the most aristocratic of Cornish surnames may record only the loot, by a Norman, of the estate of a Saxon, who dispossessed the heir of a Cornishman, who founded it and gave it his own name with Tre- before it; while the Cornish founder's heirs may still walk among us bearing, like so many Celts in Wales, some name such as Williams, Thomas, or Richards, that tells nothing of their long pedigree.'[7]

While resisting Nance's assumption – that someone whose forebears almost one thousand years ago was a Norman landowner is somehow less Cornish than someone whose contemporary ancestors were eking out their lives in splendid Celtic poverty

THE CORNISH
LANGUAGE REVIVAL

Some time around 1800, Cornish ceased to be spoken in its last centres, the fishing villages of Mount's Bay. Nonetheless, it was very soon being cherished as an important part of Cornwall's heritage. Publications of the medieval Cornish language plays, literary institution lectures and the presence of lists of Cornish words in mid-nineteenth century almanacs attest to a strong interest in the language among the middle classes in the heyday of Cornwall's industrial period. In the meantime, Cornish placenames and dialect words kept the memory of the language alive. It was a short step from antiquarian interest to active revival. In the later nineteenth century. the Reverend Lach-Szyrma of Newlyn published a short guide to the grammar of Cornish. But its was Henry Jenner, returning to an earlier interest in the language, who can be said to have kick-started the Revival by writing *A Handbook of the Cornish Language*, published in 1904. This raised the possibility of making the language live once again and provided the stimulus for the labours of Robert Morton Nance. It was he who, in the 1920s and 30s, constructed a common spelling system, known as Unified Cornish. By the 1930s, a handful of people could speak Cornish and many more write it, re-forging the chain temporarily broken at the end of the eighteenth century.

– he does have a point. As we have seen, Cornwall's unique linguistic history is reflected not just in the obvious locational and other names in the Cornish language but, as in Wales, in the ubiquity of common personal names, the residue of a relatively late process of surname stabilisation.

Turning to the more symbolic aspects of the Cornish family, we saw at the end of Chapter One that, although in many respects the late twentieth- and early-twenty-first century Cornish family has converged with families elsewhere in Britain, in theory it seems to have diverged. Despite less obvious differences, the modern Cornish family seems, paradoxically, increasingly likely to be described as 'different'. This has led to what amounts almost to a glorification of kinship links in the twentieth century. The enduring Cornish family stands in for that sense of community that many would claim has been lost, crushed by the juggernaut of selfish individualism and by demographic trends that have changed Cornish towns and villages out of all recognition since the 1960s. In an unstable world, the modern Cornish, faced by feelings confined in former centuries to exiles and emigrants, as familiar bearings shift alarmingly around them, have looked to the supposed certainties of the past to regain a sense of place, and re-orientate their changing places. Cornwall in the late twentieth century could at times resemble those intensely conservative and past-orientated societies where the power of genealogy and the claims to legitimacy that accompany it begin to take on new, and sometimes worrying, meanings. An exaggerated emphasis on kinship links has combined with another symbolic attribute of modern Cornwall – its 'Celtic' nature. Again partly in response to the everyday deluge of Anglicisation, Cornwall and its people, despite the fears of observers in the 1970s, became more 'Celtic' as the millennium reached its end. The Cornish family is not just the repository of older, cherished but now threatened values of community; it is quintessentially a Celtic family, refreshed by the renewed (and re-discovered) links with its equally 'Celtic' cousins across the seas. These two aspects, kinship and Celticity, neatly collide in events such as the Dewhelans festival, first held in 2002 and drawing Cornish people from around the world back to their homeland.

ABOVE

John Carlyon Angove and his daughter, Victoria, at their winery near Adelaide. Angove's was founded in 1886 by their ancestor, the miner's son, surgeon and emigrant to Australia, Dr W.T. Angove. Their surname has been common in Cornwall for more than five centuries.

The history of the Cornish identity: medieval identities

When we think of identity we tend to take it for granted, as having always been there, a point of stability in a changing world. And it's the same with family. But neither identity nor families come into the world fully formed. Both are produced and changed by society. Cornish identity has a history just as the Cornish family does. It's difficult, if not impossible, to know what people in the medieval period felt about themselves. Historians used to believe that before the nationalist and democratic revolutions of late-eighteenth-century France and North America, there was little sense of national or ethnic identity below the élites. Nowadays, they are not so sure. Many would now argue that such identities pre-date modernity, the period after the industrial revolution of the eighteenth century, although ethnic identities may have been 'second-order' forms of identity, less central than religious identities.[8] Whatever the situation was, and, because ordinary people left no direct record of their views on such matters before the 1600s, we can never be sure, it would be surprising if the thirteenth-century peasants breaking their fields on the slopes of Bodmin Moor would have spent much time pondering the question of their Cornishness. This was more likely just to have been taken for granted. Their world was probably divided into categories based on those people they were related to, people they met on an everyday basis, people they knew from a distance or saw occasionally, and strangers. However, one attribute binds groups together and marks them off from others – the language they speak. Distinctions were drawn in the medieval period between groups on the basis of language. In the middle of the twelfth century, a landowner such as Reginald, Earl of Cornwall, could greet his men at Launceston as 'French, English and Welsh (i.e. Cornish)', distinguishing one from another by their language.[9] Reginald's position as earl introduces another potential basis for identity loyalty to an institution based on a territory. The most obvious and powerful such institution was the monarchy and in the case of Cornwall, a cultural identity, as part of a language group co-existed with a broader 'regnal identity', that looked towards the English monarchy and the English state.

In Cornwall this regional identity was modified and mediated by the institution of, first, Earldom, and then Duchy. In the twelfth century, earls of Cornwall appear in the records, commanding huge power on behalf of the king. This concentration of power in the hands of a single landlord was unusual in the south and east of England, where it was viewed as producing dangerously over-weening subjects with the capacity for baronial rebellion. But in places such as Northumberland or the Welsh Marches or Cornwall, turbulent frontiers with a potentially troublesome population there or nearby, the Norman monarchy took the risk and delegated power to single, dominant lords. These wielded what were 'palatinate' powers, dispensing justice, retaining profits and generally

THE STANNARY PARLIAMENT

The tinners' customs were protected by the Stannary courts, themselves guaranteed by a series of royal charters after 1201. In 1508, when restoring the rights of the Stannaries, which he had suspended in 1496, Henry VII also extended the legislative powers of the Stannary Parliament, or Convocation, as it is properly titled. This charter established provision for the nomination of 24 stannators from the four towns of Lostwithiel, Truro, Helton and Launceston and gave the Stannary Parliament the right of veto over royal statutes. Some have seen this, never repealed, as giving Cornwall its own sovereign, constitutional rights, an interpretation that led to the restoration of a Stannary Convocation in 1975. The historical Stannary Parliament last met in 1752, by which time it was a body tightly controlled by the gentry and those with investments in mining. The growth of copper mining broke the central role of the Stannaries, although stannary courts continued to sit into the 1890s in judgment on mining matters.

acting as the local potentate. The Earldom of Cornwall, with great power in the twelfth and early thirteenth centuries, was gradually transformed into a tamer version, the Duchy of Cornwall, which in 1337 was formalised as the property of the king's eldest son. The Duchy, while not in possession of such a range of powers as the twelfth-century Earldom, efficiently diverted tin mining profits into the royal family's coffers, establishing its local presence, a Duchy Palace at Lostwithiel, former seat of the earls. At the same time, in the late 1200s, Cornwall moved more clearly under English jurisdiction, with the king's courts meting out justice, the payment of taxes to the Exchequer in London, and Cornish representatives in the House of Commons. All in all, Cornwall began to resemble more closely the English counties to the east of the Tamar. Nonetheless, the continuing presence of the Duchy of Cornwall, an attenuated reminder of Cornwall's earlier palatinate status, was also a visible symbol of a different constitutional position, as a conquered province of an English ruler.

The Duchy may have provided a pole for institutional loyalty, but, for most people, identities were still mapped by the language people spoke and also, perhaps, by the loyalty of tenants towards the family of their landlords. As we have seen in Chapter Two, naming customs made up a major cultural difference between the English- and Cornish-speaking language communities in Cornwall, with the strong suggestion that, by the fifteenth and sixteenth centuries, there was a particular bond between people and place in Cornish-speaking mid and west Cornwall, a close association of landscape and loyalties.

Into England: the sixteenth and seventeenth centuries

Over the course of the sixteenth century, this language community began to shrink. This decline was at the least exacerbated by the new emphasis on bible reading and the *English Prayer Book* in the now Protestant Church which resulted in a rise of literacy in English. Such a process may have drawn starker boundaries around what was by now a beleagured Cornish-speaking community and such boundaries may have strengthened the sense of identity.[10] In the later 1500s, Cornish speakers were said to foster a 'concealed envy against the English, whom they effect with a desire of revenge for their fathers' sakes, by whom their fathers received the repulse', although historian Richard Carew claimed that this feeling among 'the western people ... little by little weareth out' in the 1590s.[11] Carew himself epitomised another type of identity, a gentry allegiance to a 'county community' that was emerging in Cornwall, as well as in English counties, during the sixteenth century. This loyalty to a 'county' territory amongst the gentry was part of a trend in Protestant England, whereby gentry, perhaps especially those of Puritan sympathies (as was Carew), while embracing a new Calvinist religious theology and rejecting the old, Catholic one, seemed to compensate by delving into the past of their local places, the boundaries of which were delimited by a new Tudor emphasis on county government.

By the early 1600s, two distinct 'Cornish' identities existed. First, there was the older, ethnic identity based on language and drawing its boundaries between Cornish and English speakers. But the implications of this definition were that a considerable and growing proportion of the population of Cornwall were only ambiguously 'Cornish', at best. Secondly, there was a newer gentry identity based on the 'county' and the institutions of 'county' government. In the Cornish case, this was with the significant

THE RISINGS OF 1497 AND 1549

In 1997, the *Keskerdh Kernow* organised a walk to London to commemorate the 500th anniversary of Michael Angove's rising of 1497. This re-enactment acted as a lightning conductor for the modern sense of Cornishness, stimulating an upsurge of cultural activity. The actual historical experience was less happy. Angove's rising began in St Keverne in the early summer of 1497. His force, picking up some limited gentry support on the way, headed for London, causing no little panic in government circles. However, by the use of mercenaries and an army assembled to fight the Scots, Henry VII was able to defeat the Cornish insurgents without too much difficulty at the Battle of Blackheath. Undeterred, Cornwall was the starting point for a second rising just months later, when thousands flocked to the banner of the Yorkist pretender, Perkin Warbeck. Confronted by a superior force, Warbeck abandoned his supporters in Somerset and the second rising was dispersed. The 1497 risings were triggered by tax demands and fuelled by support for the Yorkists. In 1549 the rising was the result of the imposition of a new *English Prayer Book* and the religious changes that accompanied it and were associated with the Protestant Reformation. This time the 'rebels' laid siege to Exeter, which just about held out long enough for the government to raise an army. After several very bloody encounters the Cornish and their Devonian allies were defeated and the rising ended in the streets of Launceston with the capture of the insurgents' leaders. The 1549 Rising was followed by a much more draconian round of state-sanctioned executions than was 1497, and has been linked to the long-term decline of the Cornish language. Certainly, the number of Cornishmen who lost their lives in this rising and its aftermath was, in proportional terms, at least equivalent to the British loss of life in World War One.

addition of the extra dimension of both the Duchy government (albeit in the seventeenth century run from London by a Prince's Council), and the five Stannaries, which had overseen mining in Cornwall since at least 1100. The seventeenth century was a crucial period as the older identity seemed to disappear, overwhelmed by the unstoppable march of Englishness. And yet, with its disappearance, it was possible for the newer territorial identity to take on elements of the old. The civil wars of the 1640s (also now known as the 'wars of the five peoples' – English, Scots, Irish, Welsh and Cornish) were crucial in this process. During this decade, the previously somewhat docile gentry identity became fused with elements of that ethnic identity that during the sixteenth century had been associated with rebellion and unruliness. This fusion produced the first inklings of a more modern identity, based on the territory of Cornwall but stressing the 'otherness' of the Cornish. Paradoxically, this was to a large extent created by growing literacy and the vicious pamphleteering wars that accompanied the blood-letting of the 1640s when the Cornish had, seemingly unanimously, declared for the king. Moreover, the exploits of the first Cornish army of 1642 and 1643, led by commanders such as Bevill Grenville, Sidney Godolphin, John Trevanion and Nicholas Slanning, who became folk heroes after the wars, established the Cornish as amongst the fiercest and most effective enemies of the Parliamentary cause. Parliamentarian propagandists engaged in vicious polemics against their Cornish foes, caricaturing them as cruel, perfidious, plundering demons.[12] In response, Royalist pamphlets went equally over the top and heaped praise on the 'Cornish people'.

What both sides did by building these stereotypes of the Cornish was to draw boundaries around the whole of Cornwall and all the Cornish people. They were different from the more civilised (or more uncivilised, depending on the standpoint) English. Differences between Cornish and English speakers within Cornwall were dissolved and the whole of Cornwall became the template for the 'Cornish' identity. Now writers such as William Scawen (1600-89), from a landed family based in St Germans in the east, could incorporate Cornwall's rebellious history and its fast disappearing language, together with the British origins of its people, into their accounts of Cornish difference.[13] A recognisably modern Cornish patriotism had been created out of the traumas of the seventeenth-century wars. But Scawen was a lone voice and his brand of Cornish patriotism, with its edgy anti-Englishness, had to wait another 250 years for its full flowering.

Although Scawen linked Cornish difference to a longer tradition of rebelliousness, looking back to the 1497 and 1549 risings and to the condition of what was by the later seventeenth century a socially despised language, his gentry companions were much less keen to rattle the skeletons of Cornwall's rebellious Tudor years. Another part of Cornish 'difference' in the Restoration years after 1660, when Charles II resumed the English throne, lay in its Royalist allegiance of the 1640s. This, plus the enduring role of Duchy and Stannaries in Cornish life, with their apparent royal patronage, produced an ultra-loyalism in the gentry which endured into the next century and beyond: conservative, intensely royalist and Anglican in religion. The Cornish royalist tradition expressed its Cornishness through staunch and uncritical devotion to the monarchy and the traditional institutions of the English and (after 1707 and the Union with Scotland), British state.

The eighteenth century identity: West Barbary and industry

During the eighteenth century, two other representations of Cornwall began to challenge the Cornish royalist tradition that looked back to the 1640s for its inspiration. Both of these were, in their different ways, more contemporary, although the first, Cornwall as West Barbary, had obvious roots in the stereotypes assiduously constructed by the anti-Cornish pamphleteers of the 1640s. Of course, there is a difference between the idea of Cornwall – an image of the place and its people – and a Cornish identity – a sense of belonging to place and people. The Cornish never saw themselves as 'West Barbarians' or, as we shall see, if they did so it was only from the loftier vantage point of hindsight. The image of Cornwall as a wild and uncivilised periphery had a long pedigree. In 1506, a Venetian diplomat, Vincento Quirini, his ship holed up in the Fal estuary by stormy weather, wrote back to his masters in Italy that he was 'in a very wild place which no human being ever visits, in the midst of a most barbarous race'.[14] The seventeenth-century stereotype of the Cornish as a race of murderous plunderers reinforced this, while stories in the eighteenth century of the wreckers of Breage and Germoe, who were known to loot ships as they lay at harbour at St Michael's Mount in 1730 and 1750,[15] added their quota to the heady brew of an inhumane people living on the edge of civilised behaviour as well as the edge of the land. Present-day tourist imagery of the Beast of Bodmin Moor, transformed by the postcard industry from an elusive four-legged feline into a neanderthal, two-legged creature dressed in skins and labelled 'what we found in Cornwall', continue this representation today. Within Cornwall in the 1750s another identity was germinating which was to burst forth within a generation to become the popular identity of labouring communities and urban middle classes alike in the late eighteenth century. Founded on Methodism and deep mining, it reached its full fruition in the mining and quarrying districts of Cornwall.

Methodism was new. In 1743, its founder John Wesley (1703-91) had followed his brother, the preacher and writer of hymns, Charles, to Cornwall, bringing with him the simple, yet effective message that all could find salvation through faith. Open-air meetings fuelled the dissemination of this message of hope, albeit one transferred from the harsh reality of the present world to the promised glories of the next. Thousands flocked to Wesley's preachings as the evangelical revival that had already touched communities in Scotland, Wales and North America seared through Cornwall's hills and valleys. Methodism did not just bring the excitement of evangelism; it established an organisation that was perfectly suited to places like Cornwall, with a network of lay preachers, ordinary men and, at first, women, who spread the word in the accents of the people. Early half-hearted opposition from the Tory gentry, worried that Wesley was an agent of the Pretender, Charles Stuart, in 1744 and 45, was swept aside and after the 1760s, the small chapels of the Wesleyans began to sprout across the Cornish countryside.

If Wesleyan chapels were to become one icon of Cornwall, their twin was the engine houses, built for the engines that pumped water up out of the mines or brought ore to surface or which ran the stamps that crushed the ore at the surface. Mining and Methodism were two parts of the equation reproducing the Cornish identity. As copper became the mineral of choice and profit after the

BELOW
The celebrated Methodist preacher William 'Billy' Trewartha Bray (1794-1868), was born at Tweleveheads, near Truro. An ex-miner and a reformed drunkard, he was an energetic and witty evangelist who instigated the building of several chapels. He is buried at Baldhu Church.

1730s, mines were dug deeper in a search for that mineral, rather than the tin that had borne the weight of Cornish mining activity for a thousand years. Deeper mines meant growing problems of drainage. From the 1760s in particular, steam engines joined water-powered pumps and elaborate eighteenth-century drainage networks to help solve the problem. The cost of coal, which had to be brought by sea to Cornwall, ensured that the inventive skills of Cornish engineers were honed to a fine pitch. By the 1810s, Cornish engineers were coaxing a greater efficiency from their new high-pressure steam engine than the scientists of the day had believed theoretically possible.

Mining was no respecter of existing settlement patterns and, as new mineral reserves were exploited, new villages and hamlets sprang up nearby. Places such as Four Lanes, Carharrack, Praze and Pendeen grew rapidly. But these villages were often situated several miles away from their parish church. By the time the Church of England responded to this and built some new churches in the 1840s, it was too late. The ubiquitous Methodist chapel had become the popular resort in preference to the echoing, half-empty mausoleum that was the parish church. In 1829, at Sithney, the Anglican clergyman Richard Tyacke gloomily recorded in his diary, 'Sunday – the Church was but thinly attended, the rain pattered down so thick and fast, though at evening I observed the roads that led to the Methodists' chapel were thronged in every direction'.[17]

A Methodist 'cottage religion' emerged, one that was built upwards from people's cottages and which spoke their language. Occupationally homogenous communities dominated by the unpredictable and often dangerous callings of mining and fishing were the breeding grounds for this identity. Here, families lived out their lives relatively free from the suffocating oversight of Anglican clergyman and landlord alike, although for some, including those early emigrants of the nineteenth century, not free enough. In such independent communities, by the 1780s the religious culture had also become a revivalist culture. Mass revivals, during which fresh cohorts of converts were 'saved', blazed their way through communities at regular intervals. Perhaps the two greatest of these occurred in 1799 and 1814, marking the coming to age of this identity. And at the heart of it lay the 'Cornish customary family' that was identified in Chapter One, a unique Cornish variant of the family form of early industrial regions, but one that survived strongly into the 1840s before beginning to change.

Regional pride: the nineteenth century identity of industrialisation

This working-class cultural identity of cottage religion, customary family and mining industry overlapped in the early nineteenth century with a more public, more expressive articulation of Cornish pride. From the 1820s on, a confident regional identity was being pushed forward. Its mouthpieces were the Cornish press, especially the *West Briton*, founded in 1810, the outpouring of local magazines,

LEFT
Sir Humphrey Davy
(1778-1829) by John
Jackson, RA. Born in
Penzance, Davy's
research into testing the
effects of methane led to
his most famous inven-
tion in 1905 of the
Miner's Safety Lamp.
This was never used in
Cornish mines where
methane does not exist,
but it has been used
extensively in coal
mines worldwide.

dialect tales and, from the early 1850s, almanacs, and the lectures given in the literary institutions of the small towns. This was a more urban and more middle class variant of Cornishness, still Methodist in inclination, and still fuelled by the profits of mining shares and mining contracts, but an identity that expressed itself publicly, that moved beyond the cottage and the taken-for-granted, everyday struggles of the cottagers and their families to earn a living and keep themselves in relative decency.

The small-town Cornishness of the early nineteenth century had some things in common with the gentry territorial identity of the seventeenth, but the cloying royalism of later versions of that tradition was not so central. Instead, at its core was Cornwall's role in industrialisation, its place at the cutting edge of steam engine technology and the part being played by its miners in opening up mining fields overseas. This was a proud, assertive, secure, even arrogant identity, but it was also a regional identity in that it nestled within a larger pride in being British, in being subjects of the greatest Empire the world had yet seen. Moreover, like the gentry 'county'

ABOVE

*Many town signs in
Cornwall are now
bi-lingual.*

identity, the regional identity could look back to earlier times. Like the Cornish royalist tradition it tended to move swiftly over the rebelliousness of Tudor Cornwall with some embarrassment, bowdlerising it by transforming it into loyalty to Restoration Anglicanism, as was brilliantly done in Reverend Robert Stephen Hawker's 'Trelawny', written in the 1820s and rapidly adopted as the Cornish national anthem. Nevertheless, unlike the royalist tradition, it could look back on the Cornish language and Cornwall's British roots with more sympathy.[18]

It was this self-confidence that produced what was one of the greatest successes, in fact one of the few victories, for Cornish devolutionary sentiment in the modern period. A long, drawn-out campaign from 1846 demanded the re-formation of the Cornish religious diocese that had briefly appeared in the tenth and eleventh centuries. In 1877, this was at last successful, severing Cornwall from Devon for purposes of ecclesiastical government and finally producing a Cornish diocese and bishop. Meanwhile, copper mining had spread eastwards, first to the St Austell and St Blazey districts in the 1810s, and then twenty years on to the Caradon district near Liskeard, with a resurgence of mining in the older mining district near Gunnislake. As a result, there was a short period, from the 1830s to the 1870s, when the popular culture of Cornwall, based on mining and Methodism, almost converged with the boundaries of the historic territory of Cornwall. The county seemed more united than it had been at any time since the Black Death of the fourteenth century.

Unfortunately, this was to be short-lived. From the 1860s, the hammer blows of successive slumps fell on the mining industry, sapping the regional industrial identity and dismantling the cottage social life that had produced the Cornish customary family. In the face of economic crisis, especially profound in the 1870s and 1890s, migration became inevitable for many families rather than optional, a symbol of failure rather than a sign of dynamism and accomplishment. And yet emigration had already gone some way to produce a 'transnational' Cornish identity, one not bound by territory but linked over several continents and oceans.

The rise of Cornish transnationalism

As the Cornish migrated after the 1860s from a declining mining region, they tended to resettle in developing mining towns overseas where they could find work. Transplanting their cultural habits and behaviours to the receiving settlements, they formed distinct communities in which they continued the 'old country' way of life based largely on industrial pride and skill, underpinned by Methodism. In such 'Little Cornwalls', Methodist chapels were constructed, choirs and brass bands formed, rugby and soccer teams established, Cornish wrestling matches held and self-help societies set up, while shops sold distinctive foods such as pasties and saffron cake and Cornish dialect was heard on the streets. Burra in South Australia for example had three distinct Cornish quarters:

Redruth, Copperhouse and Lostwithiel. Cornish families at that time were sometimes accused of being 'clannish', reluctant to mix with those from other ethnic backgrounds. But of course, this comment could easily be made about any new immigrants in a foreign land who gravitate naturally to each other for protection and cultural continuity.

By the late nineteenth century, transnational migrant circuits characterised by outward migration, onward migration, return and repeat migration, linked communities in Cornwall with those overseas and overseas communities to each other. Some were of significant size. By 1850, there were already as many as 4,500 Cornish immigrants in the lead regions of Wisconsin, comprising half of the populations of Dodgeville, Mineral Point and Hazel Green, three quarters that of Linden and a quarter of the population of Shullsburg.[20] In 1898 there were estimated to have been 10,000 pure-blooded Cornish in this region and the 1890 census for Linden suggests that ninety to ninety-five per cent of residents had Cornish ancestry, many of them being from core families such as the Rules or Jewells whose ancestors came from the Camborne-Redruth area.[21]

These communities did not exist in isolation; for example Cornish people in Butte, Montana were interested in the outcome of a mining strike in South Africa in 1913, as many of the Cornish miners in Butte had worked at the mines in or around Johannesburg and might well have planned to do so again. At this time, the Cornish had a sense of belonging to a cohesive worldwide community, one that could exchange news and ideas, mobilise aid and discuss cultural issues. This was particularly well illustrated by the numerous Cornish societies and organisations that mushroomed from the 1890s and was expressed superbly by W. Guy Tickell of Bodmin, the secretary of the Cornish Association in Johannesburg, in his New Year address of 1912: 'To our kith and kin in the Homeland, and our kith and kin in all lands, I wish One and All a very Happy and Prosperous New Year'.[23]

In the United States there were Cornish societies in many of the major cities including Boston, Pittsburgh, Chicago, Detroit and New York, and in states such as California. In Canada there were societies in British Colombia, Winnipeg and Toronto and in Mexico at Mexico City. In Australia, Cornish societies were set up, too: that of South Australia was formed by James Penn Boucat and John Langdon Bonython at a banquet in the Adelaide Town Hall in 1890, with branches in Gawler, northern Yorke Peninsula, Kapunda and Clare and there was another at Broken Hill, New South Wales.

Across South Africa they also proliferated, the Cornish Association of the Rand for example having branches in Fordsburg, Germiston, Roodepoort, Krugersdorp, Randfontein, Benoni, Denver and Johannesburg. Associations were also formed at Durban and Kimberley. Not all Cornish associations were in far-flung places. Societies existed in the Midlands, Manchester, London and Cardiff and there were

ABOVE
Map Kernow ('Son of Kernow') erected at Kadina, South Australia in 1988 to commemorate the role played by the Cornish in the development of the metalliferous mining industry on the Yorke Peninsula.

also groups for expatriates from Devon and Cornwall, such as the Devon and Cornish Association at Reading. The mottos, motifs and symbols of Cornwall were adopted by many societies providing visual reminders of the connection with Cornwall and toasts to 'fish, tin and copper' were often made. The Cornish Association of British Columbia designed a lapel badge that displayed 15 golden balls on a black enamel shield, which included the Cornish motto 'One and All.'[24] 'If we took into account the Cornish and their children outside', the Cornish MP Leonard Courtney told the Midland Cornish Association in 1900, 'there is really a greater Cornwall outside than inside.' The editor of the *West Briton*, reporting the speech, noted the strong manifestation of Cornishness often displayed by those who had left Cornwall: 'the Cornish outside become more Cornish than the Cornish themselves.'[25]

Yet some Cornish associations were more than mere social clubs. That of South Africa demonstrated a remarkable degree of social and political mobilisation, organising a Cornish Sick and Benevolent Fund for the relief of distressed Cornish widows and orphans residing in the Transvaal, a Labour Bureau to help Cornishmen on the Rand find work, a scheme to put missing friends and relatives back in touch and ensured that men on the Rand continued to support their families at home through remittances. Moreover, the Association sent £40 a month

BELOW

Randfontein c. 1900 Cornish wrestlers Jack Chapman (second left) and Sydney Chapman (third left) who came from the St Columb area. The brothers also wrestled in the US and Australia.

back to the Mining Division in Cornwall (the Camborne-Redruth district) for the relief of destitute miners' families.[26] The Cardiff Cornish Association used the occasion of its 1908 annual dinner to make a collection for necessitous

Cornishmen and the Manchester and District Cornish Association also operated a benevolent fund and helped arrivals to find jobs.[27]

Industrial abroad: barbarians at home

As the classic Cornishness of industrial prowess moved overseas with the emigrants, older 'West Barbary' images re-asserted themselves at home. They had, of course, never gone away, but had been overlain in the early nineteenth century by more powerful representations of the Cornish people as the epitome of industrial civilisation and of Cornwall as a landscape of fire, a place of industrialisation.[28] Somewhat paradoxically, Cornish writers, as much as outsiders, had kept the idea of 'West Barbary' alive. It was they who were keen to measure the distance they had travelled by contrasting the state of the people of early Victorian Cornwall with their barbarous forebears of earlier centuries. Cornish Methodists were especially keen to emphasise the gap between that wrecking, rioting, raucous (and drunken) Cornwall of the West Barbary imagination and chapel-going, sober, hard-working Methodist Cornwall. The credit for this moral transformation was claimed for Methodism. But in highlighting the revolution wrought by John Wesley and his followers, Methodist historians exaggerated the debauchery of West Barbary. In all this there was little place for facts; the widespread smuggling of the Napoleonic War years in the 1790s and 1800s and the periodic food riots that were interspersed with the Methodist revivals as late as 1847 suggested that the popular culture was somewhat more boisterous than the Methodist grandees cared to admit.

And, by re-emphasising, albeit in retrospect, Cornwall as West Barbary, local writers were providing a hostage to fortune. For, after the 1870s, images of Cornwall as at the edge of civilisation made a re-appearance, this time in a different guise, cosier, less threatening and more homely, but backed up by the power of the broader Romantic movement that had colonised British aesthetic culture from the late eighteenth century. In the 1880s, Newlyn became home to a growing number of artists. Although they termed their artistic style 'social realism' this was a 'realism' that was extremely selective, choosing those elements of the 'real' that appealed to deeply embedded Victorian ideas of 'genre' painting, artworks that told a story, usually one with an uplifting moral to it. It was a realism that depicted poverty, but only if it was stoic, uncomplaining, dignified and, above all, as long as it was not ugly. By representing Cornwall to a wider metropolitan audience as a place of simple, poor people, closer to nature, living more primitive lives than the 'urban' civilisation the painters were romantically rejecting, the Newlyn School located Cornwall itself as a simpler, purer, more natural environment.

By choosing a fishing community, the painters in the process jettisoned Cornwall's proud history of industrialisation. They rendered this invisible to the trickle of visitors eager, courtesy of the Great Western Railway after the 1890s, to view this simple arcadia with their own eyes. Eventually the trickle was to grow to a landslide.

CHAPTER
FIVE

The Celtic Revival

The simple Cornwall of the Newlyn School, with its appeal to nostalgia and a lost (or threatened) past was, to some extent shared by another set of romantics, this time more home-grown. The early Cornish Revival also looked backwards for inspiration, to a Cornish-speaking medieval and 'Celtic' Cornwall. Although this version of romanticism carried the possibility of linking ideas of Cornwall into that oppositional rebellious Cornishness of the early sixteenth century, it failed to do so. As it appealed primarily to an intellectual and gentry class suffused with the remnants of the Cornish royalist tradition, the Cornish Revival trod a highly loyal

THE NEWLYN SCHOOL OF PAINTERS

In the early 1880s, a number of artists began to settle in Newlyn, the best known of which became Stanhope Forbes (1857-1947) and Walter Langley (1852-1922). Influenced by French methods – many of the Newlyn artists had spent time in Paris or Brittany – they spearheaded the new technique of *plein air* painting, working in the open air in addition to a studio. The Newlyn School became famed for their representations of fishing families going about their day-to-day lives. Known as 'social realism', their work actually fitted into a familiar Victorian genre of depicting fishing communities as being closer to 'nature' and untainted by the urban 'civilisation' that most of the artists were rejecting. Newlyn was regarded as having a special quality of light, although its nearness to the railhead at Penzance was another undoubted attraction. The artistic colony at Newlyn flourished in the last two decades of the nineteenth century and persisted into the inter-war period. The contemporary artistic colony at St Ives, on the north coast, survived into the second half of the twentieth century, in the process moving well away from 'social realism' by becoming a leading centre of 'modernism'.

path. Celts with a love of the Crown, they were quick to disown any link to that other Celtic Revival in Ireland that was demanding political independence.

Meanwhile, the mass of the Cornish people just got on with their own lives unperturbed by the seething romanticism that swirled around literary and upper class circles. Instead, they concentrated on making a living, continued to go to chapel, were more likely to express their political views in voting for Gladstonian Liberalism, watched rugby matches in the west, listened to and performed in brass bands and choirs, read the potboiler novels of the Hocking brothers from St Stephen in Brannel, and wrote to their relatives in the Cornish dispersed family overseas. In them, the classical Cornish industrial identity lived on, but it did so in a less articulate and public way than before the 1870s with one exception. In 1908, Cornwall won the English county rugby championship. Its progress had been followed by huge and excitable crowds, the victory of the Cornish team providing a lightning conductor through which an intense connection with people and place could still be displayed. It indicated that a latent Cornish patriotism was still present, but could it have any outlet other than the occasional rugby match? And could it transcend its 'English' framework?

Romance and recession

The inter-war period of the twentieth century perhaps saw the greatest divergence between external representations of Cornwall and its inner everyday life and identity. A growing guide book industry, most notably the series of books by S.P.B.Mais on *The Cornish Riviera*, provided a steady drip-feed of romanticism for a middle-class readership in southeast England which was apparently hell bent on finding King Arthur's grail west of the Tamar. As the representation of Cornwall as a romantic tourist destination seeped more deeply into the suburban sub-conscious, the Cornish people were suffering the traumas of economic restructuring. It was in the 1920s and 30s that the full impact of the recession in mining and its effects on other parts of the Cornish economy were really felt. After the Americans closed the door to mass immigration in 1919, the safety valve of overseas emigration that had eased the pressure at home was closed. Of course, people still left and the population still fell, but now the destination was as likely to be Slough as South Australia. Male unemployment rates for a time in the early 1920s and again, even more catastrophically, in the early 1930s, rose to heights of forty per cent in the Camborne-Redruth district and an amazing sixty per cent in Gunnislake by the Tamar, where the demise of mining and brick-making was exacerbated by a lack of alternative opportunities. In the 1930s, even the once buoyant china clay industry suffered from the American depression, while farmers and the fishing industry were paralysed by low prices for food.

There was cultural paralysis as well. While a small minority dallied with dreams of a Celtic Revival, most people clung to that classical nineteenth-century nonconformist, politically radical (though now socially conservative) Cornish identity created by industrialisation. By the inter-war decades this identity had become a hollow shell, as romantic in its own way as Arthurian imagery or the Cornish language revival. Cornishness was, above all, confined to family and friends and to the home. It was both a domestic and a domesticated identity, accepting of its territorial place

BELOW
Girl on a Cliff *by Penzance-born artist Harold Harvey (1874-1941).His model, local girl Cressida Tonkin (née Wearne) was the daughter of John Henry Tonkin who appeared in paintings by Stanhope Forbes.*

as subordinate to those far grander political and cultural identities of Britishness and Englishness. Cornishness in this period became strongly linked to family ties and memories; it was measured in the faces and voices of relatives and neighbours, lived through in the take-for-granted spaces of the home. When writers such as A.L.Rowse thought about being Cornish, they conjured up childhood memories, the towns and villages they had known as youngsters, the family connections that had forged them.[29] Cornishness had its epicentre in memories of family and was grounded on a close awareness of the places in which those families were located. The intimate link between the identity and the landscape survived, although this could often be very localised, feeding the parochialism that was coming to bedevil Cornish civic life, reinforced by the small-town geography of Cornwall, divided into a number of warring 'city-states'.[30] There were occasionally hints of something else; sparks of the older confidence flickered into life when Cornwall did well in the 1928 rugby championships. And in the 1930s in politics, there were attempts, both by Isaac Foot for the Liberals and A.L.Rowse for Labour, to appeal to people's Cornish patriotism in order to garner their votes.

THE CORNISH BARDS

Every year at its ceremony, the Gorseth welcomes new bards. These are either invited to become bards for their services to Cornwall or they are language bards, passing the third grade of the written examination in the Cornish language. Once initiated into the bardic circle, bards adopt a bardic name in the Cornish language in addition to their normal one. The Gorseth is led by the Grand Bard, elected for a period of office. The first of these was the redoubtable Henry Jenner, in old age every inch the bardic figure. Well-known recent bards include Paul Farmer, Bonjo Johns, Sir Richard Trant and E.V. Thompson.

Nonconformists like the editor of the *Cornish Guardian*, Arthur Browning Lyne, helped to widen the social basis of the Cornish Revival by supporting its more popular manifestation, the Old Cornwall Societies that mushroomed across Cornwall after 1925.[31] But for most Cornish people, things such as the new-fangled Gorseth, invented in 1928, remained a foreign and exotic growth, one that had little to do with their own innate sense of being Cornish. Jack Clemo, the clay-country poet and self-professed romantic, was an interesting case.

The decline of Cornish transnationalism

From a background of working class poverty and dour hardship Clemo was attracted for a short period in the 1930s to the Gorseth and the Cornish language revival, corresponding enthusiastically with its guru, Robert Morton Nance. But even for Clemo this was romanticism that went one step too far and he soon

LEFT
Dr A.L. Rowse opening
the fire station at St
Austell in 1937, sixty
years before his death.
Born at Tregonissey in
1903 he was a respect-
ed historian, author
and scholar of Tudor
England. In 1968 he
became a Bard of the
Cornish Gorseth.

rejected it, preferring the grimmer, introspective Calvinism that seemed to suit his stark and shimmering clay landscapes far better than the blue flapping gowns of the bardic circle.[32] Meanwhile, the links with the Cornish overseas were by now loosening. As was observed among the Cornish of southwest Wisconsin as early as 1898:

> '...while many of the Cornish immigrants in their lifetime keep up a correspondence with Cornwall, the second generation has almost entirely dropped it, although an occasional Cornish newspaper is received in the region. The Cornish descendants are scattering, and have almost lost their identity as a race. They do not hesitate to marry with other nationalities...'[33]

This area of Wisconsin witnessed some of the earliest migration flows outside Cornwall. By the turn of the twentieth century, most of the Cornish resident in the region had been born there and did not appear to have the same degree of psychological attachment to Cornwall that their parents and grandparents had. Indeed, family networks began to break down as immigrants and their children reared their own families and played out their lives in host communities far removed from Cornwall. Letters were written less frequently or not at all to relatives in Cornwall whom they had never met or had not seen for many years. Catherine Jane Kemp of Hayle berated her son, Josiah, resident in Utah in a letter of 1920:

> 'I can assure you that we have been wondering whatever had happened to you, why you should stop writing I could never understand for surely you could write a little oftener and let me now how you are going on

now and again for you don't know how a letter cheers me. There is Henry too its years since I have heard from him but I would like to and if you should see him at any time you can tell him that he still has a mother who thinks of him.'[34]

ABOVE

Barrie T. Kessell of North Country near Redruth in 1956, six months before he sailed for Cyprus where he did his National Service. Away from Cornwall for the first time, he recalls that it was during his National Service, when he was billeted with men from all over the UK, that he experienced his first real sense of being Cornish.

The reason for the declining links with Cornwall was largely the assimilation that occurred because of schooling, intermarriage with other ethnic groups, and social mobility. Second- and third-generation Cornish were more likely to associate their cultural identity with the area of their birth and/or formative years; thus the focal point of loyalty of those born overseas was increasingly detached from distant Cornwall, as exemplified in the minutes of the Cornish Association of South Australia in the inter-war years: 'The younger generation (have) no interest in the old Land or its traditions, having been born here in different surroundings.'[35]

But perhaps of greater significance was the cessation of mining in the 1920s and 30s, the industry that had so defined what it meant to be Cornish. Towns such as Moonta were decimated by the closure of the mines in 1923, which led to unemployment and signalled the end of Cornish immigration. Population dispersals eroded the Cornish cultural presence in mining settlements as some families moved away to find new work and some came home to Cornwall, and Methodist chapels gradually closed. Beliefs and behaviours become unfamiliar when they are no longer used regularly. Lack of exposure to news, ideas and ways of doing things brought by migrants from Cornwall resulted in a diminution of the Cornish presence in some overseas communities. One by one, the Cornish associations disbanded until only a handful remained and those immigrants who stayed in the old mining communities became increasingly nostalgic about their Cornish roots and heritage.

Social revolution

Back in Cornwall, after the shock of the Second World War, things seemed to settle back into the established routine. Some new factories were built on the wrecked surface works of former mines in the Camborne-Redruth area and unemployment thankfully receded a long way from its pre-war peaks. But the same underlying malaise persisted. Cornwall continued to export its young people; the population continued to drift downwards; local politicians remained stuck in their old petty parochialisms, fighting the battles of the pre-war period. But there were straws in the wind, perhaps the biggest – more of a haystack than a straw – was the arrival of post-war mass tourism, facilitated by the spread of car ownership down into the lower middle and skilled working classes.

The annual holiday traffic jams on the Exeter by-pass were an omen of what was to come. For, in the 1960s, much to the surprise of local planners who had confidently, but totally inaccurately, predicted that the major problem facing Cornwall was still population loss, the population began to grow again. And not just grow slowly. In the 1960s, Cornwall's population growth was 11.5 per cent, in the 1970s, 13.2 per cent and in the 1980s, another 9.7 per cent.[36] This massive growth came at a time when population increase in the UK as a whole was slowing down. From being a demographically stagnant periphery, Cornwall had suddenly shot to the top of the population growth table. Only Cambridgeshire and Buckinghamshire among English counties showed a higher rise in these same decades. But Cambridge was home to one of Britain's major research universities, and Buckinghamshire the location of Milton Keynes, Britain's biggest new town. Cornwall, in contrast, had no higher education sector, other than the specialised Camborne School of Mines and Falmouth College of Art, and no new town. The population explosion was fuelled entirely by in-migrants, a part of what demographers have termed 'counterurbanisation', as people in the 1960s began to leave the cities, or more accurately the suburbs, for the smaller towns of the countryside. This was a social trend to some extent fuelled by vague environmental yearnings.

ABOVE
The Curnow family
reunion in 1992 at
William Randolph
Hearst's mansion in
Lead, South Dakota.
One hundred American
Curnows are
assembled here, with
Howard Curnow at
the front left.

Cornwall, with its growing profile as a major tourist destination, was well placed to attract more than its fair quota of such movement as people in the 1960s and 70s began to cash in the equity made from an over-heating Home Counties property market and invest it in Cornwall.

The shock of counterurbanisation was the stimulant for a re-assessment of what it meant to be Cornish. Many Cornish people began to look more closely at what made them feel Cornish. In the face of what appeared to be the inevitable loss of a distinct identity, drowned in the rush of people westwards, the Cornish started to re-invest in their identity, to re-emphasise their difference from that anonymous English culture that seemed about to engulf them. Because of their past, part of this re-investment was inevitably directed towards the Cornish family. One thing that could be confidently regarded as guaranteeing a 'belonging' to Cornwall was the existence of ancestors here. This helped to foster a vigorous, sometimes desperate, search to prove one's Cornish roots.

The family tree stood as a visible reminder of the roots going deep into the Cornish past, tethering the apparently threatened modern family to a more certain past. Inevitably, this excavation had strong mythic dimensions. The assumption that the family was a solid bastion and a link to communal values now being destroyed was central. The danger was and is that an obsession with 'roots' diverts the gaze from the present and future. Instead of using the past as a resource for re-making the present (the hope of Morton Nance when he founded the Old Cornwall movement), the past can become an object of reverence in its own right.

The nostalgia and the reactive passivity that was a strong characteristic of Cornish identity in the twentieth century was always liable to induce an inward and backward-looking obsession with genealogical purity. For some, the iconic role of the family in Cornishness was therefore seen as irrelevant, even downright counter-productive, in view of the urgent requirement for a renaissance in all aspects of Cornish society. Or at least that was the danger. The Cornish family was, however, saved from a fate of antiquarian irrelevance by the revival of its links with that wider 'family' overseas.

The rise again of Cornish transnationalism

By the mid-twentieth century, those Cornish associations overseas which had managed to survive were mere shadows of their former selves, beset by financial difficulties and comprising small and aging memberships. In the 1960s, the future of Cornish transnationalism had never looked so bleak. But the years from the 1970s witnessed a remarkable resurgence. This is perhaps attributable to globalisation – an explosion of travel, migration and socio-economic interchange fuelled cheaper transportation and communication networks that have transformed the form and shape of human communities around the world. Globalisation has not necessarily led to the cultural annihilation predicted by some observers, where regional, ethnic or national distinctiveness vanish into a 'melting pot'. Rather it has had the opposite effect, as ethnic groups seek to reconcile the local with the global, in the process rediscovering, reconnecting, re-affirming, and celebrating their various cultural heritages.[38]

Additionally, a new multicultural awareness has impacted on Cornwall itself where different interpretations of 'Cornishness' have been steadily evolving since the Celtic Revival of the early twentieth century. A new political environment has allowed more Cornish to challenge the view that considers them to be English, leading to a heightened interest in Cornwall's 'Celtic' heritage and closer links with other Celtic nations, for example through the rash of twinning schemes with Breton communities and participation in inter-Celtic film and music festivals. This new Cornish identity is echoed among the overseas Cornish. 'What we

ABOVE

Prize-winning poet, children's author and playwright, Charles Causley CBE (1917-2003) was born at Launceston. He drew inspiration from his local surroundings and was known as 'a poet of place' - much of his life spent in and around his beloved home town.

appear to be witnessing', notes anthropologist, Amy Hale, is 'a kind of cultural feed-back resulting from a heightened awareness of ethnicity within the Celtic regions themselves…learning about the often shared experience of emigration has created new opportunities for dialogue around the Cornish world'.[39]

An important watershed in Cornish transnationalism came in 1973, with the greatest revival of Cornishness seen anywhere in the world: the three-day *Lowender Kernewek* or Cornish Festival focused on Moonta, Kadina and Wallaroo in South Australia. Musical concerts of Cornish hymns and folk songs were staged in Kadina; Wallaroo held a *Golya* or Cornish feast featuring *swanky*, a home-brewed beer once popular among the mining popula-tion there, and Moonta provided a *Fer Kernewek* (Cornish Fair). The programme included Cornish wrestling, a Methodist service, the tradi-tional Cornish Furry Dance, a pasty-making competition and a prize for the best dressed Cousin Jack and Jenny. More than 12,000 people par-ticipated in the Cornish fair, the *swanky* ran dry before the three days were over, petrol stations in Kadina sold out and one Moonta baker made so many pasties he exhausted his flour supply!

In North America too, the winds of change were blowing. In 1982, the Cornish American Heritage Society (CAHS) was formed. A confederal umbrella organisation with the aim of preserving the history and culture of Cornish people and strengthening connections between Cornish com-munities around the world, it had an initial membership of several hundred and held its first 'Gathering of Cornish Cousins' in Detroit. Through its gatherings that grew in popularity to become biennial events and its quarterly newsletter *Tam Kernewek* ('A Bit of Cornish'), the CAHS has been one of the main movers in the renaissance in Cornish culture and heritage across North America.

The year 1999 saw the inception of the Cornish Foundation for North America (CFNA). The creation of this new society marked yet another important turning point in modern Cornish transnationalism and was set up because its founding mem-bers 'care about Cornwall and our Cornish identity'.[40] Recognising that modern Cornwall has socio-economic problems resulting from the demise of mining and related industries, much the same problems in fact that face many of the old mining communities in North America, this non-political organisation aims to provide finan-cial assistance for projects in Cornwall. These relate to community regeneration, continuing education opportunities for residents in Cornwall, and the restoration and preservation of Cornwall's historical sites.[41]

Globalisation and multiculturalism cannot by themselves wholly explain the remarkable worldwide renaissance of Cornish culture and heritage. The credit for this must go to the many thousands of ordinary people with an interest in tracing their family histories, a process that had been quickening especially since the 1970s

ABOVE
Sir Terry Frost RA, who died in 2003, spent most of his life in Cornwall, his name inextricably linked with the place. Now the Frost dynasty lives on through his sons.

and accelerated more recently through access to the Internet. This electronic forum, or 'virtual community' perhaps reflects 'a hunger for community' in our modern era.[42] These are the people that make up the majority of the memberships of the revived and rejuvenated Cornish associations. Leading the way has been the Cornwall Family History Society. Indeed, it was members of CFHS who were responsible for setting up the Cornish American Heritage Society.

Researching family histories and sharing genealogical information has brought together distant branches of many family trees as Cornish Cousins, whose ancestors lost touch many years ago, share family lore and photographs and catch up on the fortunes of their distant relations. By the 1990s people such as Cornwall's Howard Curnow and Cornish-Australian historian, Pat Lay, were gathering sufficient numbers of overseas Cornish willing to participate in special genealogical and heritage tours to Cornwall. Indeed, involvement in genealogy has sometimes led to large family reunions that have reunited family name bearers from around the world who have been separated for several generations. For many people, the acme of achievement in Cornish reunions was the first *Dewhelans* ("Homecoming") in May 2002, when many hundreds of Cornish from across the world gathered for a three-day festival at Pendennis Castle Falmouth. The future

of the event has recently been secured by the granting of Objective One money. Carleen Kelemen, director of the Objective One Partnership, explains the importance of *Dewhelans* 2004 in Newquay: 'One of the priorities of the Objective One programme is to deliver economic and employment benefits based on the distinctive nature of Cornwall. *Dewhelans* 2004 will contribute directly to these aims. Not only will it help enhance understanding and appreciation of Cornish culture, it will do it in a way that is also economically beneficial.' She added: 'There is a niche tourist market for this kind of event, both in terms of the actual additional visitors it will bring to Cornwall

> ## THE GORSETH
>
>
> The Cornish Gorseth was established in 1928, the first ceremony being held at Boscawen Un near St Buryan, purportedly one of the ancient centres of Druidism in Britain. The annual Gorseth ceremony was loosely based on the already existing Welsh and Breton Gorseths. The aim was to 'maintain the national Celtic spirit of Cornwall', foster the culture of the Cornish and give recognition to those individuals or organisations whose work enriched that culture.

and in terms of the boost that the publicity generated will give Cornwall's economy and its national and international profile.'[43]

A transnational future

Dewhelans has illustrated that Cornish transnationalism has reached a new and exciting level. But why is there such an interest or even need for transnationalism? Adherence to the 'old country' which has claims on the loyalty and emotion of the Cornish worldwide has, according to academic Robin Cohen, implications for the international state system as a number of groups (like the Cornish) evince 'a "peoplehood" through the retention or expression of separate languages, customs, folkways and religions'.[44] Attempts to make the Cornish ethnically visible worldwide put transnationalism centre stage. Although Cornish associations are not meant to be political organisations, by educating their members to acknowledge their ancestry as 'Cornish' and not 'English' they are nonetheless strengthening the case for the Cornish to be recognised as a national minority within the United Kingdom.

The value of a Cornish population worldwide becomes apparent when we consider that over one and a half million people of Cornish descent are believed to reside in the US alone. This compares with Cornwall's population of just over half a million with the indigenous Cornish making up less than fifty per cent of this total. This is exemplified by a twelve-point appendix to the *Cornish National Minority Report* of 2000 that stressed the historical importance of Cornish labour migration in the creation of a modern and vibrant sense of Cornishness.[45]

ABOVE

The annual Gorseth ceremony, usually meeting on the first Saturday in September, with its circle of blue-robed bards, has now become one of the established spectacles of the Cornish year.

The most overtly political event of the 1990s was a re-enactment of the Cornish Rebellion of 1497, when thousands of aggrieved Cornishmen marched on London to be defeated by King Henry VII's army at Blackheath. The marches of solidarity planned in the US to compliment those in Britain clearly unsettled some Americans. For in the collective memory of most Cornish-Americans, Cornwall and its people were not seen as victims of English oppression and tyranny, but as skilled migrants from a successful industrial region that had contributed greatly to the economic powerhouse that was the United States of America. Cornish-American historian and Bard, Gage McKinney of California, noted that he felt uncomfortable lending support to any activity that might be construed as a gratuitous intrusion into the internal politics of another sovereign state.[46]

However, Cornish transnationalism has evolved and will doubtless continue to evolve as the Cornish in Cornwall and their cousins overseas contest, renegotiate and reinvent their common cultural heritage. For an abiding sense of Cornishness provides 'One and All' with a sense of heritage and roots in an increasingly mobile and changing world. An awareness of transnationalism has ensured that the Cornish – thrifty, sober, hard-working Celts, of good moral character, in short, archetypal nation-builders, have their place among the many threads that constitute the rich ethnic tapestry of the United States, Canada, Australia and other countries where the Cornish settled in significant numbers. Moreover, the economic benefit of preserving Cornish cultural heritage is evident from Mexico to Moonta and from Cornwall to California. But more importantly, the growth of Cornish transnationalism is acting as a vehicle to accelerate the creation of a Cornish Diaspora that has great relevance for Cornwall as its people attempt to be recognised as an ethnic minority within the British Isles.[47]

Changing identity; changing family

As Cornish transnationalism mutated and changed so, by the 1990s, clear evidence began to mount for a new, more hybrid, more dynamic and creative Cornish identity in the making at home. This erupted into wider consciousness around a familiar emblem, Cornish rugby. In 1989, "Trelawny's Army", following the Cornish rugby team on what seemed to become an annual pilgrimage to Twickenham, became itself a wider, more inclusive Cornish family. Furthermore, a new blending of previously separate Cornish sub-cultures was visible in the euphoria surrounding the success of Cornish rugby. St Piran's flags could be waved, tartans worn and the pasty eaten in an unselfconscious and eclectic new mix of cultural elements. The Cornish family retains its place as an important symbol of Cornishness, expressive of an enduring sense of place. However, in modern Cornwall, it is ultimately just one expression of being Cornish amongst many others.

Revivalist symbols such as the flag and 'Celtic' iconography now appear in all sorts of different guises, such as surf culture.[48] In addition, old symbols are used in new ways, for example the advertising of Skinner's Ales at Truro shows a creative and self-parodying attitude to Cornishness, one that seems more relevant to modern Cornwall. And old symbols are joined by new. The Eden Project has bequeathed its striking domes to visual representations of Cornwall. This may help to slowly shift external representations away from leisure-orientated landscape stereotypes towards a more dynamic imagery. However, it should be noted that it is still an image imbued with a romantic environmentalism and the economic imperatives of mass tourism. Politically, too, since the 1980s there are signs that a sense of Cornishness is now seen as relevant in new ways. It's not just something to be appropriated and patronised by political parties whose loyalties lie elsewhere, although it is still that. It can also be used to inspire multi-level lobbying in defence of Cornish aspirations or in demands for the return of Cornish institutions and recognition of Cornwall's status as an historic European region.

As we have seen in this book, the Cornish family has at various points in the past mirrored wider social differences between Cornwall and elsewhere. Cornish surnames give many Cornish families a distinct marker of identity and, more broadly, even those of us who do not bear such surnames are affected by the unique history of surname formation in Cornwall. Furthermore, the Cornish family is believed to be 'special', closer, more kin-orientated. The truth of this is less important than the stubborn belief that it is so. But, while families root us, we have to leave them eventually and form new families. It is in this changing use of family in Cornwall that its greatest significance is most likely to lie. Perhaps most important in the long run, through its links with families of Cornish descent overseas, the Cornish family can take its place as part of a more diverse, more confident, and re-articulated sense of pride in being Cornish that is noticeably emerging in the early twenty-first century.

LEFT
Some of the leading lights at work in Cornwall today (left to right from the top): Andrew George MP; Margo Maeckleberghe, painter; Bert Biscoe, poet and local politician; Karl Weschke, painter; Tim Smit, of Heligan and Eden Project; Daphne McClure, painter; Moira Tangye, Director, Cornish-American Connection and Cornish Bard; E. V. Thompson, novelist and Cornish Bard; Anthony Frost, painter; Bill Mitchell, Artistic Director, Kneehigh Theatre; Robert Jones, painter; Professor Philip Payton, Director, Institute of Cornish Studies.

TIMELINE

The aim of these pages is to give a very simplified overview of key events of Cornish and wider world history to set into context events which have directly affected the study of Cornish family history. Monarchs, presidents and prime ministers are also listed here.

9th and 10th Centuries	**838** Cornish and their Danish allies defeated at Battle of Hingston Down. Cornish rulers accept Wessex kings as overlords **936** King Athelstan's settlement fixes boundary of Cornwall **950-1100** Bodmin Manumissions (records of Cornish and other personal names of freed slaves)
11th Century	**1000s** Cornish land owning class lose their land to the Normans. First Armorican return – in-migration of high-status Breton landowners **1050** Cornwall amalgamated into Diocese of Exeter **1066** Norman Conquest. Robert de Mortain, half brother of William I, becomes Earl of Cornwall and builds Launceston Castle **1066-87** William I **1067** Arrival of the Normans in Cornwall **1086** Domesday Book **1087-1100** William II
12th Century	**1100** Old Cornish Vocabulary, an English-Latin-Cornish vocabulary **1100-35** Henry I **1100-1350** East Cornwall becomes English-speaking. Origin of many Cornish towns **1100s and 1200s** Population growth in Cornwall; settlements and farming spread into the wasteland **1135-54** Stephen **1140s** Earls of Cornwall created **1154-89** Henry II **1189-99** Richard I. Crusades **1199-1216** John
13th Century	***c*1200** Formation of Stannary courts **1201** First charter of the Stannaries **1215** Sealing of Magna Carta **1216-72** Henry III **1230s** Earl Richard builds Tintagel Castle **1272-1307** Edward I **1280s** Lostwithiel becomes chief town of the Earldom **1280-90** Cornwall shown as one of four constituent parts of Britain on *Mappa Mundi* (map of the world) in Hereford Cathedral **Late 1200s** Cornwall more integrated into English administration - in terms of parliamentary representation, taxation and justice

14th Century	**1300s** Cornish language cultural renaissance
	1305 Edward I defines privileges enjoyed by tinners in two charters
	1307-27 Edward II
	1327 Lay subsidy rolls, the first listing of Cornish taxpayers
	1327-77 Edward III
	1337 Outbreak of Hundred Years War between England and France, in which Cornish archers played a decisive role. Duchy of Cornwall established by Edward III, funnels profits from Cornwall to monarch. His eldest son, Edward the Black Prince, becomes first Duke of Cornwall
	1349 and 1360 Black Death reaches Cornwall
	1349 Black Death causes Cornish population decline of up to a third
	By 1350/1400 Most surnames hereditary in English-speaking Cornwall
	***c*1350-1500s** Language border along Camel-Fowey line
	1377-99 Richard II
	1399-1413 Henry IV
	Late 1300s-1400s Cornish Miracle Plays written

15th Century	**1400s** Cornish towns shrink in size. Cornwall's economy diversifies - fishing, shipping, textiles plus farming and mining. Growth of a Cornish gentry class
	1413-22 Henry V
	1422-61 Henry VI
	1450-1500 Second Armorican return – in-migration of Bretons, bolstering Cornish language and bringing new surnames
	1453 End of The Hundred Years War
	1455-85 Wars of the Roses
	1461-70 Edward IV
	1470-71 Henry VI
	1471-83 Edward IV
	1476 William Caxton sets up first printing press
	1480s/90s Population decline halted
	1483 Edward V. Accession of Richard III
	1485 Defeat and death of Richard at Battle of Bosworth, Leicestershire
	1485-1509 Henry VII
	1496 Stannary courts suspended
	1497 Two Cornish risings and defeat of Angove ('An Gof') at Blackheath

16th Century	**Early 1500s** *Beunans Meriasek* and *Beunans Kea* miracle plays written
	1500s Cornish defeat in Prayer Book Rebellion accompanied by decline in numbers of Cornish speakers. Cornish in decline in Pydar and Powder Hundreds
	1500s-mid 1600s Population growth
	1508 Charter of Pardon granted by Henry VII restores Stannary Parliament
	1509-47 Henry VIII
	1530s-40s Reformation, together with increased use of English Bible and Prayer Book, contributes to decline of Cornish language
	1534 Act of Supremacy, establishing Henry as head of Church of England
	1538 Thomas Cromwell, advisor to Henry VIII, initiates parish registers
	1547-48 Major mortality crisis in Cornwall caused by outbreak of plague

16th Century	**1547-53** Edward VI
	1549 Act of Uniformity, dictating one form of worship, and imposition of *Book of Common Prayer*. Glasney College closes. Cornish Prayer Book Rebellion, opposing new Protestant prayer book and its use of English language
	1553-58 Mary I
	1558-1603 Elizabeth I
	1563-1603 Poor Laws enacted
	1570s Persecution of Cornish Catholics
	1585 Colony of Roanoke (Virginia, US) founded
	1588 Spanish Armada appears off coast of Cornwall
	1590s Richard Carew writing *Survey of Cornwall*, indication of a strong 'county' identity among gentry
	1595 Last direct report of spoken Cornish in mid-Cornwall. Spanish raiders attack Mousehole, Newlyn, Penzance and Paul
	1597 Clergy ordered to keep bound copies of parish registers and Bishops' Transcripts
17th Century	**By 1600** Most surnames hereditary in Cornish-speaking Cornwall
	1600s Decay of ethnic identity based on language
	1603 Richard Carew's *Survey of Cornwall* published. Law against bigamy enacted
	1603-25 James I. Accession of Charles I (1625)
	1606 Virginia and Plymouth Companies formed by charter from James I
	1620 Mayflower sails from Plymouth for North America
	1625-49 Charles I
	1640s Last Cornish sermon at Feock. New sense of territorial identity created by civil wars
	1642-49 English civil wars. Cornish Royalist forces defeat Roundheads at Braddock Down and Stamford Hill
	1649 Execution of Charles I
	1649-60 Commonwealth. Oliver Cromwell abolishes Duchy of Cornwall and Stannary courts, and reduces Cornish MPs from 44 to 12
	1660 Falmouth founded on Cape Cod, North America
	1660-1730s 'Newlyn School' of revivalists. Population in west Cornwall grows, but stagnates in east Cornwall
	1660s-1740s Cornish Tory Royalism
	1660-85 Charles II. Duchy of Cornwall and Stannary courts restored; Cornwall regains 44 MPs
	1662 Act of Settlement, establishing rights to poor relief
	1670 Charter of Hudson's Bay Trading Company granted to English investors. British immigration to Canada begins
	1678-89 Publication of William Scawen's essay on the Cornish language
	1685-88 James II
	1687 Bishop Jonathan Trelawny imprisoned in the Tower of London
	1688 Falmouth in Cornwall granted official Packet status
	1688-89 Falmouth Packet service begins
	1689-1702 William and Mary
	Late 1600s Expansion of tin mining - gunpowder and capitalism

18th Century

Early 1700s Employment of Cornish girls and young unmarried women as 'bal maidens' (surface workers) becomes a familiar sight at many mines

*c*1700 Edward Lhuyd's visit to Cornwall

1702-14 Anne

1707 Act of Union between England and Scotland

1707-10 Sidney Godolphin, Britain's first Prime Minister

1714-27 George I

1727-60 George II

1730s Copper mining expansion begins

1731 Cornish reopen Old Darren mine near Aberystwyth

1743 John Wesley, founder of Methodism, first visits Cornwall

1750s Generalised population growth begins

1752 Last meeting of Stannary Convocation. Switch from Julian to Gregorian calendar

1753 Joseph Hornblower installs Newcomen steam engine at New Jersey copper mines. Lord Hardwicke's Marriage Act makes all marriages outside Church of England illegal

1760-1820 George III

1763 French cede Canada to British

1767 Easter Island and Tahiti discovered by Samuel Wallis

1768-71 James Cook's first voyage results in annexation of Australia and New Zealand by Great Britain

1775-83 American War of Independence

1778 William Pryce's *Mineralogia Cornubiensis* refers to Cornish men inspecting mineral deposits around Lake Superior

1780s-1810s Emergence of a working class identity in Cornwall based on mining and Methodism

1781 John Wesley preaches to 20,000 at Gwennap Pit

1786 Colony of New South Wales proclaimed by George III

1788 First British convicts arrive in Botany Bay, New South Wales

1789 Outbreak of French Revolution. Mutiny on HMS *Bounty* under Cornishman Admiral William Bligh

1789-97 George Washington becomes first US President

1790s Last Cornish-speakers in the Newlyn/Mousehole district

1791 England separates Canada into Upper and Lower Canada, New Brunswick and Nova Scotia

1794 Cornish miners working at Loxton copper mines, Somerset. Discovery of china clay in Cornwall

1794-1815 Napoleonic Wars, culminating in Napoleon's defeat at Waterloo

1795 British capture Cape Town from the Dutch during Napoleonic Wars

1797-1801 John Adams President of US

1799 and 1814 Great Methodist Revivals

1799 Foundation of Royal Cornwall Infirmary, Truro

19th Century

1800 Vivian family representatives of Associated Miners of Cornwall, arrive in Wales to found great copper smelting and mining dynasty

1800-10 Cornish newspapers published – *Royal Cornwall Gazette* and *West Briton*

1801 First national census

1801-09 Thomas Jefferson President of US

1806 British recapture Cape Town from Dutch and take over Cape Province

1807 Miners' safety lamp invented by Humphry Davy

1809-17 James Madison President of US

1810-25 Latin American Wars of Independence

c1810 Richard Trevithick invents high-pressure steam engine

1814 Formation of Cornwall Geological Society at Penzance, and of Cornwall Philosophical Society

1811 John Vivian forms company to work Mona copper mine in Anglesey, staffed by experienced Cornish miners

1815 British Government passes Corn Laws

1815-50s Period of Methodist schisms

1816 Transatlantic migration of industrial revolution in mining technology: first Cornish manufactured machinery (boiler parts from Holmans) exported to Latin America for Cerro de Pasco silver mines. Engine construction overseen by Richard Trevithick

1817 Suspension of right of Habeas Corpus. Cornish miners working Beara Peninsula copper mines, County Cork, Ireland

1817-25 James Monroe President of US

1818 Richard Trevithick sails for Peru to oversee erection of steam engines, spends 12 years in Latin America. Foundation of Royal Institution of Cornwall

1819 Cornish engine installed at Pearl Mine, Anglesey

By 1820s China clay established as an industry

1820 County Lunatic Asylum established, Bodmin

1820-30 George IV

1820s Rev R.S.Hawker writes the romantic 'Song of the Western Men', known more usually as 'Trelawny'

1820s-50s Flowering of a regional pride in Cornwall as an industrial region

1824 Gwennap parish produces more than one third of global copper ore

1824-25 London Stock Market boom. Mines reopened across Latin America

1825 Van Diemen's Land established as colony. John Quincy Adams President of US

1826 British Government Select Committee on Emigration; *Burke's Peerage* first published. Stock Market crash

1827 British Colony of Western Australia founded

1828 Foxdale Mining Company formed to work lead mines on Isle of Man. Laxley mine also attracts Cornish labour

1829-37 Andrew Jackson President of US

1830 St John del Rey Mining Co work Morro Velho gold mine, Brazil

1830-37 William IV

1830s Cornish begin to migrate to lead mining region of Wisconsin. Mineral Point founded. Two important copper mining ventures started at Cobre in Cuba. Cornish miners working copper deposits at Alten, Norway

1832 Great Reform Act. Williams family lease mines in East Avoca, County Wicklow, Ireland. Cornwall loses 27 Parliamentary seats

1833 Foundation of Royal Cornwall Polytechnic Society

1833-47 Sark Mining Company work copper and silver mines on Sark, in the Channel Islands

1834 Poor Law Amendment Act. New workhouses built.

1836 British province of South Australia established. Free and assisted emigration begins

1836-67 Copper mining on Virgin Gorda, Virgin Islands

19th Century (continued)

1837 Victoria accedes to throne. Civil registration of births, marriages and deaths. Church of England loses its monopoly on marriages. Riots at Camelford, Stratton, St Ives and Perranarworthal against the new Poor Law

1837-1901 Victoria

1837-41 Martin van Buren President of US

1838 Abolition of 'coinage' (dues paid to Duchy of Cornwall on tin mining)

1839 Cornish miners at work in gold fields in western India

1840 *Britannia*, first Cunard ship, leaves Liverpool for US

1840s 'Hungry Forties'. Population growth slows down; mass emigration begins

1841 Two Cornishmen discover silver-lead deposits at Glen Osmond. Wheal Gawler mine started. First census that recorded details for named individuals. Upper and Lower Canada united through Act of Union. William H. Harrison President of US

1841-45 John Tyler President of US

1842 South Australia becomes Crown colony

1843 Copper rush in Keweenaw Upper Peninsula, Michigan

1844 Copper mining begins at Kapunda on Yorke Peninsula - start of Australia's commercial mining industry

1845 Copper discovered at Burra, South Australia and at Callington, named by Cornish miners after town in East Cornwall. Mining begins at Kapunda. First large iron steamship driven by screw propeller, the SS *Great Britain*, crosses Atlantic

1845-49 James K. Polk President of US

1846 Bruce Mines, Ontario, attract Cornish labour. Cornish miners brought in to work ailing Magpie Mine at Sheldon, in Peak District. Cornish miners arrive in Kawaw, New Zealand, to begin copper mining

1846-48 Potato blight hits Cornwall

1846-77 Successful campaign to re-establish a Cornish diocese

1847 Last food riots

1848 Royal Niger Company stimulates tin production in Nigeria

1848-49 Economic depression sparks revolution across Europe. Cholera pandemic

1849 Gold rush in California. Cornish miners drain and reopen Guadalcanal silver mines, southern Spain

1849-50 Zachary Taylor President of US

By 1850s Methodism widespread in Cornwall

1850 Falmouth Packet service ceases. South Australia is world's third largest copper producer. Cornish miners sail for Piroc, Brittany, to work tin mines.

1850-53 Millard Fillmore President of US

Mid 1850s Cornish miners at work throughout Europe and Americas: at silver-lead mines at Pontgibaud, France; at Veraguas gold mines, Panama; Obernhof Mining Company's mines and Wildberg Consols Mine, Germany; Tuscany Copper Mining Co mines, Italy; Linares lead mines, Spain; Dalecarlia Silver-lead Mining and Smelting Co., Sweden; New Jersey zinc mines, USA; Chontales gold mines, Nicaragua; and copper mines in Jamaica.

1852 Cornish miners sent to Algeria to inspect copper mines

1853 First white baby born in Grass Valley, California to Cornish immigrants. Cornish miners arrive in Alabama from Tennessee and revive mining in search for copper

1853-57 Franklin Pierce President of US

1855 Copper discovered in Namaqualand, South Africa. Hodbarrow iron mine opened out by a Cornishman and the Hodbarrow Mining Company begins operations at Millom, in Cumberland

19th Century (continued)	**1856** Van Diemen's Land renamed Tasmania

1856 Van Diemen's Land renamed Tasmania

1857 Union Line's *Dane* leaves Southampton on 15 September inaugurating Union Line's mail service to Cape Town. Divorce Act entitling men to sue for adultery alone, whereas women had to prove other grounds as well as adultery

1857-61 James Buchanan President of US

1858 Fraser River gold rush, British Colombia

1859 Gold discovered in Colorado. Opening of Brunel's Royal Albert Bridge over the River Tamar at Saltash links Cornish and English railway systems. Copper discovered at Wallaroo, South Australia.

1860s Absolute population fall sets in. Crisis in Cornish mining industry

1860 Development of Comstock Lode in Nevada. Monument to Dolly Pentreath erected at Paul churchyard

1860-65 Maori Wars in New Zealand

1861 Moonta, South Australia, founded. Gold rush at Tuapeka River near Dunedin, New Zealand

1861-65 American Civil War. Abraham Lincoln President of US

1862 Springbok near O'Okiep, South Africa, founded. Cornish miners involved in copper mining on Loch Fyne, Scotland

*c*1865 Chile producing 44 per cent of world's copper

1865-69 Andrew Johnson President of US

1866 Failure of Overend & Gurney bank and Cornish copper mining crash, prompting further mass emigration. Alluvial gold found on Inangahua River, West Coast, South Island, New Zealand.

1867 Discovery of diamonds in Kimberley and at confluence of Orange and Vaal Rivers and of gold in Tati River, South Africa. Cornish miners begin exploitation of alluvial tin deposits in Siam. Canada becomes first independent dominion in British Empire. John Alexander Macdonald first Canadian Prime Minister

1868 Silver discovered at Park City, Utah

1869 Coast-to-coast railway in US. Suez Canal opened. Thomas J.Ismay registers his Oceanic Steam Navigation Co., also known as The White Star Line, a byword for transatlantic travel

1869-77 Ulysses S. Grant President of US

1870 Cornish miners recruited for New Almaden, California. Extensive nitrate beds found in Bolivian Atacama

1870s-80s Trade unions beginning to emerge

1871 Tin deposits discovered on Mount Bischoff, Tasmania

1872 Donald Currie's Castle Packet Company begins sailing to Cape Town. Production of tin at its peak

1873 Rediscovery of ancient Champion Lode at Kolar, Mysore State, India

1873-78 Alexander Mackenzie Prime Minister of Canada

1874 British gain control over main tin mining in Malay States. Gold discovered in Black Hills, Dakota.

Mid 1870s Cornish miners at work for the Sentien Mining Company, in France

1876 Butte, Montana, emerges as significant copper producer. Akankoo Mining Company in Gold Coast recruits Cornish miners

1877 British Government annexes the Transvaal

1877-81 Rutherford B. Hayes President of US

19th Century (continued)	**1878** Tombstone, Arizona, founded after discovery of copper. Magistrates allowed to issue separation orders in cases of aggravated assault by husbands on wives

1878 Tombstone, Arizona, founded after discovery of copper. Magistrates allowed to issue separation orders in cases of aggravated assault by husbands on wives

1878-91 John Alexander Macdonald Prime Minister of Canada

1879-83 War of the Pacific, involving Chile, Bolivia and Peru

1879-86 John Vivian publishes his *Visitations of Cornwall*, including the heralds' visitations of 1530, 1573 and 1620

1880s 'Newlyn School' of painters

1880 Cecil Rhodes founds De Beers Consolidated Mining Company, controlling diamond mining in Orange Free State. Foundation stone of Truro Cathedral laid by HRH The Duke of Cornwall

1880s-1920s Romantic imagery of Cornwall gains ground

1881 Rosario Mining Company, Honduras, and Great Zaruma Gold Mining Company, Ecuador, recruit Cornish miners. James A. Garfield President of US

1881-85 Chester A. Arthur President of US

1882 Campaigning for a Cornish Sunday Closing Bill

1884 Tin output of Perak State, Malaya, equal to whole of Cornwall's. Gold discovered on the Rand. Couer d'Alene gold rush in Idaho

1885-89 Grover Cleveland President of US

1886 Free and assisted passages to South Australia cease. Mining boomtown Johannesburg created

1889 Cornwall 'County' Council established

1889-93 Benjamin Harrison President of US

1890s Primary schooling both free and compulsory

1891-92 John Joseph Caldwell Abbott Prime Minister of Canada

1892 Ellis Island opens in New Jersey to control immigration into US

1892-94 John Sparrow David Thompson Prime Minister of Canada

1893-97 Grover Cleveland President of US

1894-96 Mackenzie Bowell Prime Minister of Canada

1895 Ashanti Goldfields Corporation established in West Africa's Gold Coast

1896 Charles Tupper Prime Minister of Canada, followed by Wilfrid Laurier. Last case heard in Stannary courts

1897 Klondike gold rush

1897-1901 William McKinley President of US

1899-1902 Anglo-Boer War

20th Century

1900 Union Steamship Company and Castle Mail Packets Company merged to form Union-Castle Steamship Company Limited

1901 Death of Queen Victoria. Inauguration of Commonwealth of Australia. Lord Hopetoun first governor-general, Edmund Barton first Prime Minister. Foundation of Cowethas, Kelto-Kernuak (Cornish Celtic Society)

1901-09 Theodore Roosevelt President of US

1901-10 Edward VII

1902 Britain completes conquest of Northern Nigeria and tin production soars. Submarine telegraph cable opened from Vancouver, Canada, to Southport, Queensland, enabling information to be sent via Morse code

1903 Alfred Deakin Prime Minister of Australia. Women's Social and Political Union, demanding votes for women, founded by Mrs Emmeline Pankhurst

1904 J.C. Watson Prime Minister of Australia
Great Western Railway introduces Cornish Riviera Limited train, opening way
for development of mass tourism. Publication of Henry Jenner's *Handbook of the
Cornish Language;* Jenner secures Cornwall's membership of Celtic Congress
1905 George Reid Prime Minister of Australia followed by Alfred Deakin
1908-9 Andrew Fisher Prime Minister of Australia
1908 Cornwall wins 'county' rugby championship
1909 Alfred Deakin Prime Minister of Australia. First state old age pensions
1909-13 William H. Taft President of US
1910 Andrew Fisher Prime Minister of Australia. Union of South Africa formed.
Louis Botha becomes Prime Minister
1910-11 Mexican Revolution
1910-36 George V
1911-20 Robert Laird Borden Prime Minister of Canada
1912 Strike in Cornwall's china clay district; mass strike of white miners in
South Africa. Sinking of the *Titanic*
1913 Joseph Cook Prime Minister of Australia
1913-21 Woodrow Wilson President of US
1914 Andrew Fisher Prime Minister of Australia. Panama Canal opened.
Mass overseas emigration ends
1914-18 First World War
1915 W. M. Hughes Prime Minister of Australia
1919 Deep depression in Australia's mining district.
1919-24 Jan Smuts Prime Minister of South Africa
1920-21 Arthur Meighen Prime Minister of Canada
1920s Cornish 'Revival' institutionalised in Old Cornwall movement
1921 End of unrestricted immigration to US
1921-23 Warren Gamaliel Harding President of US
1921-26 William Lyon Mackenzie King Prime Minister of Canada
1922 Empire Settlement Act enables Australia to take in many British immigrants
1923 Closure of mines in Moonta, South Australia. Stanley Melbourne Bruce
Prime Minister of Australia. Women now also able to sue for divorce on grounds
of adultery alone (i.e. equal rights as men)
1923-29 Calvin Coolidge President of US
1924-39 James Hertzog Prime Minister of South Africa
1925 Foundation of the Federation of Old Cornwall Societies
1926 Arthur Meighen Prime Minister of Canada, followed by William Lyon
Mackenzie King. Formation of St Ives Society of Artists
1927 Official adoption procedure introduced
1928 First Cornish Gorseth held at Boscawen-un
1929 Beginning of Great Depression. James Scullin Prime Minister of Australia
1930s High unemployment in mid and west Cornwall
1936 Edward VIII. Accession of George VI
1936-52 George VI
1939 Jan Smuts Prime Minister of South Africa
1939-45 Second World War
1940s Temporary rise in Cornwall's population
1948 Daniel Malan Prime Minister of South Africa; apartheid formally implemented

20th Century (continued)	**1950s** Mass tourism begins
	1950 Political Cornish nationalism arrives
	1951 Foundation of Mebyon Kernow (Sons of Cornwall) pressure group and political party
	1952 Death of George VI. Accession of Elizabeth II
	1960s Growth of branch plant economy. Population turnaround in Cornwall with the flight from suburban England
	1961 South Africa becomes a republic
	1960s-2000s Creeping regionalisation; loss of decision-making and jobs eastwards
	1969 Divorce Reform Act
	1976 Cornwall Family History Society founded
	1970s In-migration triggers resurgence of Cornishness. Rise in Cornish speakers
	1973 First Lowemder Kernewek - the world's largest Cornish festival - in South Australia
	From 1980s Unsustainable growth of population and economy begins
	1982 Foundation of the Cornish-American Heritage Society
	1985 Exhibition at the Tate Gallery, London: *St Ives 1939-64: 25 years of painting, sculpture and pottery*
	1986 Debate about the spelling system of Cornish
	1989-91 'Trelawny's Army' (massed rugby union football supporters) marches on
	1990s Some fusion of industrial and Celtic Cornish identities
	1993 Tate St Ives opens
	1997 Celebrations to mark 500th anniversary of events of 1497
	1999 Cornwall gains EU Objective One aid. Cornwall defeats Gloucestershire at Twickenham in Rugby Union County Championship
21st Century	**2000** Cornish Constitutional Convention.
	2001 Eden Project opens. Work begins to obstain World Heritage Site status for Cornish mining,
	2002 First Dehwelans held in Cornwall at Pendennis Castle, Falmouth
	2003 Opening of National Maritime Museum Cornwall in Falmouth
	2004 New university campus opens at Tremough for the Combined Universities in Cornwall (Exeter University and Falmouth College of Arts)

FAMILY HISTORY RESEARCH IN CORNWALL

David Holman
Chairman of the Cornwall Family History Society

This chapter will provide sources and facilities to assist readers in their research into families in Cornwall. Anyone researching families should consider all sources, particularly those with good coverage such as the censuses, but should not disregard the more obscure sources. There are three main categories of sources, personal, local and national, which will be examined below. Also included is a list of useful books and website addresses.

PERSONAL SOURCES FOR FAMILY HISTORIANS

Personal records are those that relate directly to families and are often passed on from other family members.

Oral history

This is the most useful of the personal sources. The importance of oral history is illustrated by the fact that a grandmother who remembers stories told by her grandfather about his grandmother represents six generations of oral history that can be passed down to you.

Oral history, however, is reliant on memory which is often subject to embellishment or detraction. All oral history should, where possible, be followed up with reference to other sources. Oral history can be taped or recorded on other electronic means. While this will not increase the accuracy of the story being told, it will prevent further distortions. An Oral History Project is being organised by the Centre for Cornish Studies/Kresenn Kernow (see details on pages 221 and 229) in Redruth, which aims to record stories told by people about families and local Cornish history.

Letters and diaries

Letters often provide insight into the lifestyles of our ancestors. Sadly not many letters survive. In the same vein, diaries can give a day-to-day account of what our ancestors were experiencing and feeling. Even a diary kept in a business or workplace may provide valuable clues. With the migration of Cornish families overseas many letters were sent between the separated families. Where they survive they tell tales of heartbreak and joy and often contain instructions on how those left behind were to make their way overseas to join their relatives.

Photographs

Where photographs have been preserved, they may contain no clues as to their subject matter and are often found in job lots at flea markets. Some older photographs with no specific details can be dated by looking at styles of dress and buildings. This is a skilled practice and there are people who can assist in providing a service for dating old photographs. It is also possible to take a badly damaged photograph and have it digitally enhanced by the removal of stains, blotches and scratches. This process will often reveal background details that were not previously visible.

Postcards

Postcards, like photographs, can often give a sense of time and place and many postcard sellers can be found selling cards which have been sorted by parish. Postcards are easier to date and if they were used, may have a postmark giving an exact date, a short few lines as well as an address for a recipient. Family postcards are rare and should be treasured. The earliest postcards probably come from about the end of the nineteenth century and may often be a photograph of a family member or group taken by a professional photographer and backed with a postcard format.

Postcards are held in the Valentine Archive of the University Of St Andrews Library, North Street, St Andrews, Scotland KY16 9JR. A useful book on postcards is *The Dictionary of Picture Postcards in Britain 1894-1939* by A.W. Coysh, Antique Collectors' Club Limited, 1996.

Family bibles

For the family historian the family Bible may be a valuable source of genealogical information and will often record several generations of a family. If the handwriting and ink vary with each entry it is likely that the record was updated at each event. Early entries are often in the same handwriting and ink which means that the first user of the Bible filled in previous generations to the best of their knowledge or from an earlier family Bible. These will almost certainly contain some errors and should be carefully checked against parish registers and other sources.

LOCAL SOURCES FOR FAMILY HISTORIANS

Parish registers

The most used local sources are the parish registers. These are a record of local church events. In Cornwall, these will mainly be Church of England, but other denominations will also be found, including Catholic and other non-conformist registers as well as Quaker and Jewish registers. Parish registers have been maintained by the Church of England since 1538, although not all parishes have records that date back that far. The registers record baptisms, marriages and burials. However, baptism and burial records are not the same as the dates of birth and death, but there is some mileage in estimating the main events from the church events. The time between death and burial is usually only a few days, but longer periods are recorded where after death, the body has been transported some distance to the parish of burial.

Some forenames can give very exact dates. A search of Cornwall Family History Society (CFHS) Monumental Inscriptions (the words written on a grave or other memorial) shows that the name Redvers was popular over a short period around 1900. This coincides with the Anglo-Boer War and General Sir Redvers BULLER, who as a Lieutenant Colonel was awarded the Victoria Cross in March 1879 during the Zulu War, but this does not seem to have sparked the nation into naming their children after him then. Only later, after his dismissal from the army as a General, was his name revered enough to name children after him.

Most Anglican Church registers, except those currently in use, are held at the Cornwall Record Office (CRO), which is also the Diocesan Record Office. A small number are still held by the churches. The CRO now holds most parish registers on fiche or film with a few exceptions. Many registers up to the late 1950s, when the films were first used to preserve registers, are also on film at the Courtney Library of the Royal Cornwall Museum.

Some registers of other denominations are also held by the CRO. All Methodist registers up to 1837 had to be forwarded to the Registrar-General, and are now held at the Public Record Office, approximately 871 in number, covering the whole country. The dates of church registers held at the Cornwall Record Office are listed in a CRO booklet and on the internet. New parishes have been introduced from time to time. If a particular register does not go back to 1538, it is worth enquiring whether the early registers have been lost or whether the parish has been created since that date, in which case one needs to know what the original parish was.

When examining baptism records in registers it is worth remembering that baptisms may well have been followed by the burial of a child in infancy. It is not unusual to find the same parents baptising a second child with the same forename. This may seem unusual today as parents wish to preserve the memory of their child with its unique name. In the past parents may have remembered their lost child by re-using the name for a subsequent child as a way of perpetuating their name and memory.

Bishops' Transcripts

From 1598 the incumbent vicar was required to send a copy of his registers to his Bishop. These are known as the Bishops' Transcripts. Very few survive from such an early date and in Cornwall the earliest are from 1600. Those from the periods 1600-70, 1737-40 and 1773-1837 are held at the Devon Record Office in Exeter and at the Cornish Studies Centre at tje Cornwell Centre, Redruth, with a fiche copy at the CRO in Truro. Those from the periods c1670-1736 and 1741-72 are held at the CRO.

The coverage is not complete and there are discrepancies, omissions and additions to the original parish registers. The transcripts are a useful source where there are gaps in the original registers. Some parishes in Cornwall were 'Peculiars' of the Bishop of Exeter and the transcripts for these parishes are held at Exeter with fiche copies held at the CRO in Truro. The transcripts post-1812 are held at Exeter.

Catholic records

The Catholic Church in Cornwall has kept nearly all of its records, but the CRO holds the marriage register for St Austell 1983-88. Records rarely exist before 1791. The best starting place to trace Catholic ancestors is the Catholic Family History Society (see useful internet sites on page 227).

Non-conformist records

Cornwall was a hive of non-conformism and during the 1851 Religious Census of Cornwall more than half of people attended the chapels of one of these denominations. The Anglican Church was virtually the only source of family information through its comprehensive records of baptisms, marriages and burials, until the coming of the Methodist Church in the late 1700s. From 1837 Methodists were permitted to perform marriages, but only in the presence of the registrar. At the end of the nineteenth century these churches could be licensed for the independent conduct of marriages. Baptisms and burials were conducted, but there was not the same degree of control in comparison with the Anglican Church, and few of the early Methodist registers have survived.

Jewish records

Jewish synagogues existed at Falmouth, from 1740 to 1892, and Penzance, between 1807 and 1906. There are two closed Jewish cemeteries in these towns. The CRO holds a photocopy of the Penzance Synagogue Marriage Registers for the period 1838-92. For further information, you can contact The Jewish Genealogical Society of Great Britain (see page 227).

Quaker records

The Society of Friends, known as The Quakers, has been in Cornwall since the 1600s. Quakers and Jews were the only denominations who were allowed to marry outside the Church of England before Civil Registration in July 1837. The registers of the Quakers in Cornwall are held at The National Archives in Kew. Transcripts of parts of these registers can be found at the CRO.

Transcriptions and other sources

Transcriptions are extracts or complete copies made from church registers. Research centres usually hold transcriptions of one sort or another; either printed or hand-written. Two of the best known and most extensive are those by Phillimore and Percival Boyd. Phillimore organised the transcription of the marriage records of many parishes chronologically. Boyd organised his marriage transcriptions alphabetically in 25-year periods. Both provide good coverage of the Cornish registers, but, with few exceptions, have stopped at 1812. The Courtney Library, in the Royal Cornwall Museum, holds, on film, copies of the Ross Marriage Index, which is probably the most extensive, but only gives the year of marriage. It does give some coverage to as late as 1925.

Transcripts of parish registers are available to view at the Cornwall Record Office. There are many groups and individuals who have indexed the registers to facilitate research. The first of these projects was the Phillimore Marriage series for England and many of the Cornwall marriages are listed in their printed volumes. These volumes have been entered on to computer databases and have been used to make a searchable database of the county. The caveat is that all indexes are susceptible to error and therefore where possible, indexed entries should be checked against the original document. This is, of course, only possible if a reference to the original can be found. There may well be errors in the data in Phillimore, but more useful to the researcher are the names in the transcripts that are now not readable on the original or even some names no longer present on the original parish registers due to damage.

The Church of the Latter Day Saints (also known as the Mormon Church) have used the work by Phillimore and others to provide an index of marriages and baptisms that forms a major source for family historians. This index is called the International Genealogical Index. The index is incomplete and there are gaps for many counties. The latest entries usually go up to 1837 and sometimes beyond, although a project called FreeReg may be changing this; again data are mainly before Civil Registration.

Monumental inscriptions

Graves have been marked by an inscription over them since very early times. A comparison of the index of Monumental Inscriptions and the Burials Indexes held by the Cornwall Family History Society shows that in the period 1813-37 about one in ten people were commemorated on a gravestone. The information gleaned from these inscriptions is valuable to family historians as it often gives more information than burial registers.

CFHS has an index to nearly all of the burial grounds in Cornwall. A project to photograph these has completed about one quarter of the stones and the work will continue until all are photographed. Other organisations and individuals have also been transcribing and photographing monuments and a search of the internet will find these.

Wills and probate

Wills were often dictated to a scribe and existence of a will is not evidence that a person could write. They could be nuncupative wills, which are made orally, and then signed or a mark or seal used. Some wills are quite detailed and may give quite obscure relationships.

Where a will is not made, a person is deemed to have died intestate and various legal actions are required to apportion the goods and chattels to those who would be likely to benefit where a will had been made. Whether or not a will was made, an inventory of items can be made and these do survive. An administration is a legal form that allows others to administer the effects of a deceased person and is usually found where no will is made or perhaps the executors of the will have since died. Probate is the process whereby a will is 'proved' in court. The Principal Probate Registry was formed on 12 January 1858. There is a Probate Office in Bodmin which holds indexes to the wills proved across the country.

Wills prior to 1858 can usually be found in the various county record offices. However, wills for large parts of Devon and Cornwall were destroyed during an air raid on Exeter during the Second World War. Archdeaconry of Bodmin wills were not destroyed during that air raid and about 80,000 are indexed and available on fiche at the CRO. The main problem of locating a will is knowing at which court the will was proved. The death duty registers, discussed below, may prove useful in locating the local court where a will was proved.

Taxes and tithes

The official documentation that accompanies death, either as a death certificate, a burial register, or obituary or monumental inscription, can often assist in filling in the branches of a family tree. It is likely that a birth and baptism of an individual could be recorded on a family tree without realising that the baptism or birth was closely followed by the death of the child.

As part of the estate of a deceased person taxes have to be paid. A direct tax on death was instituted as a Death Duty from 1796 and by 1811 all estates going through the Probate Courts, except those that were very

FAMILY HISTORY RESEARCH IN CORNWALL

Cornwall District Probate Registry
Market Street
BODMIN
PL31 2JW
Tel. +44 (0)1208 72279

small, would be subject to death duty. Registers of death duties will tie in with wills and show what actually happened to the estate as opposed to what was intended. Many of these registers exist at the National Archives.

Other taxes such as Hearth Tax and Window Tax were levied against property. Land Tax was levied against any holdings of land. Poll Tax was raised against the individual. Many of these taxation records exist and some have been indexed, particularly the Hearth Taxes of the seventeenth century. These indexes are available at most record offices and societies.

Linked with taxation was the requirement to provide men for the defence of the realm. Details of people who were liable are usually found in the muster rolls and military surveys. These have been indexed and show the name of a head of household, the parish and the types and number of armour and weapons available. Viewing the original may not be practical as many of the original records are damaged, poorly written and in Latin.

The Lay Subsidies of the late thirteenth and early fourteenth centuries give lists of names taxed on their personal and moveable assets. These records will show the existence of a name during that period, but at this time names were not always passed on from one generation to the next, so there is only a small chance of linking families back to this time.

Tithes began as a payment in kind, and were originally paid to the church but after the dissolution of the monasteries, in the first half of the 16nineteenth century, the payment passed over to the new owners of the land. In 1836 an Act of Parliament commuted all payments in kind into payments of money. Tithes were apportioned within a parish and maps of these apportionments exist. These are available at the CRO and at the National Archives and are in the process of being indexed and digitised.

Courts and quarter sessions

Court records could add some colour to family histories. Minor misdemeanours were dealt with at a local court. Quarter Sessions were the main judicial and administrative bodies of the English counties from the 16nineteenth century until they were replaced by County Councils in the late 19nineteenth century. Their judicial functions were not removed until 1971. Principally the archives held at the CRO relate to criminal cases. The archives contain the punishment handed down and usually details of the offence. Whole lists of jurors are also listed in the sessions.

Deeds and leases are another useful source to family historians and often a lease for 99 years was made on three lives. The CRO holds these deeds and also has collections from the estates and families of Cornwall.

Maps and Ordnance Survey maps

Maps provide a method of viewing where ancestors lived and how the local area looked. National mapping is the responsibility of the Ordnance Survey (OS) and the Cornish Studies Library, Redruth and the CRO in Truro hold copies of the OS First Edition of 1800-10. This will show how the county was laid out at that time. These maps were the basis of future Ordnance Survey mapping up to the present day.

Newspapers

Newspapers in Cornwall are available at a number of sites, including a large collection at the Centre for Cornish Studies/Kresenn Kernow in Redruth and the Royal Institution of Cornwall (RIC) Courtney Library in Truro. Newspapers will contain obituaries as well as details of other life events including births, marriages, divorces and legal proceedings, including bankruptcy and intestacy. An even more interesting record from newspapers are inquests and cases heard in the Assizes and other courts.

The Centre for Cornish Studies/Kresenn Kernow is one of the services provided by the Cornwall County Council. This is the only public library with librarians and staff who specialise in helping those who are studying Cornwall. It is not necessary to be a library member to use the Centre for research. A large collection of newspapers and periodicals is available on microfilm as are the Cornish censuses, parish registers, maps and photographs. The Courtney Library at the Royal Cornwall Museum holds about 30,000 printed volumes, 35,000 manuscripts and documents and original copies of newspapers, some dating back to 1798. The study area is open to the public and there is a small staff to provide assistance.

Directories

Directories list places and the people living in them. They differ from a census in that they list only tradespeople and the gentry in the town or village. The first example for Cornwall was produced by Pigot. Later editions were produced by commercial companies like Kelly's and called *Post Office Directories*. Kelly's produced a large range of directories well into the twentieth century. Many of these directories are now available on CD and Archive CD books (see pages 226-28).

Poll books, electoral registers and poor law records

Before the Secret Ballot of 1872, poll books in the nineteenth century recorded those individuals registered to vote and also those for whom they intended to vote Modern electoral registers have been made available as public documents and can usually be found in the porch of parish churches. They have also been indexed and made available on the internet and on CD. Earlier electoral registers are available at the Cornish Centre, Redruth, the CRO and in registers for Devon which can be found at the Westcountry Studies Library in Exeter. In Cornwall, records about the application of the Poor Law at parish level are available and include such documents and deeds as overseers' accounts; bastardy bonds; apprenticeship records; and settlement papers.

Pedigrees and visitations

Pedigrees are usually in the form of family trees and in the Victorian era were often produced by the family and may have reflected some wish to link the family to the great and good, or to royalty. They often contain factual errors or fabrications to prove that a link existed or to prove title to land. (A Holman family tree held at the Topsham Museum in Devon measures about six feet wide by four feet high.) Many pedigrees have been printed in publications such as Burke's *Landed Gentry* and Vivian's *Visitations of Cornwall* which bring together various gentry families into one publication.

Miscellaneous records

There are a large number of sources that do not fall into any particular category which include school records, vaccination records, and workhouse records. These may not all have been deposited at record offices and so any success in using them is purely fortuitous.

NATIONAL SOURCES FOR FAMILY HISTORIANS
The census

The first national census took place on 10 March 1801 and one was conducted every ten years after that, the most recent being in 2001. No census was conducted in 1941 due to the war. The censuses of 1801-31 asked for the number of houses, both inhabited and uninhabited, as well as how many families and individuals occupied them. Information on occupations, baptisms, marriages and burials by parish were also asked for.

The original records of the 1801-31 censuses were destroyed. The census of 1841 was the first to ask for more detailed information, including names and county of birth. It is generally considered as the first to be of use to family historians. Census forms would be collected from the householder by an 'enumerator' who would, in theory, assist in completing the forms and fill in extra information where necessary. The enumerator then transcribed the householders' schedules in his enumerator's book. These books are the ones used in tracing family histories. There will be problems where illegible forms had to be transcribed by the enumerator.

Records for the censuses from 1841 to 1901 are available through The National Archives. The census of 1911 will not be available for public access until 2012 as all censuses are released for public scrutiny only after one hundred years have elapsed. Microfilm versions of all these censuses are also held at the Cornish Centre, Redruth.

The national register of births, marriages and deaths

Data for births, marriages and deaths occurring after 1837 are available thanks to the introduction of Civil Registration in that year. These records are indexed both nationally and locally. Registration was not compulsory for all events until approximately 1875.

A project called FreeBMD (see useful internet links on Page 227) has an index to a growing number of the index entries. Registration is organised by districts and it is possible from the indexes only to see an entry giving name, district and the period in which it was registered. The actual certificates are stored in Southport and the indexes are stored at the Family Records Centre in London (see useful organisations on Page 230). In Cornwall a full set of indexes is held at the Cornwall Centre and the Cornwall Family History Society. Local Register Offices also hold certificates.

Ships' passenger lists

Many people left during the diaspora of the Cornish and the movement overseas was by ship. Ships that sailed during the latter three-quarters of the nineteenth century were required to have a manifest of cargo and a list of passengers. Many of these lists survive but not all have been indexed. Finding those manifests which still exist or details of ships that were plying their trade in passengers to the New World and the Antipodes is easy. A site run by Cyndi Howells in the USA called Cyndi's List is useful for this (see internet links on Page 228) and has many pointers to other sites. Newspapers, such as the *New York Times*, and many others, at both the departure and arrival ports, published lists of passengers.

Immigration records

Linked with passenger lists are immigration records which might tie in with naturalisation records for the new country. More than 22 million passengers and members of ships' crews entered the United States through Ellis Island and the Port of New York between 1892 and 1924. However, other routes from Europe to the USA were taken and a major route involved going through the Great Lakes on the US-Canadian border.

Military records

If an ancestor was attached to a military unit it could be useful to investigate what military sources are available. Sites concerning the issuing of medals are increasing and two cover the highest awards for valour and gallantry. The first of these is the Victoria Cross site at http://www.victori-across.net/default.asp. This site lists the actions of 1,354 of the medals awarded since its institution in 1856 and its subsequent antedating to 1854 to cover the Crimean War. A new site which gives details of those service and civilian personnel who have been awarded the George Cross is at http://www.gc-database.co.uk. This medal was first awarded on 30 September 1940 with the most recent being awarded on 31 October 2003. During this time 401 awards have been made. Linked with the above sites is one that has images of the *London Gazette*, where all such awards are 'Gazetted' (see internet links on Page 226).

For servicemen and women who were killed in action during the First and Second World Wars or for civilians who died during the Blitz, the Commonwealth War Graves Commission (CWGC) is an invaluable resource. This task can never be complete as many records were destroyed during the London Blitz. The PRO has started to place the index to the Medal Rolls of the war online and now has names starting with A, B, C and D up and running. There are 5.5 million entries to be entered. All surnames will be searchable on the database by the end of 2004. This resource is at http://www.documentsonline.pro.gov.uk/whats-new.asp.

Local sources available nationally

Many of the local sources listed above are also available nationally and two organisations have been at the forefront to make this information available at a national level: The Federation of Family History Societies, and the Society of Genealogists. More information on both organisations appears on pages 230 and 232 respectively.

Some potential pitfalls

When starting out to research family history your first step will probably be to talk to family members, but beware of the unreliability of oral history, as mentioned above. Firstly all facts, names, dates and places should be collated and noted down. The facts should then be verified. Dates can often be out by up to a decade, although the day and month could be correct.

The census is a good place to start looking at the family as opposed to the individual. Once an individual has been found and the family identified, it is possible to search for the family through the censuses back to 1841. With the help of indexes the process can be eased. A word of warning should be given about indexes – they are the product of people reading the documents at least a century later. There is a danger that they may not correctly interpret the handwriting. In the 1861 Census an entry was transcribed as 'BARCE', but research showed that the family was that of James and Jane PEARCE. Any entry viewed in isolation will need checking with other sources, not necessarily other census records, and where possible all data should be checked against the original or a good copy of it.

Variant spelling of surnames is another problem faced by many family historians. There are also some gentry families where a certain spelling is passed down through the generations. An example of this is the THYNNE family. They could say that they are not related to recent families who spell their name THIN. The gentry has ensured that the first spelling is continued but the original THIN family may well have spelled their name the same way as the gentry in the past, even if the two families are not related.

A single family group, for example, is that of ROTHERE, ROTHERY, ROTHERO, ROTHEROW, ROTHNOUGH, ROTHESOUGH, ROTHEROUGH, ROTHERS, ROTHERO, which illustrate how diverse the variants of a name might be.

Forenames can also be an indication of family history and where an exact year of birth is not known, trends in forenames may give some indication of a period when the name was popular.

The census records the age of people at the time of the census, which was usually around April of the year in question. The age was only recorded from 1851, while in 1841 only children aged 15 or under had their exact age recorded, and older people had their ages rounded down to the nearest five years. This did not occur in the later censuses although there is some strong evidence that people rounded off their ages because they were unsure of their exact age.

Linking individuals together into families

Once information from the various sources have been collated, the next step is to link the information to provide a family structure.

The VINGOE family from the west of Cornwall provides a useful example of a family tree that has been compiled using a variety of data sources such as the Sennen Parish Muster Rolls, baptisms, monumental inscriptions and telephone books. The linking of much of the above information produces a family tree, which would look similar to the example appearing on the following page which shows descendents of one Vingo. We can see that John L. VINGO, born in 1847, died in Mauritius - it would be an interesting branch of the tree to follow why he was there.

With this VINGOE example, there is an important point worth noting, however, which applies generally when it comes to researching family names: there may well be any number of variants in spelling. In this case, we also found VINGOE, VINGOW, VINGOWE, VINGOES, VINOGO, VINGUE, VENGO, VENGOE, VINGAE AND VINGAR. Each of these may have branched out at different times and places The Monumental Inscriptions are vital in getting some linked family details and often cover more than one generation. Any links to modern telephone book entries would probably rely on personal sources and the links back to the very early sources are probably only going to be a matter of conjecture.

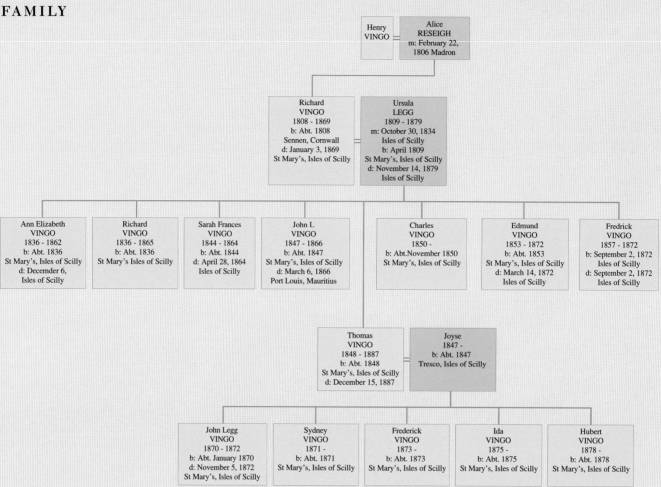

VINGO

Henry VINGO — Alice RESEIGH
m: February 22, 1806 Madron

Richard VINGO
1808 - 1869
b: Abt. 1808
Sennen, Cornwall
d: January 3, 1869
St Mary's, Isles of Scilly

Ursula LEGG
1809 - 1879
m: October 30, 1834
Isles of Scilly
b: April 1809
St Mary's, Isles of Scilly
d: November 14, 1879
Isles of Scilly

Ann Elizabeth VINGO
1836 - 1862
b: Abt. 1836
St Mary's, Isles of Scilly
d: Decemder 6, Isles of Scilly

Richard VINGO
1836 - 1865
b: Abt. 1836
St Mary's Isles of Scilly

Sarah Frances VINGO
1844 - 1864
b: Abt. 1844
d: April 28, 1864
Isles of Scilly

John L VINGO
1847 - 1866
b: Abt. 1847
St Mary's, Isles of Scilly
d: March 6, 1866
Port Louis, Mauritius

Charles VINGO
1850 -
b: Abt.November 1850
St Mary's, Isles of Scilly

Edmund VINGO
1853 - 1872
b: Abt. 1853
St Mary's, Isles of Scilly
d: March 14, 1872
Isles of Scilly

Fredrick VINGO
1857 - 1872
b: September 2, 1872
Isles of Scilly
d: September 2, 1872
Isles of Scilly

Thomas VINGO
1848 - 1887
b: Abt. 1848
St Mary's, Isles of Scilly
d: December 15, 1887

Joyse
1847 -
b: Abt. 1847
Tresco, Isles of Scilly

John Legg VINGO
1870 - 1872
b: Abt. January 1870
d: November 5, 1872
St Mary's, Isles of Scilly

Sydney VINGO
1871 -
b: Abt. 1871
St Mary's, Isles of Scilly

Frederick VINGO
1873 -
b: Abt. 1873
St Mary's, Isles of Scilly

Ida VINGO
1875 -
b: Abt. 1875
St Mary's, Isles of Scilly

Hubert VINGO
1878 -
b: Abt. 1878
St Mary's, Isles of Scilly

USEFUL INTERNET LINKS

- http://beehive.thisiscornwall.co.uk/Falwwfhg
  Fal World-Wide Family History Group
- http://www.devon.gov.uk/library/locstudy/wsl.html
  Devon Local Studies Library
- http://www.gazettes-online.co.uk/
  The London, *Belfast* and *Edinburgh Gazettes*.
- http://www.origins.net/
  English, Irish and Scottish Records – Pay Per View
- http://freepages.genealogy.rootsweb.com/~wbritonad/
  West Briton Newspaper (for the years 1836, 1837 and 1887)
- http://www.census.pro.gov.uk
  1901 Census
- http://www.regiments.org/milhist/uk/lists/bargxref.htm
  For information on finding the exact name of a UK military regiment.
- http://www.statistics.gov.uk/registration/
  Certificates from the national register of births, marriages and deaths

- http://www.genuki.org.uk/

  Genuki Genealogy for the UK and Ireland

- http://freebmd.rootsweb.com

  UK births, marriages and deaths 1837-1900

- http://www.cwgc.org/cwgcinternet/search.aspx

  Commonwealth War Graves Commission

- http://www.british-genealogy.com/resources/registers/indexf.htm

  Information about parish registers

- http://www.ffhs.org.uk/

  Federation of Family History Societies (FFHS) - Home Page

- http://www.catholic-history.org.uk/cfhs/index.htm

  Catholic Family History Society

- http://rylibweb.man.ac.uk/data1/dg/text/method.html

  Methodist Archives

- http://www.pro.gov.uk/

  The National Archives (Public Record Office)

- http://www.jgsgb.org.uk/index.shtml

  Jewish Genealogical Society of Great Britain

- http://www.documentsonline.pro.gov.uk/

  National Archives site

- http://www.sog.org.uk/

  Society of Genealogists Homepage

- http://www.cornwallfhs.com/

  Cornwall Family History Society

- http://www.a2a.org.uk/

  Access to Archives allows searches to be made of a Quarter Sessions

- http://www.devonfhs.org.uk/

  Devon Family History Society

- http://www.ordnancesurvey.co.uk

  Ordnance Survey for modern and historic maps at various scales

- http://freepages.genealogy.rootsweb.com/~kayhin/ukocp.html

  Cornish On-Line Census Project

- http://www.parishchest.com/

  The Parish Chest – One-Stop Shopping Site

- http://west-penwith.org.uk/opc.htm

  Online Parish Clerks for Cornwall

- http://uk2.multimap.com/

  Modern Maps and Air Photographs

- http://www.old-maps.co.uk/

  Old Maps of the UK

- http://www.cornwall.gov.uk
  Cornwall County Council
- http://www.bl.uk/collections/newspapers.html
  British Library – Newspaper Library
- http://www.a2a.pro.gov.uk/
  Access to Archives – Some excellent on-line data from many archives
- http://www.ancestry.co.uk/rx/content.asp?htx=List&dbid=6598
  UK 1891 Census On-line – Pay per View
- http://www.cwgc.co.uk/
  Not the Commonwealth War Graves Commission but worth a look.
- http://www.gazettes-online.co.uk/
  London, Belfast and Edinburgh Gazettes – WW1 and WW2 pages
- http://www.familyrecords.gov.uk/default.htm
  Family Records Centre
- http://www.stivestrust.co.uk/
  The St Ives Ives Trust Archive Study Centre
- http://www.familyhistoryonline.net/
  Federation of Family History Societies, publisher of the National Burial Index
- http://www.friendsreunited.co.uk/ & http://www.genesconnected.co.uk/
  Find school friends – GenesConnected for Family History
- http://www.archivecdbooks.org
  Archive CD Books
- http://www.curiousfox.com/
  A lookup page that is growing.
- http://www.ellisislandrecords.org/
  USA immigration records through Ellis Island from 1892
- http://www.dogpile.com or http://www.dogpile.co.uk
  A good search engine that searches the other engines
- http://www.cyndislist.com/
  Cyndi's List of Genealogy Sites on the internet
- http://www.cyndislist.com/writing.htm
  Cyndi's List - Writing Your Family's History
- http://www.amberskyline.com/treasuremaps/oldhand.html
  Deciphering Old Handwriting
- http://www.familysearch.org/
  FamilySearch LDS (Mormon) Internet Genealogy Service
- http://www.familyhistoryonline.net
  FFHS Online Database - Includes Cornwall – Pay Per View
- http://www.gendex.com/gendex/
  Gendex – WWW Genealogical Index

- http://www.rootsweb.com/
  A large genealogical site
- http://www.rootsweb.com/~jfuller/internet.html
  Genealogy Resources on the internet
- http://members.tripod.com/chrisuphill/cemeteries.htm
  Suezan Elliot's site of monumental inscriptions which provides links to many cemeteries in Cornwall
- http://www.ancestry.com
  Another large site that is now linked with Rootsweb
- http://www.genoot.co.uk/
  Genoot – Family History Internet Resources
- http://www.kindredkonnections.com/
  MyTrees.com - The World's Largest Pedigree-Linked Database

USEFUL ORGANISATIONS AND SOCIETIES

Cornwall Centre

When starting out researching Cornish family history, this is the place to begin. The Centre houses Cornwall's largest library of Cornish printed and published items - books, pamphlets, newspapers, serials, maps, photographs, censuses, trade directories. There are more than 30,000 volumes relating to the history, geography, customs, industries, language and other aspects of Cornish life. There are study facilities and helpful staff on hand to aid beginners.

Cornwall Centre /Kresenn Kernow
Alma Place
REDRUTH
TR15 2AT
Tel. +44 (0)1209 216760
E-mail
cornishstudies.library@cornwall.gov.uk

Cornwall Family History Society (CFHS)

The CFHS was founded in 1976 and has been at the forefront of family history research in Cornwall as well as nationally within the Federation of Family History Societies (FFHS). CFHS is a charity whose aims are to promote and encourage research into family history by providing facilities for such research. It provides a library and publishes books and indexes relating to family history in Cornwall. The 5,000 members of the society are spread across the world. The society's headquarters hold over 8,000 items in the library and are available for members and non-members.

Cornwall Family History Society
5 Victoria Square
TRURO,
TR1 2RD
Tel. +44 (0)1872 264044
E-mail:
Enquiries@CornwallFHS.com

Cornwall Record Office (CRO)

The main purpose of the CRO is to ensure that historical records relating to the people, places and organisations of Cornwall are preserved and made available for public consultation. The main repository for Cornish archives is the CRO in Truro. Held here are all historic parish registers detailing the baptisms, marriages and burials across the 200-plus parishes of the Duchy. The CRO also holds documents dating from the twelfth century to

The Cornwall Record Office
Old County Hall
TRURO
TR1 3AY
Tel. +44 (0)1872 323129
E-mail:
cro@cornwall.gov.uk

THE CORNISH FAMILY

DCLI Museum
The Keep
BODMIN
PL31 1EG
Tel. +44 (0)1208 72810
E-mail
dclimus@lightinfantry.org

The Family Records Centre
1 Myddelton Street
LONDON
EC1R 1UW
Certificate enquiries
Telephone 0870 243 77 88
(UK only)
Census, general enquiries
Tel. +44 (0)20 8392-5300
Advice for local and social historians
Tel. +44 (0)20 8392-5300

FFHS
PO Box 2425
COVENTRY
CV5 6YX
E-mail:
info@ffhs.org.uk

The General Record Office
Smedley Hydro
Trafalgar Road
SOUTHPORT
PR8 2HH
Tel. +44 (0)870 243 7788
General enquiries
E-mail
certificate.services@ons.gov.uk
For all enquiries relating to on-line ordering
E-mail:
col.admin@ons.gov.uk
Opening times:
Mondays to Fridays 8.00am to 8.00pm
Saturdays 9.00am to 4.00pm

the present day, including maps, plans, photographs, parchment documents and books that contain information on local families, businesses, schools, towns and villages.

The Duke Of Cornwall's Light Infantry (DCLI) Museum

The DCLI Museum in Bodmin is based in the Keep of the former DCLI Training Depot. The regiment no longer exists in name, although Old Comrades organisations still meet regularly. The regiment merged with the Somerset Light Infantry in 1959. The new regiment was called the Somerset & Cornwall Light Infantry (SCLI) and in 1968 this regiment formed part of the new large infantry regiment, The Light Infantry. The museum houses a large collection of uniforms, weapons, medals and other memorabilia of the DCLI and the archives hold many details on members of the regiment as well as pictures depicting regimental life.

The Family Records Centre(FRC)

The Family Records Centre houses the search facilities of the General Register Office's Public Search Room and the Census Reading Rooms of The National Archives. The Public Search Room holds paper indexes to the records of all births, deaths and marriages registered in England and Wales since July 1837, adoptions since 1927, and some births, deaths and marriages of British citizens overseas since 1761 including those of the armed forces. The centre also holds census returns from 1841 to 1891. The original registration records are not open to the public, but copies of the entries in the form of birth, marriage and death certificates can be ordered.

Federation of Family History Societies (FFHS)

The FFHS was founded in 1974 and was awarded a grant of arms in 1997. The federation is the umbrella organisation for Family History Societies and membership includes county and area societies in the UK, state societies in the USA and Australia, provincial societies in Canada, specialist societies and one-name societies. FFHS publishes books on family history and holds conferences and seminars. It also makes awards for excellence in various aspects of family history including the Elizabeth Simpson award for the best family history journal. Since 2002 the federation has provided a pay per view online service to family historians and this database contains about 20 million entries from many counties within the UK. The entire Cornwall FHS database, of about 4 million records, forms part of the online database.

The General Register Office (GRO)

The GRO for England and Wales is responsible for ensuring the registration of all births, marriages and deaths that have occurred in England and Wales since 1837 and for maintaining a central archive. The Office works in partnership with local authorities to provide a locally based service at register offices, known as the local registration service. The local registrars send birth, marriage and death register information to the GRO to make up the National Archive.

It is situated at Southport, except for the London based Family Records Centre. The Southport office deals with postal and telephone requests for certificates and the registration of all adoptions made through a court in England and Wales. At the Family Records Centre the indexes of births, marriages and deaths can be searched.

The London Cornish Association (LCA)

The LCA was founded in 1898 and has an active Family History Group that hosts conferences on a variety of family history subjects. This group was formed in 1997. Cornishmen, Cornishwomen, and members of their family by birth, marriage or descent are eligible for membership. Other persons connected with Cornwall may also be admitted as members.

The Morrab Library

This library was founded in 1818 and is located in Penzance in the west of Cornwall. More than 40,000 volumes form the basis of the library and these contain works on subjects including biography, topography, religion, history, antiquities and literature. Nearly 3,000 of the books were printed before 1801 and the library holds extensive runs of early newspapers. About 25,000 photographs, transparencies and negatives depicting life in Cornwall are held in the archives and the total is growing with new donations.

The National Archives (Public Record Office)

The Public Record Office is the National Archive of England, Wales and the United Kingdom. It preserves the records of central government and the courts of law, and is available to the public. The records span an unbroken period from the 11nineteenth century. The archives in Kew have an enormous variety of sources including military records, census returns, maps, statistical information from government departments, land conveyances, shipping records and police records. A look at their website is useful before a visit as it contains links to details and information leaflets about the records held there as well as some online data. Some government documents are opened for public inspection 30 years after the file was closed, except in a few cases where the closure period is longer.

The National Maritime Museum Cornwall (NMMC)

The NMM opened in 1937 and is based in Greenwich in London. A new branch of the NMM in Falmouth was opened to the public with its 'Sea Trials' on 4 December 2002 and is called The National Maritime Museum Cornwall (NMMC). It houses a collection of approximately 140 small craft from the past 150 years. Within the museum is The Bartlett Library, which

The London Cornish Association
Cowethas Kernewek Loundres
Secretary:
Dr Francis Dunstan
26 Sharrow Vale
HIGH WYCOMBE
HP12 3HB
Tel. +44 (0)1494 531703
www.londoncornish.co.uk

The Morrab Library
Morrab Gardens
PENZANCE
TR18 4DA
Tel. +44 (0)1736 364474
E-mail:
Enquiries@morrablibrary.co.uk
Opening times:
Tuesday to Friday: 10am to 4pm
Saturday: 10am to 1pm
Closed Sunday & Monday

National Archives (Public Record Office)
Kew
RICHMOND
TW9 4DU.
Tel. +44 (0)20 8876 3444
E-mail:
enquiry@nationalarchives.gov.uk

NMMC
Discovery Quay
FALMOUTH
TR11 3QY
Tel. +44(0)1326 313388
E-mail
enquiries@nmmc.co.uk
Bartlett Library
Tel. +44 (0)1326 214579
E-mail:
library@nmmc.co.uk

Royal Institution of Cornwall
River Street
Truro TR1 2SJ
Tel. +44 (0)1872 272205
E-mail
RIC@royal-cornwall-museum.freeserve.co.uk

The Librarian,
The Courtney Library
Tel. +44 (0)1872) 272205 Fax
+ 44 (0)1872)240514
E-mail:
courtney.rcmric@btinternet.com

SOG
14 Charterhouse Buildings
Goswell Road
London
EC1M 7BA
Tel. +44 (0)20 7251 8799

The Administrator
Victoria County History
Lansdowne
Pendower Road
Veryan
TRURO TR2 5QL
Tel. +44 (0)1872 501074

Westcountry Studies Library
Castle Street
EXETER
EX4 3PQ
Tel. +44 (0)1392 384216

houses a diverse collection of books, periodicals and archive material available to the public for reference. The library is divided into a book collection, comprising 10,000 maritime reference books, including an extensive run of Lloyd's Registers; research facilities which consist of several databases, the most important of which covers vessels built in Cornwall between 1776 and 1914; and archive material ranging from the Falmouth Harbourmaster's Daily Records from 1880 to 1990, to Acts of Parliament relating to the development of various Cornish harbours.

Royal Insitution of Cornwall (RIC)

Founded in 1818, the RIC is the home of the Royal Cornwall Museum and the Courtney Library and is the oldest established Cornish History Research Centre in the County. The study area of the Library is open to everyone, for reference only, and holds around 30,000 volumes of books, plus periodicals, newspapers, maps, posters, illustrations, parish registers and original documents dating back many centuries. Knowledgeable staff are available to assist.

The Societies Of Genealogists (SOG)

The SOG holds a vast collection of research material and gives guidance and support for those interested in family history. The SOG Library in London has a large collection of family histories, civil registration and census material, and a collection of 9,000 county sources. These include local histories, poll books and directories, topographical material, and the publications of county records and archaeological societies. Also included in the collection is Boyd's Marriage Index, which covers some 2,600 parish registers with nearly seven million names. There is a general card index which contains over three million references.

Victoria County History of Cornwall

The series of Victoria County Histories of England was commissioned in 1899 to provide a countrywide history reference work for English local history. Cornwall has a single volume produced to date and work on further volumes is being undertaken after a slumber of about 100 years.

Their website is www.cornwallforever.net/default.asp?moduleId=14

Westcountry Studies Library

This library is in the Devon Studies Centre in Exeter. It preserves non-archival documentation relating to the counties of Devon, Cornwall, Somerset and Dorset. The collection was enlarged when the old Exeter City collections were merged with the County Library's collections on the local government reorganisation in 1974.

The library contains maps, electoral registers, photographs, newspapers and more than 60,000 books about people, places and the history of the four counties. Holdings include runs of the periodical *Devon & Cornwall Notes & Queries* as well as publications of the *Devon & Cornwall Record Society*, many of which are indexes to parish registers.

SOME USEFUL BOOKS

The following list contains books that can assist in finding sources and explain how to use them. It does not contain books about specific families or areas of Cornwall.

Michael Drake and Ruth Finnegan, *From Family Tree to Family History*, Cambridge University Press, 1994

Michael Drake and Ruth Finnegan, *Sources and Methods for Family and Community Historians: A Handbook*, Cambridge University Press, 1994

Cornwall Family History Society, *Journals of the Cornwall Family History Society*, 1976-2004

Cornwall Record Office, *Index to Cornish Estate duty and Deanery of St Buryan Wills*, Cornwall County Council, 1987

Cornwall Record Office, *Sources for Cornish Family History*, Cornwall County Council, 2002

George Pelling, *Beginning your Family History*, Countryside Books, 1990

Hugh Peskett, *Guide to the Parish and Non-parochial Registers of Devon and Cornwall, 1538-1837*, Devon & Cornwall Record Society, 1979

Robert Pols, *Dating Old Photographs*, Countryside Books, 1993

Stuart Raymond, *Cornwall: A genealogical bibliography (British genealogical bibliographies)*, S.A. & M.J. Raymond, 1994

Pauline Saul & F.C. Markwell, *Tracing Your Ancestors: The A-Z Guide*, Countryside Books, 1991

T.L. Stoate, *Cornwall Protestation Returns, 1641*, T.L. Stoate, 1974

T.L. Stoate, *The Cornwall Military Survey, 1522 with Loan Books and Tinner's Muster Roll c1535*, T.L. Stoate, 1987

T.L. Stoate, *Cornwall Subsidies in the Reign of Henry VIII*, T.L. Stoate, 1985

T.L. Stoate, *Cornwall Hearth and Poll Taxes, 1660-1664*, T.L. Stoate, 1981

W.E. Tate, *The Parish Chest*, Phillimore & Co Ltd, 1983

Charles Thomas, *Views and Likenesses: Early Photographers and their Work in Cornwall and the Isles of Scilly, 1839-70*, The Royal Institution of Cornwall, 1988

Archive CD Books is publishing a number of books about Cornwall as well as copies of the Census Enumerators Books on CD A full list of publications can be found at http://www.archsdivecdbooks.org

NOTES AND REFERENCES

Introduction

1 *Cornwall Family History Society Journal* 100 (2001), 2.

2 Jose Harris, 'Tradition and transformation: society and civil society in Britain, 1945-2001', in Kathleen Burk (ed.), *The British Isles since 1945*, Oxford, 2003, 93.

3 Roy Prideaux, 'Descending lines and the search for connections in an expanding population', *Local Population Studies* 36 (1986), 8-18; Dawn Walker, 'The Cornwall Protestation Returns', *Cornwall Family History Society Journal* 100 (2001), 8.

4 For example John Titford, *Searching for surnames: a practical guide to the meanings and origins*, Newbury, 2002, 146-53.

5 P.S.Morrish, 'History, Celticism and propaganda in the formation of the diocese of Truro', *Southern History* 5 (1983), 238-66.

6 Richard Polwhele, *History of Cornwall*, London, 1806, volume 7, 6-9.

7 The method used here to calculate pre-1801 population is to take the estimates of the English population calculated from family reconstitutions by Wrigley and Schofield, *The Population History of England 1541-1871: A Reconstitution*, Cambridge, 1981, 531-35 and apply these to Cornwall, allowing for periods of faster growth. For a summary of previous population estimates see Jonathan Barry, 'Population distribution and growth in the early modern period' in Roger Kain and William Ravenhill (eds), *Historical Atlas of South West England*, Exeter, 1999, 110-17.

8 Our estimate here is somewhat higher than previous ones. For example Norman Pounds, 'The population of Cornwall before the first Census' in Walter Minchinton (ed.), *Population and marketing: two studies in the history of the south west*, Exeter, 1976, 11-30.1976; Barry, 1999.

9 Malcolm Williams, 'Why is Cornwall poor? Poverty and in-migration since the 1960s', *Contemporary British History* 17 (2003), 55-70.

Chapter One The Changing Family

1 Will Coster, F*amily and Kinship in England 1450-1800*, Harlow, 2001, 25; David Hey, *Family History and Local History in England*, 1987, 142.

2 Coster, 2001, 28.

3 P.A.S.Pool, 'The autobiography of Alexander Daniel of Alverton, 1599-1688', *Journal of the Royal Institution of Cornwall* NS7 (1977), 262-75.

4 Helen Amy, *Clemens: A Family from Cornwall*, 1986, 6-8.

5 Sir Frederick Pedler, *A Pedler Family History*, Colchester, 1984, 36.

6 Pool, 1977.

7 Ralph Budge, 'The Budges of Linkinhorne', *Old Cornwall* 7 (1971), 405-10.

8 Sennen marriage registers.

9 Edmund Vale, *The Harveys of Hayle: engine-builders, shipwrights and merchants of Cornwall*, Truro, 1966.

10 Coster, 2001, 59.

11 Polwhele, *History of Cornwall*, London, 1806, volume 7, 107.

12 Roger Burt, (ed.), *Cornwall's Mines and Miners: nineteenth century studies by George Henwood*, Truro, 1972, 68.

13 Burt, 1972, 70.

14 Burt, 1972, 68.

15 Information from Allen Buckley.

16 James Whetter, *Cornish People in the 15th Century*, Gorran, 1999, 2.

17 Todd Gray, *Harvest Failure in Cornwall and Devon: the Book of Orders and the Corn Surveys of 1623 and 1630-1*, Redruth, xi

18 Polwhele, 1806, 68.

19 Michael Tangye, *Tehidy and the Bassets*, Redruth, 1984, 15.

20 Charles Barham, *On the sanitary state of Truro*, London, 1840, 14.

21 Polwhele, 1806, 38.

22 Polwhele, 1806, 40 and 51.

23 *Register of marriages, baptisms and burials of the parish of Camborne, 1538-1837*, Exeter, 1945, 146.

24 Daniel Defoe, *A Tour Through the Whole Island of Great Britain*, London, 1962, volume 1, 257.

25 K.Theodore Hoppen, *The Mid-Victorian Generation 1846-1886*, Oxford, 1998, 328.

26 Pedler, 1984, 53.

27 Burt, 1972, 110.

28 David Gore, *A Cornish Inheritance: The Harveys of Chacewater*, Basildon, 1997, 52.

29 David Hey, *The Oxford Guide to Family History*, Oxford, 1993, 118.

30 Sharron Schwartz and Roger Parker, *Lanner: A Cornish Mining Parish*, Tiverton, 1998, 2

31 Keith Wrightson, *English Society 1580-1680*, 1982, 46 and Coster, 2001, 40.

32 Ralph Houlbrooke, *The English Family 1450-1700*, Harlow, 1984, 45-9.

33 Mary Giraut (ed.), *The Trevleyan letters to 1840*, Taunton, 1990, 71.

34 Julian Cornwall, *Wealth and Society in Early Sixteenth Century England*, London, 1988, 49 and 118.

35 Keith Skues, *Cornish Heritage*, London, 1983, 367.

36 Richard Carew, *Survey of Cornwall*, London, 1811, 179.

37 Norman Pounds, 'William Carnsew of Bokilly and his diary 1576-7', *Journal of the Royal Institution of Cornwall* NS8 (1978), 14-60.

38 Whetter, 1999, 43.

39 Richard Polwhele, *Traditions and Recollections, Domestic, Clerical and Literary*, London, 1826, 721.

40 Pounds, 1978.

41 Harry Hendrick, *Children, Childhood and English Society, 1880-1990*, Cambridge, 1997, 21.

42 Pat Griffith, 'Thomas Gwyn and friends', *Journal of the Royal Institution of Cornwall* NSII.1 (1993), 290-303.

43 Pool, 1977.

44 James Whetter, 'John and William Pearce, men with problems during the Civil War period', *Old Cornwall* 7 (1970), 250-60.

45 Llana Krausman Ben-Amos, 'Reciprocal bonding: parents and their offspring in early modern England', *Journal of Family History* 25 (2000), 291-312.

46 Whetter, 1999, 85.

47 T.H.Murrin, 'Under the badge of a white eagle – the Godolphins', *Old Cornwall* 8 (1977), 380-87.

48 James Whetter, 'Robert Hoblyn of Nanswhyden 1658-1705, clerk', *Old Cornwall* 7 (1967), 12-21.

49 Griffith, 1993.

50 Amos Miller, 'Sir Richard Grenville, Royalist general 1600-1659', *Journal of the Royal*

Institution of Cornwall NS6 (1971), 220-29.

51 Hopper, 1998, 317.

52 Anon, 'A 17th-century Cornish marriage settlement', *Old Cornwall* 9 (1979), 39-41.

53 P.A.S.Pool, 'Retirement of a Cornish farmer, 1662', *Devon and Cornwall Notes and Queries* 28 (1959-61), 25.

54 Hey, 1993, 111.

55 Peter Laslett, *The World We Have Lost*, London, 1965.

56 Coster, 2001, 54-56.

57 Census enumerators' books, 1861 and 1891.

58 David Cullum, 'Society and Economy in West Cornwall c1588-1750', unpublished PhD thesis, University of Exeter, 1993.

59 Cullum, 1993, 288.

60 David Levine, *Family Formation in an Age of Nascent Capitalism*, New York, 1977.

61 Leonore Davidoff, 'The Family in Britain', in *The Cambridge Social History of Britain*, Part 2, Cambridge, 1990, 75.

62 Davidoff, 1990, 88.

63 John Rowe, *Cornwall in the Age of the Industrial Revolution*, Liverpool, 1953, 225-26.

64 Bernard Deacon, 'The reformulation of territorial identity: Cornwall in the eighteenth and nineteenth centuries', unpublished PhD thesis, Open University, 2001, 252.

65 Charles Barham, 'Report on the employment of children and young persons in the mines of Cornwall and Devonshire', *British Parliamentary Papers* 1842 (380) XV, 753-54, sets out the various collateral aids. See also Seymour Tremenheere, 'Report on the state of education in the mining districts of Cornwall', *British Parliamentary Papers* 1841 (371) XX, 88.

66 Wally Seccombe, *Weathering the Storm: Working-Class Families from the Industrial Revolution to the Fertility Decline*, London, 1993.

67 *West Briton*, 6 February 1852.

68 *West Briton*, 2 July 1858.

69 Alice Arden and to Bill Giles: changing nightmares of intimate violence in England, 1558-1869', *Journal of British Studies* 40 (2001), 184-212.

70 Gill Burke, 'The decline of the independent bal maiden: the impact of change in the Cornish mining industry', in Angela John (ed.), *Unequal Opportunities: Women's Employment in England 1800-1918*, Oxford, 1986, 194: Sharron Schwartz, '"No place for a woman": Gender at work in Cornwall's metalliferous mining industry', in Philip Payton (ed.) *Cornish Studies Eight* (2000), 69-96.

71 Burke, 1986, 194.

72 Anna Clark, *The Struggle for the Breeches: Gender and the Making of the British Working Class*, Berkeley, 1995, 126-30.

73 Michael Anderson, *Family Structure in Nineteenth Century Lancashire*, Cambridge, 1971.

74 Barry Reay, *Microhistories: demography, society and culture in rural England, 1800-1930*, Cambridge, 1996.

75 Steven Ruggles, Prolonged Connections: *The Rise of the Extended Family in Nineteenth Century England and America*, Madison, 1987.

76 Ruth Finnegan and Michael Drake, *From Family Tree to Family History*, Cambridge, 1992, 95.

77 Thomas Collection, CSM Library, Day and night book Dolcoath mine captains, December 1822–October 1823. I am indebted to Allen Buckley for this reference.

78 John Harris, *My Autobiography*, London, 1882.

79 Sub-Registrar General's Annual Reports, *British Parliamentary Papers*.

80 Hoppen, 1998, 317.

81 Hendrick, 1997, 18.

82 Paul Thompson, *The Edwardians: The Remaking of British Society*, St Albans, 1977, 43.

83 John Burnett (ed.), *Destiny Obscure. Autobiographies of Childhood, Education and Family from 1820s to the 1920s*, London, 1982, 16.

84 Hopper, 1998, 331.

85 Hopper, 1998, 332.

86 Alice M.Brannlund, *Memoirs of a Cornish Housewife*, no date, 1.

87 Cited in Hopper, 1998, 316.

88 Harris, 1882, 67.

89 Harris, 103, 11, 5.

90 John James, 'Journal', n.d., copy in Cornish Studies Library, Redruth.

91 W.H.Hudson, *The Land's End*, London, 1908, 7 and 111-12.

92 Charles T.Trevail, *The Life and Reminiscences of Charles T. Trevail*, Bristol,1927, 16.

93 Many thanks to John Probert for furnishing the details of this fascinating case.

94 *Western Daily Mercury*, 9 January 1914.

95 Hendrick, 1997, 31.

96 Mary Buck, Lyn Bryant and Malcolm Williams, *Housing and Households in Cornwall: a pilot study of Cornish families*, University of Plymouth, 1993.

97 Michael Peplar, *Family Matters: A History of Ideas about Family since 1945*, Harlow, 2002, 4-5.

98 Lyn Bryant, 'The Cornish family', in Philip Payton (ed.), *Cornwall Since the War*, Redruth, 1993, 181-97.

99 David Dunkerley and C.Wallace, 'Young people and employment in the south west', *Journal of Interdisciplinary Economics* 4 (1992), 225-39.

100 Paul Cockerham, 'Continuity and change: memorialisation and the Cornish funeral monument industry, 1497-1660', unpublished PhD Thesis, University of Exeter, 2003.

101 Hugh Seymour Tremenheere, *Memorials of My Life*, London, 1885, 26.

102 Burt, 72, 220.

103 Harris, 1882, 10.

104 Hey, 1993, 140.

105 Family tree in the possession of John Probert, Redruth.

106 Edward Freeman, Professor of History at Oxford had dismissed the craze for pedigrees in these words in 1877 (Cited in Hey, 1993, 140).

Chapter Two By Tre, Pol and Pen Will Ye Know Most Cornishmen?

1 Oliver Padel, 'From Cornish place-name to surname in Cornwall', *Cornwall Family History Society Journal* 35 (1985), 19-20.

2 Richard McKinley, *Norfolk and Suffolk Surnames in the Middle Ages*, Chichester, 1975, 22.

3 J.A.Giggs, 'Surname geography: a study of the Giggs family name 1450-1989', *The East Midland Geographer* 17 (1994), 58-68.

4 Stephen Wilson, *The Means of Naming: A social and cultural history of personal naming in Western Europe*, London, 1998, 115.

5 McKinley, 1975, 77.

6 Richard McKinley in David Postles, *The Surnames of Devon*, Oxford, 1995, 92-95.

7 McKinley, 1995, 88-92.

8 Percy Reaney, *A Dictionary of British Surnames*, London, 1970, 42; Patricia Hanks, Flavia Hodges, A.D.Mills and Adrian Room, *The Oxford Names Companion*, Oxford, 2002, 85.

9 Hanks et al, 2002, 90.

10 Reaney, 1970, 203; Hanks et al, 2002, 383.

11 T.L.Stoate (ed.), *Cornwall Subsidies in the Reign of Henry VIII*, Bristol, 1985, 38-39. Most of the references to Cornish surnames in the 16th century in this chapter come from this source.

12 Hanks et al, 2002, 273.

13 Hanks et al, 2002, 652.

14 Hanks et al, 2002, 481.

15 Hanks et al, 2002, 530, 537.

16 Hanks et al, 2002, 280.

17 Hanks et al, 2002, 478.

18 Hanks et al, 2002, 324.

19 Hanks et al, 2002, 322.

20 Hanks et al, 2002, 537.

21 Hanks et al, 2002, 134.

22 Hanks et al, 2002, 276.

23 Oliver Padel, 'Cornish surnames in 1327', *Nomina* 9 (1985), 81-87.

24 Personal communication from Oliver Padel, December 2003.

25 Joseph Hambley Rowe (ed.), *Cornwall Feet of Fines*, Exeter, 1914, volume 1, 356.

26 Hanks et al, 2002, 477-78.

27 George Redmonds, *Surnames and genealogy: a new approach*, Bury, 2002.

28 David Hey, *Family Names and Family History*, London, 2000; David Hey and George Redmonds, *Yorkshire Surnames and the Hearth Tax Returns of 1672-73*, York, 2002.

29 Reaney, 1970, 179.

30 Oliver Padel, *Cornish Place-name Elements*, Nottingham, 1985, 258.

31 Personal communication from Oliver Padel, December 2003.

32 Hanks et al, 2002, 73.

33 T.L.Stoate (ed.), *The Cornwall Military Survey 1522 with the Loan Books and a Tinners Muster Roll* c.1535, Bristol, 1987.

34 Oliver Padel, 'Place-Names', in Roger Kain and William Ravenhill (eds), *The Historical Atlas of South West England*, Exeter, 1999, 88-94.

35 Hanks et al, 2002, 337.

36 Stoate, 1985, 142.

37 T.L.Stoate (ed.), *The Cornwall Protestation Returns 1641*, Bristol, 1974.

38 Hanks et al, 2002, 581.

39 LDS, *1881 British Census*, CD-ROM.

40 Hanks et al, 2002, 348.

41 Hanks et al, 2002, 283.

42 Cited in David Hey, *Family History and Local History in England*, London, 1987, 28.

43 Padel, 'Cornish surnames', 1985.

44 Postles, 1995, 112, 115.

45 Peter Ellacott, 'The Borlase family', *Cornwall Family History Society Journal* 92 (1999), 12-13.

46 Padel, 'From Cornish place-name', 1985.

47 Information from Peter Mariott of Mevagissey.

48 Oliver Padel, 'Geoffrey of Monmouth and Cornwall', *Cambridge Medieval Celtic Studies* 8 (1984), 1-27.

49 Oliver Padel, *Cornish Place-Names*, Penzance, 1988, 15.

50 Padel, 1988, 168-69 and 105.

51 Padel, 'Cornish surnames', 1985.

52 H.S.A.Fox and O.J.Padel, *The Cornish Lands of the Arundells of Lanherne, Fourteenth to Sixteenth Centuries*, Exeter, 2000, cxxiv-cxxxvii.

53 Fox and Padel, 2000, 51 and 118.

54 Fox and Padel, 2000, 67 and 113.

55 Fox and Padel, 2000, 78 and 122.

56 Fox and Padel, 2000, cxxxiv.

57 Fox and Padel, 2000, 126 and 83-84.

58 Fox and Padel, 2000, 69 and 113.

59 Fox and Padel, 2000, 122, 78, 116, 57.

60 Matthew Spriggs, 'Where Cornish was spoken and when: a provisional synthesis', in Philip Payton (ed.) *Cornish Studies Eleven*, Exeter, 2004, 228-269, pulls together the evidence of placenames and contemporary comments.

61 Fox and Padel, 2000, cxxix.

62 Stoate, 1987, 176.

63 Robert Morton Nance, 'Celtic personal names of Cornwall', *Old Cornwall* 4 (1943-51), 10-17 and 61-68.

64 Padel, 1988, 103.

65 P.L.Hull (ed.), *The Cartulary of Launceston Priory*, Exeter, 1987, 12.

66 Hanks et al, 2002, 523.

67 Nance, 1943-51.

68 Personal communication from Oliver Padel, December 2003.

69 Henry Jenner, *A Handbook of the Cornish Language*, London, 1904; Morton Nance, 1943-51.

70 Hanks et al, 2002, 329.

71 Nance, 1943-51.

72 Nance, 1943-51.

73 Nance, 1943-51.

74 Nance, 1943-51.

75 Padel, *Cornish Place-Name Elements*, 1985, 152.

76 T.L.Stoate, *Cornwall Hearth and Poll Taxes 1660-1664*, Bristol, 1981.

77 Fox and Padel, 2000, cxxx.

78 Wilson, 1998, 148.

79 For the argument that Cornish was only spoken west and south of Helston in the early 16th century see J.P.D.Cooper, *Propaganda and the Tudor State*, Oxford, 2003, 65 and 257. Surname evidence thoroughly refutes this.

80 H.L.Douch (ed.), *1569 Muster Roll*, Bristol, 1984.

81 Wilson, 1998, 109-11.

82 David Hey, *The Oxford Guide to Family History*, Oxford, 1993, 38.

83 Hanks et al, 2002, 629.

84 Hanks et al, 2002, 356.

Chapter Three Cornish Families on the Move

1 John Chynoweth, *Tudor Cornwall*, Stroud, 2002, 59.

2 Chynoweth, 2002, 50: Anne Duffin, *Faction and Faith: Politics and Religion of the Cornish Gentry before the Civil War*, Exeter, 1996, 18-19.

3 Chynoweth, 2002, 51; Duffin, 1996, 8-9.

4 Chynoweth, 2002, 56.

5 Chynoweth, 2002, 150; Duffin, 1996, 22.

6 Veronica Chesher, 'Some Cornish landowners 1690-1760: a social and economic study', unpublished B.Litt thesis, Oxford University, 1957, 211.

7 G.C.Boase, *Collectanea Cornubiensis*, Truro, 1890, 488-92.

8 Denys Bradford Barton, *A History of Tin Mining and Smelting in Cornwall*, Truro, 1967, 25.

9 Edwin Jaggard, *Cornwall Politics in the Age of Reform*, Woodbridge, 1999, 19.

10 Boase, 1890, 488-92.

11 Allen Buckley, *The Cornish Mining Industry: a brief history*, Penryn, 1992, 16.

12 Boase, 1890, 1252.

13 Barton, 1967, 24.

14 Cited in Boase, 1890, 1332-40.

15 Barton, 1967, 55.

16 Boase, 1890, 972-973.

17 Boase, 1890, 978.

18 Gill Burke, 'The Cornish miner and Cornish mining industry 1870-1921', unpublished PhD thesis, University of London, 1981, 118-24; Cyril Noall, *Levant, the mine beneath the sea*, Truro, 1970, 67.

19 Clive Carter, *Cornish Engineering 1801-2001: Two centuries of industrial excellence in Camborne*, Camborne, 2001.

20 Manuscript of Elizabeth Trounson, 1993, in possession of Mr John Probert, Redruth.

21 Patricia Hanks, Flavia Hodges, A.D.Mills and Adrian Room, *The Oxford Names Companion*, Oxford, 2002, 261.

22 Hanks et al , 2002, 677.

23 Oliver Padel, *Cornish Place-name Elements*, Nottingham, 1985, 206.

24 Padel, 1985, 112.

25 Padel, 1985, 66.

26 Harold Fox and Oliver Padel (eds), *The Cornish Lands of the Arundells of Lanherne, Fourteenth to Sixteenth Centuries*, Exeter, 2000, 9/10.

27 Joseph Hambley Rowe (ed.), *Cornwall Feet of Fines*, Exeter, 1914, volume 1, 320.

28 Rowe, 1914, 362, 415.

29 Hanks et al, 2002, 173.

30 Oliver Padel, *Cornish Place-Names*, Penzance, 1988, 97.

31 Bernard Deacon, '"A race apart": the fishing communities of the west in the nineteenth century', *Old Cornwall* 10 (1988), 268-71.

32 Rowe, 1914, 357, 402.

33 Padel, 1985, 188.

34 Rowe, 1914, 289.

35 Fox and Padel, 2000, 136.

36 Padel, 1985, 104.

37 Robert Morton Nance, 'Celtic personal names of Cornwall', *Old Cornwall* 4 (1943-51), 10-17 and 61-68.

38 Nance, 1943-51.

39 Rowe, 1914, 63 and 86.

40 David Postles, *The Surnames of Devon*, Oxford, 1995, 183.

41 Hanks et al, 2002, 265.

42 Hanks et al, 2002, 485.

43 Information from Mr William Harry of California.

44 Fox and Padel, 2000, 84, 126.

45 Hanks et al, 2002, 487.

46 Nance, 1943-51.

47 Hanks et al, 2002, 465.

48 Postles, 1995, 173.

49 Percy Reaney, *A Dictionary of British Surnames*, London, 1970, 30.

Chapter Four To Go or To Stay?

1 David Hey, *The Oxford Guide to Family History*, Oxford, 1993, 64.

2 James Whetter, *The Bodrugans: a study of Cornish medieval knightly family*,
Gorran, 1995, 101.

3 Oliver Padel, 'Cornish surnames in 1327', *Nomina* 9 (1985), 81-87.

4 Although the 1327 tax subsidy lists may possibly underestimate the presence of poorer
people from foreign lands, James Whetter (*Cornwall in the 13th century: a study in social
and economic history*, Gorran, 1998, 218-21) notes evidence of Irish, French, Flemings and
Jews as well as Welsh, Bretons and English in Cornwall at this time.

5 David Postles, *The Surnames of Devon*, Oxford, 1995, 63-64.

6 E.D.Lloyd, 'The Egloskerry Barons', *Cornwall Family History Society Journal* 8
(1978), 12-15.

7 Barbara Marlow, 'The Cornish Entrepreneurs', *Cornwall Family History Society Journal*
61 (1991), 38-39.

8 Ken Harrison, 'My Cogar ancestry', *Cornwall Family History Society Journal* 59
(1991), 35.

9 Joshua Behenna, 'Sir Henry Irving's Cornish ancestry', *Cornwall Family History Society
Journal* 71 (1994), 6-7.

10 G.Hugo, 'Migration and the Family', *Family: Challenges for the Future*, United Nations
Publications E.95.IV.4, 1996, 335-78.

11 Hugo, 1996, 337.

12 A.L. Rowse, *The Cornish in America*, Redruth, 1967, 35.

13 Rowse, 1967, 38-42.

14 Rowse, 1967, 59-69 and 85-114.

15 N. Rodger, '"A Little Navy of Your Own Making": Admiral Boscawen and the Cornish
Connection in the Royal Navy' in Duffy, M., (ed.), *Parameters of British Naval Power,
1650-1850*, Exeter, 1992.

16 A. Moorehead, *The Fatal Impact: The Invasion of the South Pacific 1767-1840*,
Sydney, 1987.

17 W. Bligh, *The Mutiny On Board the Bounty*, 1787, republished Guildford 1981.

18 R. Hughes, *The Fatal Shore: A History of the Transportation of Convicts to Australia,
1787-1868*, London, 1988.

19 J. Cook, *To Brave Every Danger*, 1994.

20 L. Lankton, *Cradle to Grave: Life, Work, and Death at the Lake Superior Copper
Mines*, New York, 1993, 7.

21 Dudley Baines, *Emigration from Europe, 1815-1930*, Cambridge, 1995, 26-7.
22 Dudley Baines, *Migration in a Mature Economy and Internal Migration in England and Wales, 1861-1900*, Cambridge, 1985, 158-59.
23 Baines, 1985, 158-59.
24 J.Hicks, 'The Cornish in Cardiff', *Cornwall Family History Society Journal* 70 (1993), 18-19.
25 PRO Home Office Papers 52.
26 Typescript of letter in possession of author.
27 *West Briton*, 10 February 1832.
28 Typescript of letter in possession of author.
29 *West Briton*, 10 February 1832.
30 *West Briton*, 6 April 1832.
31 Typescript of letter in possession of author.
32 http://freepages.genealogy.rootsweb.com/~cornwall/diary/rrun.htm Rundell's diary transcribed by Phil Ellery, 2000.
33 M.J.L. Wickes, *The Westcountry Preachers: A History of the Bible Christians 1815-1907*, Bideford, 1987, 52-59.
34 http://freepages.genealogy.rootsweb.com/~cornwall/diary/rrun.htm Robins' diary transcribed by Phil Ellery, 2000.
35 http://freepages.genealogy.rootsweb.com/~cornwall/diary/rrun.htm
36 Margaret James-Korany, "Blue Books' as Sources for Cornish Emigration History', in Philip Payton (ed.) *Cornish Studies One*, Exeter, 1993, 31-45.
37 Sharron Schwartz, 'Migration to the United States, 1815-1930: Preliminary Comparative Demographics for the Redruth and St Austell Registration Districts', *Cornish History Network Newsletter* 6, 1999. Some miners also worked smallholdings and this probably accounts for the high degree of movement of 'farmers' from the Redruth Registration District.
38 Bernard Deacon, 'The reformulation of territorial identity: Cornwall in the eighteenth and nineteenth centuries', unpublished PhD thesis, Open University, 2001, 218-19.
39 For more information see Bernard Deacon, 'Proto-industrialisation and Potatoes: A Revised Narrative for Nineteenth Century Cornwall', in Philip Payton (ed.) *Cornish Studies Five*, Exeter, 1997, 64-84.
40 Sharron Schwartz, 'Exporting the Industrial Revolution: Trevithick and the Migration of British Steam-Engineering Technology to Latin America', *Journal of the Trevithick Society*, 2001, 3-12
41 Sharron Schwartz, 'Exporting the Industrial Revolution: The Migration of Cornish Mining Technology to Latin America in the Early Nineteenth Century', in H.S. Macpherson and W. Kaufman (eds.), *New Perspectives in Transatlantic Studies*, New York, 2002, 143-58.
42 See Sharron Schwartz, 'Cornish Migration to Latin America: A Global and Transnational Perspective', unpublished PhD thesis, University of Exeter, 2003, chapter 4.
43 See www.ex.ac.uk/cornishlatin for a transcription.
44 www.ex.ac.uk/cornishlatin
45 *West Briton*, 30 October 1829.
46 See Schwartz, 2003, chapter 7 for details of Cornish migration networks that bound parishes in Cornwall with regions in Latin America.
47 Schwartz, 2003, chapter 9.

48 H/1/17 Jenkin Letter Books, Royal Institution of Cornwall. See Schwartz, 2003, chapter 9.

49 Thomas Malthus (1766-1834) was a curate whose ideas were highly controversial, particularly his most celebrated work, the *Essay on Population* (1798). He condemned the Poor Laws, in particular, for apparently allowing the poor too much freedom to breed.

50 Typescript of letter in possession of author.

51 Cornwall Record Office P 79/81/1.

52 See Pat Lay, 'Not What They Seemed? Cornish Assisted Immigrants in New South Wales 1837-77', in Philip Payton (ed.), *Cornish Studies Three*, Exeter, 1995, 36-37 for an explanation of these schemes. From 1835 a bounty of £20 was given to young married mechanics and agricultural labourers who wished to emigrate to Australia.

53 Lay, 1995.

54 See Philip Payton, *The Cornish Overseas*, Fowey, 1999, chapter 3 for a comprehensive coverage of Latimer and assisted passage schemes.

55 Lay, 1995.

56 E.E. Bolitho, *Reefton School of Mines: Stories of Jim Bolitho*, Reefton, 1999, 29.

57 For the chronology of mineral discoveries and subsequent settlement patterns see Philip Payton, *The Cornish Miner in Australia: Cousin Jack Down Under*, Redruth, 1984.

58 John Rowe, *Changing Times and Fortunes: A Cornish Farmer's Life 1828-1904*, St Austell, 1996, 105-13.

59 James-Korany, 1993, 38.

60 Baines, 1995, 46.

61 James-Korany, 1993, 43. She gives many more interesting examples.

62 *West Briton*, 30 August 1850.

63 A number of good examples are given in D.B.Barton, *Essays in Cornish Mining History 1*, 1968, 20-22.

64 *Daily News* 14 Jan 1879.

65 Migration to America is covered by A.C.Todd, *The Cornish Miner in America*, Truro, 1967 and John Rowe, *The Hard Rock Men: Cornish Immigrants and the North American Mining Frontier*, Liverpool, 1973. Migration to South Africa is detailed by Richard Dawe, *Cornish Pioneers in South Africa: Gold, Diamonds, Copper and Blood*, St Austell, 1998, and to Latin America by Schwartz, 2003. For the migration of stonemasons see H.Rossler, 'Constantine Stonemasons in Search of Work Abroad, 1870-1900', in Philip Payton (ed.) *Cornish Studies Two*, Exeter, 1994, 48-82.

66 Sharron Schwartz and Roger Parker, *Lanner: A Cornish Mining Parish*, Tiverton, 1998, 153.

67 Rowse, 1967, 422. The hotel went bankrupt in the depression years.

68 Rowse, 1967, 333.

69 *West Briton*, 24 September 1896; Bernard Deacon and Philip Payton, 'Reinventing Cornwall' in Philip Payton (ed.) *Cornish Studies One*, Exeter, 1993, 68.

70 A.L.Rowse, *A Cornish Childhood*, reprint Redruth, 1998, 34-5.

71 See Oswald Pryor, *Australia's Little Cornwall*, Rigby, 1962.

72 *West Briton*, 13 September 1894; Gill Burke, 'The Cornish Diaspora of the Nineteenth Century', in Marks S., and Richardson P., (eds.), *International Labour Migration: Historical Perspectives*, London, 1984, 57-75.

73 Herbert Thomas, *Mining Interviews*, Camborne, 1896.

74 Roger Burt, *The British Lead Mining Industry*, Redruth, 1984, 195.

75 Alan Pearson, 'Cornish miners in coal mines', *Old Cornwall* 9 (1981), 222-25.

76 *West Briton*, 28 Sep 1871 and 16 Oct 1873.

77 LDS, *1881 British Census*, CD-ROM.

78 John Marshall and John Walton, *The Lake Counties from 1830 to the mid-twentieth century*, Manchester, 1981, 168.

79 Bryn Trescatheric, *Roose – a Cornish village in Furness*, Barrow, 1983, 13.

80 LDS CD-ROM.

81 Information from Global Migration Programme database.

82 Trevor and Margaret Hill, 'The Baragwaneths of Towednack', *Cornwall Family History Society Journal* 65 (1992), 21-22.

83 Anon, *A Cornish Waif's Story: an autobiography*, London, 1954, 26.

84 Bernard Deacon, 'A forgotten migration stream: the Cornish movement to England and Wales in the nineteenth century', in Philip Payton (ed.) *Cornish Studies Six*, Exeter, 1998, 96-117.

85 Examples from LDS CD-ROM.

86 Data provided by the Cornish Global Migration Programme database.

87 Data provided by the Cornish Global Migration Programme database.

88 Dawe, 1998, 24.

89 Data provided by the Cornish Global Migration Programme database.

90 Data provided by the Cornish Global Migration Programme database

91 Rowse, 1967, 30-31.

92 Schwartz and Parker, 1998, 168-71.

93 http://www.greywall.demon.co.uk/genealogy/

94 As recounted to Sharron Schwartz by a family historian.

Chapter Five 'What We Belong to Be'

1 Patrick Laviolette, 'Cornwall's visual cultures in perspective' in Philip Payton (ed.), *Cornish Studies Eleven*, Exeter, 2004, 157.

2 Mary Lakeman, *Early Tide: A Mevagissey Childhood*, Redruth, 1987, 41 and 29.

3 For example Charles Phythian-Adams (ed.), *Societies, Cultures and Kinship, 1580-1850: Cultural Provinces and English Local History*, Leicester, 1993.

4 W.H.Hudson, *The Land's End*, London, 1908, 179-81.

5 A.L.Rowse, cited in Philip Payton, '"I was before my time, caught betwixt and between:" A.L.Rowse and the writing of British and Cornish history' in Philip Payton (ed.), *Cornish Studies Eleven*, Exeter, 2004, 30.

6 Although see Bernard Deacon, *The Concise History of the Cornish People*, Cardiff, forthcoming.

7 Robert Morton Nance, 'Celtic personal names of Cornwall', *Old Cornwall* 4 (1943-51), 68.

8 Colin Kidd, *British Identities before Nationalism: Ethnicity and Nationhood in the Atlantic World, 1600-1800*, Cambridge, 1999.

9 Peter Hull (ed.), *The Cartulary of Launceston Priory*, Exeter, 1987, 9.

10 For a version of this argument see Mark Stoyle, *West Britons: Cornish identities and the early modern British state*, Exeter, 2002.

11 John Norden, *Speculi Britanniae Pars: A Topographical and Historical Description of Cornwall*, London, 1728, 28; Richard Carew, *Survey of Cornwall*, London, 1811 (originally published 1602), 184.

12 Stoyle, 2002, 66-90.

13 Stoyle, 2002, 134-56.

14 Cited in Stoyle, 2002, 32.

15 John Rowe, *Cornwall in the Age of Industrialisation*, Liverpool, 1953, 36.

16 Nick von Tunzelman, *Steam Power and British Industrialization to 1860*, Oxford, 1978.

17 Diary of Richard Tyacke, 1826-29, Cornwall Record Office AD 715.

18 Fortescue Hitchins and Samuel Drew, *The History of Cornwall*, Helston, 1824.

19 Philip Payton, *The Cornish in Australia*, Redruth, 1984, 36.

20 L.A. Copeland, 'The Cornish in Southwest Wisconsin', *Wisconsin Historical Collection*
XIV (1998); *Cornubian*, 2 November 1922.

21 J. Jewell, *Cornish in America: Linden, Wisconsin*, Mineral Point, 1990, 63-64.

22 *Cornishman*, 24 July 1913.

23 *Cornubian*, 17 January 1913.

24 *Cornubian*, 19 April 1913.

25 *West Briton*, 20 February 1900.

26 Richard Dawe, *Cornish Pioneers in South Africa*, St Austell, 1998, 271-77.

27 *Cornubian*, 27 February 1908; *Cornish Post and Mining News*, 10 February 1910.

28 Bernard Deacon, '"The hollow jarring of the distant steam engine": images of Cornwall
between West Barbary and Delectable Duchy', in Ella Westland (ed.), *Cornwall: The
Cultural Construction of Place*, Penzance, 1997, 7-24.

29 A.L.Rowse, *A Cornish Childhood*, London, 1942; Ann Treneer, School House in the
Wind, London, 1944.

30 Ronald Perry, 'Cornwall circa 1950' in Philip Payton (ed.), *Cornwall Since the War:
The Contemporary History of a European Region*, Redruth, 1993, 22-46.

31 Garry Tregidga, 'The politics of the Celto-Cornish Revival, 1886-1939', in Philip Payton
(ed.), *Cornish Studies Five*, Exeter, 1997, 125-50.

32 Jack Clemo, *Confessions of a Rebel*, London, 1949.

33 Copeland, 1898, 330.

34 Typescript in possession of the author.

35 Payton, 1984, 211.

36 Published Census, 1971-91.

37 David Held, *A Globalizing World? Culture, Economic, Politics*, London, 2000, 1-2.

38 See G.Mulgan, *Connexity: Responsibility, Freedom, Business and Power in the New
Century*. London, 1998; Held, 2000.

39 Amy Hale and Philip Payton, 'The Celtic Diaspora', in *New Directions in Celtic Studies*,
Exeter, 2000, 95.

40 Cornish Foundation For North America leaflet, 1999.

41 J.Jolliffe, 'The price of success?' *Tam Kernewek* 17, 1999, 2-3.

42 H. Rheingold, *The Virtual Community*, London, 1995, 6.

43 http://www.cornwall24.co.uk/cornish/news11.htm: accessed December 5 2002.

44 Robin Cohen, *Global Diasporas*, London, 1997, ix-x.

45 Bernard Deacon, *The Cornish and the Council of Europe Framework Convention for
the Protection of National Minorities*, Redruth, 2000.

46 Gage McKinney, cited in Philip Payton, *The Cornish Overseas*, Fowey, 1999, 399.

47 Sharron Schwartz, '"Bridging the Great Divide": Cornish labour migration to America
and the evolution of transnational identity', in N. Winn and A. Thompson (eds.), *Citizens,
Nations, Cultures'*, London, forthcoming.

48 Alan Kent, 'Celtic nirvanas: constructions of Celtic in contemporary British youth
culture' in David Harvey, Rhys Jones, Neil McInroy and Christine Milligan,
Celtic geographies: old culture, new times, London, 2002, 208-226.

LIST OF SUBSCRIBERS

Adlam, Tania
Taupo, Central Plateau, NZ

A'Lee, Janet
Tiverton, Devon

Allen, Mr Jack
Taunton, Somerset

Allen, Madeleine
Houghton, West Sussex

Allen, Barbara
(Cocking)
Flint, MI, USA

Allen, Rodney J
Newquay, Cornwall

Allen, Clive David
County Wexford, Ireland

Allen, C Barbara
St Keverne, Cornwall

Alvarez-Buylla,
Mrs Mary
Guildford, Surrey

Amos, Harriet
(Hosking)
Bakersfield, CA, USA

Anderson, Patricia
Green Valley, AZ, USA

Andrew, D Pentreath
Alton, Hampshire

Andrewartha, W L
Caulfield, VIC, Australia

Andrews, Trevor
Brightlingsea, Essex

Angear, Thomas
Northwood, Middlesex

Annear, John Marshal
Dulwich, London

Annear, Nicholas
Marshall Poon
Dulwich, London

Annear, Mark
O'Donovan Poon
Dulwich, London

Annear, Richard
O'Donovan
Swansea, Wales

Annear, Tristram David
Setauket, NY, USA

Annear, Michael
William
Brandon, Suffolk

Archer, James
Bowmanville, ON, Canada

Archer (née
Kneebone), Rosemary
Trenarren, Cornwall

Argall, Squadron
Leader Ian H A
St Keverne, Cornwall

Axten, Janet
St Ives, Cornwall

Baker, Tessa
Lezant, Cornwall

Ball, D P
Camborne, Cornwall

Balls, Mrs G J
Penzance, Cornwall

Banks, (née Trewavas)
Gillian
York, Yorkshire

Bannister, A G
Padstow, Cornwall

Barbery, the family
Ladock, Cornwall

Barnes, Pauline Robbie
Richards DJJ
Godolphin Cross, Cornwall

Barnett, Pam
*Christchurch,
Canterbury, NZ*

Bartlett St Clair,
Elizabeth
Greenville, DE, USA

Bassett, Christopher
James
Truro, Cornwall

Bawden, Michael
*Rickmansworth,
Hertfordshire*

Baxter, John
Trebetherick, Cornwall

Baxter, Bill Polwin
Aberdeen, Scotland

Beale, D J
Bridgend, Cardiff

Beard, Lorraine
and Francis
Green Point, NSW, Australia

Beautyman, Paul
Aviemore, Scotland

Beckerleg, Mrs A
Newquay, Cornwall

Bellman, Daphne
Maynard
Launton, Oxon

Bellman, Brian
Maynard
Silver Spring, MD, USA

Benallack, William G
Lansing, MI, USA

Bendle, Margaret
Newquay, Cornwall

Bennett, Clive and
Lynda
Ruislip, Middlesex

Bennett, William
Gordon
Torrance, CA, USA

Bennett, Vaughan
St Ives, Cornwall

Bennett, John H
Granite Bay, CA, USA

Bennetts, Lottie
(grandmother of
Jean Gray)
Roche, Cornwall

Bernard, Karen Kent
Alexandria, VA, USA

Berriman, Norman
Montreal, QC, Canada

Besanko, Chris
*Sutton Coldfield, West
Midlands*

Bice, Christopher
Kingsbridge, Devon

Biscoe, Bert
Truro, Cornwall

Blackmore, Ewart W
Grimsby, ON, Canada

Blackwell, Alan
*Newcastle, NSW,
Australia*

Blewett, Christine
Colliver
Tywardreath, Cornwall

Body, John
Falmouth, Cornwall

Bolitho, Gordon J
Franksville, WI, USA

Bolitho, Dr Elaine
Ngaio, Wellington, NZ

Bolitho, Richard T A
Toronto, ON, Canada

Boon, Robin Edmund
Martyn
Trevone, Cornwall

Bosustow, George A
Hornsea, East Yorkshire

Botheras, Graham
St Agatha, ON, Canada

Botterill, Deryck
Torquay, Devon

Boundy, Nigel
Wanneroo, WA, Australia

Bowden, Clive Eric
Witney, Oxfordshire

Bowley, R L
Penzance, Cornwall

Bowman, Ron
Escondido, CA, USA

Bracey, S M Tingcombe
Newton Abbot, Devon

Bradley, Vivianne
Trevithick
Burnsville, NC, USA

Bratton, Alexander C
Oxford, Oxon

Bray, Harry and
Carolyn (Parsons)
Pen Argyl, PA, USA

Bray, Robert
Bradley Stoke, Bristol

Bray, Michael
Boughton Monchelsea, Kent

Brewer, Rex
Duporth, Cornwall

Brewer, Collin W
Sladesbridge, Cornwall

Brewer, Frank L
Wokingham, Berkshire

Bridges, Mrs
Shelagh J R
Ovington, Northumberland

Brieger, Lenore
Bastrop, TX, USA

Britton, Clive and June
Marke
Hanham, Bristol

Broad, David
Roswell, GA, USA

Brooke, Mr and Mrs
Justin
Marazion, Cornwall

Brooks, Derek Joseph
John
Goonhavern, Cornwall

Brown, Mrs Rosemary
St Austell, Cornwall

Brown, Cherryl
Spreydon, Christchurch, NZ

Brown, Christopher
Trevenen
Las Condes, Santiago, Chile

Brownlee, Alice M
Minneapolis, MN, USA

Brunton-Green, Cyril,
John and Josephine
Davidstow, Cornwall

Buchanan, Margaret R
(née Trewern)
Warner, QLD, Aus

Buckingham, John
Padstow, Cornwall

Burns, Barrie
Kanata, ON, Canada

Burnside RAN,
Commodore Ian
Reid, ACT, Australia

Burrow, K J
Bideford, Devon

Burt, Andrew and Toni
St Just in Penwith, Cornwall

Burt, E Laura
St Columb, Cornwall

Burwell, Marilyn
Bend, OR, USA

Busby, Graham D
St Mellion, Cornwall

Butler, Miss R
Saltash, Cornwall

C C C Celt
Jamison, PA, USA

Cannon, Maureen
Bournemouth, Dorset

Carbis, In-Pensioner
John C
Chelsea, London

Cardy, Derek and
Sharon
Carharrack, Cornwall

Cardy, Sally and
Spencer
St Saviour, Jersey

Carew Pole, Sir Richard
Torpoint, Cornwall

Carson, Elizabeth Snell
Huntington, OR, USA

Carwithen, F A
Addlestone, Surrey

Carwithen, Glenn and
Sue Miller
Lerryn, Cornwall

Case, Jane Meres
Mullion, Cornwall

Cassley, H A
Dalton-in-Furness, Cumbria

Challoner, Sally R
Helston, Cornwall

Chamberlain, R H
Flournoy, CA, USA

Chambers, Jennifer
Perran Downs, Cornwall

Chantry, P A
St Austell, Cornwall

Chapman, Mr and
Mrs Jim
Launceston, Cornwall

Chapman, W E (Ted)
Falmouth, Cornwall

Chapman, Mrs John W
Wheat Ridge, CO, USA

Chase, Mary Ann
Port Alberni, BC, Canada

Christophers, Robin
Anthony
Perth, WA, Australia

Clark, Dr Alan
Kingston, ON, Canada

Clarke, Stewart
*Bentleigh East, VIC,
Australia*

Clarke (née Annear),
Rosemary Doreen
Tavistock, Devon

Cleaver, Mrs D J
Northam, North Devon

Cleaves, Mr Stephen J
Radstock, Somerset

Clemoes, John W G
Bournemouth

Clogg, Sylvia Mary
Hertford, Hertfordshire

Cock, Owen W N
Pinner, Middlesex

Cockerham, Paul
Penryn, Cornwall

Cofer, James
Truro, Cornwall

Coleman, Ada
Forest Hill, VIC, Australia

Coleman, Mrs M C
Royston, Hertfordshire

Colwill, Mr Briant
Newquay, Cornwall

Comes, Elaine L
Concord, NC, USA

Compton, John William
Victor Harbor, SA, Australia

Connelly, Mrs Mary
(Spargo)
Worthing, West Sussex

Conner, Marlene
Chandler, AZ, USA

Cook, Elizabeth E
*Northampton,
Northamptonshire*

Cook, Mr and Mrs K H
Tavistock, Devon

Coomb, Mrs D E
Portscatho, Cornwall

Coombe, Marion
Hayle, Cornwall

Coon, George Vernon
Ashburton, Devon

Coon, Robert
Clitheroe, Lancashire

Cooper, Grace (Poad)
Pasco, WA, USA

Copsey, Brian
Bushey Heath, Hertfordshire

Corbet, Sally
St Buryan, Cornwall

Cornish Studies Library
Redruth, Cornwall

Cornwall Inscriptions Project
Redruth, Cornwall

Cothey, Ted and Win
St Ives, Cornwall

Couch, Teri
Copley, OH, USA

Coupland, Mrs Y M
Penryn, Cornwall

Courts, Carla
Sherborne, Dorset

Cousins, Valerie
Skelmersdale, Lancashire

Cowling, Graham Maurice
New Plymouth, Taranaki, NZ

Cowling, Jan Trelawney
Rock, Cornwall

Craddock, John Campbell
Verona, WI, USA

Crago, Kenneth Paul
Lostwithiel, Cornwall

Crawshaw, Edward T
London

Craze, Thomas Llewellyn
Winchester, Hampshire

Crichton-Harris, Ann
Toronto, ON, Canada

Croggon, Richard
Buninyong, VIC, Australia

Crowson, J M
Rosudgeon, Cornwall

Curnow, Howard
St Hilary, Cornwall

Curnow, William Charles
Pullenvale, QLD, Australia

Curnow, Ann L
Las Vegas, NV, USA

Curnow, Mrs G E and Mrs R Manning,
Clarks Beach, Auckland, NZ

Curnow Jr, William J
Punta Gorda, FL, USA

Dadda, Miss J A
Poole, Dorset

Dally, Lindsay J
Mt Waverley, VIC, Australia

Dalrymple, Ann F
Branchville, NJ, USA

D'arcy, Mark, Alex and Max
Newlyn, Cornwall

Davey, Susan L
Radstock, Somerset

Davidson, Pauline
Salisbury, Wiltshire

Davies, Mrs S L
Downderry, Cornwall

Davies, Ralph and Jane
El Dorado Hills, CA, USA

Davis, Joan M
Falmouth, Cornwall

Davis, Janice Rickard
Lemon Grove, CA, USA

Davy, Kay
Launceston, Cornwall

Dawe, Richard D
Enfield, Middlesex

Day, Dianne
Abbotsford, BC, Canada

Deal, Bruce E
Palo Alto, CA, USA

Deffebach, Sharon R
Belmont, CA, USA

Delaney, Mrs V L
Leominster, Herefordshire

Dennis, Stephen
Bridgetown, WA, Australia

Dill, Dixie Youren
Dietrich, ID, USA

Dingle, Mary
Bundaberg, QLD, Australia

Dinham, part of the family
South Africa

Dinham, part of the family
Cornwall

Dixon, Middy Jean
Toowong, QLD Australia

Donaldson, Lesley
Hayle, Cornwall

Dower, Averil M
Mt Waverley, VIC, Australia

Dowling, Mrs N F
Ashford, Kent

Doyle SSJ, Rev Joseph M
New Orleans, LA, USA

Drew, Christopher
Saint Crépin de Richemont, France

Drew, Robert G
Buckhurst Hill, Essex

Drew, Mrs W
Penzance, Cornwall

Drinnan, Janet (Sawle family)
Clarkville, Kaiapoi, NZ

Duance, Raymond V
Nuriootph, SA, Australia

Dudley, Terry
Newport, South Wales

Duinker, Pauline S Carveth
Mississauga, ON, Canada

Dunstan, Brian
Gisborne, North Island, NZ

Dunstan, Barbara
Broadwey, Dorset

Eade, Patricia M
Glen Waverley, VIC, Australia

Ealing-Lobb, Clive
Thompson, MB, Canada

Eastlake, Gordon
Chesham, Buckinghamshire

Easton, David
St Marys, Isles of Scilly

Ebling, Albert
Downsbarn, Milton Keynes

Eddy FRCS, FRCOG, Mr John W
Colchester, Essex

Ede, Roger M
Kingskerswell, Devon

Edhouse, Alan
Plymouth, Devon

Edwards, Ann Ryall
Burlington, WI, USA

Edyvean, P J
St Keyne, Cornwall

Eich, Clive
Luxulyan, Cornwall

Elliott, Mrs S
Penponds, Cornwall

Ellis, George A
Bendigo, VIC, Australia

Ellis, Robin
Camborne, Cornwall

Elvins, James A
Mevagissey, Cornwall

Emery, Mrs C L
Street, Somerset

Eva, Tamsin
Penzance, Cornwall

Evans, Michael and Wendy
Horsham, Sussex

Farnden (née Thomas), Mrs Muriel
Kedington, Suffolk

Fawdry, John Berryman
Devoran, Cornwall

Ferrett, Malcolm John
St Neots, Cambridgeshire

Foote, Gordon
Reno, NV, USA

Fowle (née Saunders), Gail
St Ives, Cornwall

Francis, Gina M
Lismore, NSW, Australia

Francombe, Mrs Mary Lorraine
Worthing, West Sussex

Freeman (née Hichens), Mary
Enfield, Middlesex

Friggens, Canon and Mrs M A
Gwynedd, Cymru

Frost, Peter
Jurbise, Belgium

Furse, Michael John
Witney, Oxon

Fyfe (née Christophers), Lesley Diana
Currimundi, QLD, Australia

Garland, D W and D M
Pendoggett, Cornwall

Garwood, Paul
Hinckley, Leicestershire

Gates, John
Slough, Berkshire

Gaved, Arthur E
Rilla Mill, Cornwall

Geiger, Maryellen
Croswell, MI, USA

George, Pamela
St Agnes, Cornwall

George, Richard L
North Huntingdon, PA, USA

Gerrard, Richard
New Malden, Surrey

Gilbert, Mrs Mary E
Mullion, Cornwall

Gilbert, R J
Bodmin, Cornwall

Gill, Douglas
Walnut Creek, CA, USA

Gill, Godfrey A
Plaidy, Cornwall

Gillbard, Bernard
East Grinstead, West Sussex

Gilmour, Brenda
Truro, Cornwall

Ginn, Doug
Welling, Kent

Goss, Gilbert Rowland
Bribie Island, QLD, Australia

Goudge, Bryan
Sticker, Cornwall

Gould, Mr and Mrs F Latimer
Vista, CA, USA

Govan, Thelma Maude
Ballarat, VIC, Australia

Gray, James
Norton Sub Hamdon, Somerset

Gray-Hulett, Carol F
Wadebridge, Cornwall

Greater Milwaukee, Cornish Society of
Greenfield, WI, USA

Greaves, David T
Tavistock, Devon

Greaves, M Jean
Tavistock, Devon

Green, Cordelia M
St Austell, Cornwall

Green, Roger Martin
Stalham, Norfolk

Gribben, Mrs Joan
Truro, Cornwall

Griffin, Gail I
Auckland, NZ

Griffin, George and Marie
Newquay, Cornwall

Griffin, Tristan V
Alvaston, Derby

Griffiths, Phyllis Astrid
Penzance, Cornwall

Grimes, J A
Walton-on-Thames, Surrey

Grist, Michael W
Llantwith Major, Vale of Glamorgan

Grosscurth, R P
West Buckland, Somerset

Grubb, Ronald Paul
Threemilestone, Cornwall

Grylls, Richard G
Tring, Hertfordshire

Haeusler, Mrs Coral E
Blacktown, NSW, Australia

Haigh, Amelia Jean
Padstow, Cornwall

Haines, Carolyn
Holt, MI, USA

Hall, Evelyn
Foster City, CA, USA

Hampton, Terry Chenhall
Gladstone, MI, USA

Hamylton-Jones CMG, MA, Keith
Fossebridge, Gloucestershire

Hancock, Helen P
Barry, Vale of Glamorgan

Hancock, M T G
Barry, South Glamorgan

Hansen, Mrs Arlie
Grass Valley, CA, USA

Hanson, J A
Bromley, Kent

Harris, Antony
Helston, Cornwall

Harris, Colin C
St Agnes, Cornwall

Harris, Mrs Berty
Probus, Cornwall

Harris, Valerie
Mill Hill, London

Harris, Jennifer M
Pompton Plains, NJ, USA

Harry, R E
Salt Lake City, UT, USA

Harry, William Lucas
Reno, NV, USA

Hart, Cyril
Falmouth, Cornwall

Harvey, Kevin William
Pontardawe, Swansea

Hastings, Colin and Helen
Portscatho, Cornwall

Hawke, Neil
Brighton, Sussex

Hawkey, Robert C
Calgary, AB, Canada

Hawkins, Raymond Henry
Happy Valley, SA, Australia

Hay, Richard A
Ellicott City, MD, USA

Hayes, Valerie A
Lompoc, CA, USA

Heard and family, Mr and Mrs E C
Stratton, Cornwall

Hellyar, J E
Herne Bay, Kent

Hendrickson, Glynis Dorothy
Ballarat, VIC, Australia

Henwood, Charles R
Tampa, FL, USA

Heydt, Nancy Oster
Neptune, NJ, USA

Heyward, Sandra Oates
St Austell, Cornwall

Hichens, R T S
Calenick, Cornwall

Hichens, Sheila
Newlyn, Cornwall

Hill, Ernest Douglas
Truro, Cornwall

Hill (née Pidwell), Mrs Jackie
Horfield, Bristol

Hobbs, Garfield
Kirbymoorside, York

Hocken BA, M G
Egloshayle, Cornwall

Hocken RN, Captain M R
Egloshayle, Cornwall

Hockin (Wadebridge 'Hockins'), Tim
Fareham, Hampshire

Hocking, Eleanor O
Blairstown, NJ, USA

Hocking, Dave
Carlyon Bay, Cornwall

Hocking, William R
Penzance, Cornwall

Hodge, Fred and Pam
Chatham, Kent

Hodge, Rodney James
Leeming, WA, Australia

Hodnett, Diane
Andrews
*Caherconlish, County
Limerick*

Hollingsworth, Mrs G
Mt Waverley, VIC, Australia

Holman, H
Perranarworthal, Cornwall

Holmes, Joan
Connor Downs, Cornwall

Honey, Alan
Bristol

Hooper, Mrs Jeremy
St Breward, Cornwall

Hooper Kaiser, Elaine
Valencia, CA, USA

Hooten, Rose
Hampstead, London

Hopkinson, Mrs
Christina
*Leighton Buzzard,
Bedfordshire*

Hoskins, John H
Sioux Falls, SD, USA

Howlett, Jonathan
Worthing, West Sussex

Huckins, Michael F
Westlake, QLD, Australia

Hughes, John Vivian
Port Talbot, West Glamorgan

Hulett, Kate Elizabeth
Wadebridge, Corwall

Humphrey, Mrs E L
New Polzeath, Cornwall

Humphrey, Miss P E
New Polzeath, Cornwall

Huston, Joan
Tregarthen
Silverdale, WA, USA

Hypatia Trust, the
Penzance, Cornwall

Igoe, Phyllis L
Elmhurst, IL, USA

Irby, Lois Champion
Anaheim, CA, USA

Isbell, Peter
Romford, Essex

Jacklin, Michael
Parklands, South Africa

James, John F
London

Jarvis (Bawden-
Goldsworthy-
Symons-Viant), Ann
Oakley, Bedfordshire

Jelbart, Ralph D
Catford, London

Jelbert, N H
Raumati, Wellington, NZ

Jenkin, David
and Juliet
Redruth, Cornwall

Jenkin, Ann Trevenen
Hayle, Cornwall

Jenkin, Derek William
Penzance, Cornwall

Jenkin, T C
Newlyn, Cornwall

Jennings, Ken E
Ann Arbor, MI, USA

Jewell, Chris
Bude, Cornwall

Jewell, Henry A
Great Meadows, NJ, USA

Jewell, James
Mineral Point, WI, USA

Jewell, Susan
Brisbane, QLD, Australia

Johns, Bawden
Manhattan, KS, USA

Johns, Mrs B E
Casterton, VIC, Australia

Johns, D W
Plymstock, Devon

Jolliffe, J Mike
Bracebridge, ON, Canada

Jolliffe, C C R
Ryde, Isle of Wight

Jolliffe, Ronald
and Jean
Brookfield, WI, USA

Jolliffe-Winsor, Pat
*Monks Risborough,
Buckinghamshire*

Jones, Ian
Mosman, NSW, Australia

Jones, Dr Malcolm
Garston, Watford

Jordan, Eileen
London

Jordan, Scott and
Simoné
London

Jorgensen, Joy
Kenthurst, NSW,Australia

Jose, John
Llanfarian, Aberystwyth

Joslin, Muriel
*Stockport, Greater
Manchester*

Juleff, Kitto
Appledore, Kent

Juleff, Lyn
Kedron, QLD, Australia

Keast, John
Warleggan, Cornwall

Keast, Thomas J
St Ignatius, MA, USA

Kellow, Robert S
Richardson, TX, USA

Kendall, James S
Edgbaston, Birmingham

Kent, Dr Alan M
Probus, Cornwall

Kessell, Bettina Grace
Killara, NSW, Australia

King, Clifford H
Chingford, London

King, Peter
Truro, Cornwall

King, Susan Allison
Halifax, West Yorkshire

Kingdon, Lorna
West Grimstead, Wiltshire

Kinsmen, Revd Barry
Padstow, Cornwall

Kitto, J H
Abingdon, Oxfordshire

Kitto, Robert J
West Lakes, SA, Australia

Knight, Lillian
Blacktown, NSW, Australia

Knight (née
Goldsworthy), Martine
Helston, Cornwall

Knutson, Gay Treglown
Port Angeles, WA, USA

Kotovsky, Catherine
Las Cruces, NM, USA

Lane, Peter and Lesley
Tremar, Cornwall

Lane, Miss J Carveth
Wadebridge, Cornwall

Lawrey, Margaret J
Gulval, Cornwall

Laws, Dianne
Newtown, Wellington, NZ

Lenten, R D
Dibden Purlieu, Hampshire

Leslie, Russell David
Lynwood, WA, Australia

Leveridge, Annette C
Kings Langley, Hertfordshire

Lewarne, Peter
Saltford, Bristol

Lewis (Cowlyn), Ann
St Blazey, Cornwall

Litt, Mrs Joyce P
Salisbury, Wiltshire

Lloyd, Philip E
Manchester

Lloyd, Janet E
Trowbridge, Wiltshire

Lockwood, L C
Connor Downs, Cornwall

Longley, Mrs Anne
Bude, Cornwall

Lord, Nancy Roberts
Arlington, TX, USA

Lorigan, Catherine
Reading, Berkshire

Lugg, R H
Redruth, Cornwall

Luke, Richard
Trowbridge, Wiltshire

Lutey, Peter
and Roselle
Goonhavern, Cornwall

Luxton (née Bartlett),
June
Lower Tremar, Cornwall

Lyle, Robert and
Mary Gill
Fowey, Cornwall

MacCallum, Mrs Jan
Cotton Tree, QLD, Australia

Mackie, Rachel Keigwin
London

MacKinnon, Professor
Kenneth
Ross-shire, Scotland

MacNemar, Dunbar L
Columbia, MD, USA

Maddern, Allan J
Andover, Hampshire

Malcolm, Mrs Pamela E
Newbury, Berkshire

Malone (M S Wilson),
May Enid
Gymea, NSW, Australia

Manderston-Mackrill,
Mrs Bobbie
Truro, Cornwall

Marriott TD, AIB,
Lt. Col. Peter
Mevagissey, Cornwall

Marsh (née Wills),
Mrs Ela Diana
Par, Cornwall

Marshall, Barbara
Wollongong, NSW, Australia

Marshall, Brian Roberts
Farnham, Surrey

Martin, Kevin and Judy
Fowey, Cornwall

Martin, Mrs R E
Trevone, Cornwall

Martin, Peggy
and Roger
Great Coxwell, Oxfordshire

Martyn, Michael J
Cusgarne, Cornwall

Massa, Judy
Wymondham, Leicestershire

Masterman, Mrs I J
Bude, Cornwall

Masters, Mr and
Mrs R G
Padstow, Cornwall

Matthews, Duncan Paul
Liskeard, Cornwall

Matthews, Marilyn J
Golden, CO, USA

Matthews, Sarah
Grove, Oxon

McArthur, Mary
Penzance, Cornwall

McArthur, Christine
and Graeme
Coalgate, Canterbury, NZ

McAuley, Brian
Par, Cornwall

McCarthy, Margaret
Trewren
Raunds, Northants

McDonald, Debbie
Pace, FL, USA

McGivern, Adrian
Oakley, Bedfordshire

McLean, Elizabeth
Helston, Cornwall

Meer, J A
Crownhill, Devon

Membury, Eileen J
Oxford

Menadue, Keith John
Truro, Cornwall

Meneer, T D
Penryn, Cornwall

Michell, Kenneth James
*Currabubula, NSW,
Australia*

Michell, L W
St Mary's, Isles of Scilly

Michell, Donovan H
Gorran, Cornwall

Mildren, Miss
Pamela F A
Birmingham

Mills, Trevor Arnold
London

Mitchell, Charles S
Clarendon, AR, USA

Mitchell, E Morley
St Winnow, Cornwall

Mitchell, Elizabeth
*West Melton,
Christchurch, NZ*

Mitchell, J and M
Newlyn, Cornwall

Moon, R
*High Wycombe, WA,
Australia*

Mooney, Tony
Stowmarket, Suffolk

Morcombe, Beth L
Albany, WA, Australia

Morgan, Mrs R O
West Wickham, Kent

Morgan, Lesley
Coventry, Warwickshire

Morris, William A
London

Morton, Lesley
*East Malvern, VIC,
Australia*

Moyle, Terry
South Darenth, Kent

Moyse, Barbara
*Ludgershall,
Buckinghamshire*

Mudge, Bryan C
Bembridge, Isle of Wight

Murley, Windsor B
Hopewell Jct, NY, USA

Murphy, Veronica E
London

Nankivell, Edmund
Hassocks, West Sussex

Nash, Reverend David
Falmouth, Cornwall

Needham, Peter S
Helston, Cornwall

Nethersole, Nigel E
Redruth, Cornwall

Newberry, Mike
Wellington, Somerset

Newlyn, Evelyn S
Scarborough, ME, USA

Nicholas, Hanna
Leytonstone, London

Nicholas
(née Scoble), Ann
Watford, Hertfordshire

Nicholls, Peter G
Windsor, Berkshire

Nicol, Norman Douglas
Shavertown, PA, USA

NZ Society of
Genealogists Inc,
Cornish Interest
Group of
St Johns, Auckland, NZ

Oaten, Brian
Trebetherick, Cornwall

O'Flynn, P S
Truro, Cornwall

Oke, Graham
Albury, NSW, Australia

O'Nion, Diana
Cheltenham, Gloucestershire

O'Rell, Michael
Manhattan Beach, CA, USA

Osborne, Dorothy
Kogarah, NSW, Australia

**Osborne, Lady Camilla
Godolphin**
Richmond, Surrey

Otton, R M
Panmure, Auckland, NZ

Padel, O J
St Neot, Cornwall

Painter, Philip
Oratia, Auckland, NZ

**Palamountain,
Brian Anthony**
Atawhai, Nelson, NZ

Palmer, Mrs Shirley
Dorking, Surrey

Parker, Deborah J
Newton Abbot, Devon

**Parkin, Samuel and
Catherine (née Grigg)**
*St Stephen in Brannell,
Cornwall*

Parnell, David and June
Worcester Park, Surrey

Parsons, Madeleine S
Orpington, Kent

Parsons, Maureen A
Canvey Island, Essex

Pascoe, Blair C
Domme, France

Pascoe, Bruce B
Tucson, AZ, USA

Pascoe, Holly H
Thatcher, AZ, USA

Pascoe, J D
Etobicoke, ON, Canada

Pascoe, Mary
Liverpool

Pascoe, T J
Newquay, Cornwall

**Pascoe Lhormer,
Brenda**
Sonoma, CA, USA

**Passmore-Legeza,
Louise**
Conneaut, OH, USA

Paul, Barry
Peckham, London

Paul, P T
Red Cliffs, VIC, Australia

**Paynter, Mick
and Doreen**
St Ives, Cornwall

Payton, Professor Philip
Truro, Cornwall

Peachey, Dominic
Mitcham, Surrey

**Pearce (née Pengelly),
Mrs A**
Chippenham, Wiltshire

Pelmear, Dr P L
Truro, Cornwall

Pendray, Keith J
Axminster, Devon

Pengelly, Jim
Arnold, Nottingham

Pengelly, Stephen Paul
Honiton, Devon

Pengilley, Barry
Lanivet, Cornwall

Penrose, Dominick
Stithians, Cornwall

Penrose, Peter J
Swanage, Dorset

Pentney, John
Paignton, South Devon

Pentreath, Dr R J
Bath, Somerset

Perez, Mrs G M
Bude, Cornwall

Perkins, Christopher
Falmouth, Cornwall

Perriam, Barbara M
Canvey Island, Essex

Perry, Jean
*Tettenhall Wood,
Wolverhampton*

Perry, Mrs P A
Bere Alston, Devon

Perry BA, Donald C
Pavenham, Bedfordshire

Phillipps, Mrs E
Truro, Cornwall

Phillips, Bruce
*Wembley Downs,
WA, Australia*

Phillips, Dr Gael
Herston, QLD, Australia

Phillips, John A
Kendal, Cumbria

Phillips, Paul
Helston, Cornwall

Phillips, Mr Donald E
Callington, Cornwall

Phillips, Wilfred T
Fareham, Hampshire

Pickard, Christine
Twickenham, Middlesex

Pidwell, John C
Cuyahoga Falls, OH, USA

Pinch, Richard
East Looe, Cornwall

Piper, Jenny
Porthcawl, Mid Glamorgan

Playle, Mr John
Hammersmith, London

Plint, D A
*Beckley Furnace,
East Sussex*

**Polkinghorne,
Kenneth C P**
St Agnes, Cornwall

**Polkinghorne,
Richard W**
Uley, Gloucestershire

Polkinghorne, Graeme
Warwick, QLD, Australia

Pollard, Mr C C
Porthscatho, Cornwall

Polsue, John Gwavas
London

Porte, Stuart
Stockwell, London

Prideaux-Wentz, Gary
Belleville, WI, USA

**Prideaux-Wilimovsky,
Edith**
Belleville, WI, USA

Probert, John C C
Redruth, Cornwall

Prowse OBE, Irwin
Page, ACT, Australia

Pryor, Geoffrey W
Bendigo, VIC, Australia

**Queensland, Cornish
Association of**
Wishart, QLD, Australia

Quirk, Judith
The Gap, QLD, Australia

Raddy, Darren James
West Looe, Cornwall

Raddy, Laura-Jane
West Looe, Cornwall

Raddy, Luke Adam
West Looe, Cornwall

Rashleigh, Carole Ann
Breage, Cornwall

Ratnayake, Belinda
St Ives, Cornwall

Reed, G T
Devonport, Auckland, NZ

Renwick, Shirley
Midland, MI, USA

**Repper, Brian
and Susan**
*Chalfont St Peter,
Buckinghamshire*

Reseigh, Dolores
Ingleburn, NSW, Australia

Reynolds, Michael G
Addlestone, Surrey

Richards, F Stephen J
St Tudy, Cornwall

**Richards, Geoff
and Angela**
Egloshayle, Cornwall

**Richards, Keith
and Marilyn**
*Weston-Super-Mare,
North Somerset*

Richards, Peter William
Ottery St Mary, Devon

**Richards, Stewart
Arthur**
Malvern, Worcestershire

Richards, Ted
London

**Richards-Willey,
Judith E**
Twickenham, Middlesex

**Ridpath, Andrew
Gerrans**
King's Lynn, Norfolk

Riley, M J
Forrest Hill, Auckland, NZ

Ripley, Donna
Collingwood, ON, Canada

Roberts, Colin
Trentham, Staffordshire

Roberts, Matt
Trentham, Staffordshire

Roberts, Richard W
Fremont, MI, USA

Roberts, Will
Trentham, Staffordshire

Rockley, S
East Looe, Cornwall

Rogers, Douglas A T
Camborne, Cornwall

Rogers, Jeremy
Sandhurst, Berkshire

Rogers, Mary H
Devizes, Wiltshire

**Roscorla, Charles
and Martine**
*Kingston-upon-Thames,
Surrey*

Roskrow, Paul
Bexleyheath, Kent

Rowe, Deirdre M
Wadebridge, Cornwall

**Rowe, John
and Constance**
Par, Cornwall

Rowe, Lawson
Burpengary, QLD, Australia

Rowe, Phyllis
St Austell, Cornwall

**Rowe, William
John Bernard**
St Mawgan, Cornwall

**Rowe-Parker,
Margaret Jane**
Kettering, Northants

Rule, Laurence
Camborne, Cornwall

Rule, Tony
Helston, Cornwall

Rundle, Bob
St Austell, Cornwall

Rundle, Mrs Gillian
Liskeard, Cornwall

Rutter, W
Falmouth, Cornwall

Sagar-Fenton, Michael
Penzance, Cornwall

Saltern, Ian Michael
Stratton, Cornwall

Sanders, Judy
Santa Rosa, CA, USA

**Sanderson,
Betty McCutcheon**
*Glen Waverley, VIC,
Australia*

Sandrey, Eric F
Ennis, County Clare

**Sanford (née Ellery),
Mrs Phyllis Mary**
Watford, Hertfordshire

Sargent, Mrs Muriel R
West Wickham, Kent

**Scawen, Dr and
Mrs M D**
Pendoggett, Cornwall

**Schiele (Puckey),
Donald L**
Pittsburgh, PA, USA

Schoolar, Ian R
Coventry, Warwickshire

Scoble, Mr R K
St Austell, Cornwall

Scullion, Edward G
*Peterborough,
Cambridgeshire*

Searle, Peter C
Oakwood, Leeds

**Selby-Boothroyd,
Richard**
Hayle, Cornwall

Semmens, Christian P
*Melton Mowbray,
Leicestershire*

Semmens, Patrick
St Just, Cornwall

Serpell, Nick
London

Sharland, Trevor
*Restronguet Point,
Cornwall*

**Shattock-Pascoe,
Steven George**
Mortlake, London

Sill, J A
Launceston, Cornwall

Simmons, Linda
Honolulu, HI, USA

Skewis, Charles A
Statesboro, GA, USA

Sleeman, Dr Andrew
County Dublin, Ireland

Sleep, Jean Barbara
St Austell, Cornwall

Smith, Eva
Chorley, Lancashire

Smith, Frances
Buckhurst Hill, Essex

Smith, Diana
Shortlanesend, Cornwall

Smitheram, Mary Lou
Santa Barbara, CA, USA

Smitheram, William H
Santa Barbara, CA, USA

Snell, Anthony D
Lostwithiel, Cornwall

**Solomon,
Mrs M Elizabeth**
Tuckingmill, Cornwall

**South Australia
Genealogy and
Heraldry Soc. Inc**
Hallett Cove, SA, Australia

**Speed, Mrs June
Marion**
Hornchurch, Essex

Standing, Judith
Bateman, WA, Australia

Standley, Brian
Ames, IA, USA

Stanyer, Jeffrey
Exeter, Devon

**Staughton (Hicks),
David and Olivia**
Fowey, Cornwall

**Staughton
(Hicks/Edgcumbe),
James and Emma**
Fowey, Cornwall

Stephens, Anne
Lake Hopatcong, NJ, USA

Stephens, Dr F Graham
Portreath, Cornwall

Stephens, Gary E
Alamosa, CO,USA

Stephens, John
Devoran, Cornwall

Stephens, Paul
Devoran, Cornwall

Stephens, Tom
Birchington, Kent

Stericker, Mr and Mrs P
Torquay, Devon

Stevens, Jean Barrieu
San Clemente, CA, USA

Stewart, Betty Hosking
Bakersfield, CA, USA

Stirk, Carole C
Crawley, West Sussex

**Stonell, Martin
and Heather**
Mabe Burnthouse, Cornwall

Sutcliffe, E Mary
*Whittlesford,
Cambridge*

Svensson, Carol A
Brisbane, QLD, Australia

Sweet, Dorothy A
Wickham, Hampshire

Sweetman, Debra J
Courtice, ON, Canada

SWEL Club, the
Devoran, Cornwall

Swiatek, Barbara
Slough, Berkshire

Swiggs, John Noel
Par, Cornwall

**Swisher,
Suzanne Shephard**
Pasco, WA, USA

Tamulion, Mrs Diane
Marquette, MI, USA

Tangye, Moira
Newquay, Cornwall

Taperell, K
South Benfleet, Essex

Taylor, Fred W
Launceston, Cornwall

Taylor, Josephine
Mosman, NSW, Australia

**Taylor MNI,
Captain John C**
Falmouth, Cornwall

Tellam, Rosalie
Penzance, Cornwall

Ternouth, Philip
St Austell, Cornwall

Terrell, David S
North Saanich, BC, Canada

**Thomas, Audrie
Penberthy**
Yealmpton, South Devon

Thomas, Bruce M
Forestville, NSW, Australia

Thomas, David
Nantwich, Cheshire

Thomas, Frank Eustace
Knave-Go-By, Cornwall

Thomas, Leighton
Orange, NSW, Australia

**Thomas, Mr and
Mrs Roger Jenkin**
St Erth, Cornwall

Thomas, Mrs June E
Bodmin, Cornwall

Thomas, Mrs M J
St Neot, Cornwall

Thompson, Corinne
Toorak, VIC, Australia

Thompson, Rita
London

**Thompson, Tom
and Liz**
St Agnes, Cornwall

Thomson, Tess
Pinjarra, WA, Australia

Thorne, Graham
Maldon, Essex

Tillotson, Linda Dunn
Colebrook, NH, USA

Timblin, Barbara H
Boulder, CO, USA

**Timmermeister,
Jean Richards**
Sequim, WA, USA

Tinto, Alastair
Callington, Cornwall

Toms, Don
Lead, SD, USA

Toms, Doris
Chichester, West Sussex

Tonkin, Clifford G
*Hemel Hempstead,
Hertfordshire*

Tonkin, W John
St Austell, Cornwall

Tonking, Michael J H
White River, South Africa

Toogood, G
Lightwater, Surrey

Tovey, Humphrey P
Newport, South Wales

Toy, Sam
Liss, Hampshire

Tozer, Mr P J
Wymondham, Norfolk

Tracy, Barry E
New York, NY, USA

Trebilco, Major Peter
Waterloo, NSW, Australia

Treffry, John
*Frenchs Forest,
NSW, Australia*

**Tregoning,
Penelope Susan**
Benbrook, TX, USA

Tregonning, Graham L
Standish, Lancashire

Tregonning, Melwyn J
Mona Vale, NSW, Australia

Tregonning, W J W
Penryn, Cornwall

**Trelease, Gillian
Marina**
Newlyn, Cornwall

Treleaven, Mr M A
St Teath, Cornwall

Treleven, K R
Colchester, Essex

Tremaine, Dudley
Glastonbury, Somerset

Trematick, John
Wrexham, Flintshire

Trembath, Mrs A J
St Just, Cornwall

Tremelling, John V
Lichfield, Staffordshire

Tremewan, Peter
Playing Place, Cornwall

Trenerry, William
Daw Park, SA, Australia

Trengove, Pamela
Wadebridge, Cornwall

Tresidder, Mark
Cranfield, Bedfordshire

Trethewey, Derrick
Surbiton, Surrey

**Trethewey,
W Michael L**
Grampound, Cornwall

**Trevains,
Benjamin Michael**
Chepstow, Gloucestershire

**Trevarrow (Trevorrow),
David H**
Metamora, MI, USA

Trevarthen, Alan
Vannes, France

Trevathan, Ken
Fairfield, Dunedin, NZ

Trevenen House
Helston, Cornwall

Trevenna, T J and M
Newquay, Cornwall

Trevenna, Tim
St Dennis, Cornwall

Treverrow, Barry
Devizes, Wiltshire

Trevithick, Mark E
Littleton, CO, USA

Trevivian, Jacqueline
Veryan, Cornwall

Trevorrow, Jim
Corby, Northants

Treweek, Miss S
Sutton, Surrey

Trewhella, John
Marazion, Cornwall

Trewhella, Roger
Brinkworth, Wiltshire

**Trewin, David
and Wendy**
Callington, Cornwall

Trewinnard, Gordon
Twickenham, Middlesex

Tripconey, Verna
Ponsongath, Cornwall

Trudgian, Terry
Fowey, Cornwall

**Trundle (née Angear),
Susan**
Liskeard, Cornwall

**Truscott, Clarinda
and Keith**
Bodmin, Cornwall

**Truscott B Eng.
AMImechE, Craig**
Whitemoor, Cornwall

Turner, F Joy
Lostwithiel, Cornwall

**Uren, David
Andrew Trewhella**
Salisbury, Wiltshire

Varker, Fred
Rockaway, NJ, USA

Venning, John
Barnes, London

Verso, Jean
Hurstbridge, VIC, Australia

**Victoria, the
Genealogical
Society of**
Melbourne, VIC, Australia

**Vingoe, Frank and
Grace**
Mousehole, Cornwall

Virden, Charles S
San Diego, CA, USA

Vosper, Elizabeth K
Duncraig, WA, Australia

Wake, Brian D
Sturgeon Bay, WI, USA

Wakeford, R J
Burcott, Leighton Buzzard

Walker, Mrs M Heather
Sudbury, Suffolk

Wallis, Margaret Young
St Buryan, Cornwall

**Ward (née Furse),
Alison Elaine**
Freeland, Berkshire

Watkins, Brian E
North York, ON, Canada

Watkins, Douglas W
Box Hill, VIC, Australia

Wearne, Harold
Sennen, Cornwall

Welch, Mrs H E
Liskeard, Cornwall

Wellington, Jeremy J
Lower Hutt, Wellington, NZ

**Western Australia Inc.
Cornish Association of**
Beckenham, WA, Australia

Westlake, Gary William
Bude, Cornwall

Wheeler, Angela
Dowdeswell, Gloucestershire

Wheeler, Miss Norma
Truro, Cornwall

Whiffin, June
*Blackburn South,
VIC, Australia*

**White, Betty,
and Pat and Keith
Wheeler**
*Peterborough,
Cambridgeshire*

White, Martin
Exmouth, Devon

White, Penny McGuire
Mentone, VIC, Australia

White, Roger Bodinnar
Tollesbury, Essex

Whitford, Jennie
Penzance, Cornwall

Whitford JP, Percy
Datchet, Berkshire

Wiblin, C N
Shrewton, Wiltshire

Widden, Howard J
Jonesboro, GA, USA

Wilkinson, Edna H
Pottstown, PA, USA

Wilks, David
Mosman, NSW, Australia

Willcocks, Barbara A
St Cleer, Cornwall

Williams (ACE), J L
*Hamlyn Heights,
VIC, Australia*

Williams, Col. G T G
St Tudy, Cornwall

Williams, Gerald
Whitley Bay, North Tyneside

Williams, Michael C
Probus, Cornwall

Williams, Roger
Uckfield, East Sussex

Willis, Johanna
Croydon

Willis, Mrs Pam M
Wimborne, Dorset

Willmont, Kathy
*Newbury Park,
CA, USA*

Wills, Trevor
Penzance, Cornwall

Wilson, Anne
Deniliquin, NSW, Australia

**Wilson, Helen Jeanette
Kestel**
Fernleigh, NSW, Australia

Wood, Rick
Preston, Lancashire

Woods, Mary Kinder
Grantham, Lincolnshire

Woon, Christopher
London

Wroath, Sheila Mary
Faringdon, Oxfordshire

Young, Mr Donald L
Waiau Pa, Pukekahe, NZ

GENERAL INDEX

Note: References in *italic* are to illustrations and their captions.

A

Adelaide, South Australia *178*
adultery 41
Advent (parish) *58*, 68, 118
agriculture *39*; and migration 145–6, 147–8, 149, 152, 153, 156, 168; potato allotments 40; potato blight 153; recession 146, 153, 191; service 35–6; wages 145–6; *see also* smallholdings
Alberta, Canada 168
aliases *58*, 76, 77
almshouses *65*, 98
Altarnun *43, 58*, 61, 68, 72, 133
Alverton 27
Anderson, Michael 42
Angarrack 97
Anglican Church 22, *82*, 184, 186, 213, 214, 215
Angrouse 122
Antony *58*, 68, 88
Antony House *30*
apprenticeships 35, 36, 39
art *95, 140, 141, 173*, 189, *190, 191*; portraits *19, 22, 31, 52, 69, 92, 132, 160, 185*
Arthur, King 191
Australia: Cornish societies 187; migrants to 50, *145*, 149, 153, *155, 178*; New South Wales 143, 154, 166, 168, 187; penal colonies 143; Van Diemen's Land 154; Victoria 166, 167; *see also* South Australia
Ayrshire 136

B

Baines, Dudley 155
bal maidens 42
Baldhu *183*
banking *52*, 98, 99, 100, 138, 150
baptisms 24, 214, 215, 216
bards 192, *193*, 199, *199, 200*
Bartlett Library 229–30
Batten, Carne & Carne (bank) *52*
Beast of Bodmin Moor 183
Belfast 226
Belleville, USA 143
Bewnans Meriasek 83
Bible Christian Society 149
Bibles 213
bicycles *111*
births: and baptism 24; illegitimate *18*, 23–4, 39, 40, 44, *54*; infant mortality 24, 26, 217; maternal deaths 26, 33; rate 24; registration *65*, 214, 221, 228; research

214, 219, 221, 224, 225, 228; wet-nursing 32; *see also* childhood
Biscoe, Bert *200*
Bishops' Transcripts 215
Black Death 15
Black Torrington 71
Blackheath, Battle of 181, 199
Blisland *58*
Boconnoc *58*, 67, 132
Bodilly 30
Bodmin: migration from 138, 187; parish *58*; Registration District *65*; surnames 75, 83, 86, 87, 104, 107, 115, 123, 168; taxes 146; town 15
Bodmin Moor 15, 67, 111, 183
Bodmin Priory 96
Bojewyan 37
Bolitho 99, 105, *105*
Bosavarne 94
Boscastle 56, 96
Boscawen Un 198
Boston, Mass. 187
Botallack Mine 100
Botus Fleming *58, 62*
Boyd, Percival 216
Boyton *58*, 110
Braddock *58*, 67, 111
brass bands 186, 190
Brazil 151–2
Breage: emigration scheme 155; parish *58*; placenames 119; population 156; surnames 79, 80, 82, 83, 88, *92*, 97, 108, 109, 110, 114, 115, 118, 120, 128, 133, 136; wreckers 183
Bridgerule West *58*
Bristol 138, *165*, 166
British Columbia, Canada 166, 168, 187, 188
Brittany: Breton names 62, *62*, 78–9, 80, 81, 169; in-migration from 78, 138; language 89
Bryher *39, 45*
Budock *58*, 72, 108, 120, 122
Buenos Aires, Argentina 169
burials 27, 214, 215, 216–17
Burnley, Lancashire 162
Burra, South Australia 186–7
Busveal Farm 50
Busveal Wesleyan School *130*
by-names *58*, 71–3, 72, 75, 77, *84*, 88–9, 94

C

Caerhays Castle 99, *99, 163*, 188
CAHS *see* Cornish American Heritage Society
California, USA 109, 155, 156, 160–1, 166, 187, 199
Callington *58, 82*, 146, 149
Calstock *58*, 67, 108, 122, 133
Calumet, USA *143, 168, 169*

Calumet and Hecla Mine *168*
Camborne: deaths 25, 26, 27; industry 101, 194; kinship 43; migration from 142, 149, 150, 162, 187, 188; mining 150, 188; parish *58*; population 41; surnames 80, 83, 92, 102, 103, 105, 113, 114–15, 116, 119, 120, 121, 130, 133; unemployment *43*, 188, 191, 194; weddings 23
Camborne School of Mines 195
Camelford: Registration District *65*; surnames 70, 100, 104, 111, 118, 128, 168; town 15
Cammillieri, Nicholas S. *140, 141*
Canada: Alberta 168; British Columbia 166, 168, 187, 188; Coburg 148–9; Cornish societies 187; migration to 28, 149, 153, 156; Ontario 147, 148, 166, 168, 187; Quebec 149; Saskatchewan 168; Toronto 187; Winnipeg 187
Cape Cornwall *17*, 100
Cape Town, South Africa *137*
Caradon 186
Caradon mine 120
Carbis Bay 118
Carclew 36, 96, 98
Cardiff 144, 187, 188–9
Cardinham *58*, 79, 111
Carew, Richard 29–30, *31*, 53, 88, 180
Carharrack 184
Caribbean 141–2
Carisbrook Castle 158
Carn Brea 61
Carn Brea mine 100
Carn Marth 11, *156, 158*
Carnebone 68
Carnhell Green 101
Carnmenellis 40, 83
Carnsew 72
Catholic Family History Society 215, 225
Catholicism *82*, 213, 215
Causley, Charles *196*
Celtic Revival 14, 46, 178, 190–1, 192, 196, 198, 201
census *16*, 149, 220, 222–3, 224, 225, 226
Centre for Cornish Studies/Kresenn Kernow 212, 219
CFHS *see* Cornwall Family History Society
CFNA (Cornish Foundation for North America) 197
Charles I 82
Charles II 89, 97, 182
Charles Stuart, the Pretender 183
Chicago, USA 164, 187
childhood: changing attitudes

towards 45; death and 24, 26, 27, 32; discipline 46, 49, 51; parent–child relationships 32, 34, 45, 46–9; swaddling 32; work 32, 35, 39, 42, 43
Chile 152, 167
china clay industry 191, 193
Chirgwidden 106
choirs *43*, 186, 190
Church of the Latter Day Saints 216, 226
Chyandour 99
Chygwyne 105, 106
Chynoweth 108
Chynoweth, John 94
Civil Wars 181–2
Clemo, Jack 192–3
Clies 76
Clowance 29
Coads Green *54*
coal 144, 162–3, 184, *185*
coats-of-arms *18, 20, 23, 33, 54–5, 96, 118*
Coburg, Canada 148–9
cohabitation 52
Cohen, Robin 198
Colan *58*, 114
colonies 147, 153, 154
Colorado, USA 164
Commonwealth War Graves Commission (CWGC) 222, 225, 226
community 174, 178, 191–2
'compassionate' family 45–9
Connor Downs 152
Constantine: migration from 157; parish *58*; surnames 80, 88, 102, 105, 109, 117, 120, 123, 132
convicts 143
Cook, Captain James 142
copper: fortunes 97, 98–9; mining *13*, 16, 98, 143, 150, 153–4, 156, 162, 179, 183–4, 186; smelting 22, 99, 144
Copperhouse, South Australia 187
Corn Laws 145, 146
Cornelly *58*
Cornish-American Connection *200*
Cornish American Heritage Society (CAHS) 197, 198
Cornish Arms Hotel, New York 157
Cornish army 182
Cornish associations 171, 187–9, 192, 194, 196, 197, 198, 199
Cornish 'customary family' 11–12, 39–41, 42, 53, 176, 184
Cornish Foundation for North America (CFNA) 197
Cornish Guardian 192
Cornish identity 14–15, 172, 175–6; medieval identities 178–80; sixteenth and sev-

enteenth centuries 180–3; eighteenth century 182–4; nineteenth century 184–6, 189; twentieth century 191–8, *194*, 199, 201; twenty-first century 198–9, 201; Cornish family 176–8, 191–2, 195–6, 201; 'county' identity 181; ethnic minority status 199; industrialisation 185, 189; and language 179, 181; mining 183–4; people and place 176, 180, 192; regional identity 185–6; religion 183, 184; romanticism 92, 189, 191, 192; royalist tradition *82*, 182, 190; transnationalism 14–15, 186–9, 193–4, 196–9; 'West Barbary' 182–3, 189; *see also* Celtic Revival; surnames
Cornish language: eleventh century 67, 74; seventeenth century 63; English loan words 80; geography 77–90; and identity 179, 181; last monoglot speaker 26, 92; nicknames 63–4, 81–5, *84*, 121–3, 125; occupational names 85–6, 87; Protestant Reformation and 78, 180; Revival 177, *186*; surnames 12–13, 55, 66–70, 72, 74–7, 78, 79–85, *84, 85, 86*, 86–9, *87*, 135, 176; Unified Cornish 177
Cornish National Minority Report 199
Cornish overseas *see* transnational communities
Cornish Rebellions 181, 199
Cornish Studies Library 11, 219
A Cornish Waif's Story 165
Cornish wrestling *142, 143*, 152, 186, *188*, 197
Cornishman, The 160
Cornwall, Jamaica 142
Cornwall, Julian 29
Cornwall, Norfolk Island 143
Cornwall Centre, Redruth 11, 212, 215, 219, 220, 221, 227
Cornwall County Council 226
Cornwall Family History Society (CFHS) 8, 10, 198, 214, 216, 217, 221, 225, 227
Cornwall Record Office (CRO) 214, 216, 217, 218, 219, 227–8
Cotehele 97
cotton industry 162
Courtney, Leonard 188
Courtney Library 214, 216, 219, 230
courts and quarter sessions 218, 219, 225; *see also*

legal proceedings
courtship: betrothal and pledging 22, 23; sex and pregnancy 23, 39, 44; *see also* marriages; weddings
Cousin Jacks 150, 151, 156, 197
Crackington 100
Craft, Percy Robert 95
Cragantallan 123
Crantock 58, 83
Creed 58, 67
crime 42, 143
CRO *see* Cornwall Record Office
Crowan: parish 58; surnames 76, 82, 103, 105, 109, 121, 133, 144, 156
Cuba 152
Cubert 58, 108, 113, 115
Cuby 58
Cullum, David 37
Cumberland 162, 164
Cumbria 163
Curnow, Howard 198
Cury 58, 79, 102, 103, 144
CWGC *see* Commonwealth War Graves Commission

D
Dalton-in-Furness 164
Davidstow 43, 58, 75, 80
Davy, Sir Humphrey 185
DCLI *see* Duke of Cornwall's Light Infantry Museum
De Beers 100
death: causes 24–5, 27; in childbirth 26, 33; and family size 27–8; infant and child mortality 24, 26, 32, 217; life expectancy 18, 26; rates 15, 24–5, 26; registration 65, 214, 221, 228; research 219, 221, 224, 225, 228; seasonality 27; taxes 217–18; *see also* burials; funerals; legacies and inheritances; wills and probate
Defoe, Daniel 27
Delaware, USA 141
Derbyshire 161
Detroit, Michigan 157, 187, 197
Devon 60–1, 71, 144, 188, 219, 224
Devon Family History Society 225
Devon Records Office 215
Devon Studies Centre 230
Dewhelans festivals 178, 198
diamond mines 100, 156–7
diaries 32, 33, 48, 149, 151, 212
diaspora *see* transnational communities
Dickens, Charles 50
directories 219
'dispersed Cornish family' 176
divers 80

divorce 41, 52, 219
Divorce Act (1857) 41
Dobwalls 138
Dolcoath mine 27, 43, 100
Domesday Book 15, 61, 75
Duchy of Cornwall 180, 181, 182
Duchy Palace, Lostwithiel 180
Duke of Cornwall's Light Infantry (DCLI) Museum 228
Duloe 24, 58, 70, 83, 84
Durban, South Africa 187
Durham 162–3, 164
dynasties 21

E
Earldom of Cornwall 179–80
East Cornwall Bank 99
East Hundred 60, 125
Easter Island 142
economy 38, 43–4, 51, 53, 191, 198
Eden Project 201
Edinburgh 226
education 45, 99, 195; *see also* apprenticeships; service
Egloshayle 58, 83, 97, 111, 118
Egloskerry 58, 67, 138
elderly, care of the 34
electoral registers 219
emigration *see* migration
employment: children 32, 35, 39, 42, 43; unemployment 43, 153–4, 156, 191, 194; women 39, 42, 114, 133, 145, 162, 165–6; *see also* agriculture; fishing industry; mining
Endellion 58
engine houses 183
engineering 21, 101–2, 150
England: in-migration from 138; migration to 144, 161, 162, 165; mining 161, 162
Exeter 138, 181, 217

F
Falmouth: *Dewhelans* 198; emigrants 166, 169; family life 32, 33; French visitors 92; Jewish community 215; National Maritime Museum Cornwall 229–30; parish 58; population 41; Registration District 65; surnames 104, 113, 114, 117, 118, 119, 123, 130, 150
Falmouth, Cape Cod 140
Falmouth, Jamaica 142
Falmouth College of Art 195
Falmouth Packet Service 140, 141, 142
family 11–12; care of the elderly 34; and community 174, 178, 191–2; 'compassionate' family 45–9; Cornish 'customary family' 11–12, 39–41, 42, 53, 176, 184;

Cornish identity 175, 176–8, 191–2, 195–6, 201; 'dispersed Cornish family' 176; extended family households 37–8, 43–4, 53; grandparents 27; male breadwinners 41; middle class families 41, 45, 46, 49–51; and migration 139–40, 148, 151–2; mining families 100–1; modern family 51–2; parent–child relationships 32, 34, 45, 46–9; role of father 41, 46, 53; role of mother 41, 46, 53; sentiments 30, 32, 52, 53; servants 35, 35–6; size 24, 28, 35, 36, 45, 51; social change 8, 17, 28–9, 36, 45, 51–2, 54, 174–5; solidarity 53; structure 27, 28–9, 43–4, 51, 52; 'traditional' family 41–2, 53; 'transnational aspect' 10; working class family 44, 45, 46, 49; *see also* childhood; family history research; kinship; marriage
family history research 10–11, 172, 195–6, 197–8, 212; baptisms 214, 215, 216; births 65, 214, 219, 221, 224, 225, 228; Bishops' Transcripts 215; books 231; burials 214, 215, 216–17; Catholic records 213, 215; census 16, 220, 222–3, 224, 225, 226; courts and quarter sessions 218, 219, 225; deaths 65, 214, 217–18, 219, 221, 224, 225, 228; diaries 212; directories 219; electoral registers 219; family Bibles 213; family structure 223–4; immigration records 221; Internet links 222, 224–7, 230; Jewish records 214, 215, 225; legal proceedings 219; letters 212–13; local sources 213–20, 222; maps 218–19, 225; marriages 64, 65, 214, 215, 216, 219, 221, 224, 225, 228, 230; military records 218, 221–2, 224, 228, 231; Monumental Inscriptions 214, 216–17, 223; national sources 220–2; newspapers 219, 221, 226, 229; non-conformist records 215; oral history 212, 222; organisations and societies 227–31; parish registers 64, 213–14, 215, 216, 225; pedigrees 220, 227; personal records 212–13; photographs 213, 231; pitfalls 222–3; poll books 219; Poor Law records 220; postcards 213; Quaker records 214,

215–16; shipping 221, 229–30; taxes and tithes 217–18, 231; telephone directories 94; transcriptions 216; visitations 220; wills and probate 217
Family Records Centre (FRC) 221, 226, 228
Farmer, Paul 192
fathers 41, 46, 53
Federation of Family History Societies (FFHS) 222, 225, 226, 228
Feock 58
Fernacre 15
FFHS *see* Federation of Family History Societies
first names 71, 75, 90–1, 214, 223; as surnames 62–3, 65, 73–4, 75–6, 89, 90, 125–31
fishing industry 96; economy 40, 191; fish-sellers 133; fishermen 17, 62, 95, 173, 174; marriage 21; Methodism 184; romanticisation of 92, 189, 190
Florentina (ship) 154
Foot, Isaac 192
Forbes, Stanhope 190, 191
Ford Motor Company 157
Forrabury 58, 67, 88, 132
Four Lanes 184
Fowey 58, 64, 79, 96, 143, 148
Fowey Moor *see* Bodmin Moor
FRC *see* Family Records Centre
freemasons 158, 158
friendly societies 158
Frost, Anthony 200
Frost, Sir Terry 197
Fuller, Leonard J. 160
funerals 27; *see also* burials
Furry Dance 197

G
gender relations 41–2
genealogy *see* family history research
General Register Office (GRO) 228–9
gentry: and Cornish language 89; 'county' identity 180–1; family life 32; kinship 29–30, 53–4; marriage 30; research 219, 220, 222–3; rise of the gentry 96–7; rise of the mining gentry 97–100; royalist tradition 183, 190; servants 35, 36
George, Andrew 200
Germoe 58, 80, 88, 115, 183
Gerrans 58, 67
Gibraltar 142
Gilbert, C.S. 54
Glamorgan 144
Gluvias 144
Gluyas 120
gold mining 100, 155, 157, 164
Goldsithney 136

Gorran 58, 82, 84, 88, 103, 110, 111, 123
Gorran Churchtown 76
Gorseth 192, 193, 198, 199
Grade 58, 82
Grampound 132
grandparents 27
granite quarries 129
Gray, Todd 24
Great County Adit 98
GRO (General Register Office) 228–9
guide books 191
Gulval 37, 58, 82, 119
Gunnislake 186, 191
Gunwalloe 58, 125
Gwennap: copper mining 50, 98; economy 44; migration from 144, 149, 150, 151, 153, 156, 163, 169; parish 58; surnames 50, 62, 82, 87, 98, 103, 108, 109, 114, 117–18, 119, 123, 130
Gwennap Pit 130
Gwinnear 58, 86, 114
Gwithian 26, 58, 72

H
Hale, Amy 196–7
Halifax, Yorkshire 164
Hampshire 144, 165
Harris, John 43, 46–8
Hartland 71
Harvey, Harold 191
'haves' and 'have-nots' 158–9
Hawker, Reverend Robert Stephen 186
Hayle 21, 97, 106, 193
Hayle Foundry 101, 101
health and disease 15, 24, 25, 27, 32
Hearth Tax 89, 136, 231
Hecla Mining Company, Michigan 156
Helland 58, 79, 111
Helston: migration from 144; parish 58; Registration District 65; Stannary Parliament 179; surnames 25, 73, 82, 85, 88, 104, 113, 116, 117, 118, 121, 123, 130; town 15; trade 102
Henry VII 179, 181
Henwood 111
Henwood, George 22–3, 27, 42
Hey, David 11, 65
Higgoe 80
Holman, David 10, 212
home pay 150
Horsham 14
hotels 157, 167
Hudson, W.H. 49
Hundreds 60
hunger 24
hunting 13
hurling 26–7

I
identity 14, 17, 74–5, 172, 175–6; *see also* Cornish

identity; surnames

illegitimacy 18, 23–4, 39, 40, 44, *54*

Illinois, USA 151

Illogan: migration 149; mining 100; parish *58*; place-names 61, 116; plague 25; population 44; surnames 87, 103, 117, 130

immigration records 221

Imperial Brazilian Mining Company 151

in-migration 17, 78, 138, *170*, 195

industrialisation 38–9, 42, 101–2, 185, 189, 194; *see also* china clay industry; engineering; granite quarries; mining

Institute of Cornish Studies *200*

International Genealogical Index 216

Internet 198, 222, 224–7, 230

iron mining *157*, 163

Irving, Henry 138

Ivernia (ship) 168

J

Jackson, John 185

Jacobstow *58*, 66, 79, 110, 111, 168

Jamaica 141–2

James I *21*

Java (ship) 166

Jenner, Henry 81, 177, 192

Jewish Genealogical Society of Great Britain 215, 225

Johannesburg, South Africa 161, 167, *167*, 168, 187

Johns, Bonjo 192

Jones, Robert *173*, *200*

Judaism 214, 215–16, 225

K

Kadina, South Australia *171*, *187*, 197

Kea *58*, 103

Kelemen, Carleen 198

Kelynack *111*

Kent 42, 144, 165

Kenwyn *58*, 88, 114, 115, 123, 164

Kerrier: Hundred *60*; population 16; surnames 71, 78, 82, 86, 103, 113, 120, 125, 126, 134

Keskerdh Kernow 181

Kilkhampton *58*, 103, 149

Kimberley, South Africa 100, 156–7, 187

kinship 29–30, 42–3, 51, 53–4, 176, 178

Kneehigh Theatre *200*

Kneller, Sir Godfrey *19*

knit-frocks *114*

Kronstrand, B. *132*

L

Ladock *58*, 130

Lady Mary Pelham (Falmouth packet) *140*

Lake Superior 143

Lamarth 76

Lamorran *58*, 75

Lan- 75

Lancashire 42, 60, 71, 136, 144, 162

land tenure 40

landed classes: age at marriage 18; migration 138; redistribution of assets 18, 20, 29; surnames 57, 60, 76, 77; taxes 146

Landewednack *58*

Landrake *58*

Landulph *58*, 67, 84

Laneast *58*

Langdon 110

Langley, Walter 190

Lanher *73*

Lanhoghou 80

Lanhydrock *58*, *118*

Lanhydrock Atlas 115

Lanhydrock House 96, 97

Lanivet *58*, 76, 79, 80, 106, 118

Lanlivery *58*, 109

Lanner 27, 157, 169

Lanow 80

Lanreath *58*, 67

Lansallos *58*, 116

Lanteglos by Camelford *58*

Lanteglos by Fowey *58*, 80, 84, 110, 142

Lanyon Quoit *12*

Latin America 150, 152, 167

Launcells *58*, 75, 132, 144

Launceston: migration 143, 149; rebellion 181; Registration District 65; Stannary Parliament 179; surnames 73, 103, 104, 111, 118, 128, 168, *196*; wages 146

Launceston, Norfolk Island 143

Launceston, St Mary Magdalene *58*

Lawhitton *58*, 143

Lay, Pat 154, 198

LCA *see* London Cornish Association

lead mining 187

legacies and inheritances 20, 29, 34, 49–51, 96, 99; *see also* wills and probate

legal proceedings 50–1, 219

Legossick 83

Leicestershire 38

Lelant *58*, 88, 113, 118, 121, 138

Lesnewth *58*, *60*, 117, 125, 134

Lethlean 120

letters *10*, 146, 147–8, 193–4, 212–13

Levant Mine 100

Lewannick *58*, 68

Lezant *58*, 67

life expectancy 18, 26

Linkinhorne 20, *58*, 68, 103, 111, 122, 133

Liskeard: migration 138, 164; parish *58*; Registration District 65; surnames 66, 70, 91, 104, 105, 108, 111, 118, 120, 123; town 15

literacy 26, 180, 181, 217

Little Petherick *58*

Liverpool 149, 157, 166

Lizard Peninsula 87, 117, 149, 154

locational names: distribution 65, 71–3; estate names *33*; migrating 113–15; mobile names 120–1; with multiple origins 108–9; non-ramifying 116–19; from place-names 60–2, 71, 75, 76, 78, 89–90, 176–8; ramification 102–3; topographical names 62, 106–7, 121; with two or three origins 103–8

London 138, 144, 149, 164, 165, 166, 167, 226

London Cornish Association (LCA) *163*, 187, 229

Looe 68, 112, 130

Lostwithiel 15, *58*, 91, 107, 144, 179, 180

Lostwithiel, South Australia 187

Lowender Kernewek 197

Ludgvan *58*, 83, 88, 100, 113, 144, 164

Luxulyan: migration from 149; parish *58*; surnames 49, 70, 106, 109, 120, *121*, 123, 127

Lyne, Arthur Browning 192

M

Mabe *58*, 72, *129*

Madron *58*, 99, 119, 120, 121, 133, 144

Maeckleberghe, Margo *200*

Maine, USA 141

Mais, S.P.B. 191

Maker *58*

Malpas 148

Manaccan *58*

Manchester 166, 187, 189

manumissions 75

maps *21*, *115*, 218–19, 225

Marazion 79, 97

Marhamchurch *58*

Marquis of Anglesea (ship) 169

Marriage Act (1753) *21*

marriage portions 20–1, 34

marriages 18; affection between married couples 33; age at marriage 18, 39; arranged marriages 20; choice of partner 20–1, 30; cohabitation 52; divorce 41, 52, 219; and economic circumstances 20; legality 22, 215; morality 22, 41; 'never married' 18, 39; registers *64*, 65, 112–13, 214, 221; research 216, 219, 221, 224, 225, 228, 230; second marriages 27, 32, 34, 42; separa-

tions 34; social change *54*; and social class 21, 30; transcriptions 216; violence within 34, 41–2; *see also* births; courtship; weddings

Mawgan in Meneage *58*, 76, 83, 84, 108

Mawgan in Pydar *58*, 113

Mawnan 23, *58*, 120

McClure, Daphne *200*

McKinley, Richard 64–5

McKinney, Gage 199

Members of Parliament *19*, *31*, *69*, *82*, 96, 98, 136; *see also* politics

Menabilly 96

Meneage 76, 154, 155

Menheniot *58*, 91, 105, 111, 120, 122, 156, 164

Merchant Navy 142

merchants 96, 99, 102, 138

Merther *58*, 113

Methodism: and domestic piety 39, 189; lay preachers 100, 183, *183*; marriages 215; and migration 148–9, 186, 194; popularity of 184, 197; Primitive Methodism 100, 148; Redruth 102; research 214, 215, 225; Wesley 183, 189

Mevagissey *58*, 117, 120, 174

Mexico 151, *151*, 187

Michaelstow *58*, 67

Michigan, USA 136, 143, 156, *156*, 157, *157*, 166–7, 168, *168*, *169*, 187, 197

middle classes: families 41, 45, 46, 49–51; industrial middle class 101–2; life expectancy 26; mining families 100; social pressures 45

Middlesex *145*, 165

Midland Cornish Association 188

migration: early long-distance moves 136, 138, 139, 140–1; eighteenth-century 138, 140–3; Great Migration 138–9, 143–5, *144*, 147–55, 160–1, 171; later nineteenth-century 156–7, 158; twentieth-century *137*, 157–8, 159–60, 161, 191; agricultural movement 145–6, 147–8, 149, 152, 153, 156, 168; 'birds of passage' 101, 156; 'churning' 144; families 139–40, 148, 151–2; free and assisted passages 152–5, 156; 'haves' and 'have-nots' 158–9; immigration records 221; in-migration 17, 78, 138, 170, 195; long-distance 13–14; mining 143, 149–51, *153*, 154, 168, 185; networks 139–40, 141, 147–8, 149, 151, 155, 156, 159–60, 162, 168; reasons for 44,

139, 139–43, 145–9, 153–5; religious reasons 148–9; remittances 53, 152, *152*, 155, 156, 158–9, 188; self-improvement 147–8; social unrest 146–7; 'streams of migration' 164–5; 'up-country' 144, 161–5

migration agents 154, 157

migration chains *see* migration: networks

migration industry 157–8

military records 218, 221–2, 224, 228, 231

mining 149–50; bal maidens 42; engine houses 183; fortunes 96, 97–100; funerals 27; kinship 43, 54; migration 143, 149–51, *153*, 154, 168, 185; mine captains 50, *50*, *86*, *157*; steam engines 101, *129*, 143, 150, 184, 185; surnames and 88, 92–3; and three-life leases 40; unemployment 153–4, 156, 191; up-country 161–2; wedding parties 22–3; *see also* coal; copper; diamond mines; gold mining; iron mining; lead mining; tin

Minster *58*, 132

miracle plays 83, 88

misspelling 169–70, 222–3

Mitchell, Bill *200*

mobility *see* migration

Montana, USA 156, 164, 187

Monumental Inscriptions *10*, 53, *62*, *67*, *75*, *86*, *119*, *151*, *158*, 214, 216–17, 223

Moonta, South Australia *171*, 194, 197

Mormon Church 216, 226

Morrab Library, Penzance 229

mortality *see* death

Morton Nance, Robert 79, 81, 83, 84, 87, 121, 122, 128, 177–8, 192, 196

Morvah *58*, 144

Morval 25, *58*, 61, 84, 85

Morwenstow *58*, 80, 132

mothers 41, 46, 53

Mount's Bay 177

Mounts Bay Commercial Bank 99

Mousehole *16*, *52*, 119, *119*

Mullion *58*, 122, *126*

muster rolls 78, 89, 218, 231

Mylor *58*, 67, 82, 97, 144

N

Namaqualand, South Africa 156

name-chains 29

names *see* first names; *Index of Surnames*; locational names; nicknames; surnames

Nampean 125

National Archives (Public Record Office) 214, 218, 220, 225, 228, 229

National Brazilian Mining
    Company 151
National Maritime Museum
    Cornwall (NMMC) 229–30
Nevada, USA 10, 109, 125,
    126, 156, 164
New Hampshire, USA 141, 142
New Jersey, USA 143, 168
New South Wales, Australia
    143, 154, 166, 168, 187
New York 106, 157, 187
New Zealand 154, 166, 168
Newcastle 162
Newfoundland 96, 140
Newlyn 9, 62, 95, 133, 164,
    177, 189, 190
Newlyn East 58, 109, 112,
    118, 123, 133
Newport, Wales 144
Newquay 103, 112, 114, 198
newspapers: Cornish 36, 51,
    148, 184, 193; research
    219, 221, 226, 229
nicknames 63–4, 65, 84,
    88–9; Cornish 63–4, 81–5,
    84, 121–3, 125
NMMC (National Maritime
    Museum Cornwall) 229–30
non-conformism 215; see
    also Methodism
Norden, John 21
Norfolk 60, 88
Norfolk Island 143
Norman conquest 56, 75, 78
North Hill 58, 68
North Petherwin 58
North Tamerton 58, 83
Northamptonshire 138
Northumberland 162–3, 164,
    179

O
Objective One Partnership
    198
occupational names 62, 64,
    65, 73, 85–8, 87, 131–4, 168
Ocean Mail, The (ship) 154
Old Cornwall Societies 192,
    194
Ontario, Canada 147, 148,
    166, 168, 187
oral history 212, 222
Order of Elks 158
Otterham 58, 79, 117
Overend and Gurney 156
Oxfordshire 60, 167

P
Packet Service, Falmouth
    140, 141, 142
Padel, Oliver 71, 72, 75, 76,
    121
Padstow: migration from 144,
    148, 149; parish 58; sur-
    names 64, 68, 75, 90, 106,
    131
parent–child relationships 32,
    34, 45, 46–9
parish registers 64, 213–14,
    215, 216, 225

parishes 58, 59, 119–20; see
    also Poor Law
patronymics 65; see also first
    names
Paul: households 37, 44;
    parish 58; Spaniards 81;
    surnames 81, 91, 92, 114,
    119, 121, 127, 128, 133
Payton, Philip 200
pedigrees 220, 227
Pelynt 58, 72
pen- 116
Pendeen 184
Penglaze 116
Penhallurick 117
Pennsylvania, USA 141, 157,
    168
Penryn 27, 85, 92, 99, 120,
    125, 143
Pentreath, Dolly 92
Pentreath, Richard Thomas 52
Penwarden 118
Penwarne 118
Penwith: first names 71;
    Hundred 60; population
    16; surnames 78, 113, 121,
    125, 126, 134, 166
Penzance: divers 80; family
    life 18, 27, 44, 102; house-
    holds 44; Jewish communi-
    ty 215; migration 144,
    170; Morrab Library 229;
    population 41; Registration
    District 65; surnames 44,
    82, 104, 106, 107, 113, 115,
    116, 119, 120, 121, 123,
    127, 170, 185
Penzance Rifle Volunteers 135
Perranarworthal 58, 108, 109
Perranuthnoe 58, 82, 121
Perranzabuloe 58, 113, 115,
    116, 122, 128, 149, 164
Peru 150
Phillack 58, 115, 120, 144
Philleigh 58, 87, 117, 120, 167
Phillimore marriage transcrip-
    tions 216
photographs 213, 231
Pillaton 58, 103
Pittsburgh, USA 187
Place 118
place, importance of 176–7,
    180
placenames 186; elements
    and meanings 61, 75, 166;
    as surnames 60–2, 65, 71,
    75, 76, 78, 89–90, 176–8
Plymouth 35, 138, 144,
    164–5, 166
Plymouth Company, New
    England 141
Plymouth Dock Bank 138
pol- 116
Poldice Mine 98
Poleglaze 116
Polglase 114
politics 190, 191, 192, 195,
    196, 199; see also
    Members of Parliament
poll books 219

Polperro 114
Polwhele, Richard 15, 22, 26,
    30
Pool 101
Poor Law 23–4, 25, 34, 65,
    153, 220
poor rates 145
population 15–17, 20, 41,
    139, 144–5, 152–3, 156,
    195, 199
Porthleven 136
Post Office 142
postcards 158, 213
potatoes 40, 153
Potter, John 17
Poughill 58
Poundstock 58, 118
poverty 25–6, 145, 153
Powder: Cornish language 88;
    Hundred 60; surnames 78,
    108, 113, 115, 125, 126, 134
Prayer Book Rising 25, 81
Praze 184
Predannick 115
Preston 42
Priest's Cove, Cape Cornwall
    17
Primitive Methodism 100, 148
PRO see Public Record
    Office
Probus 58, 80, 82, 83, 87, 128
Protestant Reformation 73,
    78, 82, 89, 96, 180, 181
Protestation Returns 82, 83,
    94, 116, 132, 231
Public Record Office (PRO)
    214, 218, 220, 225, 228, 229
Puritanism 22
Pydar: Cornish language 88;
    Hundred 60; Protestation
    Returns 82; surnames 75,
    78, 108, 112, 125, 126, 134

Q
Quakers 141, 214, 215–16
Quebec, Canada 149
Quethiock 58, 84, 106
Quirini, Vincento 183

R
railways 148, 157, 164, 189, 190
Rame 58
Randfontein, South Africa 188
Reaney, Percy 64, 70, 132
Reay, Barry 42
Redmonds, George 65
Redruth: death and inheri-
    tance 25, 29; family life
    43, 165; households 44;
    industry 194; Methodism
    102; migration from 144,
    149, 150, 158, 162; mining
    150; parish 58; population
    41; Registration District
    65; remittances 158, 188;
    smallholdings 40; surnames
    73, 80, 87, 91, 92, 102, 103,
    104, 106, 109, 114, 115,
    116, 117, 120, 121, 123,
    127, 129, 130, 133, 187,

188, 194; temperance 102;
    trade 102, 158; unemploy-
    ment 43, 191; see also
    Cornwall Centre, Redruth
Redruth, South Australia 187
Redruth Brewery 43
Registration Districts 65, 104
religion: Easter rites 80–1;
    non-conformism 215;
    Prayer Book Rising 25, 81;
    Protestant Reformation
    73, 78, 82, 89, 96, 180, 181;
    reason for emigration
    148–9; revivalism 184; see
    also Anglican Church;
    Bible Christian Society;
    Catholicism; Judaism;
    Methodism; Mormon
    Church; Quakers
remittances 53, 152, 152,
    155, 156, 158–9, 188
Rescorla 107
RIC see Royal Institution of
    Cornwall
Rising of 1497 181, 199
Rising of 1549 181
RMS Walmer Castle 137
Rochdale, Lancashire 162
Roche 58, 80, 88, 113, 123, 132
Rocky Mountains, USA 156
romanticism 92, 189, 191, 192
Roose, Furness 163
Roseland 103, 111
Rosevean 45
Roseveare 106
Ross Marriage Index 216
Rowse, A.L. 141, 159, 175,
    192, 193
Royal Cornwall Gazette 148
Royal Cornwall Museum 214,
    216, 219, 230
Royal Institution of Cornwall
    (RIC) 219, 230
Royal Navy 142, 165
royalist tradition 82, 182, 183,
    190
Ruan Major 58, 86
Ruan Minor 58
Ruanlanihorne 58, 67, 109, 167
rugby 186, 190, 191, 192, 201
Ruggles, Steven 42

S
Saltash 58, 79, 80, 123
Sancreed 37, 58, 82, 106,
    119, 120, 121, 144
Saskatchewan, Canada 168
Scilly Isles 39, 45, 60, 65,
    128, 144
Scorrier 36, 150
Sennen 21, 36, 58, 115, 165,
    223
service 14, 33, 35, 35–6, 39,
    45, 145, 162, 165–6
Sheviock 58
shipping 137, 140, 141, 142,
    147, 148, 148, 157, 158;
    research 221, 229–30
Sithney 58, 109, 113, 116,
    119, 133, 136, 184

Skinner's Ales 201
slate workers 157
smallholdings 38, 38, 40, 42,
    43, 146
Smit, Tim 200
smuggling 189
social change 8, 17, 28–9, 36,
    45, 51–2, 54, 174–5, 194–6
social class 21, 30, 60, 77, 86,
    89; see also gentry; landed
    classes; middle classes;
    poverty; working classes
social mobility: mining fami-
    lies 100–1; rise of the gen-
    try 96–7; rise of the min-
    ing gentry 97–100
social unrest 146–7
Society of Genealogists (SOG)
    222, 225, 230
South Africa: Cape Town 137;
    Cornish Association 187,
    188; Durban 187;
    Johannesburg 161, 167,
    167, 168, 187; Kimberley
    100, 156–7, 187; mining
    156–7; Namaqualand 156;
    Rand 187, 188; Randfontein
    188; remittances 152,
    158–9; Soweto 83; Transvaal
    157, 159, 161, 188
South Australia: Adelaide 178;
    Burra 186–7; Copperhouse
    187; Cornish Association
    194; Kadina 171, 187, 197;
    Lostwithiel 187; Lowender
    Kernewek 197; migration to
    154, 154, 155, 160; Moonta
    171, 194, 197; Redruth 187;
    surnames 166, 167, 168;
    Wallaroo 153, 171, 197;
    Yorke Peninsula 160, 187
South Crofty mine 170
South Dakota, USA 195
South Hill 58, 67, 118
South Petherwin 58, 67, 68,
    132, 138
Southampton 137, 138, 157
Southill 153
Soweto, South Africa 83
Spock, Dr Benjamin 51
St Agnes 40, 58, 72, 111, 117,
    122, 149
St Allen 58
St Anstell 149
St Anthony in Meneage 58, 117
St Anthony in Roseland 58,
    108
St Austell 193; copper 186;
    Cornish language 88; fami-
    ly life 41–2; households
    44; marriages 215; migra-
    tion from 157, 159; parish
    58; Registration District
    65; surnames 18, 70, 73,
    80, 103, 104, 106, 107, 109,
    118, 123, 131, 132, 133
St Blazey: copper 186; migra-
    tion from 145; parish 58;
    surnames 80, 103, 107,
    108, 112, 116, 128, 130

St Blazey Highway 43
St Breock 58, 114
St Breward 58, 67
St Buryan 20, 44, 58, 118, 119, 121, 128, 133
St Cleer 34, 58, 68, 106, 114, 120, 122
St Clement 58, 167
St Clether 58
St Columb 33, 55, 66, 88, 104, 109, 188
St Columb Major: burials 25; parish 58; Registration District 65; surnames 72, 78, 82, 107, 111, 114, 122
St Columb Minor 25, 58, 76, 112, 113, 114, 123
St Day 169
St Day United 100
St Dennis 58, 83, 128, 131
St Dominick 58
St Endellion 80
St Enoder 58, 112, 128
St Erme 58, 109
St Erney 58
St Erth 25, 58, 87, 107, 121
St Ervan 58
St Eval 58, 87, 131, 148
St Ewe 58, 107, 109, 111, 131
St Gennys 58, 66, 100, 118
St Germans: Cornish language 63; migration from 147; parish 58; Registration District 65; surnames 67, 68, 73, 84, 104, 106, 111, 182
St Gluvias 58, 82, 108, 120
St Hilary 38, 58, 114, 116, 123
St Issey 58, 83, 87, 114, 127
St Ive 58, 68, 118
St Ives: art 190; fishermen 174; funerals 27; households 44; migration from 138, 144, 167, 168, 168; parish 58; research 226; surnames 79, 83, 85, 87, 92, 112, 113, 116, 121, 123, 127, 133
St John 58
St Juliot 58, 67, 118
St Just 26, 128, 164, 166
St Just Easter Book 37, 37
St Just in Penwith: fortunes 100, 102; households 37, 44; migration from 162, 164; parish 58; placenames 61; surnames 86, 94, 115, 119, 123
St Just in Roseland 58, 110, 120, 123, 167
St Keverne 58, 80, 83, 102, 115, 117, 123, 181
St Kew 30, 32, 58, 118
St Kew churchtown 80
St Keyne 58
St Leonard 57
St Levan 58, 105, 121
St Mabyn 58, 82
St Martin at Meneage 109
St Martin by Looe 58, 106
St Martin in Meneage 58
St Mawes 120

St Mellion 58, 66, 118
St Merryn 58, 68, 106, 131
St Mewan 58, 67, 84, 113, 163
St Michael Caerhays 58
St Michael Penkivel 58
St Michael's Mount 58, 108, 183
St Minver 58, 61, 127
St Neot: migration 147, 148, 149; parish 58; placenames 108, 110; plague 25; social unrest 146; surnames 67, 68; windows 57, 77
St Petrock's monastery 75
St Pinnock 58, 79
St Piran's flags 201
St Sampson, Golant 58
St Stephen 144
St Stephen by Launceston 58
St Stephen in Brannel 58, 80, 103, 113, 123, 131, 190
St Stephens 67
St Stephens by Saltash 58
St Teath 34, 58, 109, 118, 168
St Thomas by Launceston 58, 66
St Tudy 58, 82, 118, 142
St Veep 58
St Wenn 58, 103, 127
St Winnow 58
stained glass windows 57, 77; see also Monumental Inscriptions
standards of living 45, 46
Stannary Convocation 179
Stannary Parliament 179, 181, 182
steam engines 101, 129, 143, 150, 184, 185
Stithians 27, 58, 76, 98, 108, 113, 117, 129, 130
Stoke Climsland 25, 58, 67, 110
stonemasons 156, 157
Stratton: first names 71; Hundred 60; parish 58; Registration District 65; surnames 68, 73, 79, 90, 104, 125, 128, 168
subsidies 66, 72, 218, 231
Suffolk 60
surnames 11, 12–13, 56, 134–5; aliases 58, 76, 77; Breton names 62, 62, 78–9, 80, 81, 169; by-names 58, 71–3, 72, 75, 77, 84, 88–9, 94; Cornish language 12–13, 55, 66–70, 72, 74–7, 78, 79–85, 84, 85, 86, 86–9, 87, 135, 176; on danger list 166–7; distribution 64–5, 70–4; English 74–5, 85–6, 90, 93, 110–12; and geography of Cornish 77–90; hereditary surnames 56–7, 60, 65, 76, 83, 89, 94; and identity 74–5; mining and 88, 92–3; misspelling

169–70, 222–3; most numerous (1861) 74, 104; new names 91–3; nucleated surnames 112–13; occupational names 62, 64, 65, 73, 85–8, 87, 131–4, 168; parish names 119–20; personal names as 62–3, 65, 73–4, 75–6, 89, 90, 125–31; ramification 94–5, 102–3, 110–12; Spanish myth 81; and status 60, 77, 86, 89; two-part surnames 75–6, 77, 78, 79; unstable names 134; variants 169–70, 222–3; see also locational names; nicknames
Surrey 144
Sussex 165
Swansea 22, 99, 144
symbols 20, 201
Symons Gazetteer 105, 109

T
Tahiti 142
Talland 58, 84, 85
Tam Kernewek 197
Tamar, River 67
Tamar, River, Norfolk Island 143
Tamar Bridge 157
Tangye, Moira 200
taxes 37, 66, 72, 89, 146, 217–18, 231
Tehidy 13, 25, 97, 101
telephone directories 94
temperance 102, 189
Temple 58
Thomas, W. Herbert 160, 161
Thompson, E.V. 192, 200
Thompson, Paul 46
three-life leases 40
tin: fortunes 96, 97, 99, 100; mining 43, 156, 162, 180, 184; smelting 97, 99, 100; streaming 38, 77; surnames 93, 98; symbols 20; see also Stannary Parliament
Tin Miners' Choir 43
Tincroft mine 100
Tintagel 58, 75, 108
tithes 146, 218
topographical names 62, 106–7, 121
Toronto, Canada 187
tourism 189, 191, 195, 198, 201
Towednack 58, 106, 113, 156, 164
trade unions 41
'traditional' family 41–2, 53
transcriptions 216
transnational communities 14, 159–60, 186–9, 193–4, 196–9
transnationalism 14–15, 186–9, 193–4, 196–9
Transvaal, South Africa 157,

159, 161, 188
Trant, Sir Richard 192
Tre- 75
Trebarveth 76
Trebilcock 113
Tregeare 138
Tregonissey 193
Tregony 68, 133, 138, 166
Tregothnan 142
Tregullow 36
Trelawne 72
Trelawney, Jamaica 142
'Trelawny' (national anthem) 186
Treliske 100
Trelissick 99
Treloar 113
Treloy 76
Tremail 75
Tremain 109
Tremaine 58
Tremar 34
Tremeer 118
Tremere 58
Trenance 123
Treneglos 58
Trengwainton 99
Trerice 73
Trescatheric, Bryn 163
Tresco 128
Tresillian 75
Tresulyan 75
Treurin 78
Trevalga 58, 127
Trevena 108–9
Trevescan 36
Trevilly 36
Trevorrow 113
Trewartha 72–3
Trewassa 43
Trewen 58
Trewern 120
Trewevas 119
Trewhela 38
Trigg 71, 71, 125
Tromadlart 24
Truro: almshouses 98; families 22, 46, 96, 97, 99, 100, 150; migration 154; population 41; Registration District 65; Stannary Parliament 179; surnames 76, 82, 83, 100, 103, 104, 113, 115, 118, 120, 123, 125, 130; town 15; trade 102
Truro, St Mary's 58
Twelveheads 183
types 12, 60–4, 70–4
Tywardreath 43, 58, 112, 127, 128, 132

U
unemployment 43, 153–4, 156, 191, 194
Unified Cornish 177
Union Castle shipping line 157
United and Consolidated Mines 150

United States of America: Belleville 143; Boston 187; California 109, 155, 156, 160–1, 166, 187, 199; Calumet 143, 168, 169; Chicago 164, 187; Colorado 164; Cornish population 199; Cornish societies 187; Delaware 141; Detroit 157, 187, 197; Ellis Island 170, 221, 226; Falmouth, Cape Cod 140; Ford Motor Company 157; Illinois 151; Maine 141; Michigan 136, 143, 156, 156, 157, 157, 166–7, 168, 168, 169, 187, 197; migration to 11, 149, 170, 221, 226; mining 156, 157; Montana 156, 164, 187; Nevada 10, 109, 125, 126, 156, 164; New Hampshire 141, 142; New Jersey 143, 168; New York 106, 157, 187; Pennsylvania 141, 157, 168; Pittsburgh 187; Plymouth Company, New England 141; Rocky Mountains 156; slate workers 157; South Dakota 195; stonemasons 156, 157; surnames 105, 118, 169; Union-Pacific Railroad 157; Utah 158, 166, 193; Virginia 141; Wisconsin 148, 149, 151, 187, 193
urbanisation 41, 113
Utah, USA 158, 166, 193

V
Van Diemen's Land 154
Van Dyck, Sir Anthony 69
Van Havermaet, K. 22
Veryan 58
Victoria, Australia 166, 167
Victoria County History of Cornwall 230
Virginia, USA 141
Voluna (ship) 149

W
Wadebridge 90, 100
Wales: in-migration from 138; migration to 144, 146, 161, 162, 164, 165; mining 161, 162; naming customs 29, 75, 77, 89; palatinate powers 179
Wallaroo, South Australia 153, 171, 197
Walsingham (Falmouth packet) 141
Warbeck, Perkin 181
Warbstow 58
Warleggan 58
weddings: folk ceremonies 21; Marriage Act (1753) 21–2; marriage portions 20–1, 34; parties 22–3; and pregnancies 23; social

change *54*; timing 21; *see also* courtship
Week St Mary *58*, 127
Wendron: migrants 146; parish 58; placenames 61, 68; smallholdings 40; surnames 82, 87, 88, 102, 105, 113, 116, 117, 119, 120, 130
Werrington *58*, 130
Weschke, Karl *200*
Wesley, Charles 183
Wesley, John 183, 189
West Briton 148, 154, 184, 188, 224
West Hundred *60*, 134
West Penwith: economy 40; households 36–8, 176; surnames 82, 87, *92*, 106, 115, 119–20, 120, 123, 126, 127, 128, 133
Westcountry Studies Library 219, 230–1
Westmorland 164
Wheal Basset 100
Wheal Fortune 97
Whetter, James 30, 33
Whitstone *58*, 127
widowhood 27
Williams, Foster and Company 99
wills and probate 32, 50, 217; *see also* legacies and inheritances
Winnianton 125
Winnipeg, Canada 187
Wisconsin, USA 148, 149, 151, 187, 193
Withiel 20, *58*, 80, 111
women: employment 39, 42, *114, 133, 145*, 162, 165–6; migrants *145*, 149, 165–6; mothers 41, 46, 53; religion 82, 183; role in family 41, 46, 152, 176
working classes: economy 40, 41; families 44, 45, 46, 49; household size 36; life expectancy 26; marriage 20; 'mum' 46
wreckers 183

Y
Yelland 103
Yorke Peninsula, South Australia 160, *187*
Yorkshire 11, 60, 65, 164

Z
Zennor *58*, 83, 133

INDEX OF SURNAMES
Note: References in *italic* are to illustrations and their captions.

A
-a 80
Allen 163
Andrewartha 72
Angell 82
Anglasse 82
Angove 85, 86, *86, 155, 178*, 181
Angwin 82
Anhell 82
Anhere *84*
Annear 82, 122
Anwyn 37
Arthur 75
Arundell 73, *73*, 76

B
Baker 104
Banks *69*
Bant 163
Baragwanath 166, 167, *168*
Baragwaneth 83, 164
Barham 25–6
Baring-Gould 46
Baron 138
Basset *13*, 25, 97, 101
Bate 104
Batten 52, 63
Bawden 34
Bazeley *132*
Beaumont 33
Behenna 138
Belman 155
Benetto 79
Benneto 81
Bennett 104, 128–9
Bennetto 66, 128–9
Berryman 132–4
Billing 141
Bingham 26
Bishop 64
Blake 157
Blanchard 92
Bligh 67, 142–3
Blight 67
Blygh(t) 67
Boaden 154, 155
Bodrugan 30, 32–3
Bolitho *105*, 141, 154
Bollytho 105
Bolythow 105
Bone 95
Bonython 96, 141, 187
Borlase 57, 69, 72
Bosavarne 94
Boscawen 142
Boteraux 56
Boucat 187
Bowden 60–1, 164
Brannlund 46
Branwell *44*, 107
Bray 60, 61, 104, *156, 183*
Brewer 104
Briand 76
Briant 76
Brodribb 138
Brontë *44*
Brown 62, 63, 104
Bryant 143
Budge 20
Buller 214
Bunney *145*
Bunster 170
Burgess 25

C
Caldwell *135*
Carew 29, *30, 31,* 88, 180
Carew-Pole *30*
Carne 55
Carnsew 30, 32, 72
Carter 86
Cathno 79
Causley *196*
Chapman 64, 104, *142, 143, 188*
Chappell 138
Chegwidden 105
Chegwin 105
Chenoweth 169
Chergwin 105
Chergwyn 105–6
Chinoweth 108
Chinowith 108
Chirgwin 105, 106
Chirgwine 106
Chudleigh *167*
Chygwyn 106
Chynoweth 167
Chynowith 108
Chywargwyn 105
Clemens 20
Clemo 66, 79, 192–3
Clemou 81
Clies 76
Cock 63, 141
Cogar 138
Cogden 83
Colshull 24
Cornawe 84
Cornish 104
Cornowe 84
Coth 82
Couch *174*
Crago 67
Cragowe 67
Crease 165
Cregow 67
Cross *54*
Curnow 83–4, *195*, 198

D
Daddow 80
Daniel 18, 20, 32
Daniell 99–100
Davey *49, 50,* 50–1, 104, 147, 148
Davies *54*
Davy 76
Dawe 104, 162
De Dunstanville 56
Deacon 54
Dingle 110, *110*
Dogoe 80
Dogow 80
Dunstan 104
Dyer 87
Dymond *54*

E
Earnshaw 162
Eddy 104, 127, 162
Edgcombe 141
Edgecombe 97
Endeves 82
Engros 122
Engrose 122
Engrous 122
Engwyn 82
Enhere 82
Enner 121–2
Ennor 121–2
Enowr 121
Enowre 82
Enys 76, 97
Epscob 82
Ergudyn 83
Eustis 25
Eva 80

F
Faull 162
Fox 141, 150
Franck *37*
Freethy 141
French 43
Frost *197, 200*

G
Gard 67, 132
George 21
Gilbert 104
Glasson 95, 121
Gluvias 120
Gluyas 62, 120, 133, 146
Goddard *135*
Godolphin *18, 19,* 33, 182
Greenaway 103
Greenway 103
Gregory 104, *142*
Grenville 33–4, 182
Grose *122*, 122–3
Growden 141
Guard 132
Guvias 62
Gweader 87, *87*
Gwennap 62
Gwyn 32, 33

H
Hall 62
Hambly 149
Hancock 63, 104
Hann 63
Harrington *143*
Harris 43, 46–8, 54, 104, 126, 141
Harry 63, 124, 125–7, *126*
Hartland 62
Harvey 21, 62, *62,* 95, 101, 104, *130, 156, 169, 191*
Harvy 37
Hawke 70
Hawken 104
Hawker 186
Hawkin 70
Hawkyn 70, *70*
Heard 104
Hegaw 80
Hegow 79, 80
Hellyar 131–2
Hellyer 131
Hender 96
Hennawood 111
Henry 63
Henwood 22–3, 27, 111–12
Herle 141
Hicca 80
Hichens 27, 63, 91
Hick 63, 70
Hickman 132
Hicks 20, 80, 89, 104, 162, 163–4
Higgoe 80
Higgow 80
Higman 132
Higow 79, 80
Hill 27, 62
Hingston 158
Hitchens 63, 91
Hoar 164
Hoblyn 33
Hocken 70
Hockin 70, 170
Hocking 70, 190
Hockyn 70, *70*
Hodge 70, 144
Holman 10, 62, 101–2, 220
Hooper 104, 149
Hornblower 143
Hoskin 104
Hosking 104
Howard 33–4
Hugo 80
Husband 149
Hygman 132

I
Inch *14, 130*
Iudicou 79

J
Jack 75
Jacka 80
Jacktom 76
Jago 66, 81, 128
James *37,* 48, 104, 144
Jane 63
Jasper 104
Jekyll 81
Jenkin *37,* 63, 152, 162
Jenkins *135*
Jenky(n) 76
Jewell 104, 165–6, 187
Joce 81
John 62, 63, 75–6, 76
Johns 104, 192
Johnson 95
Jones *173, 200*
Jope 141
Jose 81, 169

K
Kaczmarek 92
Keast 67, 148
Kellow 62, 169–70
Kelly 62
Kemp *158*, 193–4, *194*
Kessell *194*
Kest/Keste 67–8
Kestell 97
Kigoer 88

King 64, 143
Kitchen 9, 95
Kitto 79, 128
Kneebone 68
Knight 64

L

Lach-Szyrma 177
Lakeman 174
Lalean 120
Lander 100
Langdon 110–11
Lannergh 76
Lanyon 12
Latilla 14
Latimer 154, 154
Le Gros 123
Lean 151
Legassick 83
Legossack 83
Lelean 120
Lemon 97–8
Lethlean 120
Lobb 60, 61, 104
Lovett 164

M

Mablean 88
Maddern 62, 95, 119–20, 133
Madron 62, 119
Mallett 148
Mana 82
Manyghy 82
Marchant 26
Marrack 83
Martin 37, 104, 152, 169
Mastian 37
May 152, 164
Melender 87, 87
Menadue 167
Menear 41–2
Meneger 88
Merrett 151
Michell 104
Mitchell 104
Modres 75
Mollard 38
Mone 67
Moon 67
Motten 135
Mount Edgecumbe 146
Moyle 63–4, 104, 128
Mudge 107

N

Nankivell 167
Nicholas 21
Nichols 154
Nuciforo 93

O

Oates 144
Oats 100–1
Odgers 158
Olly 37
Opie 129–30
Orchard 154–5
Osborne 104
Ough 68
-ow 79–80

P

Paddy 28
Parsons 64, 104
Pascoe 38, 62–3, 80, 80–1, 81, 104, 169
Paul 135
Pearce 32, 62, 104
Pebar 88
Pedick 127
Pedler 27
Pellew 142
Pen- 91, 116
Pendarves 166
Pender 39, 45
Penelerick 117
Penglaze 116, 166
Penhallow 167
Penhallurick 117–18
Penhalurek 117
Penlerick 117–18
Pennalericke 117
Penpraze 116, 116–17
Penrice 141
Penrose 115, 142
Pentecost 123, 125
Pentreath 52, 92
Penwarden 118
Penwaren 118
Penwarne 118
Perranuthnoe 79
Perrow 66, 80
Peters 147–8
Petherick 43
Pethick 127
Phillips 169, 174
Pol- 91, 116
Pole 30
Pole-Carew 30
Polglase 114–15
Polgrean 42, 166
Polkinghorne 11, 17
Polkinhorne 35
Pollard 29
Polwhele 15, 22, 23, 26, 30
Pomeroy 56
Pope 64
Potter 17
Powell 149, 150
Prophet 28
Prout 104
Pybar 88

R

Rapson 153
Rashleigh 96, 96
Rawle 141
Rescorla 106
Richard 37, 94
Richards 63, 74, 74, 89, 90, 104, 151
Rickard 63, 104
Robartes 96, 96–7, 115
Robert 63
Roberts 96, 104
Robins 149, 162
Rodda 80
Rogers 10, 104, 154
Rooke 49
Roscorla 107–8
Roscorlan 107

Roseveare 106
Roskruge 117
Rosvear 106
Rothere 223
Rouffignac 91
Rowe 20, 62, 104
Rule 187
Rundell 148
Rundle 63, 104
Ruse 143

S

Saddler 86
Sainsbury 135
Sais 83, 84
Salmon 28
Sandercock 104, 130–1, 131, 168
Sandow 66, 79
Sara 80
Sawdy 68
Says 83, 84
Scawen 63, 182
Schuyler 143
Scoble 155
Scovarns 82
Sise 83
Size 83
Skeberiow 76
Skeberyowe 76
Skewes 103, 105
Skewis 103
Skinner 86
Skues 29
Skuse 103
Skuys 103
Slanning 182
Sleep 104
Smith 20, 37, 64, 85, 86, 86, 104, 154
Snell 104
Soady 68
Sowden 68
Sowdy 68
St Aubyn 29, 108
Stacey 104
Stephen 63, 104
Stephens 91, 104
Stevens 91, 104
Stewart 135
Symons 83, 104

T

Taborer 88
Taillefer 72
Taillor 87
Tallack 83, 84
Tancock 135
Tangye 79, 200
Tanner 86
Taylor 64, 150
Teague 100
Teake 83
Tegawe 82
Thomas 27, 28, 36, 72, 74, 74, 80, 89, 90, 94, 100, 104, 160, 161, 164
Thynne 223
Tickell 187
Tippett 111

Toms 80
Tonkin 191
Toy 50
Trahair 87, 87
Traher 87
Trayer 87
Tre- 91
Trear 87
Trebervet 76
Trebilcock 104, 113–14, 169
Tredigue 20
Tredrea 166
Treen 166
Treer 87
Treffry 118
Trefuna 108
Tregeagle 166
Tregembo 136
Tregenna 118, 166
Tregimba 136
Tregonning 109
Tregurtha 166
Tregust 166
Trehane 166
Trehar 86–7, 87
Treher 86–7, 87
Treherne 141
Trelawney 72
Trelawny 141, 166
Trelill 37
Treloar 61, 104, 113
Trelowarren 33, 33
Trelowarth 61, 113
Trelower 113
Treloy 76
Tremain(e) 109
Tremayne 36, 109
Trembath 36
Tremeer 118–19
Tremenheere 53–4
Tremer 118
Tremere 118
Tremethick 119
Tremeura 118
Tremure 118
Trenerry 169
Treowran 120
Tresadern 166
Trescatheric 163
Trescothick 167
Trescowthick 166
Treseder 102, 144
Tresidder 102–3, 166
Trethall 76
Trethewyne 117
Trethowan 117
Treuren 120
Treuryn 120
Trevail 49, 121
Trevanion 99, 99, 182
Trevarthen 26
Trevelyan 29
Trevena 108–9
Trevenen 142
Trevethan 141
Trevithick 21, 101, 150, 150
Trevivian 166
Trevorrow 112, 112–13, 168, 168
Trevorvow 113

Trevren 120
Trewarn 121
Trewavas 119, 119
Trewellard 166
Trewennow 109
Trewern 121
Treworgy 141
Trewren 120, 121
Treyer 87
Treyre 87
Trezone 166
Trockyer 87
Trounson 102, 144
Truebody 34
Truran 78, 120–1
Truscott 144, 166
Tubb 77
Tucker 64
Tyack 44, 87–8
Tyacke 184
Tyak 88
Tyar 87
Tyer 87

U

Udy 79, 127, 127
Ugalde 91
Uglow 68
Uren 169
Urin 78, 79
Uryn 78
Ustick 166
Uthnoe 79

V

Vandersluys 91
Varcoe 66, 131
Vean 84–5, 85
Vercoe 131
Vian 84, 85
Vingoe 223–4
Vivian 22, 158
Vyan 84–5, 85
Vyghan 84, 85

W

Wallis 142
Warren 62, 135
Warwick 96
Wearne 191
West 21
Whetter 28
Whitehair 63, 149
Wickett 43
Will 76
Willcock 63
William 37, 63, 166
Williams 36, 74, 74, 75, 89, 90, 98, 98–9, 99, 150, 151, 166
Winn 157
Woolcock 26

Y

Yelland 103
Yeo 103
Yeoland 103
Yolland 103